The Pulse of Sense

This volume stages a series of encounters between the French philosopher Jean-Luc Nancy and leading scholars of his work along four major themes of Nancy's thought: sense, experience, existence and Christianity.

In doing so, this volume seeks to remind readers that Nancy's *sens* has many meanings in French: aside from those that easily carry over into English, i.e., everything to do with "meaning" and "the senses"; it also includes the "way" they are "conducted," the "direction" they take, the "thrust" or "pulse" in which the circulation of sense exists. Faithful to this plural understanding of *sens*, the writings collected here aim to join Jean-Luc Nancy in the process of "making-sense" that animates his thinking, rather than to deliver a definitive summary of his position on any given issue. They are conceived of as notes "along the way," documenting "encounters" as moments of "(re)direction" and recording the "pulse" of sense that animates them. In that spirit, Nancy himself has provided each contribution with an "echo" in which he, in turn, responds to each author and thereby continues their mutual encounter. Aside from these echoes, this volume includes an original essay in which Nancy reflects upon the international trajectory of his thinking: a trajectory that is to be and undoubtedly will be continued, in many different directions, across and around the world.

The chapters in this book were originally published as a special issue of *Angelaki*.

Marie Chabbert is Research Fellow at the University of Cambridge's St John's College. Her research interrogates how contemporary French thought inaugurates new perspectives for thinking faith in the postsecular age. Her first monograph, *Faithful Deicides: Modern French Thought and the Eternal Return of Religion*, is forthcoming.

Nikolaas Deketelaere is a researcher at the Catholic University of Paris, France, and the Australian Catholic University. His research considers questions of experience and embodiment in contemporary phenomenology and philosophy of religion. He has published articles in *Literature and Theology*, *Open Theology*, and *Angelaki*.

Angelaki: New Work in the Theoretical Humanities

Series Editors: Charlie Blake, University of Brighton, UK
Pelagia Goulimari, *University of Oxford, UK*
Salah el Moncef *(Consultant Editor), University of Nantes, France*
Gerard Greenway *(Managing Editor), Oxford, UK*

New Work in the Theoretical Humanities is associated with *Angelaki: Journal of the Theoretical Humanities*, a leading international interdisciplinary journal that has done much to consolidate the field of research designated by its subtitle and which has been at the forefront of publication for three decades. This book series publishes generous edited collections across the humanities as informed by European philosophy and literary and cultural theory. It has a strong interest in aesthetics and art theory and also features work in those areas of the social sciences, such as social theory and political theory, that are informed by *Angelaki's* core disciplinary concentration. This broad latitude is disciplined by a strong sense of identity and the series editors' long experience of research and teaching in the humanities. The *Angelaki* journal is well known for its exceptionally substantial special issues. **New Work in the Theoretical Humanities** publishes vanguard collections on current developments in the energetic and increasingly international field of the theoretical humanities as well as volumes on major living thinkers and writers and those of the recent past. Volumes in this series are conceived as broad but integrated treatments of their themes, with the intention of producing contributions to the literature of lasting value.

Nuclear Theory Degree Zero
Essays Against the Nuclear Android
Edited by John Kinsella and Drew Milne

Tranimacies
Intimate Links Between Animal and Trans* Studies
Edited by Eliza Steinbock, Marianna Szczygielska and Anthony Clair Wagner

Ontogenesis Beyond Complexity
Edited by Cary Wolfe and Adam Nocek

Sloterdijk's Anthropotechnics
Edited by Patrick Roney and Andrea Rossi

The Pulse of Sense
Encounters with Jean-Luc Nancy
Edited by Marie Chabbert and Nikolaas Deketelaere

For more information about this series, please visit: www.routledge.com/
New-Work-in-the-Theoretical-Humanities/book-series/ANG

The Pulse of Sense
Encounters with Jean-Luc Nancy

Edited by
Marie Chabbert and Nikolaas Deketelaere

LONDON AND NEW YORK

First published 2022
by Routledge
2 Park Square, Milton Park, Abingdon, Oxon, OX14 4RN

and by Routledge
605 Third Avenue, New York, NY 10158

Routledge is an imprint of the Taylor & Francis Group, an informa business

Foreword, Introduction, Chapters 2, 3, 5, 6, 10-14 and 17 © 2022 Taylor & Francis

Chapters 1, 4, 7, 8, 9, 15, 16 and 18 © 2021 Respective Authors. Originally published as Open Access.

With the exception of Chapters 1, 4, 7, 8, 9, 15, 16 and 18, no part of this book may be reprinted or reproduced or utilised in any form or by any electronic, mechanical, or other means, now known or hereafter invented, including photocopying and recording, or in any information storage or retrieval system, without permission in writing from the publishers. For details on the rights for Chapters 1, 4, 7, 8, 9, 15, 16 and 18, please see the chapters' Open Access footnotes.

Trademark notice: Product or corporate names may be trademarks or registered trademarks, and are used only for identification and explanation without intent to infringe.

British Library Cataloguing-in-Publication Data
A catalogue record for this book is available from the British Library

ISBN13: 978-1-032-19881-1 (hbk)
ISBN13: 978-1-032-19882-8 (pbk)
ISBN13: 978-1-003-26130-8 (ebk)

DOI: 10.4324/9781003261308

Typeset in Minion Pro
by codeMantra

Publisher's Note
The publisher accepts responsibility for any inconsistencies that may have arisen during the conversion of this book from journal articles to book chapters, namely the inclusion of journal terminology.

Disclaimer
Every effort has been made to contact copyright holders for their permission to reprint material in this book. The publishers would be grateful to hear from any copyright holder who is not here acknowledged and will undertake to rectify any errors or omissions in future editions of this book.

Contents

Citation Information	vii
Notes on Contributors	x
Foreword	xii
Marie Chabbert and Nikolaas Deketelaere	
Acknowledgements	xiv
Introduction: The Conduct of Existence	1
Marie Chabbert and Nikolaas Deketelaere	

The Fragility of Sense

1 The World's Fragile Skin   11
Jean-Luc Nancy, trans. by Marie Chabbert and Nikolaas Deketelaere

2 Insistence, or the Force of Jean-Luc Nancy   16
Irving Goh

3 Nancy on Trial: Thinking Philosophy and the Jurisdictional   31
Peter Gratton

4 The Fragility of Thinking   41
Leslie Hill

The Poetics of Experience

5 Pir-ating the Given: Jean-Luc Nancy's Critique of Empiricism   59
Benjamin Hutchens

6 Abraham's Ordeal: Jean-Luc Nancy and Søren Kierkegaard
on the Poetics of Faith   71
Nikolaas Deketelaere

7 Interpreters of the Divine: Nancy's Poet, Jeremiah the Prophet, and Saint
Paul's Glossolalist   92
Gert-Jan van der Heiden

CONTENTS

8 Art's Passing for Hegel, Lacoue-Labarthe, and Nancy 103
John McKeane

The Corporeality of Existence

9 Jean-Luc Nancy, a Romantic Philosopher? On Romance,
Love, and Literature 117
Aukje van Rooden

10 Spread Body and Exposed Body: Dialogue with Jean-Luc Nancy 130
Emmanuel Falque, trans. by Marie Chabbert and Nikolaas Deketelaere

11 An Ontology for Our Times 143
Marie-Eve Morin

12 Affectivity, Sense, and Affects: Emotions as an Articulation of Biological Life 159
Ian James

The Emancipation of Christianity

13 Metamorphosis or Mutation? Jean-Luc Nancy and
the Deconstruction of Christianity 169
Joeri Schrijvers

14 Desecularisation: Thinking Secularisation Beyond Metaphysics 185
Erik Meganck

15 Raising Death: Resurrection Between Christianity and
Modernity – A Dialogue with Jean-Luc Nancy's *Noli me tangere* 202
Laurens ten Kate

16 The Eternal Return of Religion: Jean-Luc Nancy on Faith in
the Singular-Plural 214
Marie Chabbert

17 Nancy Is a Thinker of Radical Emancipation 232
Christopher Watkin

Coda

18 An Accordion Tune
Jean-Luc Nancy, trans. by Marie Chabbert and Nikolaas Deketelaere 249

Index 253

Citation Information

The chapters in this book were originally published in the *Angelaki: Journal of the Theoretical Humanities*, volume 26, issue 3–4 (2021). When citing this material, please use the original page numbering for each article, as follows:

Foreword
Marie Chabbert and Nikolaas Deketelaere
Angelaki, volume 26, issue 3–4 (2021) pp. 1–2

Introduction
The Conduct of Existence
Marie Chabbert and Nikolaas Deketelaere
Angelaki, volume 26, issue 3–4 (2021) pp. 4–11

Chapter 1
The World's Fragile Skin
Jean-Luc Nancy, trans. by Marie Chabbert and Nikolaas Deketelaere
Angelaki, volume 26, issue 3–4 (2021) pp. 12–16

Chapter 2
Insistence, or the Force of Jean-Luc Nancy
Irving Goh
Angelaki, volume 26, issue 3–4 (2021) pp. 17–31

Chapter 3
Nancy on Trial: Thinking Philosophy and the Jurisdictional
Peter Gratton
Angelaki, volume 26, issue 3–4 (2021) pp. 32–41

Chapter 4
The Fragility of Thinking
Leslie Hill
Angelaki, volume 26, issue 3–4 (2021) pp. 42–56

Chapter 5
Pir-ating the Given: Jean-Luc Nancy's Critique of Empiricism
Benjamin Hutchens
Angelaki, volume 26, issue 3–4 (2021) pp. 57–68

viii CITATION INFORMATION

Chapter 6

Abraham's Ordeal: Jean-Luc Nancy and Søren Kierkegaard on the Poetics of Faith
Nikolaas Deketelaere
Angelaki, volume 26, issue 3–4 (2021) pp. 69–89

Chapter 7

Interpreters of the Divine: Nancy's Poet, Jeremiah the Prophet, and Saint Paul's Glossolalist
Gert-Jan van der Heiden
Angelaki, volume 26, issue 3–4 (2021) pp. 90–100

Chapter 8

Art's Passing for Hegel, Lacoue-Labarthe, and Nancy
John McKeane
Angelaki, volume 26, issue 3–4 (2021) pp. 101–112

Chapter 9

Jean-Luc Nancy, a Romantic Philosopher? On Romance, Love, and Literature
Aukje van Rooden
Angelaki, volume 26, issue 3–4 (2021) pp. 113–125

Chapter 10

Spread Body and Exposed Body: Dialogue with Jean-Luc Nancy
Emmanuel Falque, trans. by Marie Chabbert and Nikolaas Deketelaere
Angelaki, volume 26, issue 3–4 (2021) pp. 126–138

Chapter 11

An Ontology for Our Times
Marie-Eve Morin
Angelaki, volume 26, issue 3–4 (2021) pp. 139–154

Chapter 12

Affectivity, Sense, and Affects: Emotions as an Articulation of Biological Life
Ian James
Angelaki, volume 26, issue 3–4 (2021) pp. 155–161

Chapter 13

Metamorphosis or Mutation? Jean-Luc Nancy and the Deconstruction of Christianity
Joeri Schrijvers
Angelaki, volume 26, issue 3–4 (2021) pp. 162–177

Chapter 14

Desecularisation: Thinking Secularisation Beyond Metaphysics
Erik Meganck
Angelaki, volume 26, issue 3–4 (2021) pp. 178–194

CITATION INFORMATION

Chapter 15
Raising Death: Resurrection between Christianity and Modernity – A Dialogue with Jean-Luc Nancy's noli me tangere
Laurens ten Kate
Angelaki, volume 26, issue 3–4 (2021) pp. 195–206

Chapter 16
The Eternal Return of Religion: Jean-Luc Nancy on Faith in the Singular-Plural
Marie Chabbert
Angelaki, volume 26, issue 3–4 (2021) pp. 207–224

Chapter 17
Nancy is a Thinker of Radical Emancipation
Christopher Watkin
Angelaki, volume 26, issue 3–4 (2021) pp. 225–238

Chapter 18
An Accordion Tune
Jean-Luc Nancy, trans. by Marie Chabbert and Nikolaas Deketelaere
Angelaki, volume 26, issue 3–4 (2021) pp. 239–242

For any permission-related enquiries please visit:
http://www.tandfonline.com/page/help/permissions

Notes on Contributors

Marie Chabbert is Research Fellow at the University of Cambridge's St John's College. Her research interrogates how contemporary French thought inaugurates new perspectives for thinking faith in the postsecular age. Her first monograph, *Faithful Deicides: Modern French Thought and the Eternal Return of Religion*, is forthcoming.

Nikolaas Deketelaere is a researcher at the Catholic University of Paris, France, and the Australian Catholic University. His research considers questions of experience and embodiment in contemporary phenomenology and philosophy of religion. He has published articles in *Literature and Theology, Open Theology,* and *Angelaki*.

Emmanuel Falque is Professor of Philosophy at the Catholic University of Paris, France. Furthermore, he is Honorary Chair and founding member of the International Network in Philosophy of Religion (INPR). An expert in medieval philosophy, phenomenology and philosophy of religion, his work has been widely translated.

Irving Goh is President's Assistant Professor of Literature at the National University of Singapore. He is the author of *The Reject: Community, Politics, and Religion After the Subject*, which won the MLA 23rd Aldo and Jeanne Scaglione Prize for French and Francophone Studies, and L'Existence prépositionnelle (Galilée).

Peter Gratton is Professor of Philosophy in the Department of History and Political Science at Southeastern Louisiana University, Hammond, USA, and board member of the Association for Philosophy and Literature. He is co-editor of the Edinburgh series *New Perspectives in Ontology*.

Leslie Hill is Emeritus Professor of French Studies at the University of Warwick, Coventry, UK, and the author of several books. He has also translated several of Jean-Luc Nancy's essays on literary topics.

Benjamin Hutchens has an Oxford D.Phil. and has been a Fulbright Scholar. He is the author of books about Emmanuel Levinas and Jean-Luc Nancy. His current research interests involve idealism in Plato, Paul and Augustine.

Ian James completed his doctoral research on the fictional and theoretical writings of Pierre Klossowski at the University of Warwick, Coventry, UK, in 1996. He is Fellow of Downing College and a Reader in Modern French Literature and Thought in the Department of French at the University of Cambridge, UK.

John Mckeane is Lecturer in modern French literature at the University of Reading, UK. He has published numerous articles on the relation between writing and thought.

NOTES ON CONTRIBUTORS

Erik Meganck studied philosophy, theology and psychology. As an independent scholar, he studies continental philosophy of religion and (mainly French) differential thought. In 2016, he organised a colloquium with Jean-Luc Nancy at the Institute of Philosophy in Louvain.

Marie-Eve Morin is Professor and Chair of Philosophy at the University of Alberta, Canada. She is the author of many articles on Derrida, Heidegger, Nancy, Sartre, Latour and Sloterdijk.

Jean-Luc Nancy was Distinguished Professor of Philosophy at the University of Strasbourg, France, as well as Professor of Philosophy and G.W.F. Hegel Chair at the European Graduate School. His work covers a vast array of subjects, from the history of philosophy to contemporary art or sexuality, and has been widely translated.

Joeri Schrijvers is Extraordinary Professor at the School of Philosophy at North-West University, Potchefstroom, South Africa. He received doctorates in theology (2006) and philosophy (2014) from the KU Leuven (Belgium). Dr Schrijvers has published numerous articles in the field of continental philosophy of religion and is interested in all questions pertaining to the survival of religion in our secular age.

Laurens ten Kate holds degrees in theology and philosophy. He publishes in the fields of the philosophy of culture, religious studies and globalisation theory. Ten Kate is Associate Professor of Philosophy and Religious Studies, and Endowed Professor of Liberal Religion and Humanism, both at the University of Humanistic Studies, Utrecht, the Netherlands.

Gert-Jan van der Heiden is Full Professor of Metaphysics and holds the Chair of Fundamental Philosophy at Radboud University, Nijmegen, the Netherlands. He is the author of several books.

Aukje van Rooden is Assistant Professor in Philosophy of Art and Culture at the University of Amsterdam, the Netherlands. Her work is situated at the intersection of continental philosophy, literary theory and aesthetics, and focuses on the social relevance of literature.

Christopher Watkin is Senior Lecturer at Monash University, Melbourne, Australia, where he teaches across French and Literary Studies. He is the author of a number of books in modern and contemporary thought.

FOREWORD

marie chabbert
nikolaas deketelaere

THE PULSE OF SENSE
encounters with jean-luc nancy

This special issue stages a series of encounters between the French philosopher Jean-Luc Nancy and leading scholars of his work. They are grouped along four major themes of Nancy's thought: sense, experience, existence, and Christianity. In doing so, the special issue seeks to remind readers that Nancy's *sens* has many meanings in French: aside from those that easily carry over into English, i.e., everything to do with "meaning" and "the senses"; it indicates not only the results or products of these familiar processes of making-sense, but at the same time also includes the "way" they are "conducted," the "direction" they take, the "thrust" or "pulse" in which the very circulation of sense exists. To make sense then means to conduct being through the *there* that characterises human existence as being-in-the-world: to take it, or to let oneself be taken by it, in a certain direction that is precisely determined as such in light of *where* we already "find ourselves" (as Heidegger understands the *there* in §29 of *Being and Time*). In other words, in our respective encounters with Nancy, we all come to him from somewhere. From there, we take him, and are taken by him, somewhere else. The writings collected here are then reports on this process of "making-sense," notes "along the way," documenting "encounters" as moments of "(re)direction" and recording the "pulse" of sense that animates them. They are not so much studies of as responses to Jean-Luc Nancy – and it is thus entirely fitting that several of these essays are personal in nature – , for they do not deliver a definitive summary of his position on any given issue, but rather seek to join him in the making of sense: throughout these pages, thinking

> commits itself to sense and thus to a sense that is still to come, to sense's future, rather than merely describing or delivering sense as if it were already in place. Philosophy in *this* sense exposes rather than proposes; more accurately, its propositions (its meaning or its truth) are indissociable from the exposition through which it commits itself, promises itself, and risks itself. (Nancy, *A Finite Thinking* 293)

In that spirit, Nancy himself has provided each contribution with an "echo" in which he, in turn, responds to each author and thereby continues their mutual encounter.

Aside from these echoes and a previously untranslated text, the special issue also includes an original essay by Nancy in which he retraces his international trajectory throughout his career. Indeed, this essay forms a *coda* to the issue, but these closing words do not in fact close-off anything: they retrace a path *taken*, the path of Jean-Luc Nancy and (his) thinking; a path that is to be and undoubtedly will be *continued*, in many different directions, across and around the world. Faithful to his own thinking, by way of "An Accordion Tune," Nancy here continues to "restrict myself to what is, after all, the essential: a gesture of an opening or reopening in the direction of what must have preceded all construction" (*Dis-Enclosure* 189n8). In continuing to walk this path, wherever from and wherever to, we hope to be likewise faithful to Nancy's thinking: that is not to say that we are to *follow in the footsteps* of the master, but rather that in retracing his path we are equally *proceeding in a new*

direction, we are ourselves *carrying further* what *carried us away* initially – since that is the only way for us to *make sense* (of it). At least, that is what we did at "Thinking with Jean-Luc Nancy," the March 2019 conference hosted by Balliol College, Oxford, that resulted in this special issue.

bibliography

Nancy, Jean-Luc. *Dis-Enclosure: The Deconstruction of Christianity*. Trans. Bettina Bergo et al. New York: Fordham UP, 2008. Print.

Nancy, Jean-Luc. *A Finite Thinking*. Ed. Simon Sparks. Trans. Simon Sparks et al. Stanford: Stanford UP, 2003. Print.

Issue image: Jean-Luc Nancy. Photo: Dirk Skiba. Reproduced by kind permission.

Acknowledgements

This book is the result of the three-day conference "Thinking with Jean-Luc Nancy" held in March 2019 at Balliol College, Oxford. We were overwhelmed by the interest in the event, and the conference ultimately ended up being a much bigger undertaking than what we had originally envisioned: to our knowledge, never before in the English-speaking world have so many scholars of Nancy's work been in a room together. Jean-Luc kindly agreed to join us and, even though the days were very long, personally attended and generously responded to each and every presentation. His kind presence, enthusiasm and wit made a lasting impression on all of us. Indeed, the whole conference felt warmer and more agreeable than many of these events usually do—to us as organisers, but hopefully also to everyone who attended. Without lacking philosophical rigour, conversation flowed easily and in a spirit of generosity.

We are incredibly grateful to everyone who helped make the conference possible: notably Madeleine Chalmers and Daisy Gudmunsen, who made running the whole event noticeably less stressful, and Bryony Marshall-Falland, for contributing the extraordinary organisational skills we sorely lack. Similarly, we were lucky to receive generous financial support from the following institutions: the Balliol Interdisciplinary Institute, the University of Oxford's Faculty of Theology and Religion, the Maison Française d'Oxford (MFO), the Society for French Studies (SFS) and the Association for the Study of Modern and Contemporary France (ASMCF). We also thank the Master and Fellows of Balliol College for providing us with an unforgettable venue.

Publishing some of the contributions to the conference as this book posed altogether different challenges. We would therefore like to thank Gerard Greenway and Charlie Blake at *Angelaki* for their assistance and understanding when circumstances made things difficult, as well as for being so enthusiastic about the project in the first place. Finally, we are also grateful to Editions Galilée for giving us permission to translate Nancy's essay *La peau fragile du monde* from the 2020 monograph to which it gives the title.

Finally, Jean-Luc Nancy sadly died whilst we were preparing this book for publication, even though all contributions to it were written a few years before his death and in conversation with him. As a result, this book will now have to serve not only as an encounter with him, but equally as a testament to him and his work that encourages further engagement in the future. We are grateful to have had the opportunity to work closely with Jean-Luc in assembling these essays and will always remember the great enthusiasm with which he approached the project.

Marie Chabbert and Nikolaas Deketelaere
London, August 2021

Jean-Luc Nancy is a philosopher. He is not simply a "thinker" or a "theorist" (as he himself insists below). Of course, philosophers spend their time thinking, often in the most theoretical and abstract ways possible. However, being a philosopher means something rather more specific: the philosopher is a thinker situated by a particular tradition. In the West, this tradition is the history of metaphysics. This history provides the philosopher with a field of activity, namely, the many authors – from Parmenides to Derrida – making up that history. It equally provides them with a task or vocation, as topical and pressing now as it was in the sixth century BC, namely: the thinking of being – or, as Heidegger understands it, thinking the meaning of being. In other words, the thinking of philosophy is one that accomplishes the relation of being to the human being that both is and thinks, that precisely "is" insofar as it "thinks" and vice versa, through history and as its very history.

For Nancy's generation of philosophers, however, "metaphysics" functions almost as a pejorative whose "history" requires deconstruction. If we are to believe Heidegger – that generation's sternest of teachers – , this is because the historical development of metaphysics has distorted the "essence of thinking" as it concerns the philosopher: "By and by philosophy becomes a technique for explaining from highest causes," he complains in his famous "Letter on Humanism," "One no longer thinks; one occupies oneself with 'philosophy'" (*Pathmarks* 240, 242).[1] Philosophy becomes a technique to "solve" the "problems" we can nowadays find treated in various handbooks of metaphysics (personal identity, necessity, free

INTRODUCTION: THE CONDUCT OF EXISTENCE

marie chabbert
nikolaas deketelaere

THE PULSE OF SENSE
encounters with jean-luc nancy

will, etc.), but in doing so undoes itself by neglecting its true concern (the thinking of being): "Thinking comes to an end when it slips out of its element," when it neglects "what enables thinking to be a thinking" (241).[2] Being belongs to thinking as the element in which it maintains itself as thinking: "as the belonging to being that listens, thinking is what it is according to its essential origin" (241). However, this element is precisely *being*, i.e., being beyond any determination of beingness, and as such thinking is never simply "theory": "The characterization of thinking as *theoria* and the determination of knowing as 'theoretical' comportment occur already within the 'technical' interpretation of thinking," Heidegger insists, meaning that "Being, as the element of thinking, is abandoned by the technical interpretation of thinking" (240). Our task as philosophers, then, is to "free ourselves from the technical interpretation of thinking" (241). The contributions collected here intend to demonstrate the many ways in which Jean-Luc Nancy takes to heart this task of freeing thinking from its technical interpretation so that it might be able to maintain itself in its own element and thus truly be thinking.

Yet, the mysteries animating the history of philosophy are really only wrapped up rather than unfolded in the designation of being as the element of thinking. Without pre-empting the many contributions that follow, we may therefore already provide an initial and provisional indication of the way in which the element of thinking requires further specification so as to clarify their status as texts that, we suggest, should be considered "encounters" with Jean-Luc Nancy. Sticking with Heidegger, we remember that he understands this element first of all as the being of the human being, more specifically as its *existence*: "The 'essence' of Da-sein lies in its existence," as he famously states in §9 of *Being and Time* (42/40). He repeats it in his "Letter on Humanism": "Ek-sistence can be said only of the essence of the human being, that is, only of the human way 'to be,'" meaning that "the human being occurs essentially in such a way that he is the 'there,' that is, the clearing of being" (Heidegger, *Pathmarks* 247–48). In other words, thinking must maintain itself in the element of existence, because it is through the finitude of its being-in-the-world that the human being has an understanding of being and thus that its thinking might be a thinking of being. Thinking, as a thinking of being, is a thinking of existence for Heidegger. Nancy takes a similar approach to the specification of the element of thinking but radicalises it by emphasising that, if the element of thinking is said to be finite, not only *what* it thinks is finite (existence) but so too is the *way* in which it thinks. In short, the thinking of existence, as a thinking of the finitude of being,

must itself be a finite thinking, precisely because thinking must maintain itself in its proper element (i.e., the finitude of being that is existence):

> Finitude corresponds simply to the matrix-formula of the thought of existence, the thought of the finitude of being or even the thought of the sense of being as finitude of sense. And this formula? "The 'essence' of Dasein lies in its existence." (Nancy, *A Finite Thinking* 74)

Nancy understands his vocation as a philosopher in this way, namely, producing a finite thinking of finitude, a thinking of existence from existence, of being from being-there:

> a finite thinking makes itself *adequate* to the existence it thinks. *But this adequation is itself finite*, and it is there that access to the missing sense, or its inappropriation, obtains [...] Here, thinking burrows back to its source. It *knows* this source, its very being, as what is, in itself, neither thought, unthought, nor unthinkable, but the finite *sense* of existing. (29–30)

It then likewise falls to us, contributors to this special issue, to think *about* Nancy by engaging *with* him and to a certain degree writing *to* him from wherever we happen to find ourselves. In other words, the special issue is not so much a collection of *treatises on* Nancy as it is an attempt at staging a series of *encounters with* him: abandoning any pretensions of being comprehensive, the contributions collected here can only provide an infinitely finite overview of his work.

* * *

How does Nancy think (being's) finitude in a finite way? Indeed, how are we to do so in our thinking encounters *with* him? In a magisterial essay on Heidegger's "Letter on Humanism," Nancy follows him in looking at the being of the human being, but now defines this being more specifically as *action*: if, as Heidegger suggests, "man is insofar as he has to act," then action "is not a specific aspect of his being, but his very being itself" (Nancy, *A Finite Thinking* 174). Otherwise put, because

THE PULSE OF SENSE

the human being, as being-there, is the clearing of being; it is its existence, the act by which or in which the human being is there, that creates the clearing, that makes – or, rather, clears – the space for it. This action thus expresses the relation of existence (*Dasein*) to being (*Sein*), namely, as the human being's being-there (its clearing of being). As Nancy puts it:

> because the difference between being and beings is not a difference of being (it is not the difference between two kinds of being), it is not a difference between two realities, but the reality of Dasein insofar as it is, in and of itself, open and called to an essential and "active" relation with the proper fact of being. (175)

He then continues by understanding both this act and the relation as one of *sense*, the key motif of his entire oeuvre: "This relation is one of *sense*. In Dasein, it is a matter of giving sense to the fact of being – or, more exactly, in Dasein the very fact of being is one of making sense" (175). In other words, the relation is one of sense, which is to say that the act establishing it is that of making sense. "To be is to make sense" (175), Nancy writes, and being in its finitude is thus itself likewise understood *as* sense: Dasein's relation to being, i.e., being revealed in terms of our being-there. However, we said that this being is understood as action by Nancy, so the "making" of sense that is being cannot be conceived of as production: "This 'making,' however, is not a 'producing.' It is, precisely, acting, or conducting oneself. Conduct is the accomplishment (*Vollbringen*) of being. As sense's conduct, or as the conduct of sense, it is, essentially 'thinking'" (175). So, to say that "to be" is "to make sense," is to say that existence consists in a particular way-of-making-sense (a way-of-being-there that Nancy here calls "conduct"), through which it accomplishes its relation to being and only as such lets being be (in its finitude as being). This is what thinking is, and it is in that sense that the vocation of thinking is to let being be: it does not produce being or sense, but lets it be (sensed); it ek-sists being, ex-poses it *there*.

"Making-sense is not the same as producing sense," Nancy explains:

> If action is an "accomplishment," that is because being itself accomplishes itself in it as the sense which it is. But being is itself nothing other than the gift or the desire of or for sense. So making-sense is not of sense's making; it is making being be, or *letting* it be. (177)

He summarises: "Sense's conduct – or the conduct of sense – makes being as being acted by and as Dasein" (178).

This conduct, and Nancy's emphasis on it, is a consequence of finitude: given our finitude, being is never present to us except in terms of the action that comprises the human being (namely, existence as the letting-be of being), nor is sense ever given except insofar as it is made in and by this action (namely, existence as the making-sense of being) – which are the two sides of the same coin (namely, finitude). In other words, finitude (namely, the displacement of sense or being as *given*) necessitates the accomplishment of being *as* sense (namely, the action of making sense that lets being be):

> being still has to be exposed to – and as – the action of sense as such, or as the gift of the desire of and for this action, as, in other words, the *non-given of sense*, which is the very fact of being as sense – and thus as finitude. (Nancy, *A Finite Thinking* 178)

Finitude then means existence, the human way to be, first of all understood as characterised by a desire for sense in the absence of its givenness: the action in which being ek-sists and through which sense is made. "It is 'ek-sistence,' the way or conduct of being as being 'outside' of itself," Nancy explains, "in other words, as being-to-sense, or, again, as making-sense or action" (179).

That this action (the *making* of sense or *letting be* of being) is necessitated by finitude (the non-givenness of being or sense) is the reason why Nancy understands it as "conduct" (existence's accomplishment of being *as* sense). It translates what Aristotle refers to as the *ethos* (literally, the "abode") of the philosopher – as exemplified by Heraclitus, whose ordinary and humble dwelling astonishes some visitors who had expected something rather less mundane of the great thinker (*De partibus animalium* I: 5.645a17–23). Yet, Heidegger writes in his "Letter on Humanism," this "abode" must be understood in a very particular way:

> *Ethos* means abode, dwelling place. The word names the open region in which the human being dwells. The open region of his abode allows what pertains to the essence of the human being, and what in thus arriving resides in nearness to him, to appear. The abode of the human being contains and preserves the advent of what belongs to the human being in his essence. (*Pathmarks* 269)

Nancy spells this out more explicitly by suggesting that "abode" (*ethos*) indicates, not so much a place, but an action: namely, the specifically human way of being that is being-there (existence). He explains:

> *Ethos* needs to be understood as "abode" (following Heraclitus' saying: *ethos anthropoi daimon*). The abode is the "there" in that it is open. As such, the abode is much more a conduct than it is a residence; more accurately, "residing" is principally a conduct, the conduct of being-the-there. (Nancy, *A Finite Thinking* 188)

In other words, the human being's *ethos* is the way it *conducts* itself, the way in which its being consists in the ek-sistence of being, the way in which its existence consists in being-the-there. It indicates the particular way in which human beings are: letting being be and making sense by being-there. Existence, or the human being's *ethos*, makes sense by conducting being through the *there* that lets it be in its finitude:

> "Being-the-there," however, implies that being properly ek-sists as its "clearing." By this "clearing" we need to understand not, or not in the first instance, an illumination or revelation that brings being to light, but

being itself as an opening, a spacing-out *for* possibilities of bringing to light. Being ek-sists (is) in that it opens being. The *there* is the opening in which, right at an existence *hic et nunc*, making-sense is at issue. The *there* is the place in which, on the basis of it, on the basis of its opening, something can take place: a conduct of sense. The *ek* of ek-sistence is the conduct proper to being the there in full measure [...], in which, by being the there, by being *that there is there* an existence, being *is* sense. (Nancy, *A Finite Thinking* 181)

The conduct of sense (the ek-sistence of being), then, is the response to the desire for sense (the non-givenness of being): it conducts being through the *there* and makes sense in thus conducting it (lets being be as sense).

It is this conduct, which lets being be in its finitude by accomplishing it *as* sense in the way it conducts being through the *there* of human existence, that forms the true object of a finite thinking of finitude: it maintains itself in its element (i.e., the finitude of being) either as the letting-be of being in its finitude (Heidegger) or the making-sense of being in existence (Nancy). Indeed, as Heidegger puts it, as "the thinking that inquires into the truth of being and so defines the human being's essential abode from being and toward being," this thinking precisely "ponders the abode of the human being" (*Pathmarks* 271). Thinking therefore belongs essentially to the being of the human being, specifically as a thinking of (its) being, insofar as (its) being consists in the infinitely finite conduct of sense.

* * *

Conceived in this way, thinking in general and Nancy's thinking in particular confronts anyone writing and thinking about him with an incredibly urgent question: how do we conduct ourselves when making sense of him? Here, it might be useful to remind the reader of the many meanings Nancy's *sens* has in French: aside from those that easily carry over into English, i.e., everything to do with "meaning" and "the senses"; it indicates not only the results or products of these familiar processes of making-sense, but at the same time also includes the "way" they are "conducted," the "direction" they take, the "thrust" or "pulse" in which the very circulation of sense exists. To make sense then means to conduct being through the *there*: to take it, or to let oneself be taken by it, in a certain direction that is precisely determined as such in light of *where* we already "find ourselves" (as Heidegger understands the *there* in §29 of *Being and Time*). In other words, in our respective encounters with Nancy, we all come to him from somewhere. From there, we take him, and are taken by him, somewhere else. The writings collected here can then only be reports on this process of "making-sense," notes "along the way," documenting "encounters" as moments of "(re)direction" and recording the "pulse" of sense that animates them. They are not so much studies of as responses to Jean-Luc Nancy – and it is thus entirely fitting that several of these essays are personal in nature – , for they do not deliver a definitive summary of his position on any given issue, but rather seek to join him in the making of sense: throughout these pages, thinking

> commits itself to sense and thus to a sense that is still to come, to sense's future, rather than merely describing or delivering sense as if it were already in place. Philosophy in *this* sense exposes rather than proposes; more accurately, its propositions (its meaning or its truth) are indissociable from the exposition through which it commits itself, promises itself, and risks itself. (Nancy, *A Finite Thinking* 293)

In that spirit, Nancy himself has provided each contribution with an "echo" in which he, in turn, responds to each author and thereby continues their mutual encounter.

Thinking, both for Nancy and with Nancy, is an attempt at ascertaining or sensing the very *direction of sense* (i.e., the way in which sense is made), a direction that directs or is sensed as the very *conduct of existence* (i.e., the way in which the being of human beings consists in being-the-there). In light of that, the goal of this special issue is

not to explain Nancy, but to let his thinking be, to make his work make-sense, to truly bring (his) thinking into ek-sistence as the pulse of the only thing it ever can be: an infinitely finite set of interpretations in which sense is made to circulate. In their plurality, however, these interpretations do all *share* sense in a specific way. As will become clear to the reader, each contribution draws attention to a certain force emanating both *from* and existing *as* (Nancy's) thinking: the movement or drive that carries it along and involves it in the circulation of sense as such. It is that sharing, singularly plural and infinitely finite, that makes up what we are calling the *pulse of sense*: the almost (in)tangible movement and thrust that comprises life in the world as the circulation of sense. This pulse, however, is not a "force" in the sense of a strong and inexecrable pushing forward. Instead, it is delicate and frail, forceful only in its resistance: "the powerful and fragile resonance," as Nancy describes it below in an essay entitled "The World's Fragile Skin," "of all that arouses a form or tonality of existence." Indeed, it is very much like the skin under which the animating pulse is only detected as such in the first place, secure and yet incredibly vulnerable at the same time: "Openings of blood," as Nancy writes elsewhere, "are identical to those of sense" (*Corpus* 105).

We have divided the issue into four sections. The first section deals with what we might call "the fragility of sense" in Nancy's thinking, starting with his own elaboration of it in relation to the world and the body. This is followed by a consideration of the interplay between force and fragility in Nancy's thinking of sense, wherein Irving Goh skilfully demonstrates the reciprocal nature of this interaction, namely: the fact that force lies equally *in* its own fragility. According to him, attending to the weakening or exhaustion of force – as Nancy does throughout his work – , demands courage, namely: the courage to confront, tirelessly, the fatigue of existence. Indeed, it is no less important than the cultivation of life-force, for it means attending to what is both most precarious and insistent in existence. An illuminating counterpoint to Goh's contribution is offered by Peter Gratton, who suggests that, in Nancy's thought, ontological fragility can equally be found in an indefatigable exposure to disruption. In doing so, Gratton draws attention to the juridical – indeed, jurisprudential – potential of philosophy, namely: how it exposes, through the force of judgement, both the fragility and resilience of being as a disruption that is given the full force of law. The final contribution in this section then deals with the fragility of thinking itself. Indeed, in addition to recognising the philosophical inspiration for and importance of Nancy's interest in the undecidable "in-between" as constitutive of philosophical thinking in its ongoing dialogue with literature, Leslie Hill specifically questions a potential point of fragility in Nancy's own thinking, namely: its engagement with the work of Maurice Blanchot.

The second section of the issue then moves on to a consideration of the role of experience in Nancy's thinking as the very thrust and pulse of sense. Specifically, Benjamin Hutchens elaborates Nancy's conceptualisation of the experience of freedom and interrogates the role of the empirical *within* philosophical discourse, rather than as part of a philosophical "empiricism," by way of an illuminating etymology of the word of "ex-peri-ence." It is also this notion of experience beyond "empiricism" that Nikolaas Deketelaere's contribution considers, but this time focusing on the specific though paradigmatic experience of faith. He compares Nancy and Søren Kierkegaard's respective understandings of faith in terms of how they both conceive of it as a privileged experience *of* and *as* existence itself: the pulse of existence which therefore comprises the very thrust of experience. As an experience that makes lived-experience possible, faith appears to take priority over the experiences considered by classical phenomenology, which is why he suggests turning phenomenology into a poetics. By looking at the ancient understanding of the poet as an interpreter of the gods, Gert-Jan van der Heiden then turns to the experience of speech at the limit of communication in Nancy's thinking. By comparing and contrasting the poetic *voicing* of the divine with the calling of the prophet Jeremiah and Saint Paul's reflections on the glossolalist, he interrogates the phenomenon of the double voice and the experience of inhabiting the very threshold of communication in a poetics of sense that takes its cue from Nancy. An interest in the interrupted and interruptive poetics of the double voice likewise drives John McKeane's contribution, the final one in this section. McKeane looks at aesthetic experience in the work of Nancy and Philippe Lacoue-Labarthe, interrogating their respective ways of making sense of Hegel's suggestion that, with the flight of the gods of polytheism and the rise of the monotheistic God, art essentially exhausted itself at the end of Greek antiquity.

The third section deals with the pulse of sense, of our world in its infinitely finite unfolding, in a more intimate way by seeking to embody it, to make felt the incessant movement of a vein underneath the surface of the skin, to make evident our world as the circulation of sense in the same way that a rush of blood turns the cheek pink and lively. Aukje van Rooden starts by emphasising the importance of romantic love and sex in Nancy's thinking. Nancy's philosophy of love, she suggests, should be understood in the same vein as German Romanticism insofar as it fosters a thinking of the relationship between love, thinking, and literature – i.e., a thinking of *relation* itself. This relation, along with the thinking of it, becomes explicitly *corporeal* in Emmanuel Falque's dialogue with Nancy. At the crossroads of phenomenology and theology, Falque compares his own notion of the "spread body" (*corps épandu*) to Nancy's "exposed body" (*corps expeausé*). These two notions share an understanding of corporeality as neither belonging to what is lived by consciousness nor to what remains inert in matter, but rather exposing the very fact of existence along the surface of the skin. Yet, Marie-Eve Morin asks in her contribution to the issue, should this skin be considered a *human* skin? Skilfully navigating the various "new realisms" to have emerged recently, from "speculative realism" to "object-oriented ontology," she considers their shared demand for the rejection of the privileged position of the human as the centre of the universe. Morin suggests that Nancy offers an innovative response in the form of a "flat" ontology that avoids both the pitfalls of an anthropomorphic approach to the natural world as well as those of a residual human exceptionalism that deprives human beings of any agential role in the unfolding of the world. In the final contribution to this section, Ian James further interrogates the continuity between human and non-human life. Looking specifically at how emotions are generally understood as *embodied* – insofar as they consist in subjective first-person experiences dependent on objective biological conditions – , he suggests that Nancy's thinking of sense and touch unlocks a philosophy of the emotions in terms of a fundamental affectivity proper to all biological life, whether or not this life is human.

The exercises contained in the final section continue Nancy's project of the "deconstruction of Christianity." The first two contributions of this section focus on the end and overcoming of metaphysics as a process of philosophical secularisation. Drawing on Derrida's critique of Nancy's project, Joeri Schrijvers investigates whether our present condition should be considered a continuation of or rather a break with our Christian heritage (and therefore also the history of metaphysics). Looking more specifically at the contemporary exhaustion of various theories of secularisation, and drawing on authors like Gianni Vattimo and René Girard, Erik Meganck proposes the notion of *desecularisation* as a means of thinking secularisation beyond metaphysics. Adding to Meganck's argument, Laurens ten Kate considers the extent to which the *philosophical* "return of religion" opens new *theological* perspectives and vice versa. Drawing in particular on Nancy's treatment of the resurrection and the structure of the gospels themselves, Ten

Kate articulates an understanding of truth as "parabolic," i.e., truth and falsity entangled with one another. The final two contributions consider the deconstruction of Christianity in terms of its political and anthropological significance. Refusing to debate Nancy's project on Derrida's terms, both Marie Chabbert and Christopher Watkin suggest that the former provides the impetus for a radical politics of difference and emancipation. With Nancy, Chabbert shows how the logic of "return" at play in the "return of religion" should be understood along the lines of an eternal return of difference. This would then provide us with new resources for thinking the increased fluidity and diversity of the category "religion" in our supposedly "postsecular" age. Watkin in turn explicitly engages the question of political emancipation by drawing attention to Nancy's understanding of deconstruction as a gesture of self-surpassing: the rejection of the modern narrative of emancipatory progress, he notes, results from the fact that this narrative is itself far from emancipatory. Consequently, he argues that Nancy should be considered a thinker of *radical* emancipation: a thinker whose thinking, and for whom thinking, sets us on or takes us down a path of transformation and redirection, open to both continuity and change.

Once more and for a final time, we let ourselves be carried away with and by Jean-Luc Nancy at the end of this issue. His concluding reflections retrace his international trajectory throughout his career. Indeed, they form a *coda* to the issue, but these closing words do not in fact close-off anything: they retrace a path *taken*, the path of Jean-Luc Nancy and (his) thinking; a path that is to be and undoubtedly will be *continued*, in many different directions, across and around the world. Faithful to his own thinking, by way of "An Accordion Tune," Nancy here continues to "restrict myself to what is, after all, the essential: a gesture of an opening or reopening in the direction of what must have preceded all construction" (*Dis-Enclosure* 189n8). In continuing to walk this path, wherever from and wherever to, we hope to be likewise faithful to Nancy's thinking: that is not to say that we are to *follow in the footsteps* of the master, but rather that in retracing his path we are equally *proceeding in a new direction*, we are ourselves *carrying further* what *carried us away* initially – since that is the only way for us to *make sense* (of it).

notes

1 See also Heidegger, *What is Called Thinking?* 5.

2 See also Heidegger, *What is Called Thinking?* 65.

bibliography

Heidegger, Martin. *Being and Time*. Trans. Joan Stambaugh. Albany: SUNY P, 1996. Print.

Heidegger, Martin. *Pathmarks*. Trans. William McNeil. Cambridge: Cambridge UP, 1998. Print.

Heidegger, Martin. *What is Called Thinking?* Trans. J. Glenn Gray and Fred D. Wieck. London: Harper, 1968. Print.

Nancy, Jean-Luc. *Corpus*. Trans. Richard A. Rand. New York: Fordham UP, 2008. Print.

Nancy, Jean-Luc. *Dis-Enclosure. The Deconstruction of Christianity*. Trans. Bettina Bergo et al. New York: Fordham UP, 2008. Print.

Nancy, Jean-Luc. *A Finite Thinking*. Ed. Simon Sparks. Trans. Simon Sparks et al. Stanford: Stanford UP, 2003. Print.

The Fragility of Sense

I

Some ancient philosophers compared the world to a big animal. This was vigorously opposed by modernity – the Enlightenment and the nineteenth century – , which compared it to a machine. Today, nobody would dare to set foot on this terrain. It is all too clear that first comparison presupposes an internal finality, the second an external causality; whereas we can assign neither property to the world.[1] The hypothesis of a God sometimes seems capable of overcoming both difficulties, but only does so by aggravating them through the integral and indecipherable secret to which it enjoins us to submit ourselves.

Without wanting either to dissipate the secret or attribute it to some other sacred sovereign, we can try to escape the dilemma by proposing to articulate what our time more than suggests to us, that which it rather enjoins us to consider: the world is neither an animal, nor a machine; it is we ourselves. It is neither the pursuit of an immanent finality, nor the effect of a transcendent causality. It is what humanity does (*fait*) – or undoes (*défait*) – , what humanity makes of it whilst constituting itself (*se fait*) – or undoing itself (*se défait*).

"Globalisation" (*mondialisation*) is not just the effect of a techno-economic development; it is a reshuffling, a putting back into play of the world (*le monde*) itself. It is perhaps just as much the end of a "world," in whatever way (*sens*) we understand it, as the birth of something other than a world, for which we have no name.

jean-luc nancy

translated by marie chabbert and nikolaas deketelaere

THE WORLD'S FRAGILE SKIN

II

At least one certainty imposes itself: if the world were an animal, it would present itself with a distinctive unity – even if distinguished only from a formless outside – and its distinction would display the character of a skin akin to the one where everything alive (*tout vivant*) distinguishes and presents itself. If, on the contrary, it were a machine, it would have no skin since its distinction and presentation would belong to an order different from that of its machinery.

This is an Open Access article distributed under the terms of the Creative Commons Attribution-NonCommercial-NoDerivatives License (http://creativecommons.org/licenses/by-nc-nd/4.0/), which permits non-commercial re-use, distribution, and reproduction in any medium, provided the original work is properly cited, and is not altered, transformed, or built upon in any way.

If the skin is indeed the proper character of a unity subsisting by itself and simultaneously relating to a world around it, how can the neither animal nor mechanical world of humans have a skin – i.e., a proper consistence – if there is no world outside of it (even if it understands itself as a plurality of worlds, which nonetheless remains the doing (*le fait*) precisely of the spirit and activity of men).

The question of the skin could be the one most apt to illuminating the world of men for us from the moment at which we can do nothing other than consider it as such: neither animal nor machine but world of men devoid of any world-beyond (or other world) in relation to which it could be measured, situated and receive its sense of "world." For the sense of a "world" is always precisely to make sense (*faire sens*), i.e., to allow a circulation, an economy, an operation of waypoints thanks to which all that is in this world is also what makes (*fait*) it and gives it life.

If I say "the world of musicians," I evoke a sphere or nebula in which values, techniques, fashions, images, practices and even definitions of "music" compose a possibility – or, more precisely, a compossibility – through which those who are in some sense "musicians" recognise themselves, find their way, can exchange, dispute and rival.

That it is matter of something like a skin is indicated to us by the semantic profusion through which "skin" designates as much the person as the membrane (getting under one's skin,[2] shedding one's skin); the soul as much as the body, indeed even as body (feeling good/bad in one's skin) or existence itself (to save someone's skin). It is not really a matter of metaphor or even metonym; the skin is from where a presence to the world and to oneself begins and ends: not just one's life but one's sensibility, one's activity and passivity, one's expressivity and signification.

In what way would the world have a skin if it did not have to feel, act and signify outside itself? But how could it not feel, act nor signify, if that is what a world must be? This is the question I am trying to answer, and to do that I must first consider with closer attention what a skin is.

III

The skin does not envelope a set of organs; it develops the presence to the world maintained by those organs. We are familiar with images, referred to as *écorchés* (i.e., flayed or skinned figures), displaying the arrangement of muscles, tendons, blood vessels and nerves of a body from which the skin has been taken off or lifted (*sometimes, the skinned person themselves is holding up a raised piece of skin*). Those images are often hard to look at. Nietzsche says that the skin makes the repulsive sight of the organism bearable. One can say that it is less a matter of making bearable – so, by masking – than of making presentable, i.e., visible and recognisable, what is otherwise hidden in the entanglement of organs, tissues, functions; an entanglement that, altogether, remains either incomprehensible to us, or limited to the maintenance of the body (that's the physiological and medical outlook). However, the maintenance of the organism does not exhaust the presence of an individual.

The skin is itself an organ – for the physiologist – , but this organ exceeds organicity. Playing with Artaud's famous phrase, one could say that it is the organ of a body without organs, the organ or indeed the place where a body presents itself as itself.

It does this by exposing the body to other bodies. The skin lets itself be seen, touched, heard, breathed and savoured. We know what skin is by the shaking of hands, kissing, the sight of a chin or gait. This organ therefore exceeds the proper order of the organism: it does not guarantee an interior operation of an autonomous system; it exposes (in French, one can write *il expeause*, it ex-skin-hibits) this autonomy to all possible outsides.

One could very well say that the skin is the organ of an organism's heteronomy: i.e., the organ that relates to the others what, at first glance, seems designed for relating only to itself. The individual *individualises itself* on

THE PULSE OF SENSE

the occasion of the sight, contact, smell or sound of other epidermises, i.e., enters as a distinct point in the combinatorics and co-appearance of all points. In other words, individuation is always transindividuation.[3]

IV

All exterior or indeed foreign bodies take part in what we must dare to call the *transpiration* of skins. The rock or metal I bump into or handle in turn become skins by transforming themselves into tools, shelter or jewels. Everything that encounters my skin encounters me; and without it, I would encounter nothing.

Skins are not impervious to each other: they are porous by definition, organic and metaphysical at the same time. They share (*partagent*) their secrets, making one another sensible to each other. I crumple up a herb and its scent lets itself be inhaled whilst what is crushed decomposes itself between my fingers.

The true nature and role of the skin are to be deciphered in the famous Marsyas myth. The satyr, a flutist, dared to defy Apollo, master of the lyre. Irate, the god has the satyr flayed or skinned (*fait écorcher*). The triumph of the lyre is secured. The skin of Marsyas, hung on a tree by his executioners, then finds itself lifted by the breeze and resounds with melodious accents.

To conclude, the breath, the thrust outweighs the regulated vibration of strings. The skin is not the site of a calculation nor a measurement: it is a site of passage, transit and transport, traffic and transaction. It rubs against and irritates, mixes and distinguishes, comes up against or flatters it. Skin makes hair stand on end, is exhausting, shivering, retractile, caressing, lubricating, pressing, trembling.

It makes itself into (*se fait*) the lens of the eye, eardrum, tongue, vagina, olfactory bulb, mucous membrane, papillae. It gets excited, stirred, heated, electrified, repulsed or exhaled. In all respects, the skin translates, betrays (*trahit*), transpires, transudes the palpitating singularity of the enigma of a being-to-itself insofar as it is from side to side outside itself, nearby and far-off, multiple, always floating and responding to the thrusting of the world's breezes, breaths and gusts. In all respects, it is the powerful and fragile resonance of all that arouses a form or tonality of existence.

V

If the world, for its part, cannot not have a skin; what becomes of the properties of the being-to-itself that the world nevertheless must be if it is indeed the site or the act of a whole of possible sense?

It does not have skin because it is itself nothing other than – to put it like that – the factorial of all our skins. It is and is nothing but the whole of combinations, assemblages, rubbings, pressures, caresses, violences, bruises, attractions and repulsions, avoidances, osmoses, excitations, captures, signals, signages and signatures which all our skins unceasingly exchange. At the same time, in these exchanges, they form and transform themselves, take on their traits, folds, styles and compose what we call peoples or populations, cultures, rivalries or dominations.

The world has no other skin than this turbulence and swell – sometimes ample, sometimes contracted – that make for (*font*) the histories, mores, grandeurs, decadences and revolutions. This is why, neither animal nor machine, the world has no life of its own (*vie propre*). It is indeed "the" world, but insofar as it is ours, the one where our presences and absences circulate. As physics attests, it may even be plural. It is the unitotal world of our multiplicity, as much numerical as spiritual, phenomenal or noumenal – as you like.

We can speak of it as of a skin if it develops the copresence of all that presents itself. But this presentation is unendingly resorbed in the succession of copresences. In the end, the world is a co-belonging – neither animal, nor machine – of all that resonates with all, like a breath, like the moulting of a snake or a thermonuclear fusion reaction.

It is a spinning, an interminable tangling whose destination is none other than the maelstrom in which the very idea of the world escapes in order to re-emerge, no matter where, by the will of (*au gré de*) the co-belonging without cohesion. Because it is not a skin, this expansion – this expansion of space-time, this upwelling of crystals and gas – is far more fragile than skins, skins that are always already fragile because *everything* there touches upon the extremities.

Marsyas' skin floats with the (*au gré des*) zephyrs,[4] but the world is swept away by hurricanes and icy gales. It does not resound with any harmony whatsoever. No hymn celebrates it, except for the one that says that it happens, that it takes place: the world is everything that is the case (*der Fall*, as Wittgenstein puts it). What happens, what falls down (*fallen*) from what one would have thought to be a supramundane height of the Idea: the fall (*la chute*) into what is real, what is actual.

The world is everything happening between us. That is to say, first of all ourselves and everything that happens to us, everything our touch, our sight, our breath, our movement comes to. By way of skin-to-skin referrals – from that of the insect strolling across my screen to that of the Hieronymus Bosch character reproduced within the crystals of this screen – , step by step and from surprise to imminence, from fleeting to immemorial, without knowing it, you come upon the full actuality of the world: the act of existence.

This act is made up (*fait*) of works and disasters, splendour, horror and insignificance. As long as it is ours, it is the act of an infinite arising that is in itself its whole sense and all the sense there is: a sense that unceasingly goes from skin to skin, never itself enveloped in nothing.

But if this act becomes that of an animal or a machine, of an entity enveloped in an autonomy that would have to justify (*rendre raison de*) itself, a big coagulation of functions and organs; then it is lost, it implodes, it asphyxiates like a skin whose pores are all coated with a putty of organic or technical self-sufficiency.

VI

> That it is, at any moment, possible to
> experience (*éprouver*)
> my skin as the skin of the world

> and the world as the weaving-together
> of all our sights breaths
> fumbles pressures
> the reverberation of chants murmurs
>   scansions
> and always equally to encounter
> the dull darkness thickness the silence and
>   inertia
> just like the caress and sorrow

> the palm of my hand and the water of the
>   ocean
> my tear (*déchirure*) and that of a disfigured
>   face
> my solitude and the busy crowds
> those who went astray who have gone away
>   who go hungry

> my bit (*peu*) touching upon the abundance
>   of ways gestures desires

> that that is still possible and that the skins
>   assume themselves (*se prennent*)
> divest themselves (*se déprennent*) untie
>   themselves sweat get themselves wet get them-
>   selves dry
> tattoo indulge skin themselves
> confusing forbidding interpreting
>   themselves

> without resolving itself in
>   connected interactive interfaces
> in the programming of a
>   big machine-animal

> is that too much to
>   ask – already?

disclosure statement

No potential conflict of interest was reported by the author.

notes

1 Nietzsche, *Le gai savoir* 125–26.

2 Nancy refers to the French idiom *avoir quelqu'un dans la peau* (meaning literally *to have someone in one's skin*), which does not translate into English but means to be infatuated with someone (as Edith Piaf sings about it in the eponymous song). The meaning of the English idiom *someone is getting under my skin* is something of the inverse

of the French: it indicates annoyance, being rubbed in precisely the wrong way. – Trans.

3 Evidently, a reference to Simondon is required here.

4 In Greek mythology, Zephyrus is the god personifying the west wind, considered the most favourable and gentlest of all directional winds. As a result, *zephyr* has come to mean a westerly wind, a gentle breeze, or breeze from the west. – Trans.

the inexhaustible

In this essay, I am interested in the question, or status, of force in Jean-Luc Nancy. Allow me to begin with some personal observations, or else observations on the personal. The personal dimension is not entirely (self-)indulgent here, since the force in which I am particularly interested in Nancy, that is, the force that I wish Nancy could have further pursued, or would pursue, cuts across two of Nancy's most personal texts, "L'Intrus" and "Dialogue Under the Ribs." So I begin by recalling one of my first encounters with Nancy. This was in 2009, when I traveled to Strasbourg to initiate some conversations with him, in the hope of asking him to be on my dissertation committee, a request to which he eventually very generously, as always, agreed. During the time of my visit, the conference in memory of Philippe Lacoue-Labarthe at the University of Strasbourg was also ongoing, and I saw Nancy deliver his keynote on "Philippe" in terms of a first name and its philosophico-theological implications. If I remember correctly, the keynote began very slightly after 7 p.m., and Nancy did not end till sometime after 9 p.m. If I'm not wrong too, Nancy was actually not quite done with his talk. In other words, he seemingly had to cut it short only because of a logistical issue: the auditorium had to be closed, or, one had to be mindful of those who were going to lock up the auditorium and not hold them back any longer. In any case, Nancy and I arranged to do lunch the next day, and what transpired was a meeting that lasted about four hours, where Nancy talked about the genealogy of modern French thought from its early stages, where the links

irving goh

INSISTENCE, OR THE FORCE OF JEAN-LUC NANCY

to German philosophy were explicit, to its contemporary situation in France, where there was, by 2009, the significant decline in interest in the studying of philosophy in favor of more professional fields such as business studies. If it is not already evident, given the previous evening's two-hour lecture (not to mention that Nancy attended every talk during the day too), and then the four-hour lunch meeting the next day, there is an indefatigable force in Nancy. It is a force clearly demonstrated in his energy, enthusiasm, passion, and commitment – not only in mind but also in body, in person – to philosophy, to philosophical discourse, to the discourse on philosophy. Or else, more precisely perhaps, as we will see toward the end of this essay, it is the force of (his) love of thinking. Speaking of the body, we cannot fail either to recognize Nancy's strong force to live on (or *sur-vivre*, as Derrida would say), that is, to live well beyond a certain duration expected of a patient of a heart-transplant procedure, something that Nancy acknowledges in "L'Intrus" and again in "Dialogue Under the Ribs." The force is indeed strong in Nancy, and this is not to mention his consistent productivity and prolificacy in terms of published works, which began in the 1970s and continues well today, and which also spans a wide range of topics including Being or the subject, community, freedom, politics or democracy, touch, religion, aesthetics, and, more recently, sex, or more precisely "sexistence." Undoubtedly too, there is moreover a compelling force in Nancy's writings, a force that has clearly drawn me to his works and his thought, informing my works on the "reject" and "prepositional existence";[1] I do not doubt either that this is the force that motivates all the writers in this volume to contribute to this special issue on Nancy and all other scholars committed to the works of Nancy.

From what has been said above, one could perhaps articulate force in Nancy as how it is commonly understood, that is to say, as both physical and mental energy or strength, if not fortitude, and as influence. But I also want to think of force in this essay as affect, which is to say, following Raymond Williams, as a nascent or emerging "structure of feeling" that affects the individual: something that finds its first corporeal stirrings within an individual, murmuring from within the individual, which then emanates from the individual to its outside; in other words, something that keeps the individual restless, and which therefore moves, disturbs, or rouses those around that individual as well.[2] I will want to think further about this force as (personal) affect specifically in Nancy's "L'Intrus" and "Dialogue Under the Ribs," but for now, let me say that force has not been a critical term for Nancy in his works at large, at least not as much as for Derrida (as evident in "Force and

Signification" and "Force of Law," for example) or Deleuze (especially in *Nietzsche and Philosophy*). As I see it, it is only lately, in Nancy's *Sexistence*, that the term "force" has emerged more explicitly, which also gets a further explication in *The Deconstruction of Sex*, a companion material to *Sexistence* that Nancy and I worked on together. I will make reference to *The Deconstruction of Sex* later. Meanwhile, I would say that, despite the apparent ambivalent status of force in Nancy's works before *Sexistence* and *The Deconstruction of Sex*, there is nevertheless a certain force in Nancy's thinking: a certain force inscribes – or rather, "exscribes," to follow Nancy's preferred term for writing[3] – itself through his thinking; a certain force drives his thinking. And I would articulate this force in terms of *insistence*.

insistence

At first glance, this force or insistence manifests itself rather clearly in Nancy's political writings, and this is especially so when they touch on the question of freedom. In *The Experience of Freedom*, Nancy argues that freedom, essentially, is beyond all human determinations of living, beyond all human efforts at governing living, where limits to freedom might be imposed either supposedly benevolently for the common good or malignantly in order to annihilate others whose differences are intolerable to the dominant group. Freedom insists furthermore in a way that transcends all philosophies of freedom, preceding and exceeding them; or else, it does not even need philosophy to attest to its existence or insistence in the world. According to Nancy, as long as there is the fact of existence, that is, the force that somehow ensures that we *and others* always already continue to exist, despite and in spite of the histories of violence against certain existences, the force of freedom (of existence) will always remain inextinguishable, undeniably or irreducibly insisting even when affronted by conditions that seek to deny it. What becomes clear from this, then, is that behind any political insistence on freedom is an ontological force. In my view, the insistence of (and on) a strong, undeniable ontological force of existence is underscored by Nancy no more forcefully than in the essay "Unsacrificeable." There, he would argue that in sacrifice, it is *not* existence per se that has been sacrificed but existence reified in terms of "my life," "his or her life," "our lives," or "their lives." In other words, there is sacrifice only when existence is objectified, e.g., an existent's life rendered a sacrificial object, when there is the abstraction or reduction of existence into an object deemed worthy of sacrifice. We must make this distinction between existence per se and reified life separated from existence, and it is from this distinction that Nancy insists that the ontological force of existence is such that it can never be sacrificed: existence *insists* on, if not in-sists in, its existing.[4] This is no doubt reiterated in "Dialogue Under the Ribs," Nancy's reflection on his heart transplant twenty years later, played out as a dialogue between himself and the transplanted organ. In this piece, Nancy looks back at the time when his own heart was showing signs of not beating any longer, and says he was prepared to let it be: he "really didn't care" should that heart die on him ("Dialogue Under the Ribs" 172). But then came the option of having a transplant, and for Nancy, that was a case of the resilient force of existence, the insistence of existence: a case demonstrating "life that maintains itself, transmits itself, and reboots itself" (173).

But to go back to the notion of force in Nancy's political writings, one that is always motivated or driven by the ontological force of existence: this ontological insistence subtends Nancy's engagement with the question of community too. Within this context, Nancy would argue that the sense of being-with [*être-avec*], being-together [*être-ensemble*], or being-in-common [*être-en-commun*], insists in this world. Community in that sense always already exists as long as there is this world, that is, our world here and now, where we always exist with others who have come before us, others who are contemporaneous with us, and others who will arrive after us,

whether we like it or not, and regardless if we care to acknowledge them or not. In that respect, community as the sense of the world where existence is always already coexistence with others is indifferent to any communitarian project that seeks some kind of union or fusion of beings, especially beings imagined to be similar to one another. From Nancy's resistance to such projects (and I note here that such a resistance is reiterated in *Que faire?*), one could elicit a force that may be considered negative as well, which is to say, a force that actually welcomes some form of breaking down or disavowal, without necessarily projecting or enacting any concrete negating measure, without any suggestion as to how that breaking down or disavowal could take shape. This negative force is what I see in Nancy's insistence on the "inoperativity" or "unworking" [*désœuvrement*] in relation to the thinking of community since *The Inoperative Community*. And here, I point out that this negative force is not foreign at all to the idea of insistence, if we take into account that the prefix *in-* in "insistence" can signify negation as well, as in the case, precisely, of "inoperativity."[5] While this negative force might appear passive, since, to repeat, it does not seek to enact or enforce anything concrete, Nancy reminds us that its insistence is not negligible, that it cannot be ignored. In an op-ed piece published in *Libération* in early 2019 on the topic of inventing a worldly sovereignty, Nancy would call for a form of "resistance" that involves the critique of all the "immense injustices" that entail from globalization, a resistance that calls for the "mobilizing of our civil, social, moral, and intellectual energies to invent the unprecedented [*l'inédit*], without which everything will just follow its pathetic course." We must, according to Nancy there, "resist reflexes, conformism, nostalgia [*ressassement*], and resentment [*ressentiment*]," and that "would be to resist sovereignly" ("Inventons la souveraineté mondiale"; trans. mine). Nancy's resistance here is not a militant call to arms in the literal sense; I doubt there is any claim to activist ambition or horizon either (not just in this piece but also in Nancy's writings at large).

Nonetheless, there is an insistence on *at least* doing something: *at least* an active mobilization of energies to invent something in resistance to all the ultra-conservativism that is overwhelming politics lately either in the form of reactionary populism or alt-right movements, precisely the phenomena that form the backdrop to Nancy's call for a "worldly sovereignty" in the piece. Force here might be closer to what we may call political affect, that is to say, the pressure that is growing and emerging in us – "palpable pressures" (*Marxism and Literature* 132) as Williams would say – in response, if not in resistance, to the other oppressive pressures bearing on us as emanating from political and/or economic institutions and structures.[6] What insists in Nancy's resistance, then, could be a matter of harnessing these affects, of recognizing and articulating their potentiality. As to what is to be done about them, this is where Nancy once again resists in giving them a program, goal, or end point, but that is only because Nancy understands that each of these affects has different force trajectories, and is capable of taking its own shape, of following its own course. As Nancy says in *Que faire?*:

> Politics cannot assert itself without a relation to the sense of existence. But it can only open itself *toward* this sense and *toward* its diverse modes of being and doing; it cannot even think to subsume them under a single form. (46; trans. mine)

It is in respecting these various nascent or emerging forms (which include those that are not presently recognizable as political, as Nancy will insist) and, again, in resisting a singular, regulating program, that Nancy looks to that which comes from improvisation, that which is "impossible to identify" and "without pretentions of founding, inaugurating, and beginning even," hence that which is not so much borne by a revolution (which is largely guided by some sort of singular program or organization) than that which insists, nevertheless, through a "resolution" (119).[7]

The resistance against a goal or end point, or else the resolution to let emerge yet unthought of, yet unarticulated, ways of "being-in-common," as I see it, strongly resonances with Nancy's term of *déclosion*, which has been translated as "dis-enclosure." *Déclosion* is a term Nancy deploys in the first volume of *The Deconstruction of Christianity*, which is meant to explain how a mode of thinking or practice – say, monotheistic Christianity, to follow Nancy's case study in the book – , despite desperately seeking to found itself as a monolithic institution by inscribing for itself strict boundaries, finds itself eventually exposed to elements that it ideologically resists – say, atheism – , and this is only but the movement of thought itself, which no doctrine, including its own, can contain absolutely. *Déclosion*, then, signals some form of re-opening, re-exposure, or re-exposition, whenever something closes itself up or in, or whenever something is enclosed by something else. Thus, resistance or resolution is the *déclosion* we need for new and other forms of thinking about "being-in-common" to counter dominating ideologies that have repressed or suppressed the latter. If there is a need to rethink politics today, it is this kind of open politics that we need to give shape or form. In Nancy's words, once again from *Que faire?*:

> Politics is an administration of possibilities [*des possibles*], which does not impose upon them any superior order but maintains accessibility [*ouvre les accès*] to this opening: not to that which is beyond reach, but to that which touches [*atteint*] us and which comes from nowhere and goes nowhere. (51)

The idea of re-opening, re-exposure, or re-exposition is a force of thought that insists throughout Nancy's writings, and it is undoubtedly a resilient force, as suggested not just by the thinking of resistance against the wave of populist sentiments but also by the thinking of freedom beyond all human determinations, of existence that blunts the horrors of sacrifice, and of community that undoes or disavows all insular communitarian projects. I would even add that *déclosion* can also be thought of as the reiteration of the decision of existing,[8] the decision to keep making sense in the world, the ontological force once again of insisting in existing in the world of any human, animal, vegetal, mineral, molecular, and inorganic existent, beyond the will or determination of any subject, and despite opposing forces.

the love of force

So far, it has been shown that force in Nancy tends to be a strong one. Existence, freedom, "being-in-common," resistance or resolution, and *déclosion* or re-opening all assert themselves forcefully in Nancy's writings or thinking. However, when it comes to the question of touch, a leitmotif no less (insistent) than existence or "being-in-common" in Nancy's thinking, and moreover linked to existence and "being-in-common" too, Nancy, interestingly, adopts a more tender, gentler approach. Nancy clearly does not advocate forms of touch that are actually forceful. Touch, for Nancy, cannot be a grasping that seeks to hold on to another in some firm, unrelenting, permanent way; that, Nancy tells us, would not be touch but a wound, if not even a death grip. Touch, then, must be that which knows how and when to let go; it is all a matter of tact. That is how we will be able to attain "a true touch" [*une touche vraie*] (50; trans. mod.), as Nancy calls it in *Noli me tangere*, one that does not retain (and therefore possibly appropriate) the other but lets the other free to go wherever the other desires in the other's passage in the world. In other words, touch, unlike freedom, existence, "being-in-common," resistance or resolution, and *déclosion* or re-opening, must not be an insistent force; a delicate balance between reaching toward and release is needed in the force of touch. Things get interesting when such an understanding of touch is brought to bear on the question of sex, which is Nancy's subject in *Sexistence*. In *The Deconstruction of Sex*, which follows *Sexistence*, I pointed out to Nancy that the notion of touch as gentle, or even tactful, becomes problematic in sex: as I see it, sex, especially sex that involves penetration, would involve touch

that is arguably irreducibly violent. Nancy provides a very interesting response. First, he defines force as "the act of a thrust, a pressure that is exerted on [*contre*] another force. Relation, in whatever form, constitutes a part of force: force exerts itself against/with [*contre/avec*] another force." Or, as he says later, "a force implies a relation, a possibility of relations." From there, he continues to say that "touching is the taking place [*l'avoir-lieu*] of a relation: the proximity according to which forces encounter one another, one coming to another, feeling their powers, their resistances. Touch [...] is the very act of the encounter of forces." And then in direct response to my suspicion of the violence of a penetrative touch, he would say, and I quote at length:

> It is necessary to agree on this violence. Of course, penetration in all its forms exerts a force. Even if the body is open, and in some ways it invites itself to be penetrated, it is no less gaping. Its openings are indeed real – and they have totally other functions than sexual ones – but they are in some ways latent [*potentielles*]: it is necessary to force them open. However, this amorous forcing [*forçage*] is not a violence. It is a kind of mimicry of violence. Certainly, it is not negligible that this mimicry exists, but it reveals precisely that the forcing is possible and desirable as long as it is precisely desired, that is, desired by a passivity that wants to submit itself, abandon itself, to it.
>
> This abandonment indicates that a certain welcoming and accompanying force comes to press itself on/against [*contre*] the force of penetration.

The violence of penetration, then, is deflected to be but a "mimicry of violence."[9] And tact is kept intact, as long as that penetration, which Nancy comes to call an "amorous forcing," is desired by the lover or lovers. Put another way, penetration becomes an insistence by the lover for that forcing, an insistence expressed by the opening of his or her body to the lover, an opening that is not exactly passive but presses back only in order to continue drawing the lover into himself or herself, thus insisting on the proximity of the two bodies.

The proximity of the two bodies is clearly contingent upon a rhythm of their coming together, their withdrawing, and their coming back together again – a rhythm that purportedly repeats itself. This is, of course, the optimistic take. It is also possible, though, that the lovers will not come back to each other but seek out other lovers. In that regard, I asked Nancy if both bodies, in their gradual separation, after sex, could avoid a possible heartbreak: how do both bodies maintain the force of attraction between them, rather than subsequently open themselves up to other bodies, leading to what we would typically condemn as infidelity? To that question, Nancy says that there is a "force of attachment" that actually entails sex, a force that was created when the lovers felt the mutual opening up of their bodies to the "amorous forcing" of sex. This attachment would be what sustains fidelity, an insistence on the continued relation desired by the lovers. As I see it, then, this force bears not just resilience but also optimism, which can be traced back to Nancy's earlier "L'amour en éclats," translated as "Shattered Love." There, Nancy speaks of the passage of love in the world, passing from one lover to another. As such a passage, there will inevitably, or rather inadvertently (to underscore the surprise nature of the incalculable trajectory, if not event, of love), be the "broken heart" situation, that is, the end of an amorous relation, the day where "I no longer love you," or when the promise of "I love you" is no longer kept (Nancy, "Shattered Love" 100). Certainly, one might feel that the thinking of such a love is a thinking "exposed to being betrayed," proven precisely by the "broken heart" situation (94). However, Nancy tells us that this situation need not be an all-teary affair; it need not be seen as a tragedy,[10] as the end of everything, or the end of the world as it is typically and banally put. Nancy also assures us that "that does not mean that there was no love, nor even that there was not love" (100). Instead, love is always (out) there, as long as there is always

the enunciation of "I love you," which is love's name or promise and which, Nancy continues to tell us, "says nothing (except a limit of speech), but it allows to emerge the fact that love must arrive and that nothing, absolutely nothing, can relax, divert, or suspend the rigor of this law" (100). We must have faith in the arrival of love, therefore, even though that promise "does not anticipate or assure the future" (100). To be sure, we must not have any illusion that love will arrive once and for all the next time; we must not forget that love is always passing through lovers. So:

> love arrives, it comes, or else it is not love. But it is thus that it endlessly goes elsewhere than to "me" who would receive it: its coming is only a departure for the other, its departure only the coming of the other. (98)

It is such "crossing of love" that certainly "breaks the heart" at times (98),[11] but it also offers the chance for a re-opening of oneself to others, including others whom one might think of not being able to love before. This is also how "love arrives in all the forms and in all the figures of love," hence "projected in all its splintering [éclats]" (101; trans. mod.). Thus, a more adequate translation of "L'amour en éclats," that is to say, a translation faithful to the piece's optimism, would not be so much "shattered love" as "*scattered* love."

life force

The optimism above is no doubt carried over to the question, once again, of existence, which cuts through "L'Intrus" and "Dialogue Under the Ribs." I would say that optimism is the overarching insistence of both texts, touching on the resilience of the body and the body's optimism in living on after finding out that one's own heart was failing, living on after a heart transplant, after introducing into one's body an organ that is not one's own, and further living on twenty years after that transplant. Such resilient optimism or optimistic resilience is rather evident when Nancy, in "Dialogue Under the Ribs," says that "there is nothing interesting in lasting," that is to say, in letting life run its natural course; "what is interesting," he contends, "is to reboot, to be revived, to start again," that is to say, to live anew, differently, via other means, for example, via a transplanted heart (173). That optimism does not falter even in the face of the possible expiration of the transplanted organ: when, in "Dialogue Under the Ribs" again, the transplant suggests that it might die on Nancy too, a seemingly unfazed Nancy responds by saying, "Perhaps another transplant awaits its chance? Or else an all-new nice little electric heart?" (174). I will want to critique this optimism, but for now, in relation to this particular (optimistic) insisting of existing through organ transplant, perhaps one should also recall the word "insister" as a noun, the use of which is very much obsolete today. According to the *Oxford English Dictionary*, a trace of the noun "in-sister" (spelled with a hyphen[12]) can be found in a 1644 text in Canterbury, where the term signifies "a resident female member of a fraternity or guild, especially a charitable institution." One could argue, then, that there is not only the trace of otherness but also of gender or even sexual difference in *insistence*,[13] and it is very likely in the case of an organ transplant where the chance of otherness and/or sexual difference gets played out, where one reopens oneself to the rest of the world, possibly receiving an organ from someone of a different gender and race. As Nancy says, there are no "limits of sex or ethnicity" in this case; his heart "may be a heart of a black woman" ("L'Intrus" 8).

There is definitely nothing wrong in bringing to bear an optimistic and/or resilient force on the thinking of existence, love, *déclosion*, freedom, and community, if not on thought itself. But I wonder if this optimism, or else insistence, might be a little too forceful, especially with regard to existence, such that the other aspect of force has been forgotten. I am thinking of the case of force recognizing its own weakening, its waning, the case where force finds itself losing its force, perhaps even to the point where force seeks its own

dissolution, its own disavowal: force entering into a state of entropy, precipitating into that of atrophy. To repeat, this is no less an aspect of force itself, its own insistence; its sense of exhaustion in relation to its assertion in the world, even its sense of discomfort in being in the world any longer, its sense of wanting out from any continued enactment on the world stage, and one could say that this is the pessimistic side of force. This is no doubt close to Vattimo's "weak thought," which takes into account Being's "faded trans-mission," its "taking leave of" existence or "passing away," its "waning," its "fullness of its decline" or its "fully living its weakness" (45, 46, 47, 48, 50). Or, in a nod to Agamben, one could consider this the very "impotentiality" of force itself, its insistence other than enactment, exertion, and assertion: its in-sistence, then, where the prefix signals once again to negation or negativity.[14] And perhaps we must not fight, or resist, this *other* insistence of force itself; we must also learn to acknowledge, embrace, and embody it.

In a way, the registering of the weakening of force can be found in Nancy's "L'Intrus," where he writes, in the aftermath of the heart transplant and amidst its aftereffects, of the sense of precarious existence, accompanied no less by pain and fatigue. Not only does he experience "the weakening of muscles and kidneys, the diminution of memory and of the strength [*force*] to work" but also feel the following: "one no longer knows or recognizes oneself: but here these words no longer have meaning. Very quickly, one is no more than a slackening, floating strangeness, suspended between poorly identified states, between sufferings, incapacities, lapses" (Nancy, "L'Intrus" 12, 11). And that, as Nancy adds in "Dialogue Under the Ribs," constitutes "the complicated, confused, and agitated time of [his] most proper existence" (174). We find here, then, the body and the sense of existence feeling themselves weakening, the force of both body and existence failing and flailing. To be sure, though, Nancy makes clear that this weakening of force is a consequence or effect of the introduction of a foreign organ – precisely the "intruder" [*l'intrus*], according to Nancy – into the body, after which the body has to be heavily medicated in order to support this organ, including immunosuppressants such that the body will not reject the organ. Yet it is also because of the immunosuppressants that the body's immunity is reduced, hence exposing it to other health hazards such as the zoster virus, the cytomegalovirus, and lymphoma, all of which require further medical interventions in the body, which only further weaken the body. So, with the affliction of lymphoma, which

> gnaws at the body, exhausting it, the chemo and radiation treatments also attack it and cause it to suffer in several ways: this suffering is the relation of the intrusion and its refusal. Even morphine, which calms the pain, provokes others: bewilderment, disarray. (Nancy, "L'Intrus" 11)

And this is how Nancy comes to occupy "a certain continuity of intrusion, its permanent regime," through which the body passes "from pain to pain" (12).

As said, if force is waning, if the body feels the pain of existence, or if there is a disquiet or unease [*inquiétude*] with existence, it seems that Nancy is inclined to attribute all that to an intrusion or intruder that comes from elsewhere. I am thinking, however, of the intruder within oneself, the intruder that is also oneself, without any physical intervention from the outside, say, the introduction of a foreign organ into one's body. I am thinking of the *other* me who senses the fatigue of existing, who does not share in the optimism and resilience of existence, who does not possess the strength or energy for the *déclosion* toward the "rebooting" of existence, who only suffers pain in the continuing of existence, who thus feels a restlessness [*inquiétude*] of being that only an exit from existence can quell. This is the intruder within myself, the intruder who is also myself, who perhaps senses the affect that calls for the departure from existence, i.e., who responds to the affect signaling that it just might be, as Nietzsche would say, the right time to die;

this is the *other* me the intruder who gives me only the sense of disquieting uncertainty in existence, a debilitating "wavering of the mind" between living on and what is to be done to exit from existence.[15] (One could say that the weight of the body here does not match, irreconcilably, the drifting of the mind.) "Lasting" in this case, then, is not existing imbued with the resilient optimism or optimistic resilience of life rebooting, reviving, restarting itself. Instead, it is a despairing, anguishing living on, which might also be nothing more than a posthumous existing, that is, living while feeling already dead. This *other* me who senses existence as such we sometimes call our "inner demon," to whom we like to assign blame for the negative thoughts. In other words, we tend to divest ourselves from responsibility for the latter, claiming that when we do articulate the latter, we are just "beside ourselves" or "not being ourselves." Put another way, we deny the "exscription" of this devastatingly intrusive *other* me and all the accompanying negative thoughts and forces; we tend to write them off, while they nevertheless or even irreducibly "exscribe" themselves or write themselves out,[16] because, as said, they are part of a force that *insists* in existence as well. Existing, after all, involves an exiting (through death); *exit-ence* is but part of *existence*.

We can put the above in relation to Nancy's *Listening* too. There, Nancy speaks of an "ontological tonality" of existence, an "archi-sonority" that announces existence before it presents itself through a body, hence rendering the presence of a body but the "echo of the naked figure [of existence] in the open depth" (*Listening* 4, 29 trans. mod., 4). And again, like all the writings mentioned above, this sonority or tonality announces itself with a strong force: it arrives with an "attack" in the musical sense (27). I would add, though, that all echoes fade, all sonic vibrations or reverberations lose force, eventually. To every strong, primary, or principal force of sound or voice of existence, there is also always a more subtle, a more subdued *sotto voce* or second voice, if not a *voce morente* even, that is, a dying voice, or else a *sotto voce* in *morendo* (dying away). And this *sotto voce* or *voce morente* does not need to follow from, or to come at the tail end of, the principal voice of existence; it can accompany the latter simultaneously, harmonizing (in the musical sense again) with it, which create either a resonance or dissonance. In either case, as the *other*, negative insistence of force of existence, this voice must have the equal right or freedom to "exscribe" itself. Nancy, in a way again, does seem to give expression to this voice, or to the sense of what I have called above "posthumous existence," when in "L'Intrus," he says that living with the foreign/intrusive organ in him is life as "none other than death – or rather, life/death: a suspension of the continuum of being" (7).[17] Yet, as said above too, what quickly, undoubtedly, and ultimately overwhelms this sense is the force of optimism and/or resilience. What I am arguing for, then, is a receiving of weak or waning force and its affects in a way that does not supplement them with any recuperative or reparative horizon; we must, on our part, *not* insist on this force returning, resurrecting, rejuvenating itself. In other words, if being, according to Nancy in "Shattered Love" again, is a heart, that is to say, existence as a pulsation that brings the body into presence, presenting the living body as "given over, offered to the outside, to others, and even to the self" (89), and therefore also open to love, which, as seen before, traverses the body and is capable of breaking the heart, hence possibly rendering being a broken heart too, then, this time, we must also allow for the thought of being as absolutely brokenhearted. This is being absolutely abandoned – and only "love alone can" (41) abandon as Nancy says in "Abandoned Being" – to the abyss of misery and despair, from which there is no coming up for air, no respite, no salvation. Being abandoned, according to Nancy, is also akin to the syncope of the heart,[18] but the syncope here would be more asphyxiating than Nancy would want it; it would be closer to Catherine Clément's, which dares go toward the extreme, toward unconsciousness [*évanouissement*], possibly without

a return to consciousness or life even.[19] We must recognize this absolute broken-heartedness, this absolute abandonment or "extreme poverty of abandonment" ("Abandoned Being" 36), as "existential rather than categorial" ("Shattered Love" 84), as Nancy himself would say, and I would add that this is one that no ontology, no positive or optimistic *déclosion*, not even thinking, can console or suture over: there can be no recourse to a comforting ontology or thinking that lifts abandonment out of despair and turn it to a freeing of existence from "all categories, all transcendentals," from all existing enunciations of itself, hence making it available [*disponibilité*] to yet another abundance [*l'abondance*] of ways of articulating itself as it "opens on a profusion of possibilities" ("Abandoned Being" 36, 37). The silence of this abandonment is an unbearable misery or disquiet, a real or experiential suffering or pain; the hurt is real, which no epistemology can heal.[20]

Put another way, and again in Nancy's terms, but going beyond them at the same time: we must leave weak force to its very *désœuvrement*, which is perhaps an "inoperativity" or "unworking" more negative, more radical, than what Nancy has in mind for that term. We must follow it to its dissipation, its extinguishment, which I also suspect this is not where Nancy would like to go with force. No doubt, then, that what I am suggesting (or even insisting) here constitutes an intrusion into Nancy's thinking, making it strange to itself; my thoughts here act like a transplant into his thinking that he and scholars faithful to Nancy's philosophy who follow it to the letter might reject. But this is also my love, sent from the outside to his thinking, cutting through his thought, breaking the heart of his thinking, if not his heart even.[21] This is a love seeking to elucidate the differentials or differences of force, particularly its weak, pessimistic, and negative aspect. This is perhaps love and thinking as force, that is, force in Hegel's sense in his *Phenomenology of Spirit*, which recognizes differences and precedes Understanding, and which is not that foreign to Nancy's idea in "Shattered Love" of love as thought or thought as love, which "rejects abstraction and conceptualization as these are recognized by understanding," or which "does not produce the operators of a knowledge" but "undergoes an experience" and "lets the experience inscribe itself" (83–84). Thus, when in the "confused, agitated time of [one's] most proper existence," to follow Nancy's rhetoric from "Dialogue Under the Ribs" one more time, we must also not refrain from elucidating or "exscribing" the negative affects or feelings such as sadness, melancholy, anxiety, hopelessness, shame, catatonia, depression, including suicidal depression, regret, etc. that possibly accompany such times.[22] That is admittedly something we do not see much yet in Nancy. Of course, I am *not* wishing that Nancy be afflicted by these negative feelings or affects; my love simply cannot allow that. What I wish to see in Nancy's writings is for Nancy to take into further consideration, to dwell or tarry with for a greater extent of time, weak force and its negative affects: let them develop and circulate a little more. To reiterate, weak, negative force is equally a force of existence; it *insists* as much in existence too. As part of the sense of existence, or even of the world, we must learn to abandon or expose ourselves, without reservation, to this pessimistic, self-extinguishing, or even heartbreaking force and its negative affects. "Lasting" as such can be equally "interesting."

echo by jean-luc nancy

Irving Goh regrets that I am not melancholic. He uses that term only once, and in a series of several other terms, but it may be considered the term comprising the essence of everything he finds absent in me. He is right. And he does not know how much I sometimes regret ignoring melancholia because it is, according to a long tradition, at least in the West, the mark of genius.

Characterizing melancholia as the feeling of a "posthumous existence" is certainly very apt. In Derrida and Lacoue-Labarthe, setting aside the differences between them, I have of course always noticed the presence of this feeling of living or writing after one's own death. And I have always had difficulty sharing it. If I understand it as the feeling of not being there, of not being present at my own activity of being-in-the-world and therefore of thinking and writing – i.e., of trying to give shape, precisely, to this being-in-the-world – , then I could say that for me this feeling is the feeling that it is not "me" who is there in this activity/passivity, but that is an other, the other, others, the whole mass of an "It" where my culture, my history, my language leaves to the tiny "I" the almost non-dimensional place of a point which indeed "writes," traces an exploration without subject or object, occupied only with letting itself take shape, if it can, the trace of a sensibility ...

This is very present, very sensible to me, but does not take on the "posthumous" tinge Irving Goh speaks of. To the contrary, it becomes indistinguishable from what he talks about as "force." For the force and "optimism," for which I have always been both praised and blamed (or at least warned), always appeared independent from "me." It is a question of a thrust coming from elsewhere, from nowhere or from an abyss gaping behind me. I have often noticed this when listening to comments on the strength it took me to go through many a physical, medical, and organic ordeal. For I was never conscious of nor felt myself to be mobilizing forces. It happened as it happened; I had nothing to do with it.

Of course, behind every temperament there is a labyrinth of which we know that a psychoanalysis might shed some light on without therefore leading to a conclusion. Undoubtedly, this is the reason why I have replaced psychoanalysis by writing, teaching, action ... But there are melancholics who likewise do so. I therefore end up somewhat melancholic about not knowing melancholy.

However, a slightly different accent or tone has been imposing itself upon me for some time now: the course of the world has increasingly forced me to recognize that our "world" – that of the globalized civilization plunging the world into deep turmoil – is perhaps already dead and that we have been talking in the wake of this death for a long time now. And without being able to at least avoid admitting that a real end to this civilization cannot be excluded.

Many of us – whether melancholics or not – have been thinking and working with the "death of God" (or the "end of metaphysics") behind us as something achieved. Whatever complexities we recognized in our situation, whatever restraint we observed towards progressive or revolutionary promises, we – again, whether melancholics or not – continued to be carried for some time by a certain confidence in the possibility of, let's say, "doing better." And today, this is becoming much more fragile.

And on me, it exerts something of the heartbreaking force that Irving Goh wishes me to undergo. For which I thank him.

disclosure statement

No potential conflict of interest was reported by the author.

notes

1 Kindly see my *The Reject: Community, Politics, and Religion After the Subject* and *L'existence prépositionnelle*.

2 See of course Williams's "Structures of Feeling" in *Marxism and Literature*. To be clear, locating "structures of feeling" within the personal or the individual does *not* mean that affects begin with the personal or the individual. Faithful to affect studies, I take affect *not* to be a product of a will or intention of an individual. Like Raymond Williams, Sara Ahmed, Jonathan Flatley, Lauren Berlant, and other affect theorists, I would say that there is a larger historical, social, material, and psychic field that is not only coextensive but also precedes and supersedes the individual, from which affects can form and within which they can circulate before touching the individual in ways that the latter cannot ignore.

3 "Exscription," according to Nancy (see especially the essay "Exscription" and *Corpus*), is the process by which sense gets inscribed in and as writing. However, sense is not henceforth locked in writing but exceeds writing and traverses back out in the world. That is why it is "ex-scription," which is to say, writing ("scription") that writes itself to the outside ("ex"). One could argue that there is a certain resonance between Nancy's "exscription" and Derrida's notion of writing or *écriture*, the trace of which Derrida puts it precisely in terms of *force* in "Force and Signification" and *Of Grammatology*.

4 Perhaps one could hear in this an echo of Derrida's argument in "By Force of Mourning" that force and existence are ineluctable. For Derrida there, force is something virtual that gives form to existence (and this recalls his notion of force in "Force of Law," which inaugurates everything), but it also has its "dynamo-logic" (145), allowing it to escape all presence, to be indifferent to any necessity of becoming an actuality [*passage à l'acte*], hence always remaining open to the uncalculated event of its own arrival in unexpected forms, that is, open to, in Derrida's rhetoric, its "to-come." It is force as such that, according to Derrida, it precedes, traverses, and exceeds ontology.

5 At this point, allow me to say that the way I am thinking "insistence" here with regard to the question of force in Nancy can be compared to Derrida's reading of "desistance" in Lacoue-Labarthe. For Derrida, desistance is that which is structurally "ineluctable" ("Introduction: Desistance" 1) from anything, for example, the constitution of a subject. It is something always already occurring to whatever is in the making, and therefore belongs, or is an integral part of, the latter: "a certain constitutive *desistance* of the subject" (2). But it is also outside the will or decision of the latter, and as such, its trace or "pre-inscription" or "pre-impression" (2) might even run counter to one's desire. Thus, desistance might appear to pose as an opposing force, but one must recognize that it "doesn't mark anything negative" (1). It is just the other side of the same thing. (Or, to put it as Deleuze once did with speed, acceleration and deceleration are but the two aspects of it, and one must not think that deceleration is a negation of speed.) In that respect, desistance is "a (de)constitution, rather than a destitution" (2), in the sense that it resists any illusion that the thing in question is constituted once and for all. To any such illusion, desistance is there "to cease, to stop, to leave off" (4). It exposes the unavoidable aspects of the thing, "even the worst:

mistakes, weaknesses, misapprehensions, inhibitions, omissions, compromises" (10). I hope how "insistence" shares some of these aspects of desistance will become clear as this essay progresses. For another variant of "insistence" in Nancy, it is useful to see Ian James's "The Persistence of the Subject: Jean-Luc Nancy."

6 One might see here a contest of forces, which can be found in Deleuze's *Nietzsche and Philosophy*, and Deleuze would put it in terms of active forces vs. reactive forces, strong forces vs. weak forces. Following Nietzsche, Deleuze inclines toward active/strong forces, which are "appropriating, possessing, subjugating, dominating," if not have the effect of making a body "a self and define the self as superior and captivating [*surprenant*]" (*Nietzsche and Philosophy* 42; trans. mod.). This is not the space to elaborate on the differences between Deleuze and Nancy on force, but let me just say that Nancy's conceptualization of force would take distance from Deleuze's.

7 On another note, and to be sure, this "resolution," if not the resistance of worldly sovereignty that Nancy talks about in the *Libération* piece, is *not* the decision of a single subject, that is, the singular sovereign subject. This is not the space to go into details, but for Nancy, such a subject deconstructs itself, which is to say, such a subject can be revealed to be only a fantasy, and likewise his or her supposed sovereignty, which he or she presumes to solely possess (for a more in-depth discussion of Nancy and the auto-deconstruction of the subject, kindly see my *The Reject: Community, Politics, and Religion After the Subject*). If there were such a thing as sovereignty for Nancy in this case (I leave aside his inclination toward Bataille's formulation of "sovereignty is nothing"), I would say that it inheres in the fact of existence, a fact common to all existents in the world. As Nancy says, via a reading of Heidegger, the fact of existence is "the *decision of existence*" ("The Decision of Existence" 83). In other words, quintessentially, there is no single sovereign subject that decides. There is only existence that decides, without any need to declare a state of exception but simply in its "mundanity" (82). That is also to say that there is essentially no single subject exercising sovereignty over others. Just as the fact of existence is shared by all existents in the world, sovereignty, then, is also divided or distributed among these existents. To follow Derrida here, one thinks of "another

politics" that will involve "the sharing of sovereignty" ("Le souverain bien – ou l'Europe en mal de souveraineté" 110; my translation). Such a shared sovereignty, if not a sovereignty without subject, to return to a rhetoric closer to Nancy, aligns furthermore with the idea of resolution or resistance here as political affect. Affects, as scholars such as Ahmed and Flatley remind us, are independent of the subject: preceding the subject, they are independent of the subject's will or intention. On "sovereignty without subject" in Nancy, see my essay of the same title in *Nancy Now*.

8 See previous note on Nancy's "decision of existence."

9 In my view, there is a certain blunting, if not a hasty glossing over, of the force of penetration here. It is no doubt problematic, and I tried to address it with Nancy in *The Deconstruction of Sex*. I leave aside any discussion of this problematic in this essay, therefore. What I am trying to emphasize here is the supplementary positive or optimistic perspective on violent force.

10 See "Shattered Love" 98.

11 On this point of the "broken heart," Nancy also says that "the break is nothing more than a touch [*une touche*], but the touch is not less deep than a wound" (98).

12 I note here that the hyphen, or the *trait d'union* in French, is important for Nancy in the chapter "The Judeo-Christian" in the first volume of *The Deconstruction of Christianity*, but this is not the space to go into it.

13 Here, I am also thinking of Cixous's *Insister: à Jacques Derrida*, particularly at the point where she recalls Derrida saying to her, "You are *my insister* [in English in the original]." Cixous will go on:

What pleases me wonderfully in this word, by which you allow me to come to presence [*dont tu me fais présent*], your finding [*ton trouvé*], your ingenious discovery, this feminine or masculine untranslatable, is that I can likewise turn it round on you. You too, you are *my insister* [in English in the original]. *My insister. He who insists me [Mon insisteur].* (41)

I have consulted and modified Peggy Kamuf's translation here (see page 52 of the English *Insister of Jacques Derrida*).

14 On Agamben's "impotentiality," see his "On Potentiality." Also, I am thinking of Nancy's phrase in *Hegel: The Restlessness of the Negative*: "The negative is the prefix of the *in*-finite" (12). This phrase calls for explication, which I am unable to do so here. I simply want to stress the force of the negative in the prefix *in*-.

15 "Wavering of the mind" is taken from Spinoza (*Ethics* 178), when he writes of the individual caught between two conflicting emotions or affects. I bring in Spinoza here also because the notion of affect in Nancy is one closer to a Spinozian genealogy than a Freudian one, which largely informs contemporary affect theorists such as Lauren Berlant, Sara Ahmed, and Sianne Ngai.

16 I demonstrated this in a reading of Édouard Levé (in relation to Nancy) in "Exscription, or the Sense of Failure" and in another of Eve Sedgwick and Kate Zambreno in "Auto-thanato-theory."

17 Nancy also recounts his youngest son call him a "living-dead" (13).

18 See "Abandoned Being" 41–42.

19 See *Syncope: The Philosophy of Rapture*.

20 By silence here, I am referring to what Nancy says of Being freed from all its multiple ways of enunciating itself: "*It* requires nothing that being has not already, always, arranged in its silent being" ("Abandoned Being" 38). With regard to suffering, pain, and hurt, I am thinking precisely of the section "Pain. Suffering. Unhappiness" in Nancy's *The Sense of the World*. As I read it, Nancy considers pain, suffering, and misfortune at a worldly dimension, that is to say, touching on the general (i.e., mankind at large) rather than particular, or even personal, experiences. I also find that the discussion of pain there gets abstracted to an epistemological anxiety, that is, to the pain of inadequate meaning-making. Clearly, I am resisting such abstraction of pain from the experiential and/or existential realm.

21 While Nancy in "L'Intrus" says of the intruder that comes from the outside, he will say, in "Shattered Love," that "love does not stop, as long as love lasts, coming from the outside. It does not remain outside; it *is* this outside itself, the other, each time singular, a blade thrust in me [...]" (97).

22 One could argue that Derrida, likewise, is not forthcoming with negative affects. The one moment of exhibiting one's weakness (that is, fear, or anxiety) in the face of the thought of finitude, mortality, or death, though, comes through in Derrida's final interview, published as *Learning to Live Finally*, where he confesses that the only thing that he has never learned is learning to die: "I remain uneducable when it comes to any wisdom about learning-how-to-die or, if you prefer, knowing-how-to-live" (25).

bibliography

Agamben, Giorgio. "On Potentiality." *Potentialities: Collected Essays in Philosophy*. Ed., trans., and intro. Daniel Heller-Roazen. Stanford: Stanford UP, 1999. 177–84. Print.

Cixous, Hélène. *Insister: à Jacques Derrida*. Paris: Galilée, 2006. Print.

Cixous, Hélène. *Insister of Jacques Derrida*. Trans. Peggy Kamuf. Edinburgh: Edinburgh UP, 2007. Print.

Clément, Catherine. *Syncope: The Philosophy of Rapture*. Trans. Sally O'Driscoll and Deidre M. Mahoney. Minneapolis: U of Minnesota P, 1994. Print.

Deleuze, Gilles. *Nietzsche and Philosophy*. Trans. Hugh Tomlinson. New York: Columbia UP, 1983. Print.

Derrida, Jacques. "By Force of Mourning." Trans. Pascale-Anne Brault and Michael Naas. *The Work of Mourning*. Ed. Pascale-Anne Brault and Michael Naas. Chicago: U of Chicago P, 2001. 142–64. Print.

Derrida, Jacques. "Force and Signification." *Writing and Difference*. Trans. and intro. Alan Bass. Chicago: U of Chicago P, 1978. 3–78. Print.

Derrida, Jacques. "Force of Law: The 'Mystical Foundation of Authority.'" Trans. Mary Quaintance. *Deconstruction and the Possibility of Justice*. Ed. Drucilla Cornell, Michel Rosenfeld, and David Gray Carlson. New York: Routledge, 1992. 3–67. Print.

Derrida, Jacques. "Introduction: Desistance." Trans. Christopher Fynsk. By Philippe Lacoue-Labarthe. *Typography: Mimesis, Philosophy, Politics*. Ed. Christopher Fynsk. Stanford: Stanford UP, 1998. 1–42. Print.

Derrida, Jacques. *Learning to Live Finally: An Interview with Jean Birnbaum*. Trans. Pascale-Ann

Brault and Michael Naas. Hoboken, NJ: Melville, 2007. Print.

Derrida, Jacques. "Le souverain bien – ou l'Europe en mal de souveraineté." *Derrida politique: la déconstruction de la souveraineté (puissance et droit)*. Ed. Yves Charles Zarka. Spec. issue of *Cités* 30 (2007): 103–40. Print.

Derrida, Jacques. *Of Grammatology*. Trans. Gayatri C. Spivak. Baltimore: Johns Hopkins UP, 1976. Print.

Goh, Irving. "Auto-thanato-theory: Dark Narcissistic Care for the Self in Sedgwick and Zambreno." *Autotheory Theory*. Ed. Robyn Wiegman. Spec. issue of *Arizona Quarterly* 76.1 (2020): 197–213. Print.

Goh, Irving. "Exscription, or the Sense of Failure: Jean-Luc Nancy, Tecuciztecatl, and Édouard Levé." *MLN* 135.9 (2019): 1080–97. Print.

Goh, Irving. *L'existence prépositionnelle*. Paris: Galilée, 2019. Print.

Goh, Irving. *The Reject: Community, Politics, and Religion After the Subject*. New York: Fordham UP, 2014. Print.

Goh, Irving. "Sovereignty without Subject." *Nancy Now*. Ed. Verena Andermatt Conley and Irving Goh. Cambridge: Polity, 2014. 152–70. Print.

Hegel, G.W.F. *The Phenomenology of Spirit*. Trans. A.V. Miller. Oxford: Oxford UP, 1977. Print.

James, Ian. "The Persistence of the Subject: Jean-Luc Nancy." *Paragraph* 25.1 (2002): 125–41. Print.

Nancy, Jean-Luc. "Abandoned Being." Trans. Brian Holmes. *The Birth to Presence*. Trans. Brian Holmes et al. Stanford: Stanford UP, 1993. 36–47. Print.

Nancy, Jean-Luc. *Corpus*. Rev. and complete ed. Paris: Métailié, 2006. Print.

Nancy, Jean-Luc. "The Decision of Existence." Trans. Brian Holmes. *The Birth to Presence*. 82–109. Print.

Nancy, Jean-Luc. "Dialogue Under the Ribs." Trans. Irving Goh. *Nancy Now*. 171–74. Print.

Nancy, Jean-Luc. *Dis-Enclosure: The Deconstruction of Christianity*. Trans. Bettina Bergo, Gabriel Malenfant, and Michael B. Smith. New York: Fordham UP, 2008. Print.

Nancy, Jean-Luc. *The Experience of Freedom*. Trans. Bridget McDonald. Stanford: Stanford UP, 1993. Print.

Nancy, Jean-Luc. "Exscription." Trans. Katherine Lydon. *The Birth to Presence*. 317–40. Print.

Nancy, Jean-Luc. *Hegel: The Restlessness of the Negative*. Trans. Jason Smith and Steven Miller. Minneapolis: U of Minnesota P, 2002. Print.

Nancy, Jean-Luc. *The Inoperative Community*. Ed. Peter Connor. Trans. Peter Connor et al. Minneapolis: U of Minnesota P, 1991. Print.

Nancy, Jean-Luc. "Inventons la souveraineté mondiale." *Libération* 24 Jan. 2019. Web. <https://www.liberation.fr/debats/2019/01/24/inventons-la-souverainete-mondiale_1704902>.

Nancy, Jean-Luc. "L'Intrus." Trans. Susan Hanson. *CR: The New Centennial Review* 2.3 (2002): 1–14. Print.

Nancy, Jean-Luc. *Listening*. Trans. Charlotte Mandell. New York: Fordham UP, 2007. Print.

Nancy, Jean-Luc. *Noli me tangere: On the Raising of the Body*. Trans. Sarah Clift, Pascale-Anne Brault, and Michael Naas. New York: Fordham UP, 2008. Print.

Nancy, Jean-Luc. *Que faire?* Paris: Galilée, 2016. Print.

Nancy, Jean-Luc. *The Sense of the World*. Trans. Jeffrey S. Librett. Minneapolis: U of Minnesota P, 1997. Print.

Nancy, Jean-Luc. *Sexistence*. Paris: Galilée, 2017. Print.

Nancy, Jean-Luc. "Shattered Love." Trans. Lisa Garbus and Simona Sawhney. *The Inoperative Community*. 82–109. Print.

Nancy, Jean-Luc. "The Unsacrificeable." Trans. Richard Stamp and Simon Sparks. *A Finite Thinking*. Ed. Simon Sparks. Stanford: Stanford UP, 2003. 51–77. Print.

Nancy, Jean-Luc, and Irving Goh. *The Deconstruction of Sex*. Durham, NC: Duke UP. Forthcoming.

Spinoza. *Ethics*. Ed. and trans. G.H.R. Parkinson. Oxford: Oxford UP, 2000. Print.

Vattimo, Gianni. "Dialectics, Difference, Weak Thought." *Weak Thought*. Ed. Gianni Vattimo and

Pier Aldo Rovatti. Trans. Peter Carravetta. Albany: SUNY P, 2012. 39–52. Print.

Williams, Raymond. *Marxism and Literature*. Oxford: Oxford UP, 1977. Print.

We are writing in this journal, are we not, to render a verdict on the work, if not the life, of Jean-Luc Nancy? Nancy will respond to each article, kindly, all as a way to offer an *apologia* if not a defense of his writings and his philosophy – he seemed to have been given a *mandat de comparution* or summoned to a compearance here in these pages. It is only fair and right – juridical concepts through and through – that we should speak in such juridical terms since Nancy was fair and right to ask some years ago in *L'Impératif catégorique* (1983):

> What happens when philosophy becomes [*se fait*] juridical? What happens when philosophy becomes juridical, *not* in the sense that it takes account of right [*prendre en compte le droit*] as one of its objects and assigns itself the task of a reflection or meditation on it (although philosophy cannot legitimately neglect this sort of work [...]), but in the sense that philosophy itself, as such, would be instituted, determined, and presented [*s'exposerait*] according to the concept and in the form of a juridical discourse and practice? In the sense, then, in which philosophy would be *legitimated* juridically. What would be the stakes, the nature, and the validity of this operation, which goes beyond anything that we might term a "philosophy of right"? What then of philosophy? What then of right? [*Qu'y adviendrait-il de la philosophie, et du droit?*] ("*Lapsus judicii*" 152; *L'Impératif catégorique* 35)

The task of this essay is to connect two sets of claims in Nancy's philosopher together, those about the law of existence and those about the operations of the juridical. As is well known

peter gratton

NANCY ON TRIAL
thinking philosophy and the jurisdictional

to his readers, Nancy rejects a Levinasian priority of an ethics before ontology, and with it a messianic relation to the Other, in order to think of being as being-with. Nancy's writings, however, do not divorce considerations of justice and ontology, arguing time and again that the former is nothing other than the thinking of the commonality of that which is incommensurable. But this does not mean that being has a substantiality that can ground a specific set of political claims, e.g., as one finds in the natural law tradition. Rather the lack of a ground to being, as we will see, is the law beyond all laws of being singular plural. But if Nancy hesitates to provide a specific political ontology – any grounding in nature, race, and so on, have more than a whiff of totalitarianism, for him – he nevertheless will connect his claims about the originary obligation of existence and the law of being to which we are obligated to rendering justice as we ordinarily understand it (especially in terms of where we say we render justice in a daily fashion, namely, in the law courts that are the linchpins for our punitive societies), lest his work give rise to a risible political quietism. For example, in "*La Comparution*," Nancy asks "how we can (or cannot) do [*rendre*] justice" to the obligation of our abandonment to a common existence (375). But if this thinking of being as being-with is already a praxis, as Nancy claims, it will help us to rethink how one renders justice in this or that supposedly concrete situation.

For Nancy, philosophy has been, at least since Rome, jurisprudential for reasons we will see, that is, it is parasitic on a certain Roman conception of rendering justice in the law courts. Nancy's own verdict concerning philosophy as it has come down to us institutionally is split: *for* philosophy since he designates its modus operandi, as if to tell each of us how to show up properly before the court of reason, how to be trained properly in adjudicating each philosophical case that comes before us in terms of the *as if*. But *against* philosophy since it would historicize it at the same time given that philosophy borrows on or is parasitical on a model or analogue whose meaning in the end goes beyond it and which it can never control. Either verdict would finish off or finitize philosophy's transcendent or transcendental positioning. Nancy's allegation is that philosophy became juridical not from its very beginning, as I would claim occurred once a certain notion of judging or *krinein* over a *krisis* or trial in Ancient Greece became the role of a third party above the fray in philosophy and politics (as one sees in the judgment of the statesman in Plato's *Statesman*, one whose avowed *gnosis* will never touch upon the materiality of the city he commands through his *epistemē* or science). Rather, for Nancy, this happened in the Roman translation of Greek philosophy into its own juridical idioms. Though of course we should never judge guilt by association, this has more than a whiff of the Heideggerian account that philosophical wonder and such suffered a fall once translated into Latin, an *Irrnis* or errancy of philosophy with which we still live, but which Nancy avers is not just philosophical but juridico-philosophico-political. And he is right. Right about right and all that has come with it.

Nancy's allegation is that philosophy became juridical (and vice versa) once there arose a certain judge or *iudex* who literally speaks the law or right as the one who indicates the law or right, *ius*, by his very speaking, *dicere*, and then renders a verdict, a *verum dictum*, a speaking of the truth. If I'm under oath here, I would have to admit that Nancy's account is offered in just several dense pages, in the chapter "*Lapsus judicii*" of *L'Impératif catégorique*, but at the least he adds much to Martin Heidegger's account of there occurring a major architectonic shift in philosophy from Greece to Rome in the replacement of the *logos* by *ratio* or calculative reason, all while commenting in these pages on the legalism of Kant and its Roman heritage. This legalism, again I would suggest, is one that can be found in Plato's laws, Aristotle's metaphysical appropriation of the language of the law courts for his ontological edifice, and elsewhere in Greece, but it is certainly historically true that the Romans considered their thinking of *ius* (law, justice, right, etc.) as beyond anything the Greeks considered under *dikē*, *nomos*, and so on. But if Nancy is right in that there is no Greek beginning of philosophy without a given politics, it is also true that this philosophical politics has always been juridical.

My task here will be to stop short of Nancy's reading of Kant in *L'Impératif catégorique* and concentrate on what it means that philosophy is jurisdictional through and through. As he asks, "what then of philosophy? What then of right?" But how does one judge this case of philosophy without doubling down on it, without deciding guilt or innocence regarding philosophy, without borrowing from the language and practices of the law courts? And does the decision always need to be between two? The dominant

THE PULSE OF SENSE

way that decisions are presented are as between two, as having only *two* options, though the sense of the world is never presented as such; this is only but one representation but an implacable one: we can see this is in our various for and against columns in newspapers and journals, or in applied ethics textbooks, or in Badiou's claim that *essentially* every decision is always between two. This imitation – and as we know from Nancy, an imitation is never an innocent semantic borrowing – of the state's juridical apparatus accepts too unproblematically an archetype that infects almost all areas of human endeavor. We think it natural to link the trauma of a crime and the trauma of a given punishment, the vaunted economy of the *lex talionis* that Kant argued is the categorical imperative of the political. We never question that the guilty ought to be punished, or indeed that the rule of law requires a speaking of the truth, a veridiction or verdict, over those thought deserving, and just what the status of this "truth" is – is it only a truth rendered within the language game of the courts or does it not have metaphysical pretenses? Even at the individual level, we measure our lives in terms of small writs of wrongs righted through micro-punishments and hence through a juridical thinking: the cheating partner is given time in the clichéd doghouse, the wayward employee is reprimanded and faces loss of work, the perpetually late student is given marks off her participation grade, the sloppy waiter is punished with a bad tip, etc. The list is endless. We don't judge constantly in this way, we tell ourselves, because it is in our interest or sating some desire, some will to power; it is what *everyone* or *das Man* would do. The phantasm of the objective third party is implicit in all of this and removes our own implication in the micro-punishments we mete out – indeed it is exactly what is required of Kantian deontology, as Nancy argues – since we are to judge *as if* we are not implicated in the very scenarios under review. Nevertheless, this disciplining of others implicates a long thinking of crime and punishment and hence a certain thinking of *krinein* or

judging in ancient Greece that passes eventfully, as Nancy claims, through the jurisprudentialism of the Roman era, which to this day has not ended. And we, we who call ourselves philosophers, ought to be in the dock for it.

To speak juridically is, as any law student knows, to speak Latin and to trade on the whole conceptual apparatus Rome has given us, however much we must mark the invention *ex post facto* of British common law or the Napoleonic code, for example. It is this connection, this *rapport* of the juridical *with* the philosophical that is the case before us in these pages. The Latin *casus* or case means a fall, an event, an accident. The case of *casus* falls to us all, as philosophers, as those whose jurisdiction would be *everything*, the whole of the sense of the world and its histories, we philosophers who have always wanted to have the last word on what is the world and its aims and goals. Is this not the hubris of philosophy *qua* onto-theology: to leave various sciences to this or that jurisdiction, to this or that regional science, but to have the whole of the world as ours? To have the right to exile this or that area of knowledge or art away from philosophy, all to hold ourselves in this judicial position above the fray, judging it all from a God's-eye view?

In any event, even if every *casus* or case is an event or accident, as the Latin origin notes, it will be no accident that the case of the jurisdictional and all that it means for us today in terms of how the law is applied, which is always to say, misapplied, is a task for our thought, for those who call ourselves philosophers, and so it is not just Nancy's claims and allegations that are on trial today, but philosophy itself, the philosophy cum *jurisdiction* as Nancy rightly describes it. The stakes are no doubt radical: whenever one begins to question, *de jure* or de facto, any thinking of jurisdiction, of speaking rightly, one gets accused of having no care for the victims of the trauma we call a crime, of being on the side of evil, of defending the indefensible. Indeed, there is no court that exists now that would take the case, would let it accidentally fall within its writ, yet nothing at present, I think, is more central to undoing calculative reason and the law of equivalence, as Nancy has described them well in virtually all of his books of the past twenty-five years, than to strike at the heart of this *dispositif* that is the institution of judgment and punishment that protects, extends, and yet also exposes the bourgeois state and its imposition of a certain capitalist equivalence in the age of neoliberalism.

Given what is playing out in our courts and the whole system we in the United States call the prison–industrial complex, it is urgent to dissociate all manner of thinking from this legacy of jurisdiction, all as a way of deconstructing a certain thinking of judgment the results of which are there for any contemporary eyewitnesses to see: we live in ever worsening punitive societies made operative by judgments of crime and punishment, or when one pleads guilty, the fear of them. None of us escapes this law; it is universal. But without punishment, there would be no state as we consider it, for as Kant noted well, there is no law without its execution, though Kant never took up, to my mind, how the enforcement mechanisms of the modern state operate according to their own fictions and are always exceptional to any law. If we are called to deconstruct sovereignty, to think it's NOTHING, we must not just focus, as so many recent works do, on heads of state. We must, as Foucault once put it, cut the head off the king, but not, as he wanted, to think a power *other than* the juridical, but rather how this juridical is shared out across our landscapes in the gendarmerie, police, and apparatchiks all across what we call the state and indeed within the people itself. To be a subject to the law is also to be given a jurisdiction – this is the property of the subject. But it is also to hypostasize a state logic that circumscribes and prescribes what can be said about the state, most and especially around its juridical logic. Nancy writes:

> As we know all too well, right [*le droit*] furnished the model and the ideology of the bourgeois State. But on the condition of

hypostasizing juris-diction, of making it an Essence and a Sense. On the condition of forgetting or repressing its "essential" *lapsus* [from the Latin for a fall or fault, a lapse]. And it's hardly surprising, then, that the State engenders a sometimes open, always latent revolt over the right to say – the ultimate demand *of the right to say the right of what is by rights without right* [*l'exigence ultime du droit de dire le droit de ce qui est de droit sans droit*]. ("*Lapsus judicii*" 169; *L'Impératif catégorique* 58)

I would suggest that in these few pages in Nancy – his discussion of jurisdiction ranges but fifteen or so pages in an oeuvre of many thousands – his use of the Latin *casus* takes up the borderline between all of his major distinctions that he uses and deconstructs in his work, most especially sense and signification, but also presencing and representation, *désœuvrement* and operativity, transcendence and immanence, infinity and finitude, areality and territory, the incalculable and the calculable, and so on. The *casus*, the case, before us is never foreseeable, as he notes, and philosophy has always wanted a priori to prepare for every possible case, to *declare* the law as a priori even as the law only survives on its a posteriori declarations. As Nancy makes evident in "*Lapsus judicii*," the law always presupposes "the particular case" and a *lapsus*. The law hence must "fictionalize" (derived from the Latin *fictio*, a forming or feigning, and *fictum*, a counter truth or phantasm) this *lapsus* in order for what Kant calls reflective judgment to lay claim to law's universality. In this way, as we'll see below, jurisdiction is always and already juris-fiction.

That philosophy has become juridical, that it will have wanted always to become juridical, is not just one case among others on our philosophical docket; it is not a question that belongs to some sub-area like philosophy of law, but rather gets at the law of philosophy, and we must think it through to its end, to a law beyond the law, as Nancy will call it, such that we become outlaws of a sort, as we will see as I come to my summation. The political stakes are clear and we, we who call ourselves philosophers, are fully implicated in it, co-conspirators in the jurisprudential logic that pervades our societies and does such violence in the name of what is right, orderly, and just.

Now, closer to the case at hand, that is, the writings of Nancy, it is not just one case among others that Nancy takes up, quickly, in his writings. If I can persuade beyond a reasonable doubt a jury of my peers in these pages, I will demonstrate the centrality of this thinking of *casus* to Nancy's oeuvre, even if Marie-Eve Morin and I, when editing the *Nancy Dictionary*, did not include it among his key terms. Yet, if there is to be the creation of another world beyond this *immonde* world, I would suggest we need another thinking of the juridical, that is to say, a thinking heterogenous to the juridical and its modes of judgment, and hence to take up the case of *casus* in play in Nancy's work.

As Nancy notes in "*Lapsus judicii*," any jurisdiction is where one says or declares (*dicere*) the law (*ius*). Any *dicere* or saying is inherently juridical (related as it is to the Indo-European root *deik-*, to show or indicate, which it should be noted is also the root for the Greek *dikē*), which is the determination one finds in any legal judgment: *ius* is always performative, as is well known. Émile Benveniste notes,

> What is constitutive of law [*droit*] is not doing it, but always *pronouncing* it: *ius* and *iu-dex* bring us back to this constant combination [...] All this stems from the same authority and is expressed by the same turns of phrase. It was from this act of speech, *ius dicere*, that the whole [Roman] court terminology developed: *iudex, iudicare, indicium, iuris-dictio*, etc. (398)

Just as Benveniste also describes with the Greek *dikēn eipein*, there is no *ius* without this *declaration*, without this *pronouncement*, in such a way that there is something of a redundancy between *ius* and *dicere* or within the word jurisdiction itself. As such, the *ius* or law or right is not above or outside its pronouncements and *institutions* in the active sense, which is why Nancy notes a certain

making or *facere* of jurisdiction, which he dubs the jurisfiction of any jurisdiction. There is always a *making*, a *doing by saying*, at the heart of the law and its application. This, Nancy makes clear, is not the same as the German *Dichtung*, and he is not making the facile claim simply that because there is interpretive play in the law, that it is otherworldly and sheer fantasy. He knows very well the real-world effects of these declarations on the people of this world. Nancy writes:

> *Dichtung* makes up [*compose*] a world; by definition, anything like a contingent or accidental "structure" is excluded from it – just as it is from the world of metaphysical *theōria*. If poetry fictions, it does so as a theory: a vision that produces visions. By contrast, (juridical) fiction works with [*compose*] a world, with the accidental, eventual actuality of a "worldness [*mondanité*]" that the law [*la loi*] neither produces nor sublates [*relève*]. If anything and everything can happen [*arriver*] in *Dichtung*, that's because it itself produces the unlimited field of its own production; if anything and everything can happen for right [*le droit*], it is because there's always something that exceeds the limits of its spaces [*ses aires*]. Fiction each time shapes [*façonne chaque fois*] the bringing together of the universal and the particular, of necessity and contingency, doing so in such a way that what is shaped bears the indelible mark of the *case* [*cas*], quite differently to Hegelian synthesis, where the mark is always already led toward the dialectical erasure [*entraînée dans l'effacement dialectique*] of each one of its distinctive traits, right up to its complete resolution in the Concept, beyond any figure. ("*Lapsus judicii*" 157; trans. mod.; *L'Impératif catégorique* 42)

Here, then, every *casus* or case marks that which exceeds speculative thought, and Nancy is right to put fictioning at the meeting place of the universal and particular, the necessary (the law) and the particular (*this* set of events), and so forth, until he speaks of this fashioning a certain world and its *mondanité*. Each case is unique, just this once, in this way, in its fashioning and yet each case is decided as if it arrived under no such contingency. Nancy writes:

> By stating what the law is [En disant le droit], the judex always says at the same time that the reality of the case is in conformity with the law [la réalité du cas est dans le droit] and that saying it fictions or figures the very "being [être]" of the case [cas]. Indeed, we might well be forgiven for saying that the juridical order essentially arises from a "cynicism" of fiction, from a "bare-faced lie." We proceed as if [comme si] (and the Greek word for fiction, remember, is hypokrisis), this being one of the central motifs that Kant introduces into philosophy. ("Lapsus judicii" 157–58; trans. mod.; L'Impératif catégorique 42)

This may not strike practitioners of the laws as anything but blasé; they are all too aware of the hypocrisies involved in any making of the law. Jurisprudence requires a fictioning and a finishing off, a finitude, in casting about for what law and precedents to apply to what is each time an infinity of sense in any historical or biographical trauma or milieu, always as if there were no fictioning or fashioning of the matter at hand to the law and vice versa. Every krisis or trial, then, requires this feigning or the hypokrisis of the as if, which of course, Nancy aims to show, is what lies historically behind the als ob of Kant's categorical imperative. How else to take the measure of what will be decided as a crime except the fiction that one can measure the immeasurable? The iudex needs to take this plentitude of sense that would be any given trauma and give it a signification, literally, from the Latin, to make a sign of it, to mark one indelibly, as Nancy notes, which is done in each speaking that is jurisdiction. Nancy writes:

> In fact, the relation of law to case – the relation of jurisdiction – means [signifie] that no case is the law and that a case only falls [tombe] subject to the law only on the minimal condition that the law concerning it is stated. The accident – what happens [ce qui arrive] – has to be struck by the seal [sceau] of the law [la loi] (of its utterance [énonciation]) in order not yet to be judged, but to be constituted as a case in law [constitué en cas de droit], modeled or sculpted (fictum) according to the law [selon le droit]. Juris-diction is or makes up juris-fiction [my emphasis]. Law and case come before right only if they are modeled, shaped, fashioned – fictioned [fictionnés] – in and through one another. But this necessity entails a radical implication [mais cette nécessité comporte une implication radicale]: the installation or inauguration of right [droit] must itself, as such, be fictioned. ("Lapsus judicii" 156–57; trans. mod.; L'Impératif catégorique 41)

There is also the fiction that there is an ultimate backstop or ground to the laws – the one that is said to be threatened by any case that goes unpunished – a constituting moment of the state or community that legitimates these laws, even as, as Derrida showed in his reading of the American Declaration of Independence, this performative creates the very "we" that would have been the signatories to that independence, and every constituting of a given legal system must accept this illegitimate extra-juridical, extra-constitutional performative as if there was a ground or an already formed "we" (such as the "We the people" of the first words of the US constitution, or "Le peuple français" of the constitution of the French Fifth Republic) prior to the very constitution that gives the very force to the laws that are under consideration whenever a case falls or lapses into a judge's lap ("Declarations of Independence"). There is no static prior constitution that then guides the laws that then guides jurisprudence, as is normally thought, but the opposite: the constitution is only operative – at work shaping a given community according to an ex post facto founding – through the decision and fashioning, the fictioning, of each case, which is not making some world on its own – since there, da, is the existent whose life is being decided. This fictioning of the casus intervenes and makes a world with all of those involved, signifying the

THE PULSE OF SENSE

guilty and the innocent, stamped as they are for a lifetime and all that that means.

Of course, legal fictions are well known and are Roman in origin, namely, the extension of the law to cases they did not previously cover. But this marginal use of the law, of jurisfiction, is not at all marginal to Nancy, who argues that there is always an abyss between the universal and the particular, the *ius* and the *casus*: *a* is a species of *b* and hence falls under this or that law. But de facto or *en fait*, that is surely never the case – and Nancy's *Lapsus judicii* argues that this is *de jure* or *en droit* as well.

Yet, the judicial decision, despite all appeals, has all the fictive appearance of finality as the gavel goes down: it has been decided, and we should never forget the trauma of this incision, this cut into the existence of another by every juridical decision. Like every case or *casus*, it is an event, a happening, an *Ereignis* that arrives with every *Entscheidung* or decision. The signification of sense par excellence, to use Nancy's key terms, occurs in our court-rooms by way of the making of a sign, a Sense, of the *now* criminal whose expropriation by the state is one that expropriates her expro-priation, takes away her thrownness or abandonment to being, and takes it upon itself to decide for her decision for being, as we will come to it. Here, Nancy is speaking of Kant, but this follows *mutatis mutandis* for the judging and punishing that is our focus:

> Signification operates within a signi*fiction* [*La signification s'opère dans une significtion*] [...] Signification makes jurisdiction [*La signification fait juridiction*]; it assigns or it states (and does so first of all and in each case by stating the very non-empirical possibility of statement) [*énonce (en énonçant tout d'abord, et dans chaque cas, la possibilité même, non empirique, de l'énonciation)*] the concept's area of legiti-macy, the area that traces the sensible, phenomenal condition of its figurability. ("*Lapsus judicii*" 165; *L'Impératif catégorique* 53)

The case, from the Latin *casus*, is "the fall in or through chance, through contingency, the fall

according to opportunity (an opportunity that constitutes the judge as much as the criminal); the fall, then, as accident," as Nancy notes ("*Lapsus judicii*" 157; *L'Impératif catégorique* 40). This event fashions and fictions the judge and the case at the same time, and hence there is only the fictive *proclamation* of right in and through the *casus* or fall, which in Latin is also a *lapsus*; every judgment then is a *lapsus judicii*, a lapse of judgment. As Nancy puts it,

> The *persona* of the judge and his edictum are forged from the same fictitious [*fictice*] gesture: right is said [*le droit se dit*] here of the case for which there can be no prior right, and which is the case of right. ("*Lapsus judicii*" 158; *L'Impératif catégori-que* 41)

How to appeal one fall in the name of another, a *casus* in the name of a *lapsus*, given that any judgment would face all the pro-blems that Nancy has set forth? What would this court of appeal look like and what laws would it follow, given all that we have said? After the death of God, there is only for those accused – and let there be no mistake, we are all subjects to the law and therefore accused from the very beginning, though we should never forget for an instance that right has always been written from the side of those who think communities are essential, have a given foundation, and those not of those founded communities are a priori guilty by their very existence. This is what Nancy time and again dubs evil – a violence against plural-ity itself, an application of the law to the singu-lar and unique in such a way that the singularity of the accused is erased, fashioning and fiction-ing the accused as members of a Race, Class, Sex, and so on. Nancy writes, in what for us is the aptly named essay "*La Comparution*," "to exclude, exclusion must designate: it names, identifies, gives form. 'The other' is for us a figure imposed on the non-figurable [*infigur-able*]," which of course is precisely what every court, as he argues, does (392).

We are summoned to appear, to *compear*, he writes, to witness this disfiguring in the name of all figures. The courts do this figuring, this calculation where *ratio* meets *juridiction*, par excellence in our societies. Hence the law courts operate paradoxically: they at once attach a *persona* to the singular and make each one (and by extension all in awe of this power) a subject to the law, and yet at the same time, the result of this *dispositif* is to de-singularize, de-subjectivize this or that existent in the figure of the Black, the Arab, the Jew (Nancy, "*La Comparution*" 392). The ecotechnics, the habitual regularity of this infernal machinery, should not blind us to the singularity of each one, each time, who is unique and also sacrificed as a member of this or that excluded class. No doubt, the rule of law, the *lex talionis*, the invention of the third party, was all meant to end vengeance, to repress the pleasure, as Nietzsche put it well in the *Genealogy of Morals*, that was the *raison d'être* for the invention of crime in the first place. But there is also little doubt that we cannot be called to account, be summoned by and for existence, as Nancy writes, without acknowledging the violence of this technics meant to end violence: it merely sublimates it, makes it habitable in all senses for us, giving both the judge and those viewing the spectacle and drama a feigned, hypocritical detachment from this continual lapse in judgment, this *lapsus judicii*, that every sentence and every philosophical sentence as jurisdictional carries. The constant policing of the Other in our societies, backed up by the full force of law, is, without a doubt, a barely concealed law of force against which we, we who think the "we" other than as communion, must find the right to say what is without any right to say. This is what summons us to compear here, in court or not, and bear witness to another thinking of community and indeed another future that requires the *creatio ex nihilo* of the world without foundation, without a common ground, and without a god who can save us. There is nothing that is *immonde*, no *decreatio in nihilum*, as Nancy put it in his 2016 *Que faire?*, that doesn't necessitate a juridical reasoning that has always been the sharp stick of political and economic power. What makes

this reasoning so implacable, then, is precisely, as Nancy suggests, that it is the very figure of our reasoning in the Western tradition: we can't figure our way out of it.

There is, I don't doubt, a court of public opinion that will find all of this talk beyond anything we have the right to say: all societies must punish, there is evil in the world, and we must calculate and figure our way through – and our courts do just that. No doubt, too, a Kantian court of reason would deny us any entry to make this argument: we are without rights to say what is by rights without right. But we must stand our ground, even as it is the nonground of our existence, since it is a decision for existence over and against the real yet phantasmatic sovereign decisions of our judges. Nothing sounds more irrational than to try to articulate an ex-isting, a standing out ahead and with and through one another, that occurs between two nothings: on the one hand, the jurisfiction ungrounded by each case, each occasion that befalls it and ends in an act of extreme alienation and expropriation as punishment. On the other hand, the expropriation of any originary identity or property of existence as being-with in Nancy's ontology.

Nancy's wager, as so often, is not to deny our jurifictional history, but, as he does with Christianity, community, adoration, *creatio ex nihilo*, world, ipseity, freedom, and so forth, is to use the West's key philosophemes as a means for thinking them otherwise in terms of our being with. So, too, with the juridical cum philosophical, that is, jurisdiction, whose terms litter his work, and these become integral to his thinking in a way that disrupts the jurisprudential and hence all possible final verdict over what counts as the jurisdiction of any judgment or decision. For example, here he is in *Birth to Presence* as first published in the last essay of *L'Impératif catégorique*:

One always abandons to a law [*On abandonne toujours à une loi*]. The destitution [*dénuement*] of abandoned being [*l'être abandonné*] is measured by the limitless severity of the law [*aux rigueurs sans limites de la loi*] to which it finds itself exposed [*exposé*]. Abandonment does not constitute a subpoena to appear [*à comparaître*] in court charged with this or that offence. It is constrained to appear absolutely under the law, under the law as such and in its totality. In the same way – it is the same thing – to be banished does not amount to coming under a provision of the law, but rather to coming under the entirety of the law. Turned over to [*Livré à*] the absolute of the law, the banished one is thereby abandoned completely outside its jurisdiction. The law of abandonment requires that the law be applied through its withdrawal. The law of abandonment is the other of the law, which constitutes the law [*La loi de l'abandon est l'autre de la loi, qui fait la loi*]. Abandoned being finds itself deserted to the degree that it finds itself remitted, entrusted, or thrown to this law that constitutes the law [*qui fait la loi*], this other and same, to this other side of all law that borders and upholds [*fait tenir*] a legal universe: an absolute, solemn order, which prescribes nothing but abandonment. (Nancy, *Birth to Presence* 44; trans. mod.; *L'Impératif catégorique* 149)

We are abandoned without principle, and this is the law beyond the law, which is not to say it doesn't exist here and now, within this set of laws; Nancy never errs by separating the ontic and the ontological. Indeed, he is clear that these laws are part of this abandonment – hence our responsibility and decision for *this* existence *hic et nunc*. Nancy writes in *The Experience of Freedom* that one must think the "equality of singularities in the incommensurable of freedom," that is, free in our abandonment through and with one another, singular plural, plural in our singularity and vice versa, but then adds in parentheses, but this "does not impede the necessity of having a technical measure of equality, and consequently also of justice, which actually makes possible, under given conditions, access to the incommensurable" (71). In this way, Nancy uses the language of jurisdictional philosophy to testify to our inexorable exposure without principle, without ground, without any *archē* or *telos*, in sum, he takes the *jurisfiction* of

Roman law to empty out any *natural* law theory of its bases, all to testify to the infinite abandonment from nowhere and toward nowhere of existence, in between, with, and shared out to another and all others. This is as our *partage* or lot would have it. But this also means that the incommensurable measures itself, like freedom, against *nothing*: there is no pre-given measure, no outside or beyond, no transcendental or transcendent claim upon being; this too is the lot of our abandonment, our common share. All the fictions of our legal systems – the constant chatter and rigorous filing away of the cases with all purposefulness – only testifies to it simply being a case among others, the whole of it, the whole legal system itself, measured against our common abandonment. It hovers over and is measured by the nothing. Against this nihilism – the Kafkaesque proceduralism for its own sake – we must speak for justice, which is a topic that ranges across Nancy's writings. For example, here he is a few years ago in *Que faire?* (2016), and we should hear as Nancy links a certain right with speaking, as in *juridiction*, but all as a way of thinking justice otherwise:

> The "with" [*avec*] [of being as being-with] is not a simple given fact [*une simple donnée de fait*]: it's the fact of a right [*un droit*] that must be of a right which is to be demanded [*s'exige*], called for [*qui s'appelle*], and asked for [*se demande*]. This right [*droit*] shows itself from the outset as language, and even as the tongue (of a people) and as the speaking [*parole*] (of an assembly or council) and thus as a right [*droit*] – juridiction – pronounced [*énoncé*] by the law [*la loi*], jurisprudence – *juris-prudence* – discernment of cases. The justi-fica-tion [Nancy here splits the word in two to emphasize the "making" of any justice] that stands out from this theatre of the spoken compearing [*la comparution parlante*] is not given nor can it be. And yet its justice imposes itself. (*Que faire?* 42)

Here, then, Nancy hypostatizes the making of justice, juris-fiction, as part of our abandonment to the law beyond the laws, the poverty of a given signification of being to which we are nevertheless called, in a language, to appear. The *lapsus judicii* is not a fault or fall, but is our common abandonment or lot as outlaws before the law. That is to say, he takes what he had earlier in *L'Impératif catégorique* shown to be at the heart of our jurisprudence from the Roman law courts to Kant and beyond to be our "common" ontological condition as those who compear with and among one another. To do justice to the "with" of existence, then, is to show the ontological condition of possibility of philosophy's jurisprudentialism in terms of another thinking or speaking of justice, one that speaks to our common abandonment that is the law of existence. This law is the condition of possibility (and impossibility), as Derrida would put it, of every jurisdictional regime – including the one that accuses us now for another world without these prisons that are all too mundane in our world today. This is the case to which we have been summoned to compear, to which we have been abandoned, which is not one legal case or another, but the fact of each legal case as one case in itself of a violence for which we philosophers, we who think jurisdictionally, are in no small part responsible. We are being summoned and, as philosophers, are accused.

echo by jean-luc nancy

Yes, once the Divine Judge has disappeared, we are all accused whilst in a position where nobody can present to us the law under which we are accused. Perhaps Peter Gratton's powerful reflection could be extended by saying that we ourselves are the accusers, or rather that it is the very fact of existence – that of the world, not of human beings alone – that functions as a law before which we can only fall short, for it is an incomprehensible law and thus unjustifiable. But then we are as guilty as we are innocent … Or no more guilty than innocent? How can we move on and think beyond the sword and scale accompanying it?

disclosure statement

No potential conflict of interest was reported by the author.

bibliography

Benveniste, Émile. *Dictionary of Indo-European Concepts and Society.* Trans. E. Palmer. New York: Hau, 2016. Print.

Derrida, Jacques. "Declarations of Independence." *New Political Science* 7 (Summer 1986): 7–15. Print.

Nancy, Jean-Luc. *Birth to Presence.* Trans. Brian Holmes et al. Stanford: Stanford UP, 1993. Print.

Nancy, Jean-Luc. *The Experience of Freedom.* Trans. Bridget McDonald. Stanford: Stanford UP, 1993. Print.

Nancy, Jean-Luc. "*La Comparution /* The Compearance: From the Existence of 'Communism' to the Community of 'Existence.'" *Political Theory* 20.3 (Aug. 1992): 371–98. Print.

Nancy, Jean-Luc. "*Lapsus judicii.*" *A Finite Thinking.* Ed. S. Sparks. Stanford: Stanford UP, 2003. Print.

Nancy, Jean-Luc. *L'Impératif catégorique.* Paris: Flammarion, 1983. Print.

Nancy, Jean-Luc. *Que faire?* Paris: Galilée, 2016. Print.

I

One of Jean-Luc Nancy's most characteristic philosophical gestures is to begin by stressing – and thereby confirming – the dialectical reciprocity or solidarity between opposed values, in order then to affirm an excessive third term, suitably redeemed or reconfigured, of which it may then be claimed, following what Derrida once called Nancy's "absolute, irredentist, post-deconstructive realism" (*Le Toucher* 60; *On Touching* 46), that it undercuts or outstrips each and every previous binary couple to which it is properly (or improperly) irreducible. The strategy, it is sometimes suggested, bears a similarity to the classic three-stage speculative dialectic. Its purpose is however quite different. Rather than accrediting teleological progression, the ambition is rather to uncover an origin that, having been hitherto obscured, is yet to be grasped, and to expose or expound a challenging new conceptual or, more accurately, preconceptual self-evidence or evidentiality.

In the prefatory "Coda" or tailpiece to a recent collection of papers, assembled with the help of Ginette Michaud, in which he examines the rivalry or dialogue between the literary and the philosophical, each of which is said not only to be in search of its own truth, but also, and in all senses of the word, to be forever questioning the truth of the other, Nancy begins for instance by underlining the opposed yet symmetrical characteristics of the two.[1] So far, so traditional. The point here, however, is not to

leslie hill

THE FRAGILITY OF THINKING

reinforce the stereotypical idea that the one takes precedence over the other, or that the one is but the continuation of the other by alternative means, but rather to highlight the "demande" – the title of Nancy's book – , that is to say: "the asking, wanting, appealing, beseeching, or frantic requiring" (*Demande* 9; *Expectation* 1; trans. mod.), that the literary and the philosophical each addresses to its counterpart, but with no expectation that either might deliver what its opposite number craves. True, Nancy is quick to add, philosophy and literature each have a different

---

This is an Open Access article distributed under the terms of the Creative Commons Attribution-NonCommercial-NoDerivatives License (http://creativecommons.org/licenses/by-nc-nd/4.0/), which permits non-commercial re-use, distribution, and reproduction in any medium, provided the original work is properly cited, and is not altered, transformed, or built upon in any way.

understanding of what they are seeking, which necessarily lies beyond their purview, with philosophy conceiving of truth as an "interruption of sense," and literature portraying truth as "the impossibility of interrupting sense" (*Demande* 10; *Expectation* 2), with the contrary and paradoxical rider that, while philosophy cannot stop itself, devoted as it is to the assimilation or incorporation of all that lies outside it, so literature, condemned as it is to the production of singular, discrete works, only survives by cutting into its never-ending flux.

The question of truth, Nancy insists, remains unanswerable. Were there to be an answer, he rightly argues, it would cause philosophy to lapse into the authority of wisdom (or the wisdom of authority) and literature into the finality of myth (or the myth of finality). "Philosophy and Literature," he explains, "are Wisdom and Myth once they have entered the time of asking, each having lost itself, or lost the other" (Nancy, *Demande* 12; *Expectation* 3; trans. mod.). Loss, in other words, is always already an unfolding, just as unfolding is itself always already a loss. Paradox again ensues, with wisdom (as in Socrates) ending up unfolding the truth that there is no wisdom, and myth (as in Joyce) unfolding its finality by displaying its essential incompletion. "Asking," suggests Nancy, "has perhaps to divide itself to make itself understood: from philosophy to literature and from literature to philosophy." In which case, what remains, he adds, appealing, as so often elsewhere, to the elusive and indeterminate, yet perpetually self-presenting, self-validating third term with which his thinking has become synonymous, is "simply the interminable coming of sense, synonymous with its own asking" (*Demande* 13; *Expectation* 4; trans. mod.).

The argument is elegantly put. Symmetry continues to rule. But this should not prevent one from asking whether the narrative of loss which Nancy unfolds does not itself beg a number of obstinate questions. For it will be remembered how he began his long career as a philosopher and thinker by detecting in Kant the overwhelming strength, or incalculable weakness, of the undecidable, this "sameness of the same [*la mêmeté du même*] produced by the same [*le même*] as its alteration." Which was also to say: "the dialectic of the Same, and therefore the dialectic itself, *as* its own impossibility," such that "perhaps the least untenable statement," he concluded, "is along the lines of: *the same undecides itself* [le même s'indécide]" (Nancy, *Le Discours de la syncope* 13; *The Discourse of the Syncope* 9–10). If so, it would follow that the undecidable cannot ever be avoided by any philosophical discourse whatsoever, and the possibility that it might continue to haunt Nancy's own discourse, as that discourse implies, should not come as much of a surprise. Indeed, it is one of the most properly and knowingly disruptive aspects of Nancy's thinking, and one that programmes, so to speak, the many questions – questions without answers – his work bequeaths its readers.

But since "asking" is of the essence, one cannot therefore not ask, according to the story of loss or unfolding that Nancy tells, that is, of loss as unfolding and unfolding as loss, how it might still be possible, or not, to tell the difference between, say, philosophy and wisdom, or literature and myth, or even between philosophy and literature "as such," in so far as what is most in doubt here, following Nancy's reading of Kant, as Derrida once put it, is the "as-such-ness" of the "as such" "as such"? And if the one is forever haunted by the hypothesis, threat, or would-be truth of the other, and the other by the one, how are we to decide which of the two, in its interminable coming, is presenting itself to us at all?

In the end, in a wilful, throwaway parting gesture ("Let's just all forget about 'philosophy, literature, myth, or wisdom,'" the reader is enjoined), Nancy's tailpiece abandons such questions to their imponderable fate (*Demande* 13; *Expectation* 4). The question now, he maintains, is simply how to pass beyond the fragile limit between the interrupted and the uninterrupted, the complete and the incomplete, and cross the uncertain line between a conclusion and a suspension.

Passage alone, in other words, is what asks, and passage alone is what is asked for. In only a few choice pages, and five carefully worded fragments or digressions, Nancy, then, takes his reader from dialectical symmetry to wishful transgression to self-confirming aporia, from the one and the other, or the one or the other, to the neither/nor or the in-between.

But how far is the in-between, or the passage beyond, still indebted to the reciprocity it seeks to overcome? The question, it may be remembered, was the main burden of Maurice Blanchot's discreet yet searching response to Nancy's in-between concept, excessive of immanence and transcendence alike, of "unworked" or "workless" "community," and the main reason for his principled reservations regarding the very concept of "community."[2] For if it was the case that "workless community," on Nancy's definition, based itself on a dual rejection of collectivism and individualism, i.e., both State communism and capitalist neoliberalism, in so far as the one and the other, in symmetrical and mutually complicit fashion, each embodied the same equally unacceptable figure of "immanentism," it was by virtue of a concept of dialectical reciprocity that inevitably implied the prospect or temptation of their speculative overhaul. And this was why, if some concept of "community" was worth preserving, as Nancy would continue to insist, a contention Blanchot was willing to endorse only in so far as "community" was radically emptied of all positionality, thematicism, and substantiality, then it was essential, in Blanchot's eyes, to dismantle the logic of reciprocity itself rather than aim to pass beyond it.[3] It is however noticeable that, in none of the many books, articles, or interviews Nancy devotes to Blanchot's writing, is this objection ever explicitly recognised. Which would tend to suggest that Nancy's conceptual boldness comes at a price, and that in his own thinking, in much the same way as he shows it to be the case with Kant, there is what one might call an inescapable fragility, by dint of which, as the logic of "asking" would also suggest, his thinking is at its most provocative when it is also at its most precarious. And vice versa.

If the word fragility seems appropriate here, it is because, on Nancy's own submission, as we shall see, it is one of the possible names for the neither/nor or the in-between. But before going further, let me recall another piece by Nancy, from the year 2000, also collected in *Demande*, in which the symmetrical relationship or opposition between "literature" and "philosophy" is again recounted. It has as its title a quotation and a parenthesis. The quotation, from Hölderlin by way of Heidegger, though neither author is mentioned by name, uses a kind of French historic or mythic present and reads: "Un jour, les dieux se retirent ... ," "One day, the gods withdrew ... " (Nancy, *Demande* 37–44; *Expectation* 25–30).[4] The parenthesis states more simply, with an oblique appeal to punctuation: "(Littérature/Philosophie: entre-deux)" ["Literature/Philosophy: in-between"]. Here, then, as in Nancy's 2015 tailpiece, the task is to tell a story, albeit one that, being no longer present in itself, since it is a story about the eclipse of presence, leaves in its wake two alternative possibilities, i.e., storytelling or truth, possibilities which, in their separateness, each bear witness to the same withdrawal of presence, the same unavailability of the body of the gods. It is the withdrawal of presence, in other words, that provides for the separateness or the difference between what according to this tale of origins will later become, on the one hand, *muthos*, and, on the other, *logos*, otherwise known as literature and philosophy.

Between the two, suggests Nancy, runs the violence of a cut, a kind of disentanglement that in its very possibility bears paradoxical witness to that which cannot be disentangled, told apart, or decided. At the same time, it is this disentanglement that, separating truth from narration, and narration from truth, institutes each as what it now is: literature, philosophy. "Without that separation," Nancy argues, "there would be neither truth nor narration: there would be the body of god [or the gods]" (*Demande* 39; *Expectation* 26; trans. mod.).[5] As far as these two offspring of the gods are concerned, that is, as far as these two descendants of the absence, or absent presence, of the gods are concerned, rhetorical symmetry again seems decisive. On either side of an empty tomb, "a scene of mourning and desire" comes to be staged: "philosophy, literature, each mourning and desiring the other (the other as such, the other as same [*l'autre même*]), but each also competing [*rivalisant*] with the other in fulfilling mourning and desire" (*Demande* 40; *Expectation* 27–28; trans. mod.). "The absence of the gods," Nancy has it by way of conclusion,

> is the condition of both, of both literature and philosophy, the in-between that legitimates the one and the other, both irreversibly atheological. Together, however, they are jointly charged with taking care [*prendre soin*] of the in-between: with keeping the body [*le corps*, i.e., the body of god or the gods] open, allowing it the chance of that opening. (*Demande* 41; *Expectation* 28; trans. mod.)

Inevitable tautology aside, Nancy's fable of the withdrawal of the gods and the arrival on the scene of the philosophical and the literary as adversaries and accomplices is both suggestive and economical. It remains however a story, one that, according to Nancy's own presentation, is necessarily in search of its elusive truth. Indeed, one learns,

> not only is narration liable to be found lacking in truth or suspected of being so, it is indeed deprived of it from the outset, being deprived of the present body as the mouth of its own utterance, the skin of its own exposure. (*Demande* 39; *Expectation* 27; trans. mod.)

If so, Nancy's own writing, notwithstanding its fondness for rhetorical symmetry, cannot do other than exhibit an underlying asymmetry which is in equal measure both enabling and disabling. For in order to account for the separation between philosophy and literature, and so as to posit the absent body of the divine as their secret or secretly shared condition, and even as his discourse offers itself to its readers as belonging primarily not to fiction but to thought, so Nancy, as in the case of all founding myths or myths of foundation, and in what is

also plainly a calculated move, is constrained to tell a story, present a fable, or reinvent a myth. Which cannot but leave undecided, and perpetually undecidable, the question of the status of Nancy's own presentation: is it best seen as a kind of philosophy, or as a kind of literature, or perhaps more accurately as neither, that is to say, as a sophisticated attempt to reach back, in word or gesture, towards the absent presence of the body of god or of the gods? Which would of course explain his decision, amply documented in later work, to attempt to deconstruct Christianity, always at the risk of falling into the trap, encountered by many others in the past, of *re*constructing it.

No doubt, since such is the logic of all "asking," such questions are unlikely to be answerable in one way or in another. In any case, Nancy's own writing, as readers will be aware, is in its own terms remarkably diverse: there are numerous examples of formal philosophical analysis, rigorous ontological inquiry, or historical or theological commentary. There are translations, poems, fictional or autobiographical writings, interventions responding to urgent political events, probing accounts of literary outputs, exhibitions, artistic installations, films and stage productions. There are many responses to invitations, texts written in the form of fragments, extemporary interviews, and numerous cases of collaboration with others, with thinkers, writers, artists of all kinds.

It is to a relatively well-known example of this last category that, briefly, I now turn. It again appears or, better, reappears, by now for at least the third time, in Nancy's 2015 collection. Its significance has both to do with what it argues and the way it chooses to do so. Titled "Noli me frangere," i.e., "Break Me Not," it was first published in 1982, jointly authored by Nancy and his long-term collaborator Philippe Lacoue-Labarthe, following on from the pair's anthology and analysis of texts by the Jena Romantics, *L'Absolu littéraire* (*The Literary Absolute*) of 1978. Prompted in part, the authors explain, by a section of Blanchot's 1980 volume of fragmentary writing, *L'Écriture du désastre* (*The Writing of the Disaster*), the principal focus of the paper is the question of the status of the literary fragment in Romanticism and literary modernity. Nancy and Lacoue-Labarthe's discussion is not however in any standard form of literary or philosophical exposition. Taking its cue from Friedrich Schlegel's "Gespräch über die Poesie" ("Dialogue on Poetry"), it begins as a sequence of unattributed fragments, then turns into a brief dialogue between two voices (which convention suggests one should identify with the two authors), followed by a lengthy section in which the two take on the names and roles of the interlocutors from Schlegel's 1800 dialogue, i.e., Ludovico (presumably JLN) and Lothario (presumably PhLL), after which there is a further brief exchange between the two. Taken as a whole, so to speak, the piece, at one and the same time, displays and interrogates that cleverly self-conscious, half-serious, half-ironic Witz, much prized by the Romantics, that Nancy discusses in an earlier, 1977 essay, also contained in *Demande*, where it appears immediately after the inaugural Coda under the title: "A Kind of Prologue: *menstruum universale*," and explores what Novalis once described as the phenomenon of "literary dissolution."

Once again, as in the case of numerous other inherited and inescapably metaphysical binary oppositions – literature and philosophy, *muthos* and *logos*, the religious and the secular, monotheism and atheism, myth and demythologisation, even the immanent and the transcendent – , the first task Lacoue-Labarthe and Nancy give themselves is to emphasise, and reinforce, the dialectical solidarity of a thinking of the work and a thinking of the fragment. Each in fact, it is quickly suggested, despite appearances to the contrary, is but the mirror image or photographic negative of the other. All works, it would appear, are always already fragments, and all fragments works. "Dialectics, i.e., discourse," it follows (Blanchot had argued much the same in *L'Écriture du désastre*), "is indestructible." And this is duly one of the meanings of the title of Lacoue-Labarthe and Nancy's text: "*Noli me frangere*, commands the dialectic in every

text, both in the fragmentary text as well, and in any discourse in fragments on the fragment. Break me not, fragment me not" (*Demande* 196; *Expectation* 132; trans. mod.).

But at the very moment when it would appear that all thinking of the work or the fragment is destined to be trapped in a vicious circle from which there is no way out, the dialectic having always already determined and appropriated all available alternatives, Nancy, or his partner, advances the word "fragility" to address that which, being neither the work nor the fragment, is not only irreducible to each, but, just like the absent presence of god or the gods, is also the joint, in-between condition of possibility of both. And it is a condition of possibility that is itself indestructible, not least because it precedes both the fragment (which, being always already fragmented, cannot properly be now what it purports to be), and the whole (which is likewise anything but what it claims). And being "indestructible," one learns, "*fragility*," underlined in the text, "is more tenuous, more trembling, more unbearable than any fragmentation" – while also, in acknowledging no opposition, being thereby insuperable, not to say omnipotent. Fragility at any event, write Nancy and Lacoue-Labarthe, is what there is

> in beginning to speak or to write. In opening one's mouth, or inscribing a word. There, or then, is when it breaks – nowhere else, and at no other time. The fragility of a glorious body (neither transcendent nor immanent, neither yours nor mine, neither body nor soul) breaks a throat or a hand. Thus arises a word, a discourse, a song, a writing. The glorious body will never stop repeating this command, as fragile as an entreaty: *Noli me frangere*. (*Demande* 197–98; *Expectation* 133; trans. mod.)

In the title of Nancy and Lacoue-Labarthe's text – "Noli me frangere" – , two different, contrasting, even opposed meanings compete, then, for attention. On the one hand, "break me not" are the words uttered by the dialectic, by the discourse of philosophy in general, which, from the summit of its authority, tells us that what literary history has hitherto called the fragment, i.e., that of the Romantics, of Friedrich Schlegel, Novalis, and so many others, and that of modernity, of Nietzsche, Kafka, Artaud, or Beckett – is impossible. "Break me not, fragment me not," we are told, because, however much we try, we will have failed, not least by trying to try, since to will fragmentation is always already to subordinate the fragment to the energy or the will, which is to say, to the desire for a work. On the other hand, "break me not" are (almost) the words pronounced by a glorious body, warning a human, all too human hand to refrain from retaining or capturing it. The scene alluded to here, taken from the Gospel according to John 20.17, is of course well known. In what follows, Nancy, in the guise of "Ludovico," glosses it more fully by reminding readers how, after the crucifixion, after Christ's body has been laid out for burial, Mary Magdalene goes to the empty sepulchre, and, seeing a man she takes to be a mere gardener, fails to recognise who it is. "Jesus, however, calls out to her: 'Mary!' Turning on her heels, she replies with the word: 'Rabboni!,' in Hebrew, meaning 'Master!,'" i.e., Magister, according to the Latin Vulgate text that Nancy, for reasons he explains elsewhere (in *La Déclosion* 142n2; *Dis-Enclosure* 183n19), is here closely following. And Jesus goes on, with now proverbial words: "*Noli me tangere*," "Touch me not, for I am not yet ascended to my Father" (Nancy, *Demande* 204; *Expectation* 138; trans. mod.).

Two versions, two readings, two opposing interpretations of "mastery" seem to be at stake here. Both imply the imminence, that is, both the threat and the promise of an ascent, of a dialectical raising of one thing into its other, here the fragment into the work, there the mortal body into evidence of its inalienable immortality. And in both cases, "Noli me frangere" or "Noli me tangere" enacts a prohibition, an injunction instructing us as to what is not possible, or at least not desirable, not worth wanting or willing: not possible, it would appear, to write according to the fragment, and similarly not possible to retain the transcendent. And yet, here as well

as there, is something – though, in truth, it is barely a thing at all – fragile and yet indestructible, which is to say, fragility "as such" (though one can but tremble at the idea of using the expression here, since fragility is precisely what dissolves any "as such" "as such"), or, equally well, the glorious body which, being neither immanent nor transcendent, eludes all apprehension.

There is of course at least a third function of the phrase "Noli me frangere." For it should not be forgotten it is also the title of a singular piece of writing, jointly signed by Philippe Lacoue-Labarthe and Jean-Luc Nancy, which, in its playfulness, its tongue-in-cheek irony, its allusiveness, and heterogeneous composition (fragment, dialogue, pastiche, etc.), is already an egregious example of that Romantic Witz explored by Nancy in the 1977 paper that serves his 2015 book as "A Kind of Prologue." "Witz," Nancy had explained,

> barely belongs to literature or does so, as it were, only just, and only by the back door, or in a roundabout way; it is neither a genre nor a style, nor even a figure of rhetoric. But nor does it belong to philosophy, not being a concept, judgement, or argument. And yet it has the capacity to assume all these roles, but only in an act of derision. (*Demande* 15; *Expectation* 8; trans. mod.)

This, then, "in a certain sense," he adds,

> is the lesson of the Witz: the uncontrolled – and uncontrollable – genesis of the blurring of genres, or what one might be tempted to call the "genre of the West," literature and philosophy, neither literature nor philosophy, literature or philosophy. In a word, literary dissolution – where "literary" solely means the realm of the letter and of writing in general, the scriptural West. (*Demande* 22–23; *Expectation* 13; trans. mod.)

In its French guise, as "esprit" (meaning "spirit" and "wit"), or as English "wit," suggests Nancy, Witz "is the specific modern product of the philosophical crisis of *judgement*," which itself is but "the modern restaging of a 'crisis' constitutive of all philosophical discourse," and "thus marks the element or structure of undecidability in all 'logical' decision-making itself" (*Demande* 23; *Expectation* 13–14; trans. mod.). If, on the one hand, then, "Witz may be said to be nothing other than the dialectical thought of identity, beginning with the thought of the *self-identity of 'wit' itself*," such that "the separation and total opposition between *Witz* and Reason only ever occurs so as to allow that dialectic to function," and has only ever "opposed literature to philosophy the better to maintain mastery over their divide," so, on the other, it appears that "outside philosophy, outside literature (outside of psychoanalysis too), outside the mixture or coupling of the two (or the three), Witz neither delivers nor releases anything" (*Demande* 28, 32; *Expectation* 17–18, 21; trans. mod.).

This *witzig*, "witty," or "spiritual" re-presentation of its two contradictory earlier instances of indisputable mastery – of the dialectic and of the risen Christ – has, it would appear, at least two corollaries. First, it fragilises, by derision, so to speak, or by outplaying it, the two friends' dialogue as a fragmentary discourse on the fragment (this, the reader is told, is what should be avoided at all costs). In that sense, it draws it in the direction of what no longer belongs either to philosophy or to literature, but resides in their semi-serious, semi-laughable in-between. It endeavours, in other words, to outwit – or, more properly, to out-Witz – the dialectic in the name of that fragile, glorious body that has been brought forth, leaving their presentation to plummet, as it were, into the depths of an abyss. Not for nothing does one of the pair – Lacoue-Labarthe, one may guess – joyfully exclaim: "let us dance, then, on the edge of the abyss" (Nancy, *Demande* 199; *Expectation* 134; trans. mod.), an abyss, it would seem, whose principal task is to contest the spectre of dialectical mastery.

But this, as always, is only one part of the story. For at the same time, in attempting to outwit or out-Witz the dialectic, as Nancy's commentary on the Witz duly explains, what Witz does is not to force the dialectic to unravel, but rather to strengthen it, in so far

as it is itself already but an exemplification of "the dialectical thought of identity." Even as the fragility of a glorious body seems to interrupt the dialectic, so in return the dialectic duly takes possession of that selfsame fragility of the glorious body. The rising of the one turns imperceptibly into the raising of the other. Weakness becomes strength, fragility the indestructible, the immanent the transcendent. And if this is what they all are in the end, it is surely because that is what they already were in the beginning.

What remains, however, in so far as "Witz," according to Nancy, "neither delivers nor releases anything," is a kind of performative gesture – indeed what could be more expansively performative than Nancy's and Lacoue-Labarthe's Romantic dialogue? – one which, as its closing words make clear, is both inconclusive and interminable.

So where, then, it might be asked, does this leave the attempt, desire, or will, if that is what it is, to break the closure of the dialectic, break free from its strictures, and break out into the open? As I've tried to show, following in Nancy's and Lacoue-Labarthe's footsteps, as their 1982 title already had it, the enterprise is an impossible one.

But if so, there still remains a chance – a caesura, or perhaps just a syncope – which is none other than the possibility of that impossibility. There is, in other words, in writing itself, in the dialectic, even, a fracture or fissure, a fragility, so to speak, that allows thinking – and thinking with Nancy – to continue at all. It is this no doubt that Nancy has in mind when he speaks of "the interminable coming of sense, synonymous with its own asking." And this is also why it is to that possibility of an impossibility, and to the impossibility of that possibility, that Nancy comes to devote much of his thinking. It is however essential to remember that "sense," on Nancy's idiosyncratic definition, is never given "as such." "Sense [*le sens*]," he writes,

> defies all completion. At every stage, one thinks one is positing a meaning [*poser une signification*]: sense deposes them all [*le sens les dépose toutes*] and despatches

them elsewhere, towards an outside that is both before and after. Patiently, frantically, this elsewhere inscribes, exscribes its traces. (Nancy, *Demande* 86; *Expectation* 62; trans. mod.)

Its impossible possibility, then, remains vulnerable and exposed: imponderable, undecidable, and perilously fragile.

Let me cite here an example, which, naturally enough, is anything but an example. Much of Nancy's earlier work, it may be recalled, following on from his engagement with German Romanticism, is given over to the question of myth. Myth, being tautegorical rather than allegorical, as Nancy never tires telling his readers, quoting time and again a famous passage from Schelling, itself based on a remark by Coleridge pertaining to the Gospels, is that which always already contains its own interpretation, its own explanation, its own commentary. It has no outside that is not always already another version of itself (Nancy, *La Communauté désœuvrée* 124–25; *The Inoperative Community* 49; trans. mod.).[6] But if so, Schelling, and Nancy too, if only for a fragile, flickering moment (it is of course the moment of "sense"), must nevertheless have the possibility of stepping beyond myth in order to describe it in these very terms. Myth, in other words, like time, like history, necessarily incorporates its own interruption, without which it would not be graspable at all. Whence the fundamental question that occupies much of Nancy's thinking about myth: is the interruption of myth merely a dialectical continuation of myth by other means, or is it an epochal caesura or syncope which makes it possible to set myth aside?

To this abiding question, Nancy gives, however, perhaps unavoidably inconsistent answers. Particularly revealing is his shifting account of the emblematic figure of Blanchot, whose writings, both fictional texts and critical essays, occupy a central, if discreet role in the overall composition of *Demande*. Before going further however, it is worth recalling a passage which does not feature in the collection, but in Nancy's 1986 volume, *La Communauté*

désœuvrée (*The Inoperative Community*), itself written in partial response to Blanchot's *La Communauté inavouable*. Glossing the expression Blanchot takes as his title, explicitly borrowed from Bataille (and subsequently from Derrida),[7] as many commentators, including Nancy, seemingly fail to observe, Nancy asks:

> Does the unavowable have a myth? By definition, it does not. The absence of avowal amounts neither to a manner of speaking [*une parole*] nor to the telling of a story [*un récit*]. But if community is inseparable from myth, must there not be, by paradoxical necessity, a myth of unavowable community?

To which he provides this unambiguous, decisive answer: "This is however impossible." Nancy then adds: "It bears repeating: unavowable community, the withdrawal of communion or communitarian ecstacy, are revealed in the interruption of myth. And the interruption is not a myth" (*La Communauté désœuvrée* 147; *The Inoperative Community* 58; trans. mod.).

In 2014, however, revisiting these same questions apropos of the very same text by Blanchot, Nancy chooses to argue the opposite, now insisting that the expression "unavowable community" is a tell-tale symptom of regressive nostalgia for mythic communion, linked "not necessarily to fascism, far from it," as Nancy rather coyly puts it, echoing a widespread but unsubstantiated rumour regarding Blanchot's political past, but nonetheless "most certainly to right-wing thinking." "The avowal of the unavowable," he now claimed, "is the avowal of a recourse to myth." "Such recourse," he added,

> also means that Blanchot's thinking on literature and on community are more than just closely interconnected: perhaps they should be viewed as essentially the same, if indeed there is no literary communication [according to Blanchot] other than in the register of myth [...] and no thought of the common (of community or sharing) without recourse to that register.[8] (Nancy, *La Communauté désavouée* 134; *The Disavowed Community* 62; trans. mod.)

Here then, the unavowable (and its so-called "avowal"), myth, literature, and community in Blanchot are explicitly aligned as exhibiting a single continuous thought, in a way specifically excluded in 1986, suggesting that Nancy in 1986 somehow got matters badly wrong – unless of course it is in 2014, conversely, that he loses sight of what he had expressed so trenchantly nearly thirty years earlier.

True enough, major thinkers are no more immune than others to fatal misprisions, wild assertions, false conclusions, or palinodic conversions. Philosophers too make mistakes, have second thoughts, or come to see matters differently, and there is little doubt that, just like others, they should be allowed to change their minds. This however does not necessarily imply that with maturity of age comes a firmer grasp on the truth or that relative youth be seen as an impediment to wisdom. There are, as one knows, many instances of the opposite. At any event, Nancy's change of mind is remarkable, as is the decisiveness with which, in 1986 and 2014, he felt able to put forward what are, in retrospect, two diametrically opposed interpretations of Blanchot's reliance or non-reliance on foundational myth. There is nothing however gratuitous in any such shift. For the prior condition for Nancy's contradictory pronouncements, both the readings they embody and the self-certainty with which they are delivered, paradoxically enough, is the abiding and inescapable undecidability which makes all decisions both possible and necessary from the outset, and yet, as numerous sleepless nights bear witness, inevitably precarious and fragile.

In 2015, in conversation with Mathilde Girard, reviewing the question of myth and its outside, Nancy, with admirable frankness, acknowledged as much. "The expression 'interrupted myth' I used in *La Communauté désœuvrée*," he told his interviewer, "was not challenged by Philippe [Lacoue-Labarthe], quite the opposite, it seems to me, but neither he nor I knew exactly how it should be understood. And I still do not know" (Girard and Nancy 53).

II

Given the profound turbulence and abiding indecision associated with the name Blanchot in Nancy's writing, it was to be expected that it should feature as a recurrent, if intermittent point of reference in several of the diverse essays, dating from 1977 to 2013, brought together in *Demande* under the heading of "literature." Blanchot's texts, Nancy writes, in one of the earliest of these essays, together with the works of Mallarmé, Proust, Joyce, Kafka, Bataille, Borges, and Laporte, are among those which "today," i.e., in 1977, are impossible to ignore ("incontournables"), and mark an obligatory point of passage in which it was imperative steadfastly to *"remain"* (*Demande* 45; *Expectation* 31–32). True, this early endorsement of Blanchot's writing rarely leads to more than a series of fleeting allusions on Nancy's part to signature words or phrases borrowed from Blanchot, including terms or topics such as work ("œuvre") or worklessness ("désœuvrement"), the apocalypse, the "immemorial" past, or "the terrifyingly ancien" ("l'effroyablement ancien"). More importantly, however, now under the heading of "Sense" ("Sens"), *Demande* also contains three further texts devoted to Blanchot. The first, "Noli me frangere," co-authored with Lacoue-Labarthe, and arising from a discussion of Blanchot's *L'Écriture du désastre*, as seen earlier, is chiefly concerned with the question of the fragment and with the fragility said to precede it. The two remaining texts are more explicitly in the form of detailed commentaries on motifs in Blanchot's writing, "Résurrection de Blanchot [Blanchot's Resurrection]," from 2004, and "Le Neutre, la neutralisation du neutre [The Neuter and the Neutralisation of the Neuter]," first published in 2011 (Nancy, *Demande* 253–70; *Expectation* 177–90).[9]

Within the overall structure of Nancy's *Demande*, there is however something odd, even anomalous about the inclusion of these two later essays. In his prefatory "Coda," Nancy makes the valid point that solely those texts "that relate to literature" were selected for the volume, which meant leaving out many other, occasional studies devoted to the analysis of "specific works" (*Demande* 13; *Expectation* 4), such as those by Jean-Christophe Bailly, Michel Deguy, Lacoue-Labarthe, Laporte, Shakespeare, or others, not to mention essays readily available elsewhere on, say, Flaubert, Edmond Jabès, or Michel Leiris.[10] Why then include two essays dealing quite explicitly, and in some detail, with particular aspects of Blanchot's work? The most likely answer is that, in addressing specific textual passages occurring in Blanchot's inaugural novel, *Thomas l'Obscur* (*Thomas the Obscure*, 1941) and in his post-1968 volume of fragmentary writing, *Le Pas au-delà* (*The Step Not Beyond*, 1973), Nancy was also conscious of using Blanchot's writing, albeit indirectly, in order to reflect (and reflect on) aspects of his own thinking. Prominent among Nancy's concerns from 1995, it will be remembered, and in particular during the early years of the new century, coinciding with his return to Blanchot, was his project for the "deconstruction of Christianity," in which the work of Blanchot would play a not insignificant role as symptom and illustration, so much so that "Résurrection de Blanchot," together with an essay on "Le Nom de Dieu chez Blanchot [The Name *God* in Blanchot]," initially served as a centrepiece in Nancy's 2005 *La Déclosion (Déconstruction du christianisme, I)* [*Dis-Enclosure, the Deconstruction of Christianity*].

In turn, in much the same way as the question of the interruption of myth had done two decades earlier, so the deconstruction of Christianity, as Derrida was often heard to remark, posed in acute form the question of its own possibility, not least the availability of some Archimedean lever simultaneously outside and inside Christianity, at once integral to it yet inassimilable by it, from which to undertake the task of deconstruction. That this should entail renewed scrutiny of the limits or inner or outer margins of the Hegelian dialectic was something of which Nancy and Blanchot were both intensely aware, and it is telling that in his 2011 essay on Blanchot it should be in close, and potentially dangerous proximity to Hegel (following, it is true, an indication of Blanchot's own) that Nancy should choose to locate the thought of the neuter. Also worth noting, and continuing to rumble on from the mid-1980s, was the memory of unfinished business between the pair on the subject of "community," with Nancy underlining in 2001 the extent to which he still felt *La Communauté inavouable* of 1983, as far as his own *La Communauté désœuvrée* was concerned, to be "simultaneously an echo, a resonance and a rejoinder, a reservation, or even in some respects a reproach" (*La Communauté affrontée* 38; "The Confronted Community" 40; trans. mod.).

In each of these diverse instances, it is readily apparent that the work of Blanchot, with which Nancy in 1977 deemed it essential to pause, and to which he indeed returns time and again in almost obsessive fashion, continued to function as a provocative reference point, an example of what to follow or what to avoid, even at times as a convenient lightning rod for some of the difficulties and ambiguities of his own thinking. That another author or thinker should in this way become a kind of secret sharer existing within or without one's own thinking, it may be said, is far from unusual. Indeed, such haunting of one body of work by another is intimately connected with the process of thinking itself, which is also in the form of an asking and an answering in dialogue both with the living and with the dead.

It was in that regard only logical that, in his 2004 paper, "Blanchot's Resurrection," presented as part of a series of public lectures delivered less than a year after Blanchot's death at the age of ninety-five, the topic Nancy should choose to address was precisely the question of living and dying. As the point of departure and main focus of his talk, Nancy took a brief, relatively little-known passage from *Thomas l'Obscur* in which one encounters the following sentence: "He walked on, the only veritable Lazarus [*seul Lazare véritable*] whose very death was resuscitated [*ressuscitée*]" (49).[11] While the grammatical subject of the sentence, as Nancy points out,

THE PULSE OF SENSE

is unambiguously Blanchot's protagonist, i.e., Thomas, it is readily apparent that the burden of Blanchot's formulation, as persistently elsewhere in the novel, is to put into doubt any notion that a subject might own his or her experience, or that experience be anything other than an abyssal absence of foundation. It is in this respect far from coincidental that, according to Jacobus da Varagine (or Voragine), author of the thirteenth-century *Golden Legend*, the name Thomas should signify "abyss" or "twin" (de Voragine I: 57).

Was this idiosyncratic reference to the New Testament, Nancy asks, evidence of a lingering commitment to Catholicism, as he would increasingly claim, in so far as Blanchot here was thought to want to "preserve, at least in part, the monotheistic, or more precisely Christian roots of the thought of resurrection" (*Demande* 254; *Expectation* 178; trans. mod.)? Or did Blanchot's attempted "rewriting of Holy Scripture" (*Demande* 263; *Expectation* 184) already announce something of what Nancy had come to call the "deconstruction" of Christianity? Or if it did something of the latter, did it not do so at the risk of clinging to the former, and reflect a fundamental tension, not to say an inescapable fragility inseparable from thought itself? Such, at any event, according to Nancy, was the "danger" it was necessary to avoid, and it comes as no surprise, notwithstanding Nancy's Socratic questioning of Blanchot's text, that this should also be the trap into which Nancy, in his own efforts to deconstruct Christianity, is himself sometimes thought to fall, not least by Blanchot himself.[12] Which might suggest that the consequences of the abiding fragility of thinking are less easily averted than is sometimes claimed, and have the unerring capacity of displaying themselves in places where, and at times when, they are least expected.

Nancy begins his reading of Blanchot's sentence by observing, rightly enough, that the resurrection of Thomas's death is anything but a resurrection of Thomas dead, since it substitutes for the dialectical passage from death to life, as understood in Christian, not to say Hegelian doctrine, a much more fragile

exposure to the experience or, better, the non-experience of life in death and death in life, i.e., the radical inaccessibility of the experience of dying and, by that token, of living itself, irreducibly defiant of all presence. ("Inner experience" in Bataille, it will be remembered, was similarly for Blanchot "experience of non-experience" (*L'Entretien infini* 311; *The Infinite Conversation* 210).) At the same time, even as he makes this argument, Nancy still allows himself, by sleight of hand, by attributing to Blanchot, as though they were a statement of critical or aesthetic principle, comments made in 1953 apropos of Rilke, whose poetic experience, one knows, was very different to that of Blanchot, in order to subordinate the motif of "death resuscitated" in Blanchot (much as Nancy would subsequently do with the non-concept of "unavowable community") to a still lingering concept of the artwork, albeit of "the artwork in its essential worklessness [*de l'œuvre en son désœuvrement essentiel*]" (*Demande* 253–54; *Expectation* 178; trans. mod.).[13] The formulation, as has been pointed out, owes more to Blanchot's at times severe critical assessment of the thinking of the Jena Romantics[14] than to any of his own fragmentary writings. It is nevertheless striking that Nancy, two pages later, citing the same Romantic notion of the immanence of the artwork, still felt able to suggest how, for Blanchot's Lazarus, unlike the Lazarus of the Gospels,

> truth does not consist in any such return [from death to life]: it resides in the concomitance of death and of a life within death that does not revert to life, but vivifies [*fait vivre*] death as such [*en tant que telle*]. In other words, the true Lazarus [*le vrai Lazare*: Nancy's gloss substitutes "true" for "veritable" in Blanchot] lives his dying [*vit son mourir*] just as he dies his living [*meurt son vivre*]. (*Demande* 256; *Expectation* 179–80; trans. mod.)

Nancy's formula is not without its aphoristic force. Rather surprisingly, however, it omits to take account of that indisputable fragility of living and dying in Blanchot, as a result of which neither the one nor the other is ever accessible "as such," and never available to be signified, even by an artwork, in its supposed self-identity. This in turn cannot do other than cast an aura of troubling fragility over the sternly reductive definition of "literature" with which Nancy's paper concludes, "literature," that is, as Nancy puts it, as that which, embodied in the logic of the work with which he precipitately identifies Blanchot's thinking, "writes only the present of what has always already happened to us, that is, the impossible into which our being consists in disappearing" (*Demande* 256; *Expectation* 185; trans. mod.). What one misses most of all in such a definition, which also might seem to contradict much of what is argued elsewhere in *Demande*, is any awareness of the conjectural uncertainty of any such decisive judgement and what one might rightly call its fragility, as though Nancy's own concept of fragility was in the end, for some reason, not fragile enough, and only able to reach so far and no further. "Literature," Blanchot once replied to a questionnaire in 1992, "is a potency [*puissance*] that takes account of nothing." He then added: "But when is there literature?" (Blanchot, *La Condition critique* 465). Literature, in other words, as at least some of the texts collected in *Demande* appear to agree, is inseparable from a radical questioning, an asking rather than an answering, and to that extent, as Blanchot's comment suggests, it arises only when it comes from the outside, and belongs, not to the "present," but only to the in-between or neither/nor.

But how to respond to what falls between positions, how to give it a name, and how to make its voice heard? How, then, to understand the fragile interruption of myth, power, and presence, with which "literature" is said to be synonymous? And with what words to affirm the withdrawal and absence of the god or gods?

In an effort, if not to provide an answer, then at least to prolong the demands made by such questions, Nancy in 2011 immediately chose to construe Blanchot's use of the non-concept of the neuter, this fragile trace synonymous only with its withdrawal, elision, or erasure, as

a response to the death of "God," this "surplus word," or "word too many," as Blanchot had put it in *Le Pas au-delà*, and which had somehow been allowed to "rise above language by taking control of it, perhaps by breaking it apart, at the very least by claiming to set a limit to it" (*Le Pas au-delà* 84–85; *The Step Not Beyond* 59–60; trans. mod.). Nancy follows up his remark by suggesting however that, in so far as it too, according to an earlier text by Blanchot (albeit in a very different sense), was a "word too many," so the word "neuter" in Blanchot enjoyed similar status as that of "God." In which case, it would be just another instance of a dubious master concept destined to foreclose any futural "sense." It is true, as Nancy points out, that Blanchot in *Le Pas au-delà* draws attention to the possible parallels between the "neuter" and Hegelian Aufhebung, not least, of course, to stress that the neuter was radically irreducible to Hegelian negativity, to being and to non-being alike, and only "evoked" the "movement" of Aufhebung from a suspensive and interruptive distance, without producing any dialectical result, be it in the form of an artwork or of some superior concept (*Le Pas au-delà* 101–07; *The Step Not Beyond* 72–76).

Nancy in 2011 seems however to have been less than convinced, and only too keen, in responding to the challenge of thinking the "in-between" of "sense," to resist the temptation or, better, to exorcise the threat of the covert reliance on speculative dialectics he suspects, impatiently, to be at work in Blanchot. But if the neuter, according to Nancy's 2011 presentation, runs the risk of too great a proximity to Hegelian dialectics, it seems elsewhere that the opposite is equally true. In *La Communauté désavouée*, for instance, Nancy dismisses Blanchot's commitment to the neuter as a mere "Romantico-Idealist" vestige, "more reminiscent of the negative theology of Nicolas de Cusa," far removed from the "tragic" rewriting of Hegel by Bataille (*La Communauté désavouée* 40, 84; *The Disavowed Community* 15, 35). What, in other words, seems to irk Nancy in Blanchot's thinking – and the objection is self-evidently paradoxical – is the ineradicable fragility of the neuter invoked for instance in a passage from *L'Entretien infini* partially quoted, but hastily interrupted by Nancy, in which one reads:

> The neuter: this word *too many* that subtracts itself [Nancy breaks off at this point in order to privilege negativity over dissemination] either by reserving for itself a place from which it is always missing while leaving a trace, or by provoking a displacement without place, or else by distributing itself, in multiple fashion, in a supplement of place. (*L'Entretien infini* 458; *The Infinite Conversation* 312–13)

Which was also to say that, for Blanchot, the neuter, this name without name for the always other word, the word always too few and always too many, was not only the condition of possibility of all literature, but also the reason for literature's radical fragility, or, in other words, its insuperable force and immeasurable weakness, as always other than what it is, or is not.

It is no doubt the task of philosophy, in its pursuit of truth, to assert authority over the unruliness to which literature bears witness, just as it is the business of literature to set philosophy aside and ignore its would-be foundations. If so, between the two, the undecidability of a relation without relation remains ineliminable. And if thinking is to remain possible at all, Nancy tells us, it is only in so far as it allows itself to affirm the fragility on which it relies, and which constantly traverses, and forcibly outlives it.

echo by jean-luc nancy

I thank Leslie Hill for his precise and valued attention to my fragilities. He is right to be so concerned about what inevitably makes thought come short in relation to what it thinks. It seems to me that in Blanchot there is such a recurring shortcoming, not in what he seeks to preserve – the elusiveness (*l'insaisissable*) of what is essential, the impossibility of having a "last word" – but in the fact that in the end he himself grasps this elusiveness and presents it. This movement is not always present or visible, but is in any case what drives *The Unavowable Community*. It is a political movement or impulse: a sovereign authority must ensure the truth of the discourse. The hierarchical and archi-aristocratic political model is not always active in Blanchot's work, but it is so at times, especially when he began addressing the question of "community," always affirming a "communism" (which he was more or less forced to confess "officially," so to speak, by his time – and by Mascolo in particular), which he immediately subjected to the condition of being neither communitarian nor common in general (it is here, perhaps, in the "common," in a repulsion for the common, that the deep impulse is nested). The fragility of Blanchot's thinking lies in this rejection of the common, the vulgar, and at the same time in what is given only commonly, banally, effacing itself in giving itself – not, however, to transfigure itself (like the woman-Christ in *The Unavowable Community*), but simply to confess itself in its poverty or even in its common indigence.

Leslie Hill argues that the title "The Unavowable Community" is borrowed from Bataille. He does not give a reference, nor do I have one to provide. But the "avowal" is so present in Bataille – in a way, it is even essential – that I can well imagine that he spoke of an "unavowable community" – thereby indicating what should be confessed: both the obscenity and the non-knowledge inherent in the communication of the intimate. I won't elaborate any further: that alone should suffice to indicate the considerable difference that then opens up between Bataille and Blanchot. It could be summarised as follows: the unavowable in Bataille is confessed humbly, even miserably and as if dying; in Blanchot, it slips a revelation about its secret, which is a kind of resurrection.

I also thank Leslie Hill for reminding me that I had mentioned *The Unavowable Community* in my *Inoperative Community* in 1986. I had forgotten about that, otherwise I would of course have mentioned it in 2014. Leslie says that, from one day to the next, I contradict myself. This is only partly true because what I said about Blanchot's book in 1986 was so vague and undeveloped that not much can be drawn from it. Instead, one should be surprised by this lack of precision and rather light and carefree way of treating the book with which Blanchot responded to my initial text. It is then my turn to confess: this indigent passage bears witness to the fact that in 1986 I still hadn't understood a thing of Blanchot's book (and that no one allowed me to understand it – everyone had remained mute, as I pointed out in 2014). I had only perceived a refusal and recoil from me that remained poorly determined. I didn't know what to do with it and resolved, out of perplexity and respect for Blanchot's authority, to do what is known as "going down a tangent." So I said nothing, but it is not surprising that with time and Blanchot's death my perplexity has matured, my respect shifted (not been lost!) and I have come to understand what I can now only confirm about *The Unavowable Community*.

Who would have thought that fragility sometimes husbands some unforeseen resources?

disclosure statement

No potential conflict of interest was reported by the author.

notes

1 Jean-Luc Nancy, *Demande: littérature et philosophie* (Paris: Galilée, 2015); *Expectation: Philosophy, Literature*, trans. Robert Bononno, with an introduction by Jean-Michel Rabaté (New York: Fordham UP, 2018). While the French edition comprises a total of thirty-three texts of diverse genres from different periods, its English counterpart contains only twenty-eight, to which it adds an introduction by Jean-Michel Rabaté. A coda, according to the dictionary, is "a passage of more or less independent character introduced after the completion of the essential parts of a movement, so as to form a more definite and satisfactory conclusion."

2 For a detailed account of the dispute between Nancy and Blanchot on the subject of "community," literature, religion, and politics, see Hill.

3 See Blanchot, *La Communauté inavouable* 12–13; *The Unavowable Community* 3–4. On the frequently misunderstood and widely misrepresented motif of the "unavowable" in Blanchot, see Hill 103–16.

4 Robert Bononno's over-literal English version uses an unconvincing unidiomatic present tense here: "'One day the gods withdraw ... '"

5 Nancy's original text has "le corps divin."

6 For the passage to which Nancy refers, see Schelling, *Ausgewählte Schriften* V: 205–06; *Historical-Critical Introduction to the Philosophy of Mythology* 136 and 187ne.

7 On this prior history of the term "unavowable," and for the precise reference to the source of the double quotation in Blanchot's title, see Hill 103–16.

8 It should be emphasised here that there is no truth in the much repeated but unsubstantiated allegation that Blanchot before 1940 was sympathetic to "French fascism" (or any other kind of fascism).

9 Somewhat regrettably, in translating the second of these titles as "The Neutral, Neutralization of the Neutral," Robert Bononno follows the established but misleading convention of rendering Blanchot's "neutre" or "neuter," which is primarily a linguistic or syntactical category, with the predominantly political term "neutral," one of the prime meanings of which, according to the OED, is "taking neither side in a dispute, disagreement, or difference of opinions; not inclining toward either party, view, etc.; assisting neither of two contending parties or persons." It should however be emphasised that the "neuter" in Blanchot never corresponds to such non-partisan equanimity between extremes.

10 Several other "literary" essays not included in *Demande* may be found in the English translation in Jean-Luc Nancy, *Multiple Arts*.

11 As Nancy points out, unlike some of the surrounding material, the sentence recurs unchanged in Blanchot, *Thomas l'Obscur, nouvelle version* 42. For Nancy's citation and commentary, see *Demande* 255; *Expectation* 179. According to etymology, "ressusciter," as commonly used in French translations of Matthew 28.6, means: to "reanimate" or "restore to life."

12 See Hill 193–208.

13 For the essay on which Nancy is drawing, see Blanchot, *L'Espace littéraire* 121–66; *The Space of Literature* 120–59. It is a curious feature of Nancy's reading of Blanchot (also in evidence in *La Communauté désavouée*) that he seems unwilling to distinguish between Blanchot's own thinking as a writer and his observations regarding the works of others.

14 See Blanchot, *L'Entretien infini* 515–27; *The Infinite Conversation* 351–59.

bibliography

Blanchot, Maurice. *La Communauté inavouable.* Paris: Minuit, 1983; *The Unavowable Community.* Trans. Pierre Joris. New York: Station Hill, 1988. Print.

Blanchot, Maurice. *La Condition critique: articles 1945–1998.* Ed. Christophe Bident. Paris: Gallimard, 2010. Print.

Blanchot, Maurice. *L'Entretien infini.* Paris: Gallimard, 1969; *The Infinite Conversation.* Trans. Susan Hanson. Minneapolis: U of Minnesota P, 1993. Print.

Blanchot, Maurice. *Le Pas au-delà.* Paris: Gallimard, 1973; *The Step Not Beyond.* Trans. Lycette Nelson. Albany: SUNY P, 1992. Print.

Blanchot, Maurice. *L'Espace littéraire.* Paris: Gallimard, 1955; *The Space of Literature.* Trans. Ann Smock. Lincoln: U of Nebraska P, 1982. Print.

Blanchot, Maurice. *Thomas l'Obscur.* Paris: Gallimard, 1941. Print.

Blanchot, Maurice. *Thomas l'Obscur, nouvelle version.* Paris: Gallimard, 1950. Print.

Derrida, Jacques. *Le Toucher, Jean-Luc Nancy.* Paris: Galilée, 2000; *On Touching, Jean-Luc Nancy.* Trans. Christine Irizarry. Stanford: Stanford UP, 2005. Print.

Girard, Mathilde, and Jean-Luc Nancy. *Proprement dit: entretien sur le mythe.* Paris: Lignes, 2015. Print.

Hill, Leslie. *Nancy, Blanchot: A Serious Controversy.* London: Rowman, 2018. Print.

Nancy, Jean-Luc. *Demande: littérature et philosophie.* Paris: Galilée, 2015; *Expectation: Philosophy, Literature.* Trans. Robert Bononno. Intro. Jean-

Michel Rabaté. New York: Fordham UP, 2018. Print.

Nancy, Jean-Luc. *La Communauté affrontée.* Paris: Galilée, 2001; "The Confronted Community." Trans. Amanda Macdonald. *Postcolonial Studies* 6.1 (2003). Print.

Nancy, Jean-Luc. *La Communauté désavouée.* Paris: Galilée, 2014; *The Disavowed Community.* Trans. Philip Armstrong. New York: Fordham UP, 2016. Print.

Nancy, Jean-Luc. *La Communauté désœuvrée.* Paris: Bourgois, [1986, 1990] 3rd ed. 1999; *The Inoperative Community.* Trans. Peter Connor, Lina Garbus, Michael Holland, and Simona Sawhney. Minneapolis: U of Minnesota P, 1991. Print.

Nancy, Jean-Luc. *La Déclosion (Déconstruction du christianisme, I).* Paris: Galilée, 2005; *Dis-Enclosure, the Deconstruction of Christianity.* Trans. Bettina Bergo, Gabriel Malenfant, and Michael B. Smith. New York: Fordham UP, 2008. Print.

Nancy, Jean-Luc. *Le Discours de la syncope: I Logodaedalus.* Paris: Aubier-Flammarion, 1976; *The Discourse of the Syncope: Logodaedalus.* Trans. Saul Anton. Stanford: Stanford UP, 2008. Print.

Nancy, Jean-Luc. *Multiple Arts: The Muses II.* Ed. Simon Sparks. Stanford: Stanford UP, 2006. Print.

Schelling, F.W.J. *Ausgewählte Schriften.* 6 vols. Frankfurt: Suhrkamp, 1985; *Historical-Critical Introduction to the Philosophy of Mythology.* Trans. Mason Richey and Markus Zisselsberger. Albany: SUNY P, 2007. Print.

de Voragine, Jacques. *La Légende dorée.* Intro. Hervé Savon. Trans. from the Latin by J.-B.M. Roze (1900), 2 vols. Paris: Garnier-Flammarion, 1967. Print.

The Poetics of Experience

The concept of freedom is the stumbling block for all empiricists [...]
Kant, Critique of Practical Reason 7

When we talk of "undergoing" an experience, we mean specifically that the experience is not of our own making: to undergo here means that we endure it, suffer it, receive it as it strikes us and submit to it.
Martin Heidegger, On the Way to Language 57

In his book *The Experience of Freedom*, Jean-Luc Nancy explores the relationship between freedom and experience in order to liberate freedom from what he calls the "jurisdiction of theory" and the "empire of necessity." In an etymologically rich conclusion to chapter 2, he observes,

An experience is first of all the encounter with an actual given, or rather, in a less simply positive vocabulary, it is the testing of something real (in any case, it is the act of a thought which does not conceive, or interrogate, or construct, what it thinks except by being already taken up and cast as thought, by its thought). Also, according to the origin of the word "experience" in *peirā* and in *ex-periri*, an experience is an attempt executed without reserve, given over to the *peril* of its own lack of foundation and security in this "object" of which it is not the subject but instead the passion, exposed like the pirate (*peirātēs*) who freely tries his luck on the high seas. In a sense, which here might be the first and last sense, freedom, to the extent that it is the thing itself of thinking, cannot be appropriated, but only "pirated": its "seizure" will always be illegitimate. (Nancy, *Experience* 20)

benjamin hutchens

PIR-ATING THE GIVEN
jean-luc nancy's critique of empiricism

Having referred to more or less conventional conceptions of experience as an encounter with the given and as the testing of the reality of perception, Nancy also identifies an etymological conception of experience in which there is a risky venture into the unknown based on no foundation and without any form of security as might be guaranteed by a thought that "gives" itself only what it will seize. He is fascinated by the power of the <u>pir</u>- in experience, a root whose meaning is expressed in both perilous adventure and in the illegitimate seizure of a "given," which, if explicated, would open freedom to its "anarchic" or foundationless state of expenditure. As I understand it, for Nancy it is "illegitimate" to seize freedom because any conception of freedom that is *taken as given* is already illegitimate. He argues that there is after all no "law" by which freedom may empower itself in taking only what it gives itself in an act of self-appropriation; or alternatively, it is only by means of a law that distorts the freedom which gives and takes itself originarily that this self-appropriation is justified.

It is the task of this article to explore the status of experience within Jean-Luc Nancy's exposition of freedom in order to discover his positioning of "the empirical" within philosophical discourse. It is my intention to (a) determine the coherence and viability of the etymological work relating experience to the various manifestations of the sense of pir- (PIE base *per-*), (b) survey the role of "experience" in relevant aspects of Nancy's work on freedom, and (c) propose a reading of the situation of "the empirical" within Nancy's work and, by extension, philosophical discourse generally.

It is immediately apparent that Nancy is interested in "the empirical" in philosophy, not empiricism as a philosophy. In his texts, "the empirical," or even "empiricity," is drawn from the work of Kant, Hegel, and Heidegger (even Descartes!), not that of the "classical empiricists" of whom he is certainly neglectful and possibly dismissive. For the most part, Nancy approaches classical empiricism indirectly by means of a critique of Kant's transcendentalist critique of empiricism. Arguing that Kant misconstrues the nature of empirical experience, Nancy seeks to revise empiricist notions of experience and freedom by means of what he refers to as "empirico-transcendentalism," which is the result of criticism of Kant's "transcendental idealism." Ultimately, I shall argue that, in raising empirical concepts (givenness, seizing, testing, self-evidence, factuality, etc.) up to a "transcendental" level of inquiry, Nancy's "empirico-transcendentalism" yields no fruitful understanding of classical empiricism itself. Instead, it goes well beyond the concerns of empiricism as a philosophy to consider the nature of freedom in thinking and agency, and thus the "sense" of the world.

pir-ating the meaning of experience

The etymologies to which Nancy alludes in the passage above deserve a quick glance.[1]

Experience in English and *expérience* in French both derive from the Latin *experior*, meaning to try, prove, or put to the test. (Nancy frequently uses *experitur* and *experiri*, which carries the sense in his texts of trying oneself or putting oneself to the test.) *Experior* in turn derives from the Greek περάω, meaning to pass through, attempt, or endeavor, which is relevant to his conception of limits and their transgression, as well as trying oneself. It can also derive from πόρος or passage, a concept that figures intermittently in Nancy's work on limits, transgressions, and freedom of access, and of course, πεῖρα, experience. Relevant to his conception of the relation between the law and the specificity of the empirical given is the fact that ἢ ἕκαστα πειρήσαιτο means "should examine into each particular."

His understanding of *peirates* (πειρατεύω, πειρατής) and *peiratikos* (πειρατικός – piratical) is linked with πειρατέος, meaning "one must attempt," and with ναυσὶ π., "to make an attempt by sea." "Pirate" itself derives from the Latin *pirata* (sailor, sea robber), which in turn comes from the Greek *peirates*, meaning literally "one who attacks," from *peiran*, "to attack, make a hostile attempt on," itself from *peira*, "trial, an attempt, attack," from PIE base *per-* "try."

Peiraikos (πειραικός, over the border) is also relevant to the role of limits and borders in the relation between experience and freedom. Even his sense of the "end" toward which philosophy is (or should be) directed could figure as πεῖραρ, which can mean the end or issue of a thing.

The notion of peril frequently arises in conjunction with venturing out and testing oneself in Nancy's work. "Peril" derives from the Latin *periculum*, "an attempt, risk, danger," with its instrumentive suffix *-culum* and root of *ex-peri-ri* "to try."[2]

I would argue that, given the cautious use he makes of these etymologies, Nancy is interested solely in utilizing etymological derivations that assist in extracting non-explicit meanings from philosophical terminology. In particular, in tracing "experience" back to its basic etymology he reminds us of what this concept has lost in its ordinary usage, as we shall see.

tracing "experience" in freedom

For Nancy "freedom" is understood only derivatively as empirical instances of agency and much more commonly as a matter of "access," "availability," "passage," "traversal," "trying," and "testing." For example, to insist that experience or existence is "free" is to propose that there is no limit "given" when thinking establishes limits for agency.

A fruitful point of origin for the task of exposing "the empirical" is to be found in the chapter to which the leading quotation above is the conclusion, where Nancy frames the problem of freedom in respect of the essence/existence distinction as follows. Freedom is neither a matter of rationally determined essence nor of a description of significant existence, but of the "chiasmus" of these concepts. This is so because, on the one hand, existence is free in its essence to be "abandoned" to freedom and, on the other, this essence liberates existence for the purpose of being free (Nancy, *Experience* 9). Yet, as I read Nancy, if freedom were to be conceived either in terms of the essence of existence or as the existence that determines essence, then *reductio ad absurdum*, "free" consciousness would have nothing to think and the "free" life would have no object of its own to live since neither this consciousness nor this life would be capable of experiencing anything. In other words, nothing would be given to experience, either empirically or transcendentally.

Nancy then addresses the same matter by other means. If existence were to give itself as an "empiricity" intelligible through Kantian transcendental conditions of possibility or Hegelian dialectics, then it would not be possible to think of existence as anything other than a consciousness and a life stripped of experience. But, as I read Nancy, *reductio ad absurdum* again, if it is possible to think of existence *giving itself* as a "factuality" containing in itself both its very reason for being present and the presence of its reason equally, then and only then could existence as a "fact" of "freedom" be explored as a question, not merely as a *given fact*. If it is not possible to think of freedom in terms of the *factuality* of being, then it will not be possible to liberate existence as such from an unthinking "foldless immanence" out of reach of thought. And if we were to conceive of freedom as nothing other than a Kantian Idea or "fact of reason," then the *factuality* of being and the *fact* of freedom could not be addressed as questions at all: they could not be *tested*. To understand freedom in its facticity and singularity, then, it is necessary to consider how freedom *makes itself known* through experience, an experience that has a history, in the freedom of a history that incessantly *gives itself* to thinking (Nancy, *Experience* 10–11). In other words, Nancy is asking us to conceive of existence itself as a fact of freedom, not freedom as a fact of reason, at the origin of our inquiry into freedom.

At this juncture, we might wonder how freedom is "founded," both metaphysically and historically, as empiricism would require. Historically, a limit is set to thoughts concerning being as foundation, and such thoughts will only permit freedom to be thought if it is founded on something. Only if freedom is founded on something whose limits are set by history can freedom be *taken to be given*, though that is not to say that it is given to itself freely. Metaphysically, this would mean that freedom is only founded on freedom itself, the freedom exercised in history and the freedom of history itself. This in turn would require, Nancy maintains, the positioning of a supreme being, a being founded in necessity and whose name would be the name of a necessary freedom. Yet this confluence of historically and metaphysically founded acts of freedom succeeds only in subjecting being itself along with all existences to the condition of having been "founded": freedom itself has not been "thought." It grossly distorts the concept of freedom, which, if it is anything at all for Nancy, is that which *prevents* itself from being founded. And inasmuch as philosophy itself presumes this confluence, its end "deprives us of a foundation of freedom as much as it deprives us of freedom as foundation." Nancy is emphatically clear that the proper end of philosophy is not the perfect congruity of freedom and the foundation of freedom itself by means of "God" and historical pre-conceptualization, but instead the *deliverance* of freedom from foundation (*Experience* 11–12). As he writes later, "the fact of freedom is this de-liverance of existence from every law and from itself as law," right to the point that the "fact of freedom is indistinguishable from the reality of existence." It "delivers itself *for* reality" (Nancy, *Experience* 30–31; italics mine), which is to say that philosophy's "end" is to emancipate itself from its end by *handing itself over* to its own unfounded freedom. As I understand it, this would require that philosophy hand itself over to the *peril* of acknowledging both the fact that existence itself is freely disseminated and the fact that being is free in its singularity.

This has far-reaching consequences. The task of philosophy in respect of the problem of freedom, Nancy avers in contradiction to empiricism, is to find a way to "liberate freedom from the immanence of its own infinite foundation," and to liberate it therefore from its own "infinite projection to infinity, where transcendence (existence) itself is transcended and thereby annulled" (*Experience* 14). And he is insistent that this would require accepting the fact that freedom is only freedom if it surprises itself, which is not to say merely that it is *capable* of doing so. What is needed is a conceptualization of freedom beyond being and history that permits the understanding that freedom is only freedom when it is singularized without foundation, and this is only conceivable when freedom is understood to surprise itself. This would only be possible when philosophy carves out within itself a certain "spaciocity," the "opening of a new space for meaning"

alone capable of receiving meaning. This would be a space within which freedom can exist. It could be freed from the constraints of conceptualization or even renounced by means of it (*Experience* 18–19). Freedom, inasmuch as it must account for itself, is at stake in existence as a *risk* and as the challenging necessity of *testing*. One might say of this that existence does not precede freedom so as to precondition its form any more than freedom precedes existence in order to precondition the manner in which it is lived. Existence cannot be conceived at all, one might hazard, except as the *peril* of unfounded freedom asserting itself to establish such a foundation whilst persisting in spite of its failure to do so. And this is precisely the point where Nancy presents the leading quote of this article. The experience of freedom must be brought to light as a theme in the same step in which it is *put at risk* as a praxis of (free) thought.

The stakes must be high indeed if a proper comprehension of the free dissemination of existence requires an understanding of the plurality and singularity of unfounded freedom, which in turn requires an understanding of experience as the peril of venturing out into being without foundation or security, seizing experience and giving freedom to oneself. The role of understanding here is suspect, since as he writes later in *The Experience of Freedom*, "keeping a space free for freedom might amount to keeping oneself from wanting to understand freedom, in order to keep oneself from destroying it in the unavoidable determinations of an understanding." What requires sensitivity in approaching freedom is a "respect for and a preservation of the free domain of freedom," a respect that is lacking in any metaphysical approach to freedom which has already surreptitiously comprehended it before freedom is even reached because freedom is positioned solely within the "self-knowledge of a subjectively determined freedom" (Nancy, *Experience* 44). In other words, we must resist the temptation to illegitimately "pirate" the concept of freedom in a "free" act of comprehending that gives itself only that "freedom" it intends to *seize* for itself. A theory of freedom is answerable to the same criteria as the exercise of freedom itself is.

givenness and the generosity of being

Nancy approaches experience in terms of the givenness of being and the seizure that makes it accessible to philosophical discourse. My task now is to consider those many places in *The Experience of Freedom* where Nancy understands freedom in respect of experience, but especially where experience "gives" or "seizes" something, including itself, and where it "escapes" the law and "cuts itself free from" foundations, placing itself "in peril" by venturing without security. The goal here is to consider what conception of experience would enable us to "understand" freedom without illegitimately "pirating" it.

In order to do this, Nancy transforms the notion of "givenness" so that it is no longer merely a standard empiricist concept. Of course, in empiricism "the given" means several things, of which two are pertinent here. On the one hand, the "given" of classical sense-datum theory is that object of experience that is simply there in its reality, pre-existing its experience yet "given to" experience, an experience that may serve as evidence that the given is there in its reality, as with Locke's theory of causal perception. On the other hand, basic experiential beliefs are justified, not in reference to further beliefs or external states of affairs, but by appealing to states of intuition, direct apprehension or immediate experience that stand in some intimate, first-person relation to thinking. For Nancy, the problem of the given originates with Kant and the critique Heidegger levels against him. Kant presents givenness in the *Critique of Pure Reason* as follows: to "give" an object is merely to relate its representation to experience, so that the very possibility of experience is "that which gives all of our cognitions a priori objective reality" (282). Heidegger in *Kant and the Problem of Metaphysics* finds this notion of givenness impoverished. He

writes in reference to this very passage that, for Kant, "to give an object means to present it immediately in intuition," a givenness whose significance is captured by Kant with the notion that such representations relate to actual and possible experiences. But for Heidegger this "relating-to means that in order for an object to be capable of being given, there must take place in advance an orientation toward that which is capable of being 'called up'" (*Kant and the Problem of Metaphysics* 122). This act of orientation toward something is the condition of the possibility of experience. Later in that work, Heidegger notes that intuiting something means "to receive that which offers itself. Pure intuition gives to itself, in the receptive act, that which is capable of being received." Such "reception of" something is applicable to pure intuition and not to empirical intuition, yet pure intuition, as illustrated by the passing of "the now" in time, cannot be the reception of something that is present (178–79). In this case, Heidegger wonders whether pure intuition is in fact actually pure imagination.

Whether understood as a mind-independent object awaiting experience or a non-inferential state of experience, as in the Kantian "pure intuition" Heidegger criticizes, Nancy approaches givenness from the other side, that is to say, ontologically rather than epistemologically, as an act of *generosity* in which thinking *gives to itself* this object that is simply *taken to be* there in its reality. A few examples, admittedly de-contextualized here, may illustrate this relationship between the given and the gift. In *The Sense of the World*, Nancy writes of "entering into" the sense of the world, "into this gift of sense the world itself is" (8–9). The world, he proposes, is not *given* to us. It is *offered* as a gift from an infinite distance (43). He also observes that this generosity of being opens a disjuncture between a desire for the gift and the gift of desire, each of which participates in a regime of signification made possible by the fact that the world "is" sense. This generosity offers the gift of meaning to desire and the desire for meaning to the object it desires (52–53).

Furthermore, he writes there of a "sense of direction" in relation to the objects of the world that presumes a "sense of orientation" that is not given to experience itself (77–78). So, as may be apparent in these examples, "the given" is a concept that carries within itself an obvious aporia: what is given as a "gift" of being is external to thought and awaits its appropriation by experience and makes that appropriation possible; yet precisely this mind-independent state is the object of an act of thinking that gives to itself what it takes as having already been given. Thinking *gives itself* that object it takes as *having been given* to it by experience itself in the generosity of being. The task in Nancy's project, as I understand it, is to offer an exposition of the manner in which existence itself is already receptive to this generosity of being, and indeed, that free existence itself has already been given by this generosity of being. This leaves Nancy to wonder about the freedom of thinking itself. Is it the very intrinsic limit of thinking itself?

Freedom's groundlessness in experience and its foundationlessness in theory provide a pre-originary limitation to thinking itself. The "there is" of existence already serves as a limit-lessness that permits limitations to be set by thinking, limitations that enable freedom to be unleashed in a manner that is *given* to thinking just as empirical objects of experience are. However, the freedom that permits objects to be experienced at all is more intimate and "free" than any experience of such objects. Freedom is no more something that springs spontaneously from a "pregnant enclosure" than it is a definite, enduring substance (Nancy, *Experience* 55).

Nancy is arguing, then, that empirical objects are already "free" to be experienced in a state of *generosity* of being. And the "free" thinking of such objects is already "free" to experience this generosity. Neither this thinking nor this object is grounded in some state of being or fixed as some existential state. "Givenness," then, is not some stable and immutable state of action or reception of being, but something that is discernible solely

in an act of giving: the giving of thought to experience "freely" and the giving of experience to thought "freely." In the singular event of giving, the self is *given over to* the thinking of experience and the experience of thinking. As Nancy sees it, this generosity is not merely a simple positing of "the given," but the *abandonment of the generous to generosity*, an unleashing of freedom towards being without any possibility of appropriating it.

Conceiving this generosity behind the gift of the given enables Nancy to situate the empirical given in a special way. The illegitimate "pirat-ing" of the given consists in the simple positing of an empirical object preceding and awaiting experience. What is given, I would suggest, is that which has been given in an act of giving, not by thinking or freedom, but in the free space of signification opened up by the generos-ity of being itself. Abandoning the generous to generosity is to conceive of the given in such a way that it cannot be pir-ated, illegitimately taken to be precisely what it is given as being.

Now, if givenness is intelligible in terms of the generosity of being, then the grasping, the seizure, of the given is an illegitimate act of vio-lence. The given has been seized, not merely grasped. Frequently in his work the notion of seizure is associated with that of risk. In *The Sense of the World*, Nancy writes of the neces-sity of "seizing" the infinite chance and risk of being in the world, even if there is nothing there at all to seize (26). There he writes also that existence itself is exposed to a "risk" of being in the world, which he understands to be a risk that is neither imposed from outside nor simply part of the "adventure in the element of the foreign." Existence is exposed to and in the world, as a risk (33). However, in conjunction with the notion of freedom, Nancy writes that the risky venture of free experience is neither the "in itself" of the object grasped (this is my freedom) by means of thinking nor of the act of grasping (my freedom is exemplified by this act of seizing its own conditions of possibility). In the quote at the beginning of this article, Nancy likens risky experience to a passion for a foundation-less object in which existence is "exposed like the pirate (*peirātēs*) who freely tries his luck on the high seas" (*Experience* 20). Experience itself – which in its act of founding is "the act par excellence of *experiri*, of the attempt to reach the limit, to keep to the limit" – does not produce or gather anything but on the contrary "decides a limit" and "decides its law before setting it, making it exist without essence, transcendent without a transcending immanence" (*Experience* 84–85). Experience is a transgressive moment in that a limit is thought and surpassed even before it is set. He explains:

> We have related, through concepts and languages, "experience" to "piracy." But foundation always has something of piracy in it, it pirates the im-propriety and formlessness of a *chora* – and piracy always has something of foundation, unrightfully disposing rights and tracking unlocatable limits on the *chora* of the sea. In order to think the experience of freedom, one would have to be able ceaselessly to contaminate each notion by the other, and let each free the other, pirating foundation and founding piracy. (*Experience* 85)

As I understand Nancy, even the foundation to which freedom illegitimately appeals in thinking already figures within that *chora*, the "high seas" where the piracy of experience is already free. To establish a foundation is an *act of venturing out into being and taking a risk with freedom*. And piracy itself is the act of founding one's own freedom in reference to no foundation. For Nancy, *chora* designates not an undetermined place, but the possibility of places where the foundation takes place, where freedom qua "foundation of foundations" takes a place in being (*Experience* 84). The freedom of piracy, one might say, consists in being cut free of all legal and illegal foundations alike, with only the foundation of foundations which is the free act serving as a limit to be thought, crossed, and set pir-atically. In experience, existence is able to "try itself" (*experiri*), to give itself over to the world in an act of generosity of being, testing freedom's very chance of existence. The act of founding

itself cut loose from safe harbor is the act of affirmatively pirating itself, trying itself out in the world, free on the *chora* of the sea that is the space where freedom itself is first founded in an act of demarcating the "experienceable" world. This *chora* is discernible in the very relationship between being and the existent. As he writes,

> being frees itself for existence and in existence in such a way that the existence of the existent does not comprehend itself in its origin and finally never comprehends itself, but is at the outset grasped and paralyzed by this freeing which "founds" it (or "pirates" it). (*Experience* 93)

The act of experiencing something freely "pirates" it in a foundational act by liberating it from the indeterminacy of the *chora*, by carving out a space within the *chora*'s formlessness, particularizing the object, subsuming it under self-created laws, and subordinating it to thinking. And according to Nancy, there is no object more freely pirated in this way than freedom itself.

the positioning of "experience" in philosophy

Having traced the notion of experience in Nancy's exposition of freedom and explored the notions of givenness and seizure in the conception of experience, it now remains to pull things together with a general positioning of experience in philosophy. As mentioned in the introduction above, Nancy professes a desire to liberate freedom from the "jurisdiction of theory" and its enclosure in the legality of "assumed necessity" because it is the "factuality" of what is not completed or made into a fact and thus has no "Idea" (*Experience* 47). To argue that factuality escapes philosophy, or to maintain that its "praxical factuality" is irreducible to the "theoretical" (*Experience* 60) requires that Nancy position freedom's experience in relation to the essence/existence, subjectivity/objectivity, and foundation/end dichotomies. Loosely speaking, because freedom's experience qua thinking and praxis precedes and accompanies the development of such theoretical constructions, he is able to identify those points of engagement between theory and praxis: first, where the logic of expenditure involved in freedom is irreducible to the *logos* of philosophy and second, where the "free" domain of signification is irreducible to the logical space of reasons.

Freedom, as Nancy points out, is construed as nothing but a "problem" by philosophy, when in fact its *factuality* constitutes a "fact," or a "gift" (as in the given), or a "task" (as in *experiri*) (*Experience* 60). As such, freedom requires that its concept be "kept free" from the destructive (or at least reductive) *grasp* of the determinations of an understanding of the concept of freedom. When philosophy's "metaphysics of freedom" encloses it within the jurisdiction of theory and the empire of necessity, freedom itself is imprisoned within the problematic of the knowledge of a subject. From this prison freedom should be liberated so that a proper respect for the free space of freedom can be acknowledged (*Experience* 44).

With this in mind, Nancy insists that there has never been and should not be "a philosophy of freedom," since all such philosophy would be de-liberative: it would decide in advance what would constitute the concept of freedom in a manner constrained by conceptuality. In fact, he argues, freedom itself appears to philosophy to fold back upon itself by means of empirical experience. Philosophy desires to cross limits: it ventures out in an act of pir-acy in order to affirm itself transcendentally, but succeeds only in trapping itself in the immanence of the ideal of itself. Nancy takes philosophy to task for failing to acknowledge its indebtedness to the experience of freedom. If philosophy were taken to be an effort to provide formal foundation to knowledge by means of an organization of concepts, then it is necessary to pre-understand how concepts can be freely organized. The concept of "concept" itself is something that is "free" and enables access to representation itself. I take Nancy to be arguing that, before one is able to conceive of the philosophical concept of freedom, there is

the *traversal* of thinking from the concept of "concept" to the concept of "freedom" itself, a passage that is not only free, but freedom itself in thinking. And this *traversal*, of course, is the experience of freedom itself. It comes in the form of a fact, the factuality of the free possibility of having a world in the first place, or being available to that world. Having access to a world to which one is available is the existential condition of traversing limits without any "given" to be pir-ated apart from the generous gift of being itself. Nancy explains this in some detail as follows:

> Thought is specified as *logos*, and *logos*, before designating any arrangement of concepts and any foundation of representation, essentially designates – within this order of the "concept of concepts" and "foundation of foundation" to which its dialogic and dialectic are devoted – *the freedom of the access to its own essence. Logos* is not first the production, reception, or assignation of a "reason," but is before all the freedom in which is presented or by which is offered the "reason" of every "reason": for this freedom only depends on the *logos*, which itself depends not on any "order of reasons" but on the "order of matters" whose first matter is nothing other than freedom, or the liberation of thought for a world. (*Experience* 62)

In other words, *logos* is first of all designated as the freedom of access it has to its own essence. This essence is not determined by the nature of a reason that could determine the essence of freedom, but by the nature of freedom itself. What concerns the logos itself is not what reasons it can provide, as if it were folded up with its own ideality in the way that philosophy is; what concerns it is the freedom of access to its own essence, which I would venture to suggest is understood as an undertaking across limits, a gift or a task. And this access (freedom) is always *put at stake* whenever the *logos* either renounces the notion that freedom has any reason or strives to master freedom by means of logic. The *logos*, whether it strives to master or to renounce the rationality of freedom, is always already "seized" (taken, grasped, etc.) by freedom in an act of pir-ating its own givenness for philosophy. Philosophy itself would not have "a logic" of freedom at all if the *logos* were not seized by the freedom to which it is necessarily *given*. That is to say, philosophy, rather than laying foundations on which to render freedom intelligible, is merely the way that freedom folds back on itself, defining logos by means of access to its essence. Since freedom cannot be grasped as an object of the thought of an experience, it reveals itself in the exercise of "thinking" as a "fold" where thought itself may test itself. One might notice again the empirical motif of "testing" raised up to refer to thought's relation to itself as free. Nancy concludes:

> Thus philosophy does not produce or construct any "freedom," it does not guarantee any freedom, and it would not as such be able to defend any freedom [...] But it *keeps open the access to the essence of the logos* through its history and all its avatars. In this way it must henceforth keep the access open – freedom – beyond the philosophical or metaphysical closure of freedom. Philosophy is incessantly beyond itself [...] because "philosophizing" consists in keeping open the vertiginous access to the essence of the logos, without which we would not have any idea of even the slightest "logic" [...] But this maintenance is not an operation of force or even of preservation: it consists in *testing in thought* (which means: inscribing in language) this fold of freedom that articulates itself and that never appropriates itself. (*Experience* 64; last italics mine)

"Keeping open the access to the essence of the logos": I understand this to mean that philosophy is the empirical exercise of testing the linguistic articulation of freedom by which this access is kept open in the act of resisting logico-rational appropriation. Nancy clarifies this empirical basis by pointing out that it is the *praxis* of the *logos* (or "practical reason") which brings the *logos* to its limit where it "grasps" that it is the freedom of existence that gives it ("masters") and strips it of

("renounces") its own essence of logos. One might notice that bringing *logos* to its limit presumes the articulation of the pir-acy of *experiri*, a limit it "grasps" only by means of the assumption of a "fact." The *logos* itself is either "given" an essence or its essence is "seized" from it by the freedom of existence itself, the aforementioned access to a world to which this freedom is available. Only an empirical understanding of experience can assist in grasping the *logos*; or alternatively, only such an understanding can keep open its access to its essence, an access that is "free."

conclusion

Nancy affirms predictably that his conception of experience is decidedly not that of what he calls "classical empiricism." Yet, although this seems true, the reasons presented in defense of this claim could be disappointing. For example, when asserting that the *experience* of the "thing itself" is also a "thing itself," Nancy's exposition becomes somewhat unbalanced. This experience is not the experience of "classical empiricism" because it is the "experience of experience" and therefore always the "experience of thinking." He emphasizes the question of "thought as experience," which is as much empirical as transcendental, even though this transcendental is "the empirical"! Presumably this is what he means by the "empiricity of thought" in which thinking cannot think its own conditions of possibility "without at the same time materially touching on this very condition of possibility" (Nancy, *Experience* 89). Interestingly, immediately prior to this assertion Nancy considers the question of freedom's self-evidence. "Its self-evidence beyond all evidence, its factuality more undeniable than that of any fact" stems from the fact that "freedom proves itself by testing itself" and is thus "anterior to every empirical certitude" without being transcendental. Instead, he argues, "freedom is a transcendental experience or the transcendental of experience, the transcendental that is experience" (*Experience* 87). In his exposition of freedom, he understands that freedom is a transcendental force that comes in the form of a material actuality. It is a force of the materially actual thing or act that can produce relations of force amongst things subject to causality without being absorbed into immanent being or into the succession of changes (*Experience* 102). If we can conceive that experience is already transcendental because it is empirical, we still need to be clear where the difference between his own empiricism and the "classical" conception can be found. Unfortunately, Nancy provides the following suggestion instead of the required clarification:

> If freedom gives thought to thought – even more than it simply gives it something to think about – this happens in the materially transcendental experience of a mouth at whose opening – neither substance nor figure – a nonplace at the limits of which thought passes into thought – thought tempts chance and takes the risk (*experiri*) of thinking, with the inaugural intensity of a cry. (*Experience* 90)

Of course, as I have already noted Nancy identifies the importance of language for any empirical theory. However, in order to answer our question it might have been enough to propose that the manner in which thought is given over to thinking is one in which a "risk" takes place, a perilous limit of experience freely crossed by thinking without the dubious notion of a "materially transcendental experience of a mouth" where this risk is empirically situated (James 60–63). It is an interesting idea, but philosophically unsatisfactory, until we can identify precisely what is "empirical" in Nancy's work here, especially when it is entangled with the transcendental.

I propose to explain this as follows. When Nancy writes of the given and giving, taking and the taken, seizure and seizing, testing, evidence, factuality, and of course the etymology of *peirates* and *experiri*, he is describing transcendental processes by means of transcendentally explicated terms of empiricism. In other words, instead of speaking of the "given" in the "experience" of classical empiricism, he

speaks of experience itself as "given," though this givenness is, as we have just seen, a "factuality anterior to every empirical certitude." Thinking, freedom, and experience itself have been given to existence in a generosity of being without which nothing could be posited or appropriated. In reference to another example, "testing" is not understood as some experiment to prove something (or oneself), but rather testing as a traversal of limits within experience, and experience as a crossing of thresholds. This testing is understood to be a "testing in thought," which means nothing other than an act of "inscribing in language," though in this case there is no obvious sense in which this carries any of the aforementioned "material transcendentality" (Nancy, *Experience* 64). One can also see this in his claim that the "proof of freedom" reveals itself through testing or experience, not through "demonstration" because "freedom cannot be the object of a question," but rather the "putting into question of an affirmation of itself" (*Experience* 23). Thinking "tests" thinking and freedom "tests" freedom: this testing is not done *within* experience "empirically," but rather *by* experience "transcendentally." So, the concepts of "classical" empiricism are being used to describe processes that transpire transcendentally.

As I see it, the question remains whether Nancy's work can be described as "empiricist" and, if so, what relation this empiricism has to what he calls "classical empiricism."[3] When he asserts that experience's self-evidence and factuality are more self-evident and factual than that of empirical experience itself, it seems that Nancy not only wishes to utilize empirical concepts transcendentally, but in doing so to remove his work from the tyranny of empirical philosophy altogether. As long as empiricism itself is an exercise in pirating the given illegitimately, it shares all of philosophy's worst tendencies in its expositions of experience and freedom. What empiricism does to experience and freedom is different only in kind from what any other philosophical orientation does to them. Philosophy seizes experience in "illegitimately" empirical ways, and empiricism represents philosophy in its efforts to establish foundations for freedom and experience. In other words, empiricism provides to philosophy generally merely an opportunity to conceive of experience and freedom by "illegitimate" forms of givenness, seizure, testing, self-evidence, factuality, and the crossing of limits. In extracting these concepts and the theoretical constructions they imply from the jurisdiction of philosophy, Nancy takes himself to have liberated it from its "bad" empirical presuppositions by raising up the possibility of a transcendental task for these concepts. Without subordinating freedom and experience to law, he has nonetheless articulated a "legitimate" empiricism that is as intertwined with the transcendental as existence is with essence.

The question is why we should bother to refer to this philosophical approach as "empiricist" at all if it (a) is critical of all empiricism, (b) raises empirical conceptuality up to a transcendentalist register, (c) counts empiricism as merely one of many forms of philosophy that are not sufficiently "empirico-transcendental," and finally (d) reveals no special relationships between the "classical empirical" constructions and his own that would shed light on either. Given the fact that he does not even refer to the classical empiricists by name or engage with their texts, it is considerably less than clear where his own texts stand in relation to theirs. If there had been an engagement with the empiricists themselves in Nancy's work, then it might have been possible to resolve a certain issue: if Nancy identifies and revises what is empirical in philosophical conceptions of experience and freedom, then surely it would be in classical empiricism that one might find this illegitimate "empiricity" at its worst. Linking empiricist philosophy with the empirical in philosophy would have definitively proven a point that Nancy is only able to gesture toward in the absence of any such link. Raising the "empirico-transcendental" of freedom above "transcendental" conditions of empirical freedom by means of tropes of empiricism in philosophy enables Nancy to show what can be done to and by means of revised concepts of experience and freedom, yet it does not permit him to fulfill the promise of the endeavor.

All philosophy, we might remember, is an "empirical" testing of the free movement of the concept of freedom, and thus the free passage of things. But empiricism appears to be as ignorant of this traversal and passaging as any other philosophy, perhaps because it involves the experience (in thinking) of what reveals experience as a conceptual possibility. Empiricism, in the end, is merely an illustration of what is illegitimate in the philosophical effort to enfold freedom, and especially free thinking, in a conceptualization of the limits of thought. Perhaps it is empiricism that has given philosophy the mandate to legitimize the reduction of freedom to a concept of thought without attending to the "free" manner in which even reduction is done.

echo by jean-luc nancy

I am very impressed by the considerable effort Benjamin Hutchens has devoted to unpacking and interrogating my attempt at making possible a conception of experience that, as an experience of "freedom," is neither empirical nor transcendental in an abstract sense, anterior to experience itself – which is never that of Kant himself, but rather that of a superficial understanding of him.

Besides, it is entirely from Kant and his affirmation of the presence of freedom in experience that I draw my guiding motif. Kant himself presents a difficulty in this regard, and I am well aware of the additional difficulties in my own attempt that Hutchens points out. However, I am having a bit too much trouble deciphering his very learned English to be able to grasp the various points.

It seems to me that it is ultimately a question of the very idea of experience. It is always necessarily understood as the undergoing, the encounter, the trial, or the practice of some object by a subject. "I" form an experience "of" ... But isn't there another register, where the "subject" rather forms an experience of itself, which is therefore not an object and of which it is thus neither the subject? And would this be the experience of freedom par excellence – and which would equally be that of necessity (being unable not to experience it).

Is this not what Kant's famous "I rise from my chair … " is all about?

From this point onwards, the very idea of "empiricism" loses its validity. For here, there is no distinction between "a priori" and "a posteriori" …

disclosure statement

No potential conflict of interest was reported by the author.

notes

1 These etymologies are derived from a comparison of the Lidell and Scott Greek–English Lexicon and Nancy's own usage of the terms.

2 A similar presentation of the etymologies of experience, peril, and piracy is to be found in Claude Romano's *Event and World*.

3 It should be clear that my position is quite different from Peter Fenves', whose excellent foreword to *The Experience of Freedom* remains the window into the subject outlined here. For Fenves, Nancy is a "good empiricist" because he understands that neither language nor experience can ever be secured (*Experience* xxxi). For Fenves, the point where Nancy encounters empiricism most clearly is in Hume's notion of the imagination, which enables the self to conceive of states of affairs beyond the limits of experience. Nancy does not follow Hume in trying to make the frighteningly specific into something familiar, but wants to retain a sense of its uncanny specificity (*Experience* xxi).

bibliography

Heidegger, Martin. *Kant and the Problem of Metaphysics.* Trans. James S. Churchill. Bloomington: Indiana UP, 1962. Print.

Heidegger, Martin. *On the Way to Language.* Trans. Peter D. Hertz. New York: Harper, 1971. Print.

James, Ian. *The Fragmentary Demand.* Stanford: Stanford UP, 2006. Print.

Kant, Immanuel. *Critique of Practical Reason.* Trans. and ed. Mary Gregor. Cambridge: Cambridge UP, 1997. Print.

Kant, Immanuel. *Critique of Pure Reason.* Trans. and ed. P. Guyer and A.W. Wood. Cambridge: Cambridge UP, 1997. Print.

Nancy, Jean-Luc. *The Experience of Freedom.* Trans. Bridget McDonald. Stanford: Stanford UP, 1993. Print.

Nancy, Jean-Luc. *The Sense of the World.* Trans. Jeffrey S. Librett. Minneapolis: U of Minnesota P, 1997. Print.

Romano, Claude. *Event and World.* Trans. S. Mackinlay. New York: Fordham UP, 2009. Print.

Since this perception is an event of our historical life, it is actual only as our deed, and as such it makes our life. *In our experiences we are always questioned, put to the test.* We cannot *have* them as a possession. We have them only in the doing.

Bultmann, What Is Theology? *152*

I introduction

From Plato to Derrida, Jean-Luc Nancy has constantly developed his own thinking by way of creative and stimulating engagements with other authors, leaving out almost no major figure from the philosophical canon. I say *almost,* for on one author Nancy maintains a fairly constant silence: Søren Kierkegaard. This is remarkable, given both the fact that there is a natural affinity between their respective understandings of Christianity as well their shared interest in matters of philosophical style,[1] each always articulated in a constant engagement with German Idealism. In what follows, I will therefore illustrate how reading both thinkers together can serve to illuminate their shared understanding of an important element of Christian life: namely, faith. In particular, I will seek to develop a *phenomenology of faith,* that is to say, an analysis of the experience of faith as comprising the most fundamental questions of genetic and existential phenomenology. Of course, I must immediately admit that neither Kierkegaard nor Nancy are "phenomenologists," even though one of them certainly anticipated the phenomenological tradition whilst the other inherited it. This enterprise is therefore undertaken in the full awareness of the limits of classical phenomenology, which perhaps become particularly

nikolaas deketelaere

ABRAHAM'S ORDEAL
jean-luc nancy and søren kierkegaard on the poetics of faith

evident when phenomenology comes into contact with Christianity, as Derrida has observed.[2] For this reason, the phenomenology presented here will take on the form of a (quasi-phenomenological) *poetics of faith,* since for Kierkegaard as well as Nancy, faith is not primarily a question of appearing (*phanein*) but of doing (*poiēsis*). I will proceed in four steps: the first step consists in an exposition of the phenomenological framework used; the second and third steps consist in applications of said framework to Kierkegaard's understanding of faith; the fourth and final step draws on Nancy to spell out the consequences of the preceding analysis.

My main point of reference will be Kierke-gaard's *Fear and Trembling*, of which I will thus give a phenomenological reading, for it offers one of the most penetrating, though equally controversial, analyses of faith ever to have been articulated. Following Paul (Romans 4.16–17; Galatians 3.7–9), the book hails Abraham as the father of faith by way of a reading of the Old Testament narrative of the binding of Isaac (Genesis 22), a cruel story where God tests Abraham's faith by demanding that he sacrifices his only son. Abraham passes the test, showing himself willing to kill Isaac, though God ultimately pro-vides a lamb to be sacrificed instead. Abraham is then the father of faith, *Fear and Trembling* suggests, because of his blind obedience to God, even though God's command did not make any sense: Kierkegaard emphasises that Abraham only has faith because he acts "on the strength of the absurd" (65), because his actions were senseless – not simply in them-selves, but through the accompanying faith that even by demanding the sacrifice of the son of promise, God will keep his promise that Abraham would be the father of many nations through Isaac (Genesis 17.4, 21.12; Hebrews 11.17–19). In the book, a troubling "teleological suspension of the ethical" then accompanies faith, seemingly implying that the duty to God supersedes "ethical" duties: the universal character of morality would be suspended in one's singular confrontation with the absolute through faith (84–95).

The book's identification of the religious enthusiasm of faith with the insanity of the madman may therefore appear jarring: the man of faith is indeed insane,[3] religious passion has detached him from worldly ration-ality; however, many contemporary readers have misinterpreted what this means, reproach-ing Kierkegaard for gleefully embracing faith as irrational, which carries obvious dangers.[4] Even John Caputo, one of his most creative readers, distances himself from Kierkegaard here:

> For Kierkegaard, the moral of this story is that the ethical rule admits of exception,

because God, who is the author of this moral law, can suspend any given law if God so chooses. That is a profoundly danger-ous position to take [...] *Fear and Trem-bling* appears to realize the worst fears of those who are troubled by Kierkegaard's view that "truth is subjectivity." Is some-thing true just so long as you are deeply and passionately convinced that it is true? Is that not the very definition of fanaticism?[5] (*How to Read Kierkegaard* 46)

This is an odd statement coming from the author of a book entitled *Against Ethics*, throughout which he celebrates *Fear and Trem-bling*'s pseudonymous author, "Johannes de Silentio, whom I have taken as a certain mentor" (5). Of course, there are disturbing statements in *Fear and Trembling*, as Caputo rightly points out, like the following casual declaration: "If faith cannot make it into a holy deed to murder one's own son, then let the judgement fall on Abraham as on anyone else" (60). However, just a few sentences further down, we discover that the book is not about ethics, but about faith: indeed, Kierke-gaard says, "if you simply remove faith [...] there remains only the raw fact that Abraham was willing to murder Isaac, which is easy enough for anyone without faith to imitate," but "if one makes faith the main thing – that is, makes it what it is – then [...] it is only in respect of faith that one achieves resemblance to Abraham, not murder" (60–61). Kierkegaard is thus not *arguing* that faith allows one to do immoral things; he is rather *showing* what it means to have faith.

II traversing ex-per-ience

It is then a *phenomenology* that we are dealing with here: what the book aims to achieve is not an argument, but rather *an experience*, namely that of faith. The kind of experience at issue here, I would suggest, is what Philippe Lacoue-Labarthe finds in poetry or "the singular event that the poem relates," namely, "'experi-ence,' provided that we both understand the word in its strict sense – the Latin *ex-periri*, a crossing through danger – and [...] avoid associ-ating it with what is 'lived,' the stuff of anecdotes. *Erfahrung*, then, rather than *Erlebnis*" (18).[6] This *ex-periri* is thus distinct from the *lived-experience* (*Erlebnis*) of classical phenomenology, which he dismisses as anecdotal. Here, Gadamer's historiography of the term *Erlebnis* can help clarify what Lacoue-Labarthe means: conceived in this way, "something becomes an 'experience' not only insofar as it is experienced, but insofar as its being experienced makes a special impression that gives it lasting importance" (Gadamer 53). It is an experience imbued with meaning. The term *lived-experience* (*Erlebnis*) thus does not simply denote the cognitive process of experiencing (*erleben*), but instead brings it into view in terms of its result, the reality *lived* (*das Erlebte*) within it. Lived-experiences thus deliver us *phenomena*, stable "unities of meaning" (56), intentionally constituted out of the stream of conscious experience (*Erlebnisstrom*) that is sensation: "A lived experience is a distinctive and characteristic mode in which reality is there-for-me," Dilthey writes, it "is there-for-me because I have a reflexive awareness of it" and "possess it immediately as belonging to me in some sense" (VI: 312/223).[7] It implies "that every part of it is connected with the other parts in one consciousness," whilst simultaneously "it can be isolated within the household of my life because it belongs to it structurally as a function" (VI: 314/224).[8] Lived-experience thus puts the emphasis on the thing that is *lived* (*erlebt*), what consciousness is consciousness *of*, through which it stabilises the stream of consciousness into a self-same, immediately given and present, unity of sense: lived-experience "has a definite immediacy," Gadamer concludes, for "everything that is experienced is experienced by oneself, and part of its meaning is that it belongs to the unity of this self and thus contains an unmistakable and irreplaceable relation to the whole of this one life" (58).

Yet, Gadamer feels that these unities of meaning, these phenomena, these lived-experiences, do not constitute the *whole* of experience: "There is something else quite different that needs to be recognized in the concept of 'experience,'" he says, namely "its inner

relation to life." The model of lived-experience seems unnecessarily limited:

> If something is called or considered an *Erlebnis*, that means it is rounded into the unity of a significant whole. An experience is as much distinguished from other experiences – in which other things are experienced – as it is from the rest of life in which "nothing" is experienced. An experience is no longer just something that flows past quickly in the stream of conscious life; it is meant as a unity and thus attains a new mode of being *one*. (Gadamer 57–58)

It may be that in the rest of life, or in life itself (*Leben*), nothing is experienced (*erlebt*), insofar life itself is without intentional object; however, it does not follow that this is not itself an experience or at least an experienc*ing*. Does phenomenology not forget the *life* (*Leben*) by focusing on *what-is-lived* (*das Erlebte*) in its *lived-experience* (*Erlebnis*)?

According to Gadamer, life is an *adventure* in the sense that it "is by no means just an episode," a lived-experience; rather, it "lets life be felt as a whole," it "is 'undergone,' like a test or trial from which one emerges enriched." As adventure, life consists in "venturing out into the uncertain" (Gadamer 60), in *living through* (*fahren*) something, *facing a danger* (*Gefahr*): the adventure of life is an *experience* (*Erfahrung*).[9] Here, the emphasis is not on the *thing that is lived* (*das Erlebte*), but on the *life* (*Leben*) on the basis of which things are lived. This is still an experience, as Claude Romano suggests, though not an experience that I have (*avoir*), but rather an experience that I am or undergo (*faire*). The former concerns the ordinary phenomenological notion of lived-experiences as stable unities of sense constituted against an intentional horizon through which I come to know the world: it is an *empirical* experience of repeatable innerworldly facts that makes the world predictable. The latter concerns a singular and unrepeatable experience or ordeal, not of innerworldly facts against an intentional horizon, but of the (trans)formation of that very horizon against which the world appears, and as such involves facing a danger or traversal from self to self: the experience of being changed by what happens to me such that how the world appears to me is also changed, for it appears to a different *me*, against a different horizon, on different terms.[10] Between the two selves there is radical incommensurability: I no longer recognise myself in the person I have become because I have *lived through* something, made it through an *ordeal*, and been transformed by it, which subsequently changes how I *live* or *experience* everything else.[11] This second sense of experience therefore denotes a transcendental rather than empirical experience: not of innerworldly facts, indeed, not *of* anything; but rather the event of experien*cing* that makes worldly the world, its disclosure by way of my being-in it.[12] As the experience in which the self is formed by what happens to it, as the life on the basis of which things are lived, it "is not itself 'knowledge' but is rather *a way of understanding oneself*" (Romano, *Event and World* 148). For Romano, it is then this second, transcendental sense, which is the "primary phenomenological sense" of experience (146): since *I am* changed by the experience, the way in which *things appear to me* is also changed, and this question must be settled first since it concerns the very basis on which there is appearing. Experience in this primordial sense consists in "a nonempirical undergoing," in the ordeal of phenomenalisation itself (*erleben*), "only accessible from events, which put it to the test, and through which – at the risk of itself – it shows itself," which Romano calls "*ex-per-ience*" (*Er-fahrung*) (148).

It is also this primordial ex-per-ience that Nancy has in mind when he writes about freedom as "the inaugural experience of experience itself," in a passage worth quoting at length:

> The "foundation of foundation" supports itself alone, having nothing to support it, not even "itself," since "itself" comes to light, or to the world, in a founding gesture, sustaining itself only on its existence [...] Here (and now), existence tries itself (*experiri*) before and beyond itself, it

traces and crosses the limit of its being-thrown-into-the-world, it tests its every chance of existence: it founds itself and pirates itself at the same time, which amounts, furthermore, to saying that *existence makes itself its own chance to which, at the same time, it lets itself be given over*. This is why the "foundation of foundation" is experience itself: experience does not experience anything, but it experiences the *nothing* as the real that it tests *and* as the stroke of luck it offers [...] But the experience of experience is nothing other than experience itself: trying the self at the self's border. (*The Experience of Freedom* 86–87)

It is the experience in which *nothing is given* to hold on to and provide security – where there is *no object to live*, except the experience itself undergoing itself in the ordeal of (its) experiencing, its going to the limit of itself as itself – , that is or forms the self: *ex-per-ience*, which is to say, *ex-istence*; being put to the test, venturing-out into the uncertain. Or again:

> To undergo an experience is, then, to *be* experience. Were this not the case, we would never *undergo* anything but instead merely represent it, imagine it, talk about it [...] Experience, what I am here calling a movement or a journey, is a matter that moves through itself, from one side to the other. (Nancy, *Multiple Arts* 208–10)

For Nancy, experience is a question of existence, of going, living, making it *through* something: "existence is experience." This means, most obviously, that every experience is experienced in a particular way, (in)formed by a particular existential situation: my life (*Leben*), the orientation (the intentionality) with which I live it, determines how things are lived in experience (*er-lebt*). More fundamentally, it means that every world-disclosure is a question of being-in-the-world, in the sense that "it does (*fait*) nothing else but expose itself to the unforeseeable, the unheard of of its own event. Experience simply [...] 'events' (*s'évenir*), 'comes forth of itself'" (Nancy, *Dis-Enclosure* 79).

For Nancy, too, then, "this is not empiricism's experience" (*The Experience of Freedom* 89). It is, instead, an experience that, "proves itself by testing itself," which "does not refer to any introspection, nor to any intimate sentiment," but that is, rather, "anterior to every empirical certitude, without being, properly speaking, on the order of the transcendental" as "*a transcendental experience* or *the transcendental of experience*, the transcendental that *is* experience" (87). At issue here is thus that non-empirical undergoing in which ex-per-ience exists, which ex-istence experiences, and makes all subsequent lived-experiences possible by setting the terms on which things are lived: namely, existence itself, the life on the basis of which things are lived in experience, the being-in-the-world through which Dasein's being is world-disclosure. Romano therefore understands this primordial ex-per-ience as a "transcendental *a posteriori*."[13] It shapes all particular lived-experiences, and is thus transcendental in the sense that it makes them possible, but is at the same time itself experience or experien*cing*, and thus a posteriori: it is the experien*cing* that shapes, by making possible, all subsequent lived-experiences (e.g., like how the *ex-per-ience* of being bitten by a dog as a child causes dogs to *appear* as a threat later in life). As such, it runs parallel to what Caputo calls the *predelineation of experience*:

> These are possibilities whose essential content has been [...] predelineated [...] by actual experience [...] Such predelineation makes all subsequent experience possible. It is a universal law of intentionality, therefore, that every object of possible experience depends upon a prior projection of its essential type or [...] a prior understanding of its Being. This prior projection is no Kantian a priori, for it is drawn from [...] the actual course of experience, and [...] subject to ongoing temporal revision [...] In other words, it is a gradually accumulated a priori, the product of [...] the regularities of experience, and not some [...] a priori form or pre-existent idea. (*Radical Hermeneutics* 45)

This life on the basis of which all experience is lived, this ex-per-iencing that predelineates all lived-experiences, then takes priority in phenomenological investigation as the *originary form of experience*.

The primordial sense of experience as *experiri* is thus not a particular lived-experience (*Erlebnis*) but rather the *life* (*Leben*) on the basis of which things are lived (*erlebt*) that is itself a matter of ex-per-ience (*Er-fahr-ung*): the *ordeal* (*épreuve*) of going through life, the *trial* (*épreuve*) in which it exists, the *undergoing* (*épreuve*) of what happens to me. I will thus follow Romano in radically distinguishing what is *undergone* (*éprouvé*) in ex-per-ience (*Erfahrung*) from what is *lived* (*vécu*) in experience (*Erlebnis*).[14] The experience at issue is the *ex-per-iencing* of experience, *the life that makes for the lived-experience*. It aims at what is called *faire l'expérience* in French, or *eine Erfahrung machen* in German, namely the undergoing (*Leben*) on the basis of which I experience (*erleben*) things.[15] In setting the terms on which things are lived, in predelineating lived-experiences, this ex-per-ience is phenomenologically primary.

In the case of Abraham, the *ordeal* (*épreuve*) traversed, the *experience* (*épreuve*) undergone, is that of faith: namely, the *trial* (*épreuve*) of Abraham's life, the way he (in his faith) is *put to the test* (*éprouvé*) by God, the fear and trembling he lives through. Kierkegaard deals with this ordeal as the *singular event* of Abraham's life, for what happens to him is precisely not an empirical development. "The important thing here is not the idea of acquisition," say of the divine will, as Romano puts it in a secular context nevertheless perfectly befitting of Abraham;

> but, on the contrary, the idea of being put to the test, which is at the same time a transformation: I can only *undergo* an experience because it happens to me unsubstitutably, by allowing me to advene to myself, always anew, differently, unforeseeably. (*Event and World* 144)

The point of Abraham's *ex-per-ience of faith* is not the experience *of* a transcendent object (e.g., the divine will), but rather a particular way of being open to the world, another way of living life (*leben*), another way of experiencing (*erleben*), as a result of the ordeal he has lived through (*widerfährt*): it is not the appearing of phenomenology (*phanein*), but rather the experience born out of, as Aeschylus puts it (177), the *personal suffering* (*to pathein mathos*) of making it through something.[16] Indeed, referring to Abraham in his *Upbuilding Discourses*, Kierkegaard declares that "experience is the fruit of spiritual trial" (95),[17] rather than of what appears to intentional consciousness. As such, the experience of faith might be the experience par excellence returning us to the Latin root of *experiri*, for as Caputo observes, "'ordeal'" is precisely "the category of Job and father Abraham" (*Against Ethics* 106). It is not a phenomenon, not a given of lived-experience, but nevertheless shows itself in and as the exper-ience in which Abraham's life consists and out of which he experiences the world: his faith.

Here, phenomenology then takes on the form of a poetics or a discourse on creative forms, not an ontology or a discourse on the ground of being: the question is that of the relation between life and experience, not being and appearing. We are considering a form-of-life, rather than the transcendental existentiality making it possible: namely *faith*, a way of being-in-the-world (form-of-life), which *forms* or predelineates world-disclosure, how things are lived-in-experience (form-of-experience). *Fear and Trembling* wants to make us *experience the experience* (*faire l'expérience*) of faith: the *ordeal of faith* Abraham undergoes, in which his existence exists, that makes-up or forms (*fait*) his life. The (quasi-) phenomenology put forward here is thus one of this non-empirical undergoing, this ex-per-ience (*Er-fahr-ung*), *this life* – the risk and danger (*Gefahr*), the ordeal (*épreuve*), in which Abraham engages himself, finds himself, and without which "Abraham is not the one he is" (Kierkegaard, *Fear and Trembling* 60).

III the clash of forms

Kierkegaard's poetics of faith consists in staging the confrontation between two forms-of-life and thus two ways-of-experiencing: between Abraham, who has faith, and Johannes de Silentio, *Fear and Trembling*'s pseudonymous author, who does not.[18] The analysis thus offered by Kierkegaard is that of a clash of forms: not *what* is experienced (the command); but *how* it is experienced, the basis on which it is lived (faith or unfaith). Kierkegaard offers this analysis by having Johannes ponder *the ordeal of faith*, namely, Abraham's life. Two things are thus going on simultaneously: Kierkegaard is staging a clash of forms-of-life (the difference between Johannes and Abraham), whilst Johannes is analysing the experience of faith Abraham's life presents him with (from the position of unfaith). It is navigating the difference in form that is the task of a poetics.

Johannes is impressed by Abraham, impressed by how he could perform such an appalling act, not simply because God demanded it (in resignation), but because Abraham believes he will receive Isaac anew through it (in faith) – which is absurd, he has no reason for thinking this. Thus, "while Abraham arouses my admiration," Johannes says, "he also appals me" (Kierkegaard, *Fear and Trembling* 89). The point of the book is then not to *justify* (by giving reasons) Abraham's absurd actions, but to *show* (through illustrations) what it means to have faith, to make us undergo the ex-per-ience of faith, to make us live through it for ourselves: through Johannes, Kierkegaard dares us to perform the move Hegel resists, namely *stopping* to experience (*faire l'expérience de*) the intellect being stupefied by the unintelligible, feeling the fear and trembling of faith, undergoing its passion.

As a result, Johannes warns us, "the present author is not a philosopher, he is in poetic and well-chosen terms (*poetici et eleganter*) a supplementary clerk [...] who pledges neither anything about the System nor himself *to* it" (Kierkegaard, *Fear and Trembling* 43). The discourse offered illustrates faith rather than making it understandable, presenting its findings *poetici et eleganter*, as a particular *form-of-life*: Abraham's ordeal. Through his use of pseudonymity, Kierkegaard cunningly performs a quasi-phenomenological reduction: by making Johannes elaborate his mutual admiration of and disgust for the man, he points out that we only have access to the *form* (how) of Abraham's experiences, not the actual *content* (what). We have no way of knowing whether what Abraham lives in his experience is God; the only thing we can say is that, because he lives his life and experiences his experiences through it, faith recognises God in them. Otherwise put, we cannot adjudicate whether Abraham is delusional or actually in touch with God, and thus we cannot possibly justify (i.e., give reasons for) his actions.[19] We can only say something about the form of Abraham's life (faith), the terms on which he lives things in experience. In turn, through his use of pseudonymity, Kierkegaard places this in contrast with Johannes' own form of life (unfaith), which lives (and thus experiences) the same differently.

The experience Johannes relates is the stupefaction we undergo, the horror we live, when faced with the paradox of Abraham's life – namely, his *faith* that he would receive his son anew precisely in killing him – , from the position of unfaith. The experience itself, of faith from the position of unfaith, thus constitutes a *paradox*. As Johannes puts it:

> I am all the time aware of that monstrous paradox that is the content of Abraham's life, I am constantly repulsed, and my thought, for all its passion, is unable to enter into it [...] I strain every muscle to catch sight of it, but the same instant I become paralysed [...] The hero I can *think* myself *into*, but not Abraham; when I reach that height I fall down since what I'm offered is a paradox. (Kierkegaard, *Fear and Trembling* 62–63)

Since faith is a paradox (an impossibility), it cannot (possibly) be understood what it means to have faith; it can only be shown (by

an experience), when it becomes an event in one's singular existence, when it (trans)forms one's entire life: "Even if one were able to render the whole of the content of faith into conceptual form," Johannes says, "it would not follow that one had grasped faith, grasped how one came to it, or how it came to one" (43). In other words, the forms of life are incommensurable, and the clash between them makes for the paradox.

The teleological suspension of the ethical illustrates this clash: rather than Kant's morality (*Moralität*), it suspends what Hegel calls *Sittlichkeit* (*Sædelighed*), unhelpfully rendered in English as *the ethical sphere*.[20] In the *Genealogy of Morals* (188), Nietzsche calls it the "morality of mores" (*Sittlichkeit der Sitte*): arbitrary social rules ensuring the smooth functioning of society by applying universally to its members.[21] Merold Westphal's "Abraham and Sacrifice" captures the idea accurately as "the laws and customs of one's people" (320).[22] Here, it is not a question of goodness, but decency: a situation where, as Hegel puts it, "virtue displays itself as the individual's simple conformity with the duties of the station to which he belongs, it is *rectitude*" (193; trans. mod.). It is not immoral to refrain from shaking someone's hand when meeting them, but it certainly is universally frowned upon – one stands out, asserts oneself as an individual, precisely by defying the established social order: "The ethical as such is the universal, and as the universal it applies to everyone," Johannes therefore concludes, "it rests immanently in itself, has nothing outside itself that is its *telos* but is itself the *telos* for everything outside." Meanwhile, the "single individual," through which alone one comes to faith, is ethically speaking "the particular that has its *telos* in the universal," his task being "always to express himself in this, to abrogate his particularity so as to become the universal." Indeed, from the moment "the single individual wants to assert himself in his particularity, in direct opposition to the universal, he sins, and only by recognizing this can he again reconcile himself with the universal" (83).[23] Ethics (*Sittlichkeit*) achieves the singular through the universal (one's place in the *Gesellschaft*, one's station); morality (*Moralität*), meanwhile, achieves the universal via the singular (one's experience of the moral law within oneself).

What is suspended in relation to God through faith is thus not *morality*, but the *rationality* providing the universally understandable terms for public discourse by grounding the single individual in the communality of society. What is suspended is not the morality that Kant described as a fact established by itself, the experience of being bound by duty that Caputo calls *obligation* (an originary ex-per-ience of reason); but, rather, the formal system of *ethics* that derives from it and whose universal validity is grounded in the transcendentality of reason (an *ex post facto* inference justifying that fact).[24] Faith, because it is a paradox, displaces ethics from within by short-circuiting rational justification in the name of the brute facticity of our obligation (to God) in what Caputo has called "a kind of Abrahamic *Befindlichkeit*" (*Against Ethics* 27). Obligation to God is the bind Abraham finds himself in, as incommensurate with the ethical: "faith is just this paradox," Johannes says, "that the single individual is higher than the universal" (Kierkegaard, *Fear and Trembling* 84), or that Abraham "exists as the particular in opposition to the universal" (90). Faith suspends the ethical since universal public reason cannot recover this paradox: Abraham's faith wrenches him out of respectable society, withdraws him from the universal, releases him from his station. However, rather than absolving him from the singular obligation in and by which he finds himself (bound by duty), that obligation has made him so completely himself that he has become a stranger to society, it has singularised him to the extent that he has entirely disappeared from view.

Faith, therefore, cannot be understood universally, rationally, in principle, as one of reason's transcendentals or Dasein's existentials (a priori); instead, it requires ex-per-ience, an event taking place in one's singular existence that at the same time determines that existence (a transcendental a posteriori). As such, it is resistant to the universal whose

categories strip it of its (singular) meaning and thereby turn it into a paradox: "This position cannot be mediated, for all mediation occurs precisely by virtue of the universal; it is and remains in all eternity a paradox, inaccessible to thought. And yet faith *is* this paradox" (Kierkegaard, *Fear and Trembling* 85). Rational mediation exists in, mediates by way of, universalisation (which is, in turn, always rationalisation): making something understandable by explaining it in terms that transcend the singular event at issue, appropriating it into the universal by giving reasons. However, since faith can only be understood in its singularity – there are no reasons for faith, precisely because it requires a singular ex-per-ience – , it cannot be understood at all, for understanding proceeds by way of the universal and the rational. Only in that sense does Abraham suspend the ethical, namely: the universal terms or shared language in which we justify or make ourselves understandable to others, for my singular encounter with God defies such terms.

This suspension is what Caputo means by thinking *against ethics* (and thus also against transcendental phenomenology): not against moral obligation, but against ethical reason. He explains:

> Abraham is the father of all of those who dare raise their voice against ethics [...] For de Silentio, this is the story of a daring teleological suspension of ethics, of suspending understanding and hanging ethical knowledge out to dry, of lifting the force of the universal and putting it in *epochē*. For Johannes it is a story not about the suspension of obligation but about the suspension of the fine name of ethics in the name of obligation, about suspending the fine name of universality in the name of the heterogeneity and incommensurability of the singular individual and of going one on one with the Absolute. (Caputo, *Against Ethics* 9)

The singularity of obligation resists reduction to a reason or an ethic because it belongs "to the irreducible realm of that facticity which Heidegger showed, against pure phenomenology, does not submit to neutralization,"

THE PULSE OF SENSE

because it "is part of my *Befindlichkeit*, the fix I find myself in," the duty by which I ex-per-ience myself bound (25). The obligation is the bind in which Abraham finds himself, which he does not try to explain away, for he precisely *finds himself* in it (*there*): forced to do the impossible, he does not question this, but merely replies "Here I am" (Genesis 22.1). The point is thus not to make Abraham under-standable, to justify his actions; but, rather, to appreciate the impossible bind he finds himself in (faith) and to undergo his ordeal for ourselves (fear and trembling).

In short, the impossibility of what God commands Abraham to do cannot be mediated by giving reasons, either by justify-ing it (ethics) or grounding it in the trans-cendental structures of consciousness (phenomenology). Something else is needed: against the universal (ethics and phenomenol-ogy), Caputo proposes a *poetics of obligation* to think the singularity of what happens, the bind Abraham finds himself in, *his form-of-life* or the impossible *ordeal he lives through* (faith). Its task is

> to grapple with the impossible, not in order to see how it may actually be possible after all, to unearth its most hidden conditions of possibility, but in order to proclaim that it happens, as a matter of factical fact, and to provide it with a suitable idiom. (Caputo, *Against Ethics* 126)

Kierkegaard provides this horrifying impossi-bility with a suitable idiom by staging the clash of forms between Abraham and Johannes, by having Johannes describe his admiration and disgust.

IV the form of faith

Fear and Trembling offers a description of the form of faith (Abraham's ordeal), from Johannes' position of unfaith. However, Johannes first establishes that Abraham did indeed have faith. An earlier chapter of Genesis illustrates this. When God makes his promise, that Abraham and Sarah will conceive a son in old age whom many nations will descend from, Sarah reacts quite differently

from Abraham: she laughs (Genesis 18.10–14). Abraham, however, Johannes points out, "did not laugh at it, as Sarah had laughed when the promise had first been proclaimed." He believed God, for "it was faith," which Sarah lacked, "that made Abraham accept the promise." Moreover, "as time went by," Johannes continues, "he did not cast suspicious glances at Sarah, fearing she was growing old," as would have been understandable; instead, "Abraham believed and held firm to the promise," in the face of its absurdity, for according to worldly reason it was impossible (Kierkegaard, *Fear and Trembling* 51–53). Ultimately, God then gave them Isaac, thus keeping his promise despite its impossibility.

This event, this experience of the im-pos-sible, of the conditions of possible experience being challenged by the ex-per-ience of pos-sibility itself, redefines the realm of the possible for Abraham, reorganises the conditions of possible experience, transforms its predelinea-tion. Yet, this is entirely a question of faith – that is, of ex-per-ience – , we cannot reason our way up there from the absurd: faith means to cling to an im-possible possibility (Derrida); it is an event that transforms possi-bility (Romano and Falque); it is an experience calling out to us from beyond the real and the possible, calling out the real (what-is) in the name of the hyper-reality (what-can-be) of the promise (Caputo).[25] As Kierkegaard explains:

> The absurd is not one distinction among others embraced by understanding. It is not the same as the improbable, unexpected, the unforeseen. The moment the knight resigned he was convinced of the impossi-bility, humanly speaking; that was a con-clusion of the understanding [...] In an infinite sense, however, it was possible, through renouncing it [as a finite possi-bility]; but then accepting that [possibility] is at the same time to have given it up, yet for the understanding there is no absurdity in possessing it, for it is only in the finite world that understanding rules and there it was and remains an impossibility. On this the knight of faith is just as clear: all that can save him is the absurd; and this he grasps by faith. Accordingly he admits the

impossibility and at the same time believes the absurd. (*Fear and Trembling* 75–76)

To have faith is to hold out for the im-possible, without it ever appearing possible, but paradoxically hearing its call and feeling its promise nonetheless. After all, Abraham is *surprised* when the im-possible comes to pass, he is over-taken (*sur-pris*) by events. He has no *reason*, not even hope, to attach any reality to the promise, all he has is *faith*: "He believed on the strength of the absurd, for all human calculation had long since been suspended" (65).[26] The ex-per-ience of the promise – a call from beyond the possible and beyond the real – calls into question worldly reason and possibility, making the hyper-reality of the promise paradoxically more real than the reality of the world it suspends, just like the single individual becomes more real than the rational system of the universal.

Because Abraham has now experienced possibility beyond actuality for himself (promise), lived through its event and been transformed by it (faith), he experiences worldly possibility differently: in the ex-per-ience that things do not have-to-be as they are, things cannot stay as they are. "The suspension," Kierkegaard therefore concludes, "consists in the individual finding himself in a state that is the exact opposite of that required by the ethical," for "he relates to actuality not as possibility but as impossibility" (*Concluding Unscientific Postscript* 224). Faith is therefore a paradox: its event is attached to the world, whilst its logic opens-up the world from within onto an outside that remains obscure, making us tremble in fear. In short, "it was by his faith that Abraham could leave the land of his fathers to become a stranger in the land of promise," by his ex-per-ience of the hyper-reality and im-possible possibility of the promise "he left behind his worldly understanding and took with him his faith" (Kierkegaard, *Fear and Trembling* 50). As such, Abraham can experience (*erleben*) what remains absurd and paradoxical to Johannes: they have lived different lives (*Leben*), been through or ex-per-ienced (*er-fahr-en*) different

things, and therefore now also live or experience (*er-leben*) things in different ways.

Having established that Abraham had faith, we can now consider the form this ex-per-ience or this life takes on and how it in turn forms or predelineates all subsequent lived-experiences. Johannes paints Abraham's faith as both *silent* and *performative*. Starting with the former, he observes that Abraham immediately sets off to perform the sacrifice, without ever attempting to explain or justify himself: "He said nothing to Sarah, nothing to Eliezer. After all, who could have understood him? Hadn't the test by its very nature exacted an oath of silence from him?" (Kierkegaard, *Fear and Trembling* 55). Not that Abraham does not *want* to justify his actions, he simply *cannot*: he has no justification other than faith, which makes it absurd, for faith is not a reason. Faith is rather what Kierkegaard calls an "abyss of inwardness" (*Concluding Unscientific Postscript* 220): the complete lack of any outward justification or of anything given to stand upon, which must be leapt over in order to act on faith instead. Faith in itself, its paradox, is not a justification: its very nature is to resist universalisation and rationalisation, to resist reduction to what Derrida calls the "familial or public, ethical, or political space" (*The Gift of Death* 128). This makes-up (*fait*) the ordeal of faith, its fear and trembling, as Kierkegaard explains:

> Faith itself cannot be mediated into the universal, for in that case it would be cancelled. Faith is this paradox, and the single individual is quite unable to make himself intelligible to anyone [...] If there is any more precise explanation of the idea behind the sacrifice of Isaac, it is one that the individual can only give to himself. (*Fear and Trembling* 99)

Thus, because faith is a question of the singular, whilst speech and justification are matters of the universal, Johannes de Silentio – the pseudonym that "keeps silent" (Derrida, *The Gift of Death* 59) – shows us that faith is characterised by *silence*:

Abraham is silent – but he *cannot* speak, therein lies the distress and the anguish. For if when I speak I cannot make myself understood, I do not speak even if I keep talking without stop day and night. This is the case with Abraham. He can say what he will, but there is one thing he cannot say and since he cannot say it, i.e. say it in a way that another understands it, he does not speak. The relief of speech is that it translates me into the universal.[27] (Kierkegaard, *Fear and Trembling* 137)

The point of his silence is not that Abraham could not think of the right thing to say, but rather that there is nothing to say or no reasons to give – *nothing to see* – , nothing that would make anyone else understand his actions, for they are absurd by virtue of faith (not based on publicly accessible reasons), and thus particular to his own singular existence: "Abraham cannot be mediated, which can also be put by saying he cannot speak. The moment I speak I express the universal, and when I do not no one can understand me" (Kierkegaard, *Fear and Trembling* 89). Nobody understands me, because the moment I express myself, the singular *me* that is offered to the understanding in universal terms is dissolved therein. When it comes to one's singular relation to God, because it is singular, this simply cannot be done: Abraham's entire life (his faith) exists in the internal displacement of the practice of *giving reasons* (the ethical). This is faith's teleological suspension of the ethical: an irreducible ex-per-ience of a singular event that cannot be mediated without becoming discourse, and that event is nothing other than existence itself in its resistance to rationality and conceptuality (to anything *given*); as the singular defying the universal, I achieve my sense of self as ultimate responsibility in the absence of anything given, like the safety net of ethics. Is this not what the experience of morality consists in? Is this not what the experience, the adventure, of going-through life ex-ists in?[28] This *resistance of existence* makes-up (*fait*) its *ex-per-ience*: the experience of faith, its ordeal, its fear and trembling, its passion.

In the precluding speech, Kierkegaard establishes the divine as a matter of one's singular existence (its ex-per-ience) rather than any innerworldly fact (an intentional state). The divine is not a worldly object given in lived-experience, but rather forms a way of being-in-the-world in terms of which it is disclosed: instead of being experienced or lived, the divine is to be lived-out, lived-through, undergone, in faith. The second aspect of faith Johannes thus illustrates using the story of Abraham is its *performative* character: it exists in actions, a way-of-living-life (*leben*) resulting in a corresponding way-of-experiencing (*erleben*) the world. "This faith," Nancy says in a comment on Abraham, "is but the 'conviction' that gives itself over in act – not even to something 'incomprehensible' (according to the logic of the 'I cannot understand but I must or I may still believe,' and still less according to a logic of the *credo quia absurdum*)," as Caputo suspects, "but to that which is another act: a commandment" (*Dis-Enclosure* 53). Faith coincides entirely with action, it expresses itself in what Abraham does, in his life, in how he passes the test. It would be entirely understandable if Abraham were to doubt the command's authenticity (like Kant suggests),[29] beg God to change his mind, or pray that it wasn't true. However, Abraham does nothing of the sort – which is incomprehensible (impossible!) – , as a father he *did the impossible*:

But Abraham had faith and did not doubt. He believed the absurd [...] He did not beg for himself in hope of moving the Lord [...] But he did not doubt, he did not look in anguish to left or right, he did not challenge heaven with his prayers. He knew it was God the Almighty that tried him, he knew it was the hardest sacrifice that could be demanded of him; but he also knew that no sacrifice was too hard when God demanded it – and he drew the knife. (Kierkegaard, *Fear and Trembling* 142)

Abraham simply makes himself available to the God he does not understand: "Here I am" (Genesis 22.1, 11). Faith, as a kind of

Abrahamic *Befindlichkeit*, forms the *there* where Abraham finds himself, the orientation he lives-out (of), without which "Abraham is not the one he is" (Kierkegaard, *Fear and Trembling* 60).

V the experience of faith

In his "On the Judeo-Christian (on Faith)," Nancy's silence on Kierkegaard is deafening. It reads the Epistle of James, perhaps the single most import Christian text for Nancy (James is depicted on the cover of the English edition of *Dis-Enclosure*). He shares this preference with Kierkegaard, who referred to the epistle as "my first, my favourite, text" (*Journals and Papers* VI: 6769/416).[30] Though Nancy never mentions Kierkegaard, the story of Abraham and the Dane's *Upbuilding Discourses* resonate clearly throughout his own reading of James.[31]

Faith (*pistis*) is understood by James *ek tōn ergon*, by its works (2.18). We only hear the Word insofar as we are *poiētai logon*, doers of the Word (1.22). Faith thus exists in the *doing* (*poiēsis*) of the Word (1.25) – making this the only New Testament text to use that Greek word. According to Nancy, this *poiēsis* must be understood "in the sense of 'practice' (thus, of '*praxis*'), that is, if *praxis* is indeed action in the sense of *by* or *of* an agent and not the *praxis* exerted *upon* an object" (*Dis-Enclosure* 51).[32] This *poiēsis* is then not simply the production of an object adequate to its concept, but precisely the internal displacement of the productive operation as governed by a worldly logic:

> One might say: *pistis* is the *praxis* that takes place in and as the *poiēsis* of the *erga* [...] I would say that faith, as the *praxis* of *poiēsis*, opens in *poiēsis* the inadequation to self that alone can constitute "doing" (*faire*) and/or "acting" (*agir*) [...] Extrapolating from here, I would say that *praxis* is that which could not be the production of a work adequate to its concept [...], but that *praxis* is in every work and it is *ek tou ergou*, that which exceeds the concept of it [...] Faith would thus be here the *praxical*

excess of and in action or in operation, and this excess, insofar as it aligns itself with nothing other than itself, that is to say, also with the possibility for a "subject" (for an agent or for an actor) to be more, to be infinitely more and excessively more than what it is in itself and for itself.[33] (*Dis-Enclosure* 52)

This inadequation (in) which faith operates is difficult to grasp, but Nancy illustrates it with Abraham:

> But faith, according to James, is effected entirely in the inadequation of its enactment to any concept of that act [...] The work of Abraham is the acting or the doing of this inadequation: a *praxis* whose *poiēsis* is the incommensurability of an action (to offer Isaac up) and of its representation or its meaning (to immolate his son). (*Dis-Enclosure* 54)

The work of faith, thus, consists in "the inadequation of the work or the inadequation at work" (*Dis-Enclosure* 57), in the doing whose production displaces its own product, for *the doing itself* exceeds or is incommensurate with *what is done*. In his own reading of James, Graham Ward has similarly captured this idea by declaring "the Christian act" (*ergon*) the site where "the activity of God crosses through the activity of being human," and as such "realizes an unfathomable paradox in which that which is created in the image of God is crossed by that which is God himself," an inadequation that thus "finds a unique singular expression as praxis" in that very act ("*Kenosis, Poiesis and Genesis*" 172).[34] In faith, human activity is displaced by divine activity *as* human activity (*theopoiesis* or *theosis*). Faith is thus the inadequation of self to self, of doing to action, for doing "exceeds itself and *makes* itself in the act, or *makes itself* exceed itself" (Nancy, *Dis-Enclosure* 54).

This makes faith a way of being-*in*-the-world whilst *at-odds-with*-the-world; whereby, as Bultmann puts it, "the world is annulled *within* the world" (*The Gospel of John* 508)[35] in an act of "desecularization," meaning "detachment within the world from the world" (*Theology of the New Testament II* 86). Without abandoning the world, faith expects more from it: living not out of the real, the world-as-it-is, but out of the hyper-real, the world-as-it-can-be (as it was promised). As Nancy puts it:

> "Christianity" is life in the world outside of the world. Nietzsche [...] understood it perfectly. This despiser of "backworlds" knew that Christianity [...] consists in being in the world without being *of* the world. That is to say that it does not limit itself to adhering to inherence, to what is given [...] Two of Nietzsche's well-known figures illustrate what he sometimes claims to be the "experience [*Erfahrung*] at the heart" of Christianity: the tightrope dancer and the child playing with dice. Neither relates to the world as a given [...]; on the contrary, they relate to that in the world which makes an opening, rift, abyss, game, or risk.[36] (*Adoration* 23–24)

Faith is a state of the heart, an ex-per-ience at the heart, a way-of-life: a being-*in*-the-world without being-*of*-the-world.[37] It is an ex-per-ience that "restores us to the world, and it sets (us) into the world anew, as new" and "according to the novelty of an experience that is not of this world," whereby its subject "withdraws from the world in the very midst of that world," and "becomes the site of an experience" like faith (Nancy, *Dis-Enclosure* 78).

Phenomenologically, faith becomes a particular orientation of intentionality: a seeing of things not as-they-are, but in terms of the discrepancy, the inadequacy, the gap opening-up between how they are (what is) and how they could-be (what was promised). Intentionality *leaps* ahead of itself, goes where it has no *reason* to go, where there is nothing *given* for it to work on. In that sense, Abraham's life (a being-in-the-world without being-of-the-world) offers more than Johannes (immersed in worldly possibility and reason) can conceive, and it is thus only what Jean-Luc Marion calls "saturated" in that sense: saturation, a blinding refraction of light, is what happens in the clash

of incommensurable forms-of-life or ways-of-experiencing.[38] Nancy explains:

> Faith consists in relating to God [...], to the extent that God and his love are not present, shown – [...] not present in the modality of a monstration [...] The greatest [...] analyses of the Christian faith show that faith is [...] *the adhesion to itself of an aim without other*. I will say, in phenomenological terms, the adhesion to itself of an aim without a correlative object, or with no fulfilment of sense but that of the aim itself. One could perhaps say that faith is pure intentionality, or [...] the phenomenon of intentionality as a self-sufficient phenomenon, as a "saturated phenomenon," in Jean-Luc Marion's sense. I understand perfectly well that Marion [...] is not talking about a phenomenon like faith, but rather of phenomena [...] that would entail faith; nevertheless, I leave open the question of whether faith might not be such a "saturated phenomenon," or even, perhaps, saturation itself. (*Dis-Enclosure* 152–53)

Faith does not access saturated phenomena in a *theophanic revelation* (a lived-experience, a phenomenon); rather, faith, as a *theopoetic act* (an ordeal, a life), is itself a saturated phenomenon: a way of being-*in*-the-world that is not *of*-the-world, that *does* the im-possible, because it is oriented towards what exceeds the world (as-it-is) in terms of world (as-it-can-be), without having any (worldly) reason for this. Faith is intentionality without correlative object; intentionality *leaping*, i.e., venturing and adventuring,[39] ahead of itself: a seeing where there is nothing to be seen, nothing given, nothing publicly accessible. Faith, Merleau-Ponty says, "is an adherence that goes beyond the guarantees which one is given and therefore excludes an ever-present sincerity" (176).

Kierkegaard calls this intentionality "the expectancy of faith" (*Upbuilding Discourses* 7–29),[40] namely a willingness to face the radical open-endedness of the future: an openness to a singularly new event, living in the awareness of the radical unpredictability of the world, in the ex-per-ience of actuality's contingency and the impossible's possibility. Precisely this, Gadamer says, is a matter of ex-per-ience (*Erfahrung*), namely, "to have the insight that all the expectation and planning of finite beings is finite and limited" (351).[41] According to Kierkegaard, faith is lived *in* this ex-per-ience, rather than *despite* it:

> The believer, however, says: I expect victory [...], victory in all [...] spiritual trials, because experience had taught that there would be battle. But with the help of faith, it expects victory in all of them. Only for a moment does it pause. "It is too much," it says. "It is impossible; life cannot be that glorious; no matter how golden youth was in its supreme happiness, this surely surpasses the most joyous hope of youth." – Yes, it certainly does surpass even youth's most joyous hope, and yet it is so, even if not exactly as you suppose. (*Upbuilding Discourses* 21)

Faith lives out (of) the ex-per-ience, the ordeal, of the world's contingency, which it embraces precisely in faith rather than in resignation: it expects the im-possible, since nothing is impossible for God (Luke 1.37). Without making the impossible possible, justifying the unjustifiable, rationalising the absurd (we cannot even hope); faith suspends reason and possibility teleologically in an openness to the singularly new, but not therefore foreseeable. Rather than neglecting the world in favour of an otherworldly promised kingdom, faith sees and performs its coming within world: exposing the world from within to what exceeds it in terms of world. "What expectation expects, then, is not this or that finite good," as George Pattison summarises it in *Kierkegaard's Upbuilding Discourses*, "it is the self's expectation that in any and every finite situation it will be able to renew its relation to the eternal, to God, and in that relation, but under the conditions of temporality, [...] become itself" (50).

Faith expects more than is given without having any *reason* to do so, which secures its performative character: action follows from the realisation that things do not *have-to-be*

the way they *are*. Faith, being-*in*-the-world without being-*of*-the-world, means *experiencing* the world not as-it-is (reality in itself) but as-it-can-be (its excess as promise): if existence is experience, then "existence consists in having (*faire*), in the world, the experience of what is not of this world, without being another world for all that," instead opening "*within* the world an *outside* that is not a beyond-the-world, but the *truth* of the world" (Nancy, *Dis-Enclosure* 78–79). This truth is a matter of action, the world is something to be done: not *given* in lived-experience, but *formed* by the ordeal of going-through life that makes it true. It is the constant displacement of the world-as-it-is, which becomes untenable in (light of) the ex-per-ience of the world-as-it-can-be: "Faith resides in inadequation to itself as content of meaning," Nancy says, and as such "it is truth qua truth of faith or faith as truth and verification," of *doing* truth or *making* it (come) true (*poiēsis*), "not sacri-fication but veri-fication" (*Dis-Enclosure* 53). In a rare reference to the Dane, Nancy observes that this is what Kierkegaard – for whom truth and faith are coextensive – understood perfectly:

> The truth is nothing that can be known. It is to be lived (*est à être*) [...] This truth to which Kierkegaard devotes his word; this truth that cannot content itself with being said, since it is not true but as existing in the actual existence of this or that, which [...] veri-fies it; this truth that cannot be said without being done (*fait*), as if this saying functions as performative of an action which would be nothing other than the saying itself as living (*être*) – being making itself (*être se faisant*) in this world stranger to the world, detached from it and any attachment, absolute. ("Un mot d'accompagnement" 9)

It is not a truth that elevates itself, a truth of the world beyond the world; but rather a truth that makes itself true in the doing of truth (*veritatem facere*), and in doing so makes come about the world as world (i.e., makes the kingdom come).[42]

In summary, then, the poetics of faith Kierkegaard articulates in *Fear and Trembling* forms a (quasi-) phenomenology of faith, insofar as it is "a phenomenology that is theological, but not theophanic" (Nancy, *Dis-Enclosure* 49). Without offering a lived-experience of God *through* faith, it analyses the ex-per-ience *of* faith itself: a life lived in the world, like the ordeal Abraham makes it through, that challenges the world from within in the name of the kingdom that is coming, that opens up the *what-is* of the world to the promise of what *can-be* but *is-not-yet*. The experience of Abraham's faith, its ordeal, as Caputo puts it, is not one of "'seeing God,' although it gives faith a quality of 'truth' in this sense of *facere veritatem*," but means rather "testifying [...] to the love of God, doing something, a deed" (*On Religion* 116). This testimony, in which the ex-per-ience or the ordeal of faith exists, is found in lives in which the name of God becomes an event by taking on the flesh of existence in such a way that a particular being-*in*-the-world without being-*of*-the-world constitutes the kingdom's coming (*to* the world, *in* the world, *as* world). In this sense, phenomenology itself becomes a *poetics of faith*: a consideration of how the form-of-life (the ordeal of faith) makes-for (*fait*) the lived-experience, or sets the terms on which the world is disclosed (the creation of the world).[43]

echo by jean-luc nancy

Nikolaas Deketelaere exerts a pressure on phenomenological intentionality that could undoubtedly be considered a violence. I do not have the required competence to evaluate this gesture (besides, I admit that neither am I concerned with safeguarding the integrity of phenomenology which is foreign to me in any case). In one way, it is a violence because it is not certain that an intentionality could be devoid of an object (as he asserts). In another way, however, if the proper content of this intentionality lies within the tension (and intensity) rather than in the intended (another way of calling the "object" into question), there is

nothing to prevent this tension from tensing itself disproportionally, i.e., beyond anything intended, thus beyond any relation of the subject to the object.

This perspective, it strikes me, overflows the framework of phenomenology; but, from me, that is not a critical remark. Here, it may be a question of an "overflowing" of which the possibility, even the necessity, is perhaps in one way or another inscribed in Husserlian intentionality itself. That, in any case, is a possible extension of this work.

It seems to me that another opens up through the motif of the im-possible. The necessity of dividing this word so as to distinguish it from the "not-possible" demonstrates that we ought to achieve an exit from the semantics of the possible. But perhaps that is not ... possible! In any case, Nikolaas Deketelaere knows what it is all about!

disclosure statement

No potential conflict of interest was reported by the author.

notes

1 Though on either of these fronts, the influence of Nietzsche, who occupies a more visible place in Nancy's work, should not be underestimated either. Indeed, there is a major parallel between Nietzsche and Kierkegaard on these two issues (undoubtedly provided by Luther). Ultimately, however, we are left to guess at the actual source, since – to my knowledge – no extensive comparison of Nancy and Kierkegaard exists. Peter Kline has nevertheless made fruitful use of Nancy in his *Passion for Nothing: Kierkegaard's Apophatic Theology*. Though my own perspective differs quite considerably from Kline's, I am grateful to him for kindly sending me a copy of his interesting book.

2 See *On Touching – Jean-Luc Nancy* 233.

3 In his *Kierkegaard's Critique of Reason and Society*, Merold Westphal therefore rightly speaks of Kierkegaard's "logic of insanity" (see 85–103). Indeed,

one wonders to what degree Kierkegaard's Abraham is all that different from Nietzsche's Madman.

4 Kierkegaard's two most famous critics on this point are Alasdair MacIntyre (see *After Virtue* 49) and Emmanuel Lévinas (see *Proper Names* 68–72).

5 This is a constant complaint by Caputo, see further: *Against Ethics* 139–46; *On Religion* 28; *Truth* 157–58.

6 Nancy often echoes this same idea, see especially: *The Experience of Freedom* 20, 81–95; *The Birth to Presence* 3, 200; *Corpus* 101, 113, 134–35, 140; *Multiple Arts* 208–10.

7 See also Husserl, *Logical Investigations II* 101–02.

8 See also Husserl, *Cartesian Meditations* §14, 70–72/31–33; *Ideas I* §36, 64–65/73–75.

9 Though he does not cite Gadamer, this idea is echoed by Claude Romano's *Event and World* 148. See, nevertheless, Agamben's important nuance in *Infancy and History* 28–29.

10 See not only Nancy and Romano, but also a number of recent phenomenological contributions: Romano, *Event and World* 144–50; Nancy, *The Experience of Freedom* 20; Falque, *Le livre de l'expérience* 21–22; Pattison, *A Phenomenology of the Devout Life* 202; Stiegler, *Nietzsche et la critique de la chair* 42. Lacoue-Labarthe and Romano both cite Roger Munier's helpful etymology "Réponse à une enquête sur l'expérience" 37:

> *Experience* comes from the Latin *experiri*, to test, try, prove. The radical is *periri*, which one also finds in *periculum*, peril, danger. The Indo-European root is *per*, to which are attached the ideas of *crossing* and, secondarily, of *trial, test*. In Greek, numerous derivations evoke a crossing or passage: *peirô*, to cross; *pera*, beyond; *peraô*, to pass through; *perainô*, to go to the end; *peras*, end, limit. For Germanic languages, Old High German *faran* has given us *fahren*, to transport, and *führen*, to drive. Should we attribute *Erfahrung* to this origin as well, or should it be linked to the second meaning of *per*, trial, in Old High German *fara*, danger, which became *Gefahr*, danger, and *gefährden*, to endanger? [...] The same is true for the Latin *periri*, to try, and *periculum*, which originally means trial, test, then risk, danger. The idea of experience as a crossing is

etymologically and semantically difficult to separate from that of risk. From the beginning and no doubt in a fundamental sense, *experience* means to endanger.

11 See, for example, Romano on the experience of illness in *Event and World* 149. For a theological account of this idea, see Bultmann, *What Is Theology?* 76: "*Revelation is an event* that sets me in a new situation, brings to light possibilities previously veiled from me [...] In crime, for example, abysses of human nature are disclosed to me. Through an experience my 'eyes are opened.'"

12 For examples, see Nancy, *The Muses* 19–20; Romano, *Event and World* 163.

13 This is a central theme of Romano's work as a whole, see especially: *There Is* 62; *Event and Time* 152; *Event and World* 150–57, 162–63. For commentary, see my "The Event of Faith."

14 See *Event and World* 144.

15 For examples of the French, see Falque, *Le livre de l'expérience* 15, 21–23; Romano, *Event and World* 144–46. For the German, see Heidegger, *On the Way to Language* 57:

> To undergo an experience (*eine Erfahrung machen*) with something [...] means that this something befalls us (*widerfährt*), strikes us, comes over us, overwhelms and transforms us. When we talk of "undergoing" an experience, we mean specifically that the experience is not of our own making; to undergo (*durchmachen*) here means that we endure it, suffer it, receive it as it strikes us and submit to it.

16 A phrase picked up by: Romano, *Event and World* 161; Falque, *Le livre de l'expérience* 16; Gadamer 350–51.

17 On experience in Kierkegaard, especially on the problematic notion of *religious* experience, see Pattison, *Kierkegaard's Upbuilding Discourses* 56–62.

18 The guiding intuition for this method is captured by Kierkegaard in his *Upbuilding Discourses* 22: "When two people learn different things from life, it can be because they experience different things, but it can also be because they themselves were different."

19 See Caputo, *Against Ethics* 26.

20 See Hegel, *Elements of the Philosophy of Right* §145/189.

21 In Nietzsche, too, "being [...] ethical means obeying ancient established law or custom" (*Genealogy of Morals* §96/169), whilst the origin of these mores is the idea that "society is worth more than the individual" (§89/174). By contrast, *Moralität*, in Kant as in Hegel, is always primarily *individual*, the universal that reveals its reality to me as *singular individual* (subjectively and experientially) – i.e., borrowing an expression from Romano (*Event and World* 160), it is an *undergoing* that makes me "universal *by virtue* of being singular." For examples, see Hegel, *Elements of the Philosophy of Right* §106/135; Kant, *Critique of Practical Reason* 5: 8/12.

22 Caputo, too, has identified this correctly, see *Against Ethics* 11–12.

23 See further Kierkegaard, *Concluding Unscientific Postscript* 224–25.

24 For Kant, morality is a *fact* (*Faktum*) of reason: not an experience given *to* us from without (empirically), but nevertheless experience generated *by* reason from within (rationally); something reason *does*, in the sense of *facere* and thus a *factum*, the very *action* in which reason exists. On this, see Kant, *Critique of Practical Reason* 5: 6/9, 5: 31/45–46; Nancy, *A Finite Thinking* 143–45. Caputo, too, constantly stresses this idea, ultimately ascribing to it the structure of our facticity along the lines of Heidegger's *Befindlichkeit*, in *Against Ethics* 5–7, 15, 18–19, 22, 25–27, 70 (22): "Here I am (*me voici*, Levinas), faced with a fact, as it were (Kant), in a pregiven factical situation (Heidegger)."

25 For an account of experience in terms of the possibility of the im-possible, see Derrida, *On the Name* 43; *Psyche I* 15; "A Certain Impossible Possibility of Saying the Event" 451. For an account of experience in terms of a transformation of possibility (Romano) or metamorphosis of finitude (Falque), see Romano, *Event and World* 31; *Event and Time* 185–92; Falque, *The Metamorphosis of Finitude*. For an account of experience in terms of the hyper-realism of the call, see Caputo, *The Weakness of God* 9–12, 102, 112, 121–24.

26 That surprise is a mode of experience characteristic of the event is a widely shared observation

(Derrida, Caputo and Romano), but is especially well described by Nancy in *Being Singular Plural* 159–76.

27 Of course, Abraham does say something to Isaac (Genesis 22.7–8), but this does not mean that he *breaks the silence*. As Derrida writes in *The Gift of Death* 60:

> But even if he says everything, he need only keep silent on one single thing for it to be concluded that he hasn't spoken. Such a silence takes over his whole discourse [...] He speaks in order not to say anything about the essential thing that he must keep secret [...] To that extent, in not saying the essential thing, namely the secret between God and him, Abraham doesn't speak, he assumes the responsibility that consists in always being alone, retrenched in one's own singularity at the moment of decision.

28 On this, see Nancy, *A Finite Thinking* 12, 74–76; but especially Romano, *Event and World* 161–62:

> asserting that the humanity of a human being [...] is ex-per-ience, signifies that a human being's humanity is never a "given," a generic essence that transcends individuals, but is what is reached with great struggle at the price of an ordeal [...] A human being does not have experiences; ex-per-ience is rather what makes it possible to conceive of her in her humanity.

29 See Kant, *Religion with the Bounds of Bare Reason* 87/98.

30 This is somewhat remarkable, as Luther famously described the text as an "epistle of straw." For more on Kierkegaard as a reader of James, see Richard Bauckham's *James* 159–74.

31 The actual influence on Nancy might be Nietzsche, however. Compare, for example, the following quotations, which all go back to James. Nietzsche, *The Anti-Christ* §39/35: "only the *practice* of Christianity is really Christian, *living* like the man who died on the cross [...] *Not* a believing but a doing, above all a *not*-doing-much, a different *being*." Kierkegaard, *Upbuilding Discourses* 173 (my emphasis):

> As long as he merely hears the Word, he is outside it, and when the proclaimer is

silent, he hears nothing; but when he *does* the Word, he continually hears what he himself is proclaiming to himself. And any hearing of the Word is infinitely more imperfect than the *doing*.

Nancy, *Dis-Enclosure* 52–53:

What James [...] would have us understand is that faith is its own work. It *is* in works, it *makes* them, and the works *make* it [...] Contrary to Paul (Romans 4), James maintains that Abraham is justified by his work, designated as the offering of Isaac [...] According to Paul, what is important is that Abraham *believed* that God could give him a son, against all natural evidence. His act thus depended on a knowledge postulate [...] For James, on the contrary, Abraham *did*. He offered up Isaac. It is not said there that he judged, considered, or believed [...] James' Abraham is not in the economy of assurances [...] Abraham is neither persuaded nor convinced: his assent is not in the *logismos*. It is only in the *ergon* [...] The reasons that this faith has "to believe" are not reasons.

Kierkegaard, *Upbuilding Discourses* 24:

You perceived that you had not based your faith on the circumstance that you could explain what happened, since in that case your faith would have been based on your insight and, far from being a devotedness, would instead have been a confidence in yourself.

32 See also Agamben, *The Man Without Content* 42–57.

33 See also Nancy, *The Experience of Freedom* 85.

34 See further Ward, *How the Light Gets In* 166–70.

35 See further Bultmann, *New Testament & Mythology* 123.

36 Nancy alludes to Nietzsche, *The Anti-Christ* §34/ 32.

37 See John 17.13–19, especially as developed by Augustine, *Tractates on the Gospel of John, 55–111* 107–08/273–82; Bultmann, *The Gospel of John* 507–08; *Theology of the New Testament II* 75–79, 85–86.

38 See the competing accounts of Marion and Caputo: Marion, *The Visible and the Revealed* 18–48; Caputo, "The Hyperbolization of Phenomenology" 67–93. For a discussion of this debate in relation to Nancy, see my "Givenness and Existence."

39 See Bultmann, *Existence and Faith* 63–66.

40 For Nancy's account of expectation in a different context that nevertheless resonates with Kierkegaard insofar as it centres expectation around a "hope to achieve the freedom of the narrative or myth, which no concept can touch" (vii), see his *Expectation*.

41 Bultmann offers a theological version in *Theology of the New Testament I* 334: "For freedom is nothing else than being open for the genuine future, letting one's self be determined by that future."

42 On this Augustinian motif picked up by Caputo and Derrida, see Caputo, *The Prayers and Tears of Jacques Derrida* 282–339; *On Religion* 28, 115, 127; Derrida, "Circumfession" 47–49.

43 This poetics of faith thus gives way to a poetics of creation, which I have articulated in my "Imagining the World Otherwise."

bibliography

Aeschylus. *Aeschylus II: Agamemnon, Libation-Bearers, Eumenides, Fragments*. Trans. Herbert Weir Smyth. Cambridge, MA: Harvard UP, 1960. Print.

Agamben, Giorgio. *Infancy and History: On the Destruction of Experience*. Trans. Liz Heron. London: Verso, 2006. Print.

Agamben, Giorgio. *The Man Without Content*. Trans. Georgia Albert. Stanford: Stanford UP, 1999. Print.

Augustine. *Tractates on the Gospel of John, 55–111*. Trans. John W. Retting. Washington: Catholic U of America P, 1994. Print.

Bauckham, Richard. *James: Wisdom of James, Disciple of Jesus the Sage*. London: Routledge, 1999. Print.

Bultmann, Rudolf. *Existence and Faith: Shorter Writings of Rudolf Bultmann*. Ed. and trans. Schubert M. Ogden. New York: Meridian, 1960. Print.

Bultmann, Rudolf. *The Gospel of John: A Commentary.* Trans. G.R. Beasley-Murray. Oxford: Blackwell, 1971. Print.

Bultmann, Rudolf. *New Testament & Mythology and Other Basic Writings.* Ed. and trans. Schubert M. Ogden. London: SCM, 1984. Print.

Bultmann, Rudolf. *Theology of the New Testament.* Vol. I. Trans. Kendrick Grobel. London: SCM, 1953. Print.

Bultmann, Rudolf. *Theology of the New Testament.* Vol. II. Trans. Kendrick Grobel. London: SCM, 1955. Print.

Bultmann, Rudolf. *What Is Theology?* Ed. Eberhard Jüngel and Klaus W. Müller. Trans. Roy A. Harrisville. Minneapolis: Fortress, 1997. Print.

Caputo, John D. *Against Ethics: Contributions to a Poetics of Obligation with Constant Reference to Deconstruction.* Bloomington: Indiana UP, 1993. Print.

Caputo, John D. *How to Read Kierkegaard.* London: Granta, 2007. Print.

Caputo, John D. "The Hyperbolization of Phenomenology: Two Possibilities for Religion in Recent Continental Philosophy." *Counter-Experiences: Reading Jean-Luc Marion.* Ed. Kevin Hart. Notre Dame: U of Notre Dame P, 2007. Print.

Caputo, John D. *On Religion.* London: Routledge, 2001. Print.

Caputo, John D. *The Prayers and Tears of Jacques Derrida: Religion without Religion.* Bloomington: Indiana UP, 1997. Print.

Caputo, John D. *Radical Hermeneutics: Repetition, Deconstruction and the Hermeneutic Project.* Bloomington: Indiana UP, 1988. Print.

Caputo, John D. *Truth: The Search for Wisdom in the Postmodern Age.* London: Penguin, 2013. Print.

Caputo, John D. *The Weakness of God: A Theology of the Event.* Bloomington: Indiana UP, 2006. Print.

Deketelaere, Nikolaas. "The Event of Faith: The Transformation of Philosophy by Theology in Rudolf Bultmann." *Open Theology* 5.1 (Mar. 2019): 259–77. Print.

Deketelaere, Nikolaas. "Givenness and Existence: On the Possibility of a Phenomenological Philosophy of Religion." *Palgrave Communications* 4.1 (2018): 1–13. Print.

Deketelaere, Nikolaas. "Imagining the World Otherwise: Jean-Luc Nancy and John Caputo on the Poetics of Creation." *Literature and Theology* 34.1 (Mar. 2020): 1–18. Print.

Derrida, Jacques. "A Certain Impossible Possibility of Saying the Event." Trans. Gila Walker. *Critical Inquiry* 33 (Winter 2007): 441–61. Print.

Derrida, Jacques. "Circumfession: Fifty-Nine Periods and Periphrases." In Geoffrey Bennington and Jacques Derrida. *Jacques Derrida.* Chicago: Chicago UP, 1993. Print.

Derrida, Jacques. *The Gift of Death, Second Edition & Literature in Secret.* Trans. David Willis. Chicago: Chicago UP, 2008. Print.

Derrida, Jacques. *On the Name.* Ed. Thomas Dutoit. Stanford: Stanford UP, 1995. Print.

Derrida, Jacques. *On Touching – Jean-Luc Nancy.* Trans. Christine Irizarry. Stanford: Stanford UP, 2005. Print.

Derrida, Jacques. *Psyche: Inventions of the Other.* Vol. I. Ed. and trans. Peggy Kamuf and Elizabeth Rottenberg. Stanford: Stanford UP, 2007. Print.

Dilthey, Wilhelm. "Fragments for a Poetics" (1907–1908). Trans. Rudolf A. Makkreel in *Selected Works,* Vol. V: *Poetry and Experience.* Ed. Rudolf A. Makkreel and Frithjof Rodi. Princeton: Princeton UP, 1985. Print.

Falque, Emmanuel. *Le livre de l'expérience: D'Anselme de Cantorbéry à Bernard de Clairvaux.* Paris: Cerf, 2017. Print.

Falque, Emmanuel. *The Metamorphosis of Finitude: An Essay on Birth and Resurrection.* Trans. George Hughes. New York: Fordham UP, 2012. Print.

Gadamer, Hans-Georg. *Truth and Method.* Trans. Joel Weinsheimer and Donald G. Marshall. London: Continuum, 2004. Print.

Hegel, G.W.F. *Elements of the Philosophy of Right.* Trans. H.B. Nisbet. Cambridge: Cambridge UP, 1991. Print.

Heidegger, Martin. *On the Way to Language.* Trans. Peter D. Herz. New York: Harper, 1971. Print.

Husserl, Edmund. *Cartesian Meditations: An Introduction to Phenomenology.* Trans. Dorian Cairns. The Hague: Martinus Nijhoff, 1960. Print.

Husserl, Edmund. *Ideas Pertaining to a Pure Phenomenology and to a Phenomenological Philosophy I*. Trans. F. Kersten. The Hague: Martinus Nijhoff, 1983. Print.

Husserl, Edmund. *Logical Investigations*. Vol. II. Ed. Dermot Moran. Trans. J.N. Findlay. London: Routledge, 2001. Print.

Kant, Immanuel. *Critique of Practical Reason*. Trans. Werner S. Pluhar. Cambridge: Hackett, 2002. Print.

Kant, Immanuel. *Religion with the Bounds of Bare Reason*. Trans. Werner S. Pluhar. Cambridge: Hackett, 2009. Print.

Kierkegaard, Søren. *Concluding Unscientific Postscript*. Trans. Alastair Hannay. Cambridge: Cambridge UP, 2009. Print.

Kierkegaard, Søren. *Fear and Trembling*. Trans. Alastair Hannay. London: Penguin, 1985. Print.

Kierkegaard, Søren. *Journals and Papers*, Vol. VI: *Autobiographical Part Two (1848–1855)*. Ed. and trans. Howard V. Hong and Edna H. Hong. Bloomington: Indiana UP, 1978. Print.

Kierkegaard, Søren. *Kierkegaard's Writings*, Vol. V: *Eighteen Upbuilding Discourses*. Ed. and trans. Howard V. Hong and Edna H. Hong. Princeton: Princeton UP, 1992. Print.

Kline, Peter. *Passion for Nothing: Kierkegaard's Apophatic Theology*. Minneapolis: Fortress, 2017. Print.

Lacoue-Labarthe, Philippe. *Poetry as Experience*. Trans. Andrea Tarnowski. Stanford: Stanford UP, 1999. Print.

Lévinas, Emmanuel. *Proper Names*. Trans. Michael B. Smith. Stanford: Stanford UP, 1996. Print.

MacIntyre, Alasdair. *After Virtue: A Study in Moral Theory*. London: Bloomsbury, 2007. Print.

Marion, Jean-Luc. *The Visible and the Revealed*. Trans. Christina M. Gschwandtner et al. New York: Fordham UP, 2008. Print.

Merleau-Ponty, Maurice. *Sense and Non-Sense*. Trans. Hubert Dreyfus and Patricia Dreyfus. Evanston: Northwestern UP, 1992. Print.

Munier, Roger. "Réponse à une enquête sur l'expérience." *Mise en page* I (May 1972): 37. Print.

Nancy, Jean-Luc. *Adoration: The Deconstruction of Christianity II*. Trans. John McKeane. New York: Fordham UP, 2013. Print.

Nancy, Jean-Luc. *Being Singular Plural*. Trans. Robert Richardson and Anne O'Byrne. Stanford: Stanford UP, 2000. Print.

Nancy, Jean-Luc. *The Birth to Presence*. Trans. Brian Holmes et al. Stanford: Stanford UP, 1994. Print.

Nancy, Jean-Luc. *Corpus*. Trans. Richard A. Rand. New York: Fordham UP, 2008. Print.

Nancy, Jean-Luc. *Dis-Enclosure: The Deconstruction of Christianity*. Trans. Bettina Bergo et al. New York: Fordham UP, 2008. Print.

Nancy, Jean-Luc. *Expectation: Philosophy, Literature*. Trans. Robert Bononno. New York: Fordham UP, 2018. Print.

Nancy, Jean-Luc. *The Experience of Freedom*. Trans. Bridget McDonald. Stanford: Stanford UP, 1994. Print.

Nancy, Jean-Luc. *A Finite Thinking*. Ed. Simon Sparks. Trans. Simon Sparks et al. Stanford: Stanford UP, 2003. Print.

Nancy, Jean-Luc. *Multiple Arts: The Muses II*. Ed. and trans. Simon Sparks. Stanford: Stanford UP, 2006. Print.

Nancy, Jean-Luc. *The Muses*. Trans. Peggy Kamuf. Stanford: Stanford UP, 1997.

Nancy, Jean-Luc. "Un mot d'accompagnement." In Søren Gosvig Olesen. *Avec Kierkegaard: La philosophie dans le texte*. Paris: Mimésis, 2017. Print.

Nietzsche, Friedrich. *The Anti-Christ, Ecce Homo, Twilight of the Idols, and Other Writings*. Trans. Judith Norman. Cambridge: Cambridge UP, 2005. Print.

Nietzsche, Friedrich. *On the Genealogy of Morals and Ecce Homo*. Trans. Walter Kaufmann and R.J. Hollingdale. New York: Vintage, 1967. Print.

Pattison, George. *Kierkegaard's Upbuilding Discourses: Philosophy, Literature and Theology*. London: Routledge, 2013. Print.

Pattison, George. *A Phenomenology of the Devout Life: A Philosophy of Christian Life, Part I*. Oxford: Oxford UP, 2018. Print.

Romano, Claude. *Event and Time*. Trans. Stephen E. Lewis. New York: Fordham UP, 2013. Print.

Romano, Claude. *Event and World*. Trans. Shane Mackinlay. New York: Fordham UP, 2009. Print.

Romano, Claude. *There Is: The Event and Finitude of Appearing*. Trans. Michael B. Smith. New York: Fordham UP, 2016. Print.

Stiegler, Barbara. *Nietzsche et la critique de la chair*. Paris: PUF, 2001. Print.

Ward, Graham. *How the Light Gets In: Ethical Life I*. Oxford: Oxford UP, 2016. Print.

Ward, Graham. "*Kenosis, Poiesis* and *Genesis*: Or the Theological Aesthetics of Suffering." *Encounter Between Eastern Orthodoxy and Radical Orthodoxy: Transfiguring the World Through the Word*. Ed. Adrian Pabst and Christoph Schneider. Farnham: Ashgate, 2009. Print.

Westphal, Merold. "Abraham and Sacrifice." *Neue Zeitschrift für Systematische Theologie und Religionsphilosophie* 50.3–4 (2008): 318–30. Print.

Westphal, Merold. *Kierkegaard's Critique of Reason and Society*. Macon: Mercer UP, 1987. Print.

1 introduction

"This means it is the gods who make us speak" (Nancy, *Adoration* 68). With this sentence, Jean-Luc Nancy concludes a reflection on the excessive dimension of human speech in *Adoration*:

> Excessive speech speaks indefinitely, in the exuberance of literary inventions, the profusion of fictions, and the proliferation of discourses, but it also speaks infinitely – and then one no longer hears it, there is nothing more to hear. It resonates only in the voice itself, in a murmur, a rubbing of the voice against itself, hesitating on the threshold of speech. This is the extreme intimacy of the voice, the buried heart of language, a groaning of suffering or of jouissance, a brushing up against sense. (67)

The excess of language, found in literary inventions, fictions, and discourses, thus borders on a deficit or absence of language. Excessive language exceeds what the human ear can hear and makes language withdraw in a particular muteness or murmur on the threshold of speech. The figure of the threshold is marked by a basic ambiguity. On the one hand, it is the passageway and the opening up towards another space, another room, another horizon, another discourse, another person. On the other hand, and this is what Nancy emphasizes in the quotation, the threshold marks the border separating language from its "buried heart," from the *phōnē*, the mere animal voice "groaning of suffering or of jouissance" that did not

gert-jan van der heiden

INTERPRETERS OF THE DIVINE
nancy's poet, jeremiah the prophet, and saint paul's glossolalist

yet enter the realm of sense but is "brushing up against sense," coming close to touch it and become significant.

This reflection on the threshold of speech concludes with the sentence I started with: "This means it is the gods who make us speak" (Nancy, *Adoration* 68). Apparently, it is there were the gods, in relation to language, are to be found, at the heart of human speech, "effaced in speech, confused with call and response," as Nancy adds. The question is: how to bear witness in language to this "buried heart of language"?

This is an Open Access article distributed under the terms of the Creative Commons Attribution-NonCommercial-NoDerivatives License (http://creativecommons.org/licenses/by-nc-nd/4.0/), which permits non-commercial re-use, distribution, and reproduction in any medium, provided the original work is properly cited, and is not altered, transformed, or built upon in any way.

In this essay, I think with Nancy to see what is at stake in the figure of a voice on the threshold of speech and communication. I consider how the figure of the gods that make us speak is brought into play to elucidate the threshold of language and how this figure, as that which makes us speak, somehow offers the crossing of this threshold. To this end, I want to discuss three different figures or scenes in which the gods make us speak. The first one is found in Nancy's work. The ancient Greek experience of the poet's speech, as we can find it in the opening of Homer's *Iliad* and in Socrates' interrogation of the rhapsode *Ion* in Plato's dialogue of the same name, offers a paradigm for the divine inspiration of human speech. There are, however, other figures whom the gods make speak. In particular, the figure of the prophet Jeremiah and the scene of his calling and Saint Paul's reflections on the glossolalist in the First Letter to the Corinthians, offer us two different interpreters that further elucidate the phenomenon of gods making us speak and that problematize certain aspects of the poetic figure and scene. (For a more extensive analysis of the relation between poet, prophet, glossolalist, and interpreter, see Van der Heiden, *The Voice of Misery* 179–90.)

2 nancy's ancient greek poet

In "Answering for Sense," Nancy unfolds the particular hermeneutic structure of the poet's voice that he discerns in the opening sentence of Homer's *Iliad* – "Sing, o goddess, the anger" or "The wrath sing, goddess." As Nancy comments:

> Homer does not write himself: He lets the divine voice sing. Him, the *aède*, he sings in as much as he interprets the divine song – this song that he asks her to sing [...]: He does in this way what he expects her to do in order for him to eclipse himself in this song – his own (hers) becoming his own (his), yet always remaining this divine song. He thus lets the voice sing, or else he makes it heard, he recites it. ("Answering for Sense" 84–85)

As the essay progresses, Nancy weaves the different elements that demonstrate the complexity of poetic speech. The poet sings, but goddess sings; the divine voice dictates and calls the poet to commitment, but the divine voice is only heard in and by the poetic response to this demand, that is, in the poet's enactment of this commitment. As Nancy notes: "[The poet] shares the commitment of an outside voice," and "[the poet] commits to it when his turn comes, he renders polyphonic the voice that came to him as a soliloquy" (86). The divine voice is a promise – a *Zusage* in Heidegger's sense of the word – to grant both the voice that sings and the words that need to be sung, but it is a promise which can only be redeemed by and in the poet's actual singing for the goddess. The poetic voice appears, thus, from the very first sentence of the *Iliad*, as two-voiced, double-tongued if you like, because there are always two voices at least: *aede* and *thea*; singer and goddess. Neither of these voices can be said to come first. A voice is never alone, as Nancy notes:

> A voice in itself is not a voice: It's a silence that does not even have the space of an address, it's a muting enclosed in its buzzing, in its roaring or in its murmur (the repetition of a mute *mmm – mutum*). A voice is always two voices at least, always polyphonized somehow. (86)

This results in the following description of the *hermeneutic* activity of the poet, in which hermeneutics and interpretation is directly understood as a form of bearing witness:

> He bears witness to *thea's* existence and he takes upon himself his desire: the desire he has for *thea* and the desire that *thea* is herself.
> Witness to *thea's* existence, he declares his own self as being her *aede*, that is, also her hermeneut. The hermeneut is not first the one who deciphers and who decodes significations, even if he has to, at times, do just that [...] The hermeneut is not first the one who signifies *what is* said: He is the one who carries the desire to say further. The hermeneut supplements the subject with his desire: He presents *thea* and makes her

be heard in the very voice – her own voice – by which he convokes her [...] he also bears witness to her nature, and to how the latter is entirely made of this sharing of voices of whom *he*, he who writes (or she), is a part, a moment, an accent, and a sense beside so many others. (Nancy, "Answering for Sense" 90–91)

Let me unfold a number of elements that this longer quote offers and connect them to some themes we find elsewhere in Nancy's work.

(1) Nancy offers here a particular sense of hermeneutics or interpretation modelled on the poet's activity. With this suggestion, he remains faithful to his account to develop a primordial sense of hermeneutics as suggested in, for instance, "Sharing Voices" and "The Forgetting of Philosophy" (see also Van der Heiden, "Reading Bartleby, Reading Ion" and *Ontology After Ontotheology* 74–92). This account takes its point of departure in a hint that we can find in Heidegger's *On the Way to Language* where in the latter he distinguishes hermeneutics in the sense of the art of interpretation from a more primordial sense of "the hermeneutical," which still resounds in the Greek verb *hermēneuein* and the noun *hermēneus*, or interpreter, as it is used in Plato's *Ion*. Adopting Plato's playful relation of hermeneutics and the god Hermes, Heidegger suggests that "the hermeneutical" concerns "the bearing of message and tidings" (29). The interpreter carries, bears, and brings the message to convey it to the listeners. Note that in the French, the verb *porter* translates the German *bringen*: "'Hermès porte l'annonce du destin,'" as Nancy quotes Heidegger's "[Hermes] bringt die Botschaft des Geschickes" (Nancy, *Le partage des voix* 82; Heidegger, *Unterwegs zur Sprache* 115). Similarly, the German *zur Sprache bringen* is translated as *porter à parole* (Nancy, *Le partage des voix* 30). I will return to the importance of *porter* below.

The reader of Heidegger has to wait until Nancy's "Sharing Voices" to find a genuine account of this Heideggerian hint. In this text, Nancy offers a genuinely hermeneutical alternative to the more classical senses of hermeneutics developed by authors such as Gadamer and Ricoeur, for whom hermeneutics remains the art of interpretation, that is, an art that presupposes a particular signification that attracts the interpretation and that generates hermeneutic desire. Nancy fully acknowledges that hermeneutics understood as the unfolding or the deciphering of a particular signification has its own epistemological significance, but it cannot reach into the sense of hermeneutics that is attained in the ancient Greek understanding of poetic speech.

The poet-interpreter is not someone who deciphers and explicates significations. Rather, poets are enthusiasts who speak not by their own knowledge (*epistēmē*) or skills (*technai*), but because the gods make them speak. The poets receive – but never possess – the ability "to compose that to which the Muse has stirred him" (534c), as Socrates suggests in the *Ion*. Their task is first and foremost to hand down and hand out the *theia moira*, the divine dispensation – *le partage divin* as Nancy translates, thus coining his usage of *partage* – that moves them. To emphasize the distance between *epistēmē* or *technē* and the activity of the poets, Socrates emphasizes that as long as a human has its mind "in him," he "is powerless to indite a verse or chant an oracle" (534b). The poets are interpreters of the divine voice only when they are possessed by a divine force – *theia dunamis* – and when they are out of their minds; in Greek: *nous*, which is the same term used in Saint Paul's 1 Cor. 14.

When the poets sing, they do not know what they sing, they have no understanding of what they sing. In this sense, when the poet is called a *hermēneus*, an interpreter of the gods, this cannot refer to someone who seeks to explicate or decipher the words of the gods. To be an interpreter means to voice the words of the gods, to lend one's own voice so that the gods may speak with it. With the fortunate distinction between divine force and signification, the *Ion* suggests that poets do not communicate significations that can be understood, but rather a divine force or power by which they themselves are possessed. Moreover, it is this being-possessed (or being-inspired: *entheos*) that is handed down to the audience. Those who listen to the songs of poets and rhapsodes are captivated as well. They share in the inspiration that makes the poet's voice speak. As Socrates notes in the *Ion*: "the god himself is the one who speaks, and he gives voice through them to us" (534d). The voice of the poet is thus also in the *Ion* a double voice – the poet sings, but the gods sing. Because there is no divine voice outside of the human voice of the poet, as Nancy emphasizes in his reading of this dialogue, the divine voice *is* only as this voice doubled in the poet's voice. For purists, it will therefore always remain unclear who speaks, either the poet or the god, because they always speak together, at the same time, with this one tongue and one mouth that combines poetic and divine voice.

To hand down, to transmit, and to carry further thus form for Nancy the basic sense of hermeneutics in the ancient Greek paradigm of the poet. As he insists in "Sharing Voices," even the rhapsode, although he appears to be second in rank, does not diminish in any sense the *theia dunamis*, the divine power that he passes on: "the divine force is transmitted intact – but exactly as it *is to be transmitted*, and it is with the second ring that it manifests entirely this property" (237–38). Hence, the rhapsode demonstrates even more purely or univocally that the hermeneut is a passageway that is the very condition of possibility of communicating the divine power. The hermeneut enables the transmission and circulation of the divine force, allows it to move from one towards the other.

In turn, this determination of hermeneutics affects Nancy's account of sense. The following quote from *The Sense of the World* mirrors the two forms of hermeneutics – explication vs. transmission – in two senses of sense: "Sense is consequently not the 'signified' or the 'message': it is *that something like transmission of a 'message' should be possible*. It is the relation as such and nothing else" (118). We find a similar difference in "Sharing Voices": "[meaning] is abandoned to [*abandonner à*] the sharing [*partage*], to the hermeneutic

law of the difference between voices, and that it is not *a gift*, anterior and exterior to our voices and our orations" (244). The signified and the message are the forms of sense that are sought for when explicating or deciphering. A more primordial sense of sense, however, concerns transmissibility itself, the movement towards the other, the movement of making communal. When a voice, in Nancy's vocabulary of *Adoration*, brushes up against sense, it finds itself on the brink or the threshold of this transmissibility, about to reach the other. In the Socratic paradigm of the iron rings, the magnetic force itself, *theia moira, theia dunamis*, accounts for this transmissibility.

(2) For Nancy, desire is bifurcated by the same difference that traverses hermeneutics and sense. If hermeneutic desire is understood as the desire to decipher or explicate a pre-given signification, hermeneutics basically repeats an onto-theological structure, which Nancy therefore calls *onto-theo-eroto-logy* (*The Sense of the World* 51). This term refers to the *presupposition* of meaning – or of a transcendental signified – that generates the desire for meaning as the desire for something that *can be* appropriated, although it is always postponed and deferred.

There is, however, another form of desire, not one that desires to appropriate but rather to hand down, to pass on, and to relate "one toward the other." It is desire in this second sense, thought on the basis of a primordial hermeneutics that we encounter in the quote from "Answering for Sense." Here, Nancy determines the basic mood of the poet's responsiveness as desire; the poet "carries the desire to say further" – the poet is the *porte-voix* of the goddess "porte plus loin le désir de dire" (see also Nancy, "Sharing Voices" 45n29, 71n51). The motive of carrying, *porter*, is inscribed in the subsequent determination of poetic speech as *bearing witness*; the poet is the witness, *témoin*, of the existence of the goddess and of her nature, *le partage des voix*, the sharing of voices. The desire to *carry* the goddess in her existence and her nature, which is itself a carrying further or a carrying on of the desire to speak, marks this other form of *porter*, which in English we render as "to bear," namely to *bearing* witness, *porter témoignage*. The existence and the nature of the goddess, so this primordial scene of poetic speech suggests, is not without this motive of the *porte-voix qui porte plus loin, qui porte témoignage et qui porte en lui-même*. The poet is, thus, not the witness who merely sees or experiences, but the witness who brings the goddess's existence and nature to a certain completion by carrying it (cf. also Agamben 148–50).

This relation of the poet and the goddess, which concerns a carrying that carries outward and carries further, does raise the question of where exactly the voice brushes up against sense and where it is only running up against the threshold of a speech that transmits and carries further. How is the hermeneutic desire evoked and to which deficit does it respond if it is not the absence of a hidden signification? Two other figures, that of the prophet and the glossolalist, offer two different scenes of gods making humans speak which both concern the realm preceding the actual transmission, that is, a realm in which transmissibility is not yet given but genuinely longed for.

3 the prophet's calling

Although the Homeric poet is dictated and somehow called by the goddess, the *Iliad*'s song opens with the poet speaking and calling on the goddess to sing. The first word, here, is the poet's. The biblical scene of a comparable figure, the prophet Jeremiah, offers another beginning. The first chapter of Jeremiah depicts the stages preceding any opening sentence of a poetic song or a prophetic declaration. Among the group of divine hermeneuts, Jeremiah stands out, perhaps, exactly because the story of his calling itself is narrated. If you like, the particular structure of "dictation" is unfolded: the story of becoming the one who carries the divine voice is told.

(1) Jeremiah is called to be a prophet. What is the temporal structure of such a call? It is not simply confined to the moment or the event of the actual address. The call's temporal structure is more complicated. In fact, so the story goes, the calling precedes the prophet's very existence. He is called from before he was born and even from before he was formed in the womb of his mother (Jer. 1.5). Although the call cannot reach the prophet himself in these prior stages of and to his existence, it is clear that this call somehow forms the horizon of this existence – it is like the murmur in which his existence is embedded, although he does not (yet) hear or understand it. Here, the call genuinely remains on the threshold, not reaching the one who is called, not yet addressing the prophet. This immemorial dimension of the calling, which is not heard and does not yet actually address, is supplemented – perhaps even completed – at the moment when the address reaches its addressee. The moment discloses another temporal dimension of the call: it is an event taking place here and now – here and now I am called, as Jeremiah experiences. Yet, the content of this announcement is not only this here and now; rather, the call makes itself known as a call older and more ancient than existence, as a calling which apparently was there, always already, immemorial, on the threshold of an actual address, but still holding itself in reserve, brushing up against sense, awaiting the moment to cross the threshold and transform into a call that actually reaches the prophet's ear and understanding. The call has the capacity to call to another existence, but at the same time this is the existence to which the prophet has always already been called, from before his existence, with a murmuring call awaiting the event of its transformation into sense.

(2) When the call reaches Jeremiah, his very first response – because there is a *first* response in this story – is not to hand down towards others and to carry the desire to say and to call further, which is the prophet's task. Rather, he responds: "I cannot speak" (Jer. 1.6). It is important to emphasize that this response is not the expression of a will, that is, of a reluctance or a resistance to speak. It rather speaks of an incapacity. The reason the prophet provides to substantiate his response is that he is too young. He is too young

compared to the ancient call that finally reaches him. Over against this immemorial call to speak, the prophet's capacity to speak for that which calls before and beyond himself is a mere nullity; he is in the state of the infant, the non-speaking-one. Hence, at the very moment when the ancient, divine calling, transforms from an immemorial mute murmur surrounding the prophet's existence into a call that finally makes itself heard, it is this incapacity that manifests itself first and to which the prophet bears witness first; it turns out that he carries this incapacity in himself. When called, he first experiences an *obstruction* with respect to the genuine prophetic task "to carry the desire to say further."

What is the significance of this obstruction? The story, as it unfolds, confronts us with a point of indecision that forces us to interpret, to decipher the meaning of this obstruction. Let me offer two possible interpretations, which together mirror and displace the difference that traverses, according to Nancy, the sense of hermeneutics.

(a) The first reading finds the significance of this incapacity to speak in its service, its subservience to a particular divine economy. After all, as one might suggest, the prophet's incapacity to speak is not a drawback at all, but rather the basic condition of possibility for the divine speaking machine to function properly. God, as the story tells us, subsequently touches the prophet's mouth and puts the divine words in it. The human incapacity to speak and the human's utter insignificance before this God and his call turns out to be the best of fortunes. Because Jeremiah has nothing to say himself, of himself and for himself, his own voice does not add anything to the words that Yahweh puts in his mouth. His mouth, breath, and tongue become – purified from all wanting-to-say, *vouloir-dire*, from all self-contributed meaning – the *pure* vehicle for divine messages and tidings. It is the sovereign God who is fully in control of the prophet's tongue, so that nobody needs to doubt the divine origin of the words that leave the prophet's mouth.

Such a reading, one might suggest, repeats an onto-theo-eroto-logical gesture: the desire

of the prophet to become nothing is introduced here so that the longed-for purified word of God can manifest itself without reserve and without contamination. It is as if the story of this original calling and the prophet's original response are introduced as a fictional origin to ward off or to neutralize the basic experience of the *hearing* of the word of God that Derrida so strikingly describes in *The Gift of Death*:

> I hear tell what he says, through the voice of another, another other, a messenger, an angel, a prophet, a messiah or postman [*facteur*], a bearer of tidings, an evangelist, an intermediary who speaks between God and myself. (91)

From the perspective of the hearer of prophetic words, there are always messengers, go-betweens who impose themselves in between the hearer and the divine voice. As both Nancy and Derrida suggest in their own way, there is no first, pure or purified divine voice that is simply given and to which the interpreter should simply give way without obstruction. It is with respect to this particular contamination of the divine voice by the go-betweens, which is itself the very condition of possibility of carrying the divine voice further, that the story of the calling offers a supplement – that is, a second supplement in the form of a story of the origin to neutralize the contamination of the supplements that are necessary to hand down the divine words. A supplement to overcome the doubt in the hearers generated by the fact that they only hear the divine voice mediated by others and never immediately.

(b) A second reading focuses on the phenomenological sense of the "I cannot speak" for the prophet himself. It is, in the first place, the acknowledgment and affirmation of a particular lack. This lack does not simply concern the prophet's linguistic capacity as such. Although he thinks he is too young, he can speak – after all, he does speak. It is, however, with respect to the call addressing him that a specific deficit is disclosed and recognized. One might, perhaps, suggest that the divine call can only arise from the immemorial mute murmur that always already surrounded the prophet's existence to an actual call that reaches the addressee *when* the prophet is ready for and capable of recognizing and proclaiming his own incapacity. One might, perhaps, say, to use the distinction Nancy refers to in "Answering for Sense," that the call as mere *phōnē* has to be transformed in an *audē*, in an address, in a voice that can be heard by a human (86). The "I cannot speak" bears witness not to the prophet's incapacity to speak himself or to speak for himself, but rather to his incapacity to speak for the other that calls on him. Confronted with the call to speak for God, the prophet experiences his own capacity to speak as a limited capacity: he can merely speak for himself and not for any other. Exactly in this sense, the "I cannot speak" bears witness to the call and to the having heard the call.

All desire, if one may believe Socrates in the *Symposium*, follows from the recognition and the experience of a deficit as deficit. Desire is marked by a distance and this not only the distance of a signification: "*Desire* [...] *is the empty signifier of the distant signified*, or of the distance of meaning" (Nancy, "The Forgetting of Philosophy" 32). The desire to speak the other (voice) and to speak for the other is born, as desire, from the experience of this deficit, of the incapacity to speak for the other, to reach or touch the other. The call that addresses and that reaches the addressee is therefore to be understood in both its activity and passivity. Actively, it calls the prophet to speak for the other; passively, it only reaches the prophet in whom the desire to speak for the other is (being) born. This active–passive dimension of the call fits perfectly with Nancy's determination of sense: "To think sense as the in-appropriative encounter of desire and gift, as the excellence of the coming of the one toward to other, this is the task" (*The Sense of the World* 52) Actively, the call is a gift to the prophet; passively, the call can only be received in and by an awakened desire in the prophet. Only together, they form the event of the sense of the call.

The awareness that makes the prophet say "I cannot speak" is thus placed in a particular horizon that opens up the prophet's perspective to the promise of a particular displacement of his capacity to speak. This promise announces itself in this incapacity: "Perhaps I can also not speak only myself and only for myself." This possibility is first given as a desire that understands what it lacks. To the expression of this desire in the words of the prophet "I cannot speak," the divinity now indeed responds with a promise that it will grant the words. Touching the prophet's mouth, displacing and cutting in two the tongue, forking the tongue that could only speak for itself, and putting the words in the mouth of the prophet.

The God of Jeremiah, like the poet's Muse, promises, in the Heideggerian sense of *Zusage*, to grant the words that are necessary to speak for the other. Yet, in turn – and here we see the poetic-prophetic "to and fro"-movement – the words are only *actually there* and the promise is only actually redeemed when the poet-prophet speaks them out, carrying the desire to say further. Here, indeed, the prophet bears witness to the existence of the god and their call, by carrying and carrying out the promise that this call harbors from immemorial times onwards.

4 the glossolalist's interpreter

The scene of the prophet's calling concerns the provenance of the hermeneut's speech and desire. This scene needs to be complemented with one that does not concern how hermeneuts themselves are addressed, called, and dictated, but rather how the hermeneut addresses – or to use the imagery of Plato's *Ion* and Nancy's "Sharing Voices": how the hermeneut affects the adjacent iron ring.

To describe how the poet is addressed and affected by the divine voice, Nancy writes: "he shares the commitment [*il partage l'engagement*] of an outside voice" ("Answering for Sense" 86). It is, however, perhaps not self-evident that such a sharing in the divine allows for a further sharing and communication. There seems to be a difference traversing the sense of the outside voice. In fact, the commitment of an outside voice can also constitute a particular sense of inwardness, of a closed dialogue limited to two spirits alone that refuse to communalize their mutual communication to any outsider. This particular circumstance marks the figure of the glossolalist that we find in Saint Paul's 1 Cor. 14. Through the reference to glossolalia, the speaking in tongues, in Kierkegaard's *Fear and Trembling* (114–16) and Derrida's analysis of this phenomenon as a form of sharing what cannot be shared in *The Gift of Death* (73–77), as well as the comparison between the poet's and the glossolalist's speech in Agamben's *Remnants of Auschwitz* (113–15), this phenomenon goes to the heart of the import and reach of Nancy's notion of *partage*. I want to rethink this discussion here in terms of the relation between the Greek poet and the Pauline glossolalist.

The distinguishing feature of glossolalist and prophet concerns exactly the difference in their capacity to address, to communalize or to build up a community or communality. Let me note in passing that this sense "upbuilding," sometimes translated in English as "edifying," but that is in fact a somewhat unfortunate translation, is one of Kierkegaard's most cherished terms. The verb "to build up" translates the Greek *oikodomeō*, the building up of a house, a realm to dwell in and to inhabit together. It stems from Saint Paul's letters, is used in particular in 1 Corinthians (1 Cor. 8.1; 1 Cor. 10.23) and plays a crucial role in 1 Cor. 14, where it is used at least four times, to distinguish between the fertile speech that builds up the community, that is, that allows the divine voice and address to communalize, from the speaking in tongues that, under particular circumstances, does not allow for such a communalization. As soon as we read this, bearing in mind Nancy's critical assessment of the conception that approaches community as a work in *The Inoperative Community*, we know that we have to be attentive to how the "upbuilding" character functions as a demarcation criterion in Saint Paul's considerations.

The distinction between glossolalist and poet does not mean that the glossolalist is not engaged in or committed to the divine voice. Quite the contrary. The remarkable character of glossolalia consists for Saint Paul exactly in the fact that it constitutes a kind of immediate interaction between the human spirit (*pneuma*) and the divine. This in itself is a positive phenomenon, as Saint Paul notes: "Those who speak in a tongue build up themselves" (1 Cor. 14.4). Yet, he distinguishes and hierarchizes between this speech that does not address others from the speech of the prophet. It is therefore that he advises that one keeps one's speaking in tongues to oneself – after all if nobody knows what you say, when you address the others in utterly foreign tongue, you speak into the air, as he suggests. The only exception to this rule is when someone is present who can interpret this incomprehensible speech – the verb used here is *diermēneuō*. In addition to the spirit's private communication with the divine, an interpreter is needed, someone who can draw this divine dialogue outside of itself and who can indeed "carry the desire to say further." "Therefore," as Paul adds, "one who speaks in a tongue should pray for the power to interpret" (1 Cor. 14.13). Again, there is a call here, a demand and a prayer for the power to interpret. Sharing in the divine voice itself is, for Paul, a way of speaking with a foreigner's voice: this voice cannot be understood by the people who hear the glossolalist, but also not by the glossolalist him or herself. This makes this passage even more interesting: Paul distinguishes between *pneuma* and *nous*. *Pneuma* is the spirit that prays to and communicates with the divine when speaking in tongues, but the *nous*, the mind, is not part of this communication; it is excluded from it.

Thus, it truly mirrors and displaces the situation in Plato's *Ion* where the poets, when speaking or singing, are out of their minds. Yet, in Saint Paul's case, the divine spirit does not inspire the others; it remains foreign to them; they do not share in it; the divine dispensation does not hand out to them, neither to their *nous* nor to their *pneuma*. Differently put, the divine spirit in 1 Cor. 14 does not affect like a magnetic force that can be carried further. It is in this situation that Saint Paul says: "Therefore, one who speaks in a tongue should pray for the power to interpret" (1 Cor. 14.13). Apparently, the phenomenon of sharing in the divine voice does not simply have the power to interpret and address. It needs a hermeneutic supplement that draws it out of itself and carries it outward so that it can, indeed, communalize. Hence, while the *Ion* ultimately plays with the difference between force and meaning – the divine magnetic force that can be communicated without the mind being operative – arguing that communicability is attached to such a divine, magnetic power itself, 1 Cor. 14 suggests that the interaction with the divine spirit, without an operative mind, without the capacity to render intelligible, remains mute and simply foreign to the others – a mute murmur, a mute gibberish that in itself lacks communicability.

Hence, there is a force at work here, but one that only utters a mystery, a secret, thus separating the glossolalist from the bystanders. Let me emphasize that this experience of the foreign character of the language thus uttered – this experience is in itself divided between the inward experience of the glossolalist and the outward experience of those who hear without spirit – is not simply a *negative* one. Rather, this experience produces the call and the prayer for interpretation, for the hermeneut. Interpreters are thus called to *intervene* in a duality that separates the language that communalizes from the divine language, and places themselves in and on this threshold to make the two languages communicate and communalize. Since Paul argues that the interpretation aims at the upbuilding of the community, as opposed to its confusion, it would seem to go against the basic tenet of his remark to argue that the interpreter is brought in only to *reduce* the divine communication to that of the universally understood language, or to that of a fixed language of the community and the significations that can already be expressed in it. If upbuilding would be understood in this way, the work of the community would once more be that of a unification that allows for no plurality. Saint Paul seems to be pointing out that another form of *building up* of the community and of communality is at stake; the upbuilding means that the divine spirit and the divine voice with which no communication seemed possible, become significant and is communicated. The interpreter mediates between *pneuma* and *nous*, enabling communication. Therefore, it seems more likely that the interpreter is indeed concerned with creating new ways of hearing and understanding that transform the community: the community and its language are changed, opened up to another significance.

5 conclusion

When Gadamer in *Truth and Method* speaks of the hermeneutic experience, which basically is the experience that the other has something meaningful to say that I have not, in any way, anticipated, his analysis remains too much within the boundaries of an operative *nous* or mind. The genuine hermeneutic challenge is to be found at the limit of this *nous*, where another significance addresses us. This, one could summarize, is one of the basic insights that guide Nancy's rethinking of a primordial sense of hermeneutics based on the Greek poet's enthusiasm. Yet, the experience of the foreign – or *l'épreuve de l'étranger* – that imposes itself also complicates the sense of transmissibility and the passage that the poet-interpreter exemplifies. These complications are encountered especially in those variations of the figure of the poet in which the hermeneut does not speak or does not yet speak. The story of the prophet's calling as well as Saint Paul's assessment of the glossolalist show a particular complication of the *porter*, the carrying to which the interpreter is called.

The scene of the prophet's calling shows in which sense the call precedes the prophet becoming a *porte-voix qui porte plus loin* the god's call and demand. Before the prophet speaks, he bears witness to the call on the threshold of speech: on the one hand, preceding any address, truly brushing up against sense as the movement of "one toward the other" as a call that precedes each and every aspect of the prophet's existence; and on the other hand, in its kairological structure, addressing, reaching the other. This form of bearing witness, however, does not carry the call further, but is first and foremost articulated in a testimony that bears witness to the prophet's incapacity to carry further. The call, thus reflected in the prophet's incapacity to speak for the other, let's the desire to speak for the gods, to be their *porte-voix*, be born in the prophet by which the "I cannot speak" becomes the capacity that "I can also not speak for myself alone."

On the other side, the interpreter carrying the desire to say further, the phenomenon of the glossolalist confronts us with another threshold. The glossolalist is, par excellence, the one who bears witness in their speech to the god's address, but the glossolalist does not bear witness to this address and call as a call to be carried further. Rather, the glossolalist is so taken up with the divine call and the dialogue between their spirit and the divine spirit, that no transmission ensues. Only a bystander, one who is not possessed or attracted by the divine spirit in the same way but one who is rather, in a certain sense, repelled by the attraction of the glossolalist (cf. Kierkegaard 33), has the capacity to carry the experience of the pure witness, the glossolalist, further and let others share in it by not letting them share in it. Here, the interpreter is truly found on the threshold, belonging neither simply to the realm of the glossolalist nor simply to that of the community, but exactly in this way allows for the two realms to brush up against each other, allowing them to touch and communicate.

echo by jean-luc nancy

To me, Gert-Jan van der Heiden's remarkable exposition calls above all for an extension: "the experience of the foreign" (*l'épreuve de l'étranger*) must be fully appreciated on the basis of the fact that the "foreigner" (*l'étranger*) does not speak our language, nor do we speak theirs, and that as a result there is an innate impossibility of "getting along"

(*s'entendre*). We can "understand" one another (*se comprendre*), but we never hear (*entend*) the other's language as our own. Certainly, it is possible to "hear" several languages according to each time different regiments and registers of "ownness," yet for all that the threshold separating languages is not removed. In this respect, it makes no difference whether the divine language is another language or other than language: in both cases, otherness (and therefore "ownness") is other than the language itself.

But this other-than-language-in-language is constitutive of language (*la langue*) (and of the fact that there are only languages in the plural). Language (*le langage*) always indicates an outside of which it can say nothing. But it equally indicates the non-existence of any outside about which anything is to be said or kept silent.

Such is the divine: non-existent outside and yet substantive (*consistant*) or resistant ...

disclosure statement

No potential conflict of interest was reported by the author.

bibliography

Agamben, Giorgio. *Remnants of Auschwitz: The Witness and the Archive*. Trans. Daniel Heller-Roazen. New York: Zone, 2002. Print.

Cooper, John M., ed. *Plato: Complete Works*. Indianapolis: Hackett, 1997. Print.

Derrida, Jacques. *The Gift of Death*. Trans. David Wills. Chicago: The U of Chicago P, 1995. Print.

Heidegger, Martin. *On the Way to Language*. Trans. Peter D. Hertz. New York: Harper, 1971. Print.

Heidegger, Martin. *Unterwegs zur Sprache*. Frankfurt: Klostermann, 1985. Print.

Kierkegaard, Søren. *Fear and Trembling. Repetition*. Trans. Howard V. Hong and Edna H. Hong. Princeton: Princeton UP, 1983. Print.

Nancy, Jean-Luc. *Adoration: The Deconstruction of Christianity II*. Trans. John McKeane. New York: Fordham UP, 2013. Print.

Nancy, Jean-Luc. "Answering for Sense." *A Time for the Humanities: Futurity and the Limits of Autonomy*. Ed. James J. Bono, Tim Dean, and Ewa Ziarek. New York: Fordham UP, 2008. 84–93. Print.

Nancy, Jean-Luc. "The Forgetting of Philosophy." *The Gravity of Thought*. Trans. François Raffoul and Gregory Recco. Atlantic Highlands: Humanities, 1997. 5–71. Print.

Nancy, Jean-Luc. *The Inoperative Community*. Trans. Peter Connor, Lisa Garbus, Michael Holland, and Simona Sawhney. Minneapolis: U of Minnesota P, 1991. Print.

Nancy, Jean-Luc. *Le partage des voix*. Paris: Galilée, 1982. Print.

Nancy, Jean-Luc. *The Sense of the World*. Trans. Jeffrey S. Librett. Minneapolis: U of Minnesota P, 1997. Print.

Nancy, Jean-Luc. "Sharing Voices." *Transforming the Hermeneutic Context: From Nietzsche to Nancy*. Ed. Geyle Ormiston and Alan D. Schrift. Albany: SUNY P, 1989. 211–59. Print.

Plato. *Statesman, Philebus, Ion*. Trans. Harold North Fowler and W.R.M. Lamb. Loeb Classical Library, Vol. 164. Cambridge, MA: Harvard UP, 1925. Print.

Van der Heiden, Gert-Jan. *Ontology After Ontotheology: Plurality, Event, and Contingency in Contemporary Philosophy*. Pittsburgh: Duquesne UP, 2014. Print.

Van der Heiden, Gert-Jan. "Reading Bartleby, Reading Ion: On a Difference between Agamben and Nancy." *International Yearbook for Hermeneutics* 12 (2013): 92–108. Print.

Van der Heiden, Gert-Jan. *The Voice of Misery: A Continental Philosophy of Testimony*. Albany: SUNY P, 2020. Print.

The works of the muse lack the force of the spirit which, from out of the crushing of the gods and of man, has engendered its certainty of itself. They are now what they are for us – beautiful fruit broken off from the tree, a friendly fate passing those works on to us as a gift, in the way a young girl might present that fruit; the actual life in which that fruit existed no longer exists, nor does the tree that bore them, nor the earth and the elements that constituted their substance, nor the climate that constituted their determinateness, nor the alternation of the seasons that governed the process of their coming-to-be.[1]

I introduction

For long-time collaborators Philippe Lacoue-Labarthe and Jean-Luc Nancy, the question underpinning aesthetic philosophy is less *what is art?* than *what was art?* This apparently simple shift creates a narrative centred on the scene of art's dissolution or passing. Of course, such a narrative predates these two thinkers, notably in the work of G.W.F. Hegel, and it is by engaging with this philosopher that they develop their views on the issue.[2] The broader Hegelian or post-Hegelian frame is the way in which the different periods of history are interpreted as the phased march of spirit realizing or fulfilling itself. But Lacoue-Labarthe and Nancy devote particular efforts to understanding what effect the scene of art's disappearance has, both within this frame, and insofar as art's disappearance allows such framing to be overspilled.

john mckeane

ART'S PASSING FOR HEGEL, LACOUE-LABARTHE, AND NANCY

As these two thinkers assess Hegel's claims about one phase of the historical dialectic passing to the next, therefore, it is crucial to understand what we might call the passing presence of art, the presence of art as it passes or passes away.

What might it mean to claim that art *was*, but *is* not? Hegel's claim looks to ancient Greek culture and the sense of oneness uniting art, religion, and society that it allegedly enjoyed. Hegel's term "æsthetic religion," cited by Nancy, refers precisely to this oneness.[3] And if ancient art is thus defined as a central vector of ancient society, modern art

---

This is an Open Access article distributed under the terms of the Creative Commons Attribution License (http://creativecommons.org/licenses/by/4.0/), which permits unrestricted use, distribution, and reproduction in any medium, provided the original work is properly cited.

by extension is thought to have lost this role, having become fragmentary and marginal rather than plenary and unifying. Early German Romanticism, on which Lacoue-Labarthe and Nancy wrote extensively (not least in *The Literary Absolute*), reacts to these characterizations of ancient and modern art by a nostalgia for the former state of affairs, but also by a desire to forge art anew, re-founding its importance.[4] Thus Lacoue-Labarthe and Nancy write about the Jena Romantics' philological backgrounds and Friedrich Hölderlin's work on the Greeks, but also about Romanticism's programmatic element, its desire to found a new mythology, to reunite art, religion, and politics under the ægis of an infinitized or absolutized Subject. It is thus possible to see a common thesis in both Hegel and the German Romantics: art *was*, but *is* not. The difference, however, comes with the question of whether art's passing must be seen as definitive or not. For Hegel, it is definitive, and art – having reached its apogee with the Greeks – has been replaced by other manifestations of spirit: either revealed religion or philosophy (depending on where he makes the claim, as we shall see). For the Romantics, art may yet be refounded, and creating the conditions for this to occur is a task that artistic movements and groups must pursue.

This initial difference between Hegel and the Romantics, regarding the future of thought, also led to a second difference, this time found in (even) murkier waters. For where the Romantics' fusionalism led them to advocate something like a practice of life-as-art, involving collaborative, anonymous writing and the explosion of the traditional sexual order, Hegel disapproved of their activities. Lacoue-Labarthe describes him as critiquing the Romantics' "æsthetic and moral [...] 'nihilism,'" which, he tells us in French, "ne 'passe' pas – ou *passe trop*."[5] In using the verb *passer*, Lacoue-Labarthe thus indicates that for Hegel such alleged aesthetic and moral nihilism, first, must not be accepted (*passe*), but second, that this is the case precisely because it *passe trop*, i.e., it "escapes

and evades being mastered by the dialectic," is too much inclined towards movement and flightiness.[6] Romanticism for Hegel represented liberality, dissolution or dissoluteness, or what Nancy names in an eponymous essay *menstruum* (letting-go or discharge).[7] On this view, Romantic promises of re-founding a mythology are pie-in-the-sky, and it is better, faced with art's passing, to work with and through the more solid categories of revealed religion and/or philosophy.

In attempting to unpack these notions more fully, we shall begin with a Nancy text named "The Young Girl who Succeeds the Muses (the Hegelian Birth of the Arts)," which deals with the Hegelian thesis of art's passing and presents us with the enigmatic figure in which the thesis is incarnated: a young girl offering up a fruit. We will then move on to Lacoue-Labarthe's oeuvre, reading his long early essay "The Unpresentable," which addresses Hegel and Romanticism, the ancient (complete) and modern (incomplete) instantiations of art, and the question of veils, revelation, and presentation in and through both artistic form and worldliness in general.[8]

2 nancy, "the young girl who succeeds the muses (the hegelian birth of the arts)"

It is difficult to set limits on any discussion of æsthetics in Nancy's oeuvre. There is little clear boundary between his æsthetics, his phenomenology, and his philosophy of religion, for instance, in *Visitation: Of Christian Painting*, *Noli me tangere*, *The Pleasure of Drawing*, or elsewhere.[9] Similarly, where might we even attempt to draw a line between Nancy's thinking of æsthetics and the entire line of thinking around touching, sensation, and sense? And which of the philosophers he has written on, from Kant to Nietzsche to Heidegger, is not also a major aesthetician in his own right?[10]

But in *The Muses* he does discuss one particularly beguiling figure: that of a young girl who is presented as the successor to the

Muses who held sway over ancient conceptions of art.[11] This young girl is thereby associated with the ending of that ancient dispensation, and with the onset of a modern appreciation of the arts (or of modernity's non-appreciation of the arts). Her arrival or appearance on the scene therefore intervenes at a critical juncture as we follow Hegel's narrative of art's role in the historical dialectic and the eventual self-realization of spirit. In other words, the scene on which she arrives is the Hegelian one of art's passing, constituted by the claim that *art was*, rather than *is*. In introducing the topic, Nancy is careful to distinguish what Hegel states and does not state, as well as drawing a distinction between the statements made in two different works:

> It is now well established that what is attributed to Hegel as the declaration of the "end of art" is only the declaration of an ending to what he called "æsthetic religion," which is to say art as the site for the appearance of the divine. Doubtless, the religion that is abandoned in this way is the Greek religion, and the one that succeeds it (notwithstanding the episode of Rome, to which we shall return), "revealed" or Christian religion, is *de jure* beyond art. However, things are far from being this simple in Hegel himself. Indeed, whilst he does not mention Christian art in the *Phenomenology of Spirit* (in which, by contrast, we find the episode of the "young girl" we will be discussing), the importance of art in the *Æsthetics* is well known, indeed art represents its central moment (the centre of this centre in turn being painting). But in the *Æsthetics*, it is not revealed religion that succeeds art, but philosophy or the element of pure thought. (M 75–76)

Here Nancy begins by stating that Hegel's thesis of the passing of art does not in fact exclude the continued existence or practice of art, but merely strips it of any religious status, notably the unified, plenary status that art enjoyed in ancient Greece. This is to say that after this key scene of its passing, art can very well carry on de facto but it will not exist *de jure*. Nancy then distinguishes the two mutually exclusive narrative developments provided by Hegel: according to the first, revealed religion will be what succeeds this aesthetic religion, with art now only having a subsidiary or illustrative role, rather than being a true manifestation of spirit. According to Hegel's second narrative, philosophy or pure thought is what takes up the baton from aesthetic religion. It seems likely that this can be taken to mean philosophy not as our contemporary academic discipline, but as the broader search for truth, incorporating natural science as well as humanistic thought, as it did for any number of figures from Pythagoras to Pascal.

Having established this general account of Hegel's views, and thereby of the founding principles of the modern science of æsthetics, Nancy zooms in on the figure of the young girl carrying the fruit. She succeeds the Muses, meaning that she represents the closure or the passing of the ancient understanding of art as falling under their powers. But what might she instead represent, what alternative way of relating to art? Does she allow for any relation to art at all, or instead symbolize the passing of art's relevance to spirit: art's passing? Glossing her appearance, Nancy writes as follows:

> The young girl who is at once the infinitely fragile extremity of art and the infinitely sustained passage of beautiful form as form is transformed into truth – this young girl has no existence other than that of the fruits that she presents. (M 96)

The notion of art being at once fragile and extreme, either in its thematic content or in the sense of operating or occurring whenever there are extremities or endings, is reasonably well-established within the alternative canon that we can imagine Nancy reading (Sade, Nietzsche, Bataille, Blanchot). The statement on the young girl representing "the infinitely sustained passage of beautiful form as form is transformed into truth" is slightly more complex: it is tempting to focus on the transformation into truth, which would place us firmly back into the former, ancient aesthetic religion (with artistic form communicating directly with truth, the girl being an allegory and as such enjoying epistemic privileges). However, the words "the infinitely sustained passage" undermine this reading. They suggest that, whilst the destiny or purpose of form might well be to transform into truth, this passing or passage is in fact stretched out infinitely, never completed. In other words, "beautiful form" must always remain at a distance from truth, unable to unite with it. Even though "beautiful form" may seem to be a classicizing rather than radically modern category, Nancy identifies it as a surplus or remainder, forever excluded from its purpose.

But what has happened to the fruits? Both in this text and in another collected in *The Muses* ("Why are there Several Arts and not Just One?"), Nancy interprets these as representing art in the modern rather than ancient dispensation. This is to say that the plural fruits represent the plural arts in the modern (i.e., not ancient) age, over and against the unified aesthetic religion of Athens.[12] The bucolic image of the young girl bearing fruit is turned to Nancy's purpose: the descriptive detail of the fruits underlines the sheer *thereness*, patency or worldly existence that these fruits share with the arts (we can read: "that there should be *several arts*, that is something that is exposed as patency" (M 62; original emphasis)). These fruits/arts just *are*, they are in the world, without any connection to the gods that is directly understood, felt, or culturally sanctioned. As such the bucolic or painterly qualities of the figure of the young girl serve to subtract her from Hegel's dialectic as it remorselessly motors on to the next stage in the development of spirit (and it seems possible that his depiction of this figure as a young girl served to underline the lack of significance in his eyes). In any case, Nancy will confirm the fruits' (i.e., the arts') connection with mortality – rather than with immortal divinity – when he writes that "the 'fine fruits' are detached from the tree, and the fact of their presentation consents to this being-detached, this being mortally immortal." This leads him to ask: "And if art was only ever the art, necessarily plural, and singular, of consenting to death, of

consenting to existence?" (M 97). In other words, the fruits' separation from the plant tells us not only that they are ripe for eating, but that at this very moment of ripeness or perfect culmination, decay and death are setting in. The fruits are delicious, but they are time-limited pleasures for now, rather than something stored for later (one meaning of the classically Hegelian term *aufgehoben*). They exist fully in the here and now, thus representing a sort of finitude or worklessness, rather than any dialectical carrying-over or afterlife. Nancy's formulation is instead a Heideggerian one, insisting in its double shape on the co-extensiveness of existence and mortality: "the art [...] of consenting to death, of consenting to existence."[13]

In sum, whilst the move away from aesthetic religion could be understood as a loss, with the attendant nostalgia for lost unity, it can also be seen as a gain: we gain an understanding of our being-in-the-world, a relationship to finitude and mortality that the Greeks always already sublated into a religious system. But this modern understanding is difficult to hold on to, and the dual temptations of nostalgia and refoundation are strong. The Romantics bear testament to that, with their dream of a generalized or infinitized art that would unify not only the separate modern arts, but also domains including religion and politics. Let us now turn to Lacoue-Labarthe to explore this aspect in greater detail.

3 lacoue-labarthe, "the unpresentable"

Published as forty large-format, small-type pages in 1975, this piece shows a strikingly mature level of reflection not only on the topics of Romanticism and æsthetics on which Lacoue-Labarthe would later publish much, but also on the (post-)Heideggerian notions of appearance, coming-to-presence, and being-in-the-world that are more easily associated with his collaborator Nancy. Let us begin by looking at the article's characterization of modern art (via the question of whether art's

THE PULSE OF SENSE

connection to its epoch is direct or indirect). We can then explore what is said about the ancient art of statuary, which allows Lacoue-Labarthe to interrogate Hegel on his understanding of art's passing.

The article is constructed around various references by Hegel to Schlegel's unfinished free-love novel *Lucinde*, which he takes to reveal a deep-seated frustration with – or fear of – the Romantics' lifestyle and ambitions. Lacoue-Labarthe's sympathies clearly lie with the Romantics, with their project of realization of spirit in and through poetry, rather than with Hegel's sublation of that sensible art-form into a metaphysical system. Nonetheless he is clear-eyed about which side of the debate went on to have the greater recognition in the history of thought, and the terms he uses to describe Hegel's victory are brutal ones. Lacoue-Labarthe writes: "let us say, between Hegel and alchemy, that the (silent, clandestine) dissolution, the *Auflösung* of literature left a remainder, a residue, – a stunted specimen: Hegel's *text* [...]" (IMP 55; original emphasis). This victory was Hegel's, with literature driven from the field in disarray, although an implicit trace of it remains with Hegel's text being seen – in the melancholy light of what literature could have been – as a "remainder, residue, – a stunted specimen."

It is against such a backdrop that he will later continue:

> Hegel's *question* is the following: can what is to be thought, whatever it might be (Being, truth, thought itself), be presented *as such*, can it appear *in its own element*? For what is to be thought, might being presented as such and appearing in one's own element – ultimately – come down to *not being presented or appearing at all*? (Lacoue-Labarthe, IMP 75; original emphases)

These rhetorical questions imply that Hegel would prefer "what is to be thought" to find a form proper to it, without having to deal with the external possibilities afforded by art and/ or worldly reality (or art as worldly reality). The questions then go on to imply that to keep its hands clean in such a way would be

to pursue an unrealistic quest for purity, because by definition all presentation must include an element of alienation – or dirtying – of whatever is being presented. For Lacoue-Labarthe, the rivalrous other informing Hegel's intervention in this debate is Romanticism: the Jena Romantics' projects such as the *Athenaeum* review, the mode of collective, fragmentary writing they explored, and the model of community that briefly underpinned it. Let us move to see how this rivalry played out, with particular reference to the question of art's passing.

3.1 modern art: out of time

Hegel as he is glossed by Lacoue-Labarthe in "The Unpresentable" is highly sceptical about the Romantics' claim to make a return to ancient religion, and thereby to do no less than found a new mode of existence (both epistemic and communitarian). If Hegel also believes that "art counts no longer as the highest mode in which truth procures existence for itself," i.e., that modern art is not the equal of its ancient predecessor, then his view of Romanticism plants it firmly within that modern category, denying the claim that it is any different.

Although he is not directly associated with the Jena group usually taken as Hegel's interlocutor by Lacoue-Labarthe, Friedrich Schiller is mentioned at various points in the article in a way that makes clear the role modern art plays in Hegel's claim about art's passing. Ventriloquizing Hegel's view of Schiller's book *The Gods of Greece*, Lacoue-Labarthe writes that:

> *The Gods of Greece* [...] *does not mark any epoch* [...] it can even be understood, in a certain way, as illustrating this "absence of epoch" that characterizes all the art of the Moderns (as well as its unseasonal nostalgia for its bygone age). (IMP 59; original emphasis)

Although the Schiller work mentioned addresses the Greek gods, it nonetheless forms an example of modern art's predicament, namely, that it is no longer aligned with the movement of spirit in its age (whether that means in terms of religion, politics, or other domains). This means that, paradoxically, art from the modern age ultimately belongs to no age: it is cosmopolitan, rootless, liberal, not significant in any terms beyond its own. Shortly afterwards, Lacoue-Labarthe expands on his theme, again mentioning – in opposition to Hegel – Schiller, but now bringing in the Jena Romantics too. In Hegel's view, we read,

> Schiller de-limits the pre-speculative moment which precedes philosophy's *uplift* [*levée*] (the philosophical *relève* of philosophy itself), this fringe (less undecided than contradictory, and therefore "fecund") in which a certain poetic truth of philosophy (and a philosophical truth of poetry), insofar as it takes itself for its own object, *summons* the absolute Idea, the truth represented by *the identity of identity and difference*, the identity of the sensible and the intelligible. It is still too early to clarify what this truth, which we can call *poïetic*, actually is. What is important is that nothing in Romanticism has ever been able to gain access to it – and least of all, let us come back to this point, the Schlegels. The reason for this is, quite simply, that Romanticism is *more* than Schiller's negative: it is the corrosive "milieu" in which, indistinctly but irreversibly, the possibility of philosophy recognizing its own and "conserving" anything at all is dissolved, art having (finally) understood, even whilst continuing its stubborn denials, that *as such* it is no longer *of its epoch*, and has not been so for a long time. (Lacoue-Labarthe, IMP 60; original emphases)

In other words, the object of Hegel's search, the identity of identity and difference, that which he believes allows him to rise above the relativistic mess of history, is only referred to indirectly in Schiller's work. Any allusion to it remains debatable, poetic, a second-hand glimpse of the significance of philosophy, rather than a full self-realization. Schiller's claim thus having been rejected in a measured way, Lacoue-Labarthe then depicts how Hegel deals with Romanticism – this time, the rejection is more brutal. Rather than not fully stating or realizing a goal that nonetheless is

also shared by Hegel, the Romantics' activities are said to actively militate against this goal. These activities are corrosive and dissolute, both epistemically and, it is implied by the strength of the terms being used, morally as well. The end result is that modern art, to which the Romantics for Hegel belong, "is no longer of its epoch, and has not been so for a long time." The modernity to which this art belongs is therefore not a category simply mirroring the ancient era; instead, it is a paradoxical epoch where time is out of joint, whose artistic productions only belong to the age insofar as they do not belong to it, which is to say loosely, without direction, by default. Art in its ancient role having passed away, modern art is the art of passing, leaving us only with passing thoughts, with the anonymity and superficiality of passers-by.

3.2 ancient art: statuary

If early German Romanticism looks nostalgically towards ancient Greek art, this does not mean that its rival, Hegel, underestimated the importance of this art. For him, it presented a full realization of everything that art was capable of (even as some tasks or roles remained impossible for art, which is one of his points of disagreement with the Romantics). In Hegel's *Æsthetics*, Greek aesthetic religion is primarily identified with statuary and its celebration of the (athletic) human form as divine or quasi-divine. Lacoue-Labarthe discusses this in terms of the questions of gender, sexuality, and the moral scandal (for Hegel) raised by the Romantic Friedrich Schlegel's novel *Lucinde* which, Lacoue-Labarthe ventriloquizes, is "an *affront to modesty* [*pudeur*]" (IMP 70; original emphasis).[14] We have already seen that the article focuses on the notions of arrival, presentation, and ultimately on Hegel's claim that "what is to be thought" might be "unpresentable." Ancient statuary intervenes at a particular moment in these debates, with the nudity of Greek male statues being contrasted by Hegel with the robed or veiled female statues. If, under the sway of the aesthetic religion then in force, art represented the actions of spirit in the historical world, then nudity in art presents a tendency towards revelation, whilst modesty or pudeur in art displays the opposite tendency, towards withdrawal and secrecy (but also, paradoxically, the exhibition of that secrecy itself).

Lacoue-Labarthe addresses these questions in the third section of his article, titled "Immodesty: The Veil and the Figure." Here he makes it clear that Hegel does not simply take the plastic arts (and in this case statuary) to straightforwardly represent the sensible, and as such as something to be simply overcome by moving towards the spiritual. Instead, art is of interest because it represents a conflict between the sensible and the spiritual. In the first of two Hegel quotations given by Lacoue-Labarthe that we shall look at, we can read:

> if it is true that from the point of view of sensible beauty, all our preferences must be for the nude, it is nonetheless the case that sensible beauty does not represent the ultimate goal that sculpture pursues; thus the Greeks were not wrong to (re)present the majority of feminine figures as wearing clothes, whilst the majority of masculine figures were (re)-presented nude. (IMP 71)

Secondly: "'art's task is precisely to make this opposition between matter and spirit disappear, to make the body beautiful, to make this form more perfect, to animate and spiritualize it'" (IMP 71). Taken together, these passages show that art cannot simply be identified with the sensible, but instead as something like the destination of the sensible, the way that it is given force or direction. The sensible body would thus be perfected, animated, or spiritualized by art, being both itself and responsive to something beyond itself, being leavened or seasoned, and ultimately finding self-fulfilment.

On Lacoue-Labarthe's reading, Hegel therefore is not guilty of any straightforwardly sexist preference for male form (e.g., that of a naked athlete) over female form. Instead, the sexism is of a second, quite possibly more pernicious kind, consisting in the praise given to the ancient Greek practice of producing robed or veiled statues of women. In Hegel's argument, according to Lacoue-Labarthe's account, "femininity is only beautiful, in an ideal sense, when clothed, veiled, partly withdrawn from the gaze" (IMP 71). This complex gesture – about which that other interpreter of the supposedly mysterious Sphinx, Freud, would doubtless have had much to say – is in fact classically dialectical.[15] The movement of *relève* or sublation is one that both suppresses and maintains its object, removing it from present circulation or use in order to store it for later (again: the lofty Hegelian *aufheben* is also what one does, in German, to pickles or preserves). This is what happens to female nudity on Hegel's reading: it is both stored away, given over to the cause of its own spiritualization, and seemingly destined to return to haunt Hegel despite or precisely due to this sublation. For Lacoue-Labarthe, Hegel's visceral reaction to the Romantic novel *Lucinde* was due to the fact that this work leaves this sublation radically incomplete, instead opting for sexual explicitness and revelation. The technical grounds for this disapproval – if indeed we want to accept that such things can be purely technical – are that due to its emphasis on the sensible, rather than as something working towards the spiritual-in-the-sensible, the novel simply does not qualify as art. As Lacoue-Labarthe sweepingly states (to summarize Hegel's view), "modesty [*pudeur*] is the essence of art" (IMP 70). This is expanded upon shortly afterwards: "Modesty figures the figure: it is a sensible veil cast over the sensible, a negation of the negation of the spiritual, through which the spiritual begins to appear. – It is art itself" (IMP 74). For Hegel, modesty or propriety – *la pudeur* – thus allows a way of understanding the role that is proper to art, insofar as it engages with the sensible without having it as its ultimate horizon, and allows for the figure to be figured in a self-referentiality or *mise-en-abyme*.

Whilst Lacoue-Labarthe, with his sympathies for the Romantics, certainly does much to suggest that Hegel's reaction to *Lucinde* might be reducible to a straightforward sense of moral disapproval, he also reaches for a more properly philosophical way of understanding the episode. He rejects the notion of representation as a category based on metaphysical, binary logic, whereby there are some things that have form, and others that do not, with the latter being able to instantiate themselves in and through the former. Instead of such a view, Lacoue-Labarthe is sceptical regarding the existence of any pure thematic- or content-matter that, from the outside, could come to inhabit form. Picking up the terms of robing and veiling that he has been discussing with Hegel's account of statuary as part of Greek aesthetic religion, he writes that:

> The ethical scandal will always have been, in reality, an æsthetic scandal, *the scandal of æsthetics*, which like all scandals in the eyes of Knowledge and Spirit, unveiled that *there was nothing to unveil*. Or at least that it is possible that there might be nothing to unveil. In unveiling the figure in its self-sufficiency, in *showing* Venus, – in showing that Venus has nothing to hide, but that she is simply exhibiting herself (for the sake of doing so) and that that is enough for her beauty (that is enough in order for beauty to exist), æsthetics will have come close to definitively giving the figural over to immodesty. (Lacoue-Labarthe, IMP 86; original emphases)

On this view, there is nothing truly external to art or the world, and therefore nothing that can subsequently make an appearance in that art or world, and ultimately very little substance in the category of appearance itself. If there is anything to be found there, it doubtless lies in a secondary or zero-degree definition whereby any revelation is a revelation of nothing.[16] This is precisely what, he argues, so irked Hegel: the fact that this episode unveiled that "there was nothing to unveil." More than this, Lacoue-Labarthe states that this scandal is the scandal of æsthetics itself. This is to say that this entire area of philosophy (and the one that represented the day jobs of both Lacoue-Labarthe and Nancy, as professors of æsthetics) would be constructed without reference to any particular subject-matter that it would attempt to reveal (it would be, as it were, a

theology with no creed). This is quite different to Hegel's view of æsthetics as the gradually unfolding drama of the self-realization or fulfilment of spirit. Because the alienation of spirit is ultimately overcome, this spirit can be classed as a sort of caffeine hit that the historical dialectic ultimately delivers. By contrast to this unfolding drama, Lacoue-Labarthe prefers to offer a freely associated series of female figures including Antigone, the Sphinx, and robed Greek statues, and ultimately concluding with the contented self-presence of Venus in her immodest beauty.[17] The claim made, over and against Hegel, by the Romantics and by Lacoue-Labarthe in their wake, is not simply that the sensible serves to slow or interrupt the dialectical realization of spirit, but instead that the sensible must play a full role in the new mythology, founded on beauty as truth and truth as beauty.

4 conclusion: "the gleam of her self-conscious eye"

We have sought to unpack two associated readings of Hegel's views on "æsthetic religion," having broadly summarized the latter with the phrase *art was, but is not*. The first reading was Nancy's, which focused on the mechanism by which art had been said to pass on the work of the spirit to other, better-equipped discourses. For Nancy, this linear temporality needs to be deconstructed, and this passing-on is in fact "infinitely sustained," constituting a middle or milieu in which we are still, and always, located. When taken together with the additional aspect of the fruits presented by the young girl representing mortality, this comes to resemble a (post-)Heideggerian, even existentialist reading: we are always already and always still dying, a situation in which art can help us "consen[t] to death, consent to existence."

The second reading of the view that *art was, but is not* is that of Lacoue-Labarthe. Dramatizing the interaction between Hegel and contemporary Romantic thinkers, he too presents art as associated with nothingness – a dissolution or lack of substantiality that Hegel was at pains to cover up, but which the Romantics embraced in a more mindful way. For both the question of form was key, the disagreement arising over whether one emphasizes the march towards and into self-fulfilment in, through, and ultimately beyond form; or whether one instead remains haunted by the absurdity of creation *ex nihilo*, a haunting that nonetheless pushes Romanticism towards its programmatic aspect.[18]

As a final thought, let us return to the figure of the young girl bearing fruit as it is used by Hegel to characterize art's passing: the passage from a world in which art was governed by the Muses and (allegedly) played a plenary role in society. In the same section of the *Phenomenology* quoted in our epigraph, Hegel writes:

> the young girl who presents us the plucked fruits as a gift is more than the nature that immediately provided them, more than the nature that unfurls into their conditions and elements, into the trees, air, light, etc., while in a higher way she gathers all this together into the gleam of her self-conscious eye and her offertory gesture; just as she is more than that nature, so too the spirit of the fate that provides us with those works of art is more than the ethical life and actuality of that people, for it is the inwardizing-recollecting of the spirit in them that was still alienated.[19]

This seems in fact to contradict the gloss we saw Nancy giving to the figure of the girl – namely, that she "has no existence other than that of the fruits that she presents" (M 96). We can recall that this was Nancy's jumping-off point for his reflections on existence and mortality, with the detachment of the fruits from the tree – i.e., that of the arts from the civic life that nourished them – forming an irreversible step, quite possibly a tragic one. In Hegel's text, however, the fruits are detached from the tree only to be framed in an alternative setting: the girl "gathers all this together into the gleam of her self-conscious eye [...] the spirit of the fate that provides us with those works of art [...] is the inwardizing-recollecting of the spirit in them that was still alienated." In

other words, the detachment of the fruits is no tragedy but instead a fitting end. The fruits want to be eaten and the æsthetic religion wants to be overcome: which is to say that ancient Greek æsthetic religion does not merely service the needs of its social setting, but by doing so, drives the spirit of history forwards, producing the dialectic.

Hegel's dramatization of art's passing in the figure of the girl shows that he is not just a forger of concepts, someone deaf to the charms of literature.[20] Rather than a stiffly allegorical figure, the girl bearing fruit is a beguiling one. Her gleaming eye gives life to the dynamics of presentation themselves, drawing attention away from whatever the existence, properties or characteristics of the fruits (i.e., the arts) might be, and instead causes us to question what proto-psychoanalytical game of projection and transference, good objects and bad objects, we are playing when we discuss ancient art. This is to say that she causes the gaze we cast upon the fruit to become problematic: perhaps it is not always or not only the other who wallows in mythology while we rest assured of our logical objectivity.

Lacoue-Labarthe and Nancy react to such epistemic unsettledness in different ways: for the former, it is not clear that we have ever fully purged our discourse of the patterns of piety and observance usually ascribed to religious thinking; he writes of modern literature's self-conceptualization as a "'new mythology,'" with its "endless procession of priests and sectaries, mystics and martyrs, clerics and inquisitors, accursed and apostates, soldier-monks and heretics, prophets, saints and schismatics, blasphemers and profanes."[21] In short, he writes, "the entire Church repeated itself in Literature, as well as all the ancient forms of worship."[22] Here we see the importance of Romanticism for him – ultimately, all modern literature, knowingly or not, falls into a paradigm seized on at Jena.

With Nancy, on the other hand, his work provides a formidable resource for rethinking the triad of tree, fruit, and girl (i.e., ancient society, its æsthetic religion, and the way it is presented or comes down to us). It is beyond the capacities of this essay to say whether in sabotaging the transcendence of the spiritual he gives an outsized role to the materiality of the world and/or art, or whether he ultimately follows Hegel in seeing the entirety of modern (i.e., post-classical) art as a Christian phenomenon based on a structure of incarnation. It remains important to note that close readers of his work have found reason to suspect it of something like a new materialism.[23] Nonetheless, his insistence on a metaphorics of space – opening, stretching, folding, touching, moving – means that his work can be of great assistance as we attempt to think outside linearity and beyond the economy of ends.

echo by jean-luc nancy

With its often-refined language, it is rather difficult for me to find my way into this text – although I believe I can roughly follow the reading and analysis of Hegel's "young girl carrying fruit." I must say that, since the period in which I wrote the texts so well examined by John McKeane, this young girl has often continued to give me food for thought. I think I did not pay enough attention to the very gesture by which Hegel extracted a figure – very concretely – , from a book of engravings depicting the frescoes of Pompeii (a book I have seen a copy of). I commented on the figure itself without dwelling on the fact that Hegel spotted and retained it. Yet, it is a work of art in question (its exact historical and artistic connection with the great classical Greek art, especially sculpture). It is itself a work of the art, which it thus not merely presents as preservation of the past, but also as the very presence of the bearer of offerings. Priestess of a new cult – that of the museum, which is not described without irony, with its libation of dust – the young girl nevertheless fulfils a real office, and thus in some way a real presentation that is, together with that of the fruits, I repeat, that of the young girl herself. Undeniably, she finds a real presence there and her image in the museum animates a graceful movement that catches the eye of the philosopher. She catches it precisely by way of her own "self-conscious eye," making her a spiritual principle, as Hegel says. But what he does not say is that it is itself an artwork – an artwork of the past preserved and reproduced, much more so than a document, for it communicates to us an "interiorisation," Hegel says, of the art's spirit. This young girl forms a kind of intermediary between the sculptures of classical art and the person of Christ. This can be understood both as a succession in the surpassing of art and as the preservation (and the taking over?) by the memory of art right up to the edge of "revealed religion," in which – as we know from the *Aesthetics*, even if it is absent from the *Phenomenology* – art will be no less present.

This extension can only be made on the basis of Hegel's outlook on a bearer of offerings drawn after a fresco from Pompeii: on the basis of an aesthetic (and sentimental-erotic) emotion thus, experienced at the heart of thought busy overcoming the aesthetic. And in Hegel, much else bears witness to this emotion ...

This is the extension I propose to John McKeane, or at least to his project, to thank him for having, in his turn, awakened the young girl in us.

disclosure statement

No potential conflict of interest was reported by the author.

notes

1 Hegel §753, 432.

2 The following statement can be found in Hegel's work: "For us art counts no longer as the highest mode in which truth procures existence for itself" in *Aesthetics. Lectures on Fine Art*, trans. T.M. Knox, Vol. I (Oxford: Clarendon, 1975) 103.

3 Nancy, *Les Muses* 75 (trans. by Peggy Kamuf as *The Muses*). Future references to this French edition will be abbreviated M. Due to this piece

being finished during the Covid-19 lockdown of 2020, this is my translation, as are all those that follow, unless stated otherwise.

4 Lacoue-Labarthe and Nancy; amongst other texts, see Lacoue-Labarthe and Nancy, "Noli me frangere" (1982) collected in Nancy, *Demande: Littérature et philosophie* (trans. by Robert Bononno as *Expectation: Philosophy, Literature*).

5 Lacoue-Labarthe, "L'imprésentable" 53–95 (63; future references will bear the abbreviation IMP). Lacoue-Labarthe also writes that:

the "application" to art of the Fichtean principle of the absoluteness of the (abstract) self means that "nothing appears to have any proper value but only that imprinted on it by the subjectivity of the self." In the same way, the Romantic artist's transformation, setting-in-form, figuration, or even fictioning (*Gestaltung*, *Bildung*, etc.), of his life leads to something that cannot be "taken seriously." (IMP 62)

6 Ibid.

7 Nancy, "*Menstruum universale*: La dissolution littéraire" (1977), *Demande*, op. cit. (trans. by Robert Bononno as "*Menstruum universale*: Literary Dissolution," *Expectation*, op. cit.).

8 Nancy, "La jeune fille qui succède aux Muses (la naissance hégélienne des arts)," *Les Muses*; "The Young Girl who Succeeds the Muses (the Hegelian Birth of the Arts)," *The Muses*, op. cit., 41–55.

9 On the confluence of aesthetics and phenomenology, see Nancy, *The Pleasure of Drawing*:

Drawing is not a given, available, formed form. On the contrary, it is the gift, invention, appearance, or birth of form. "That a form comes" is drawing's formula, and this formula implies at the same time the desire for and the anticipation of form. (3; trans. mod.)

10 Other discussions of the topic can be found in Heikkilä 26–28 and James 202–30.

11 See also James's discussion of "Le Portrait de l'art en jeune fille" ("Portrait of Art as a Young Girl"), in *The Fragmentary Demand* 206ff.

12 Such is the interpretation given of Nancy's (modern) aesthetics by Martta Heikkilä: "Just as

there is no being in general but only the singular existence of existing things, there is no art 'in general' which would grant a uniqueness or a unity of origin to art" (26).

13 Jacques Rancière also mentions the fruits' detachment:

The young girl of whom Hegel speaks, the one who succeeds the Muses, offers us the fruits picked from the tree, the veiled memory, "without effectiveness," of the life that carried the artworks. But, precisely, these works are such only because their world, the world of nature fulfilling itself in culture, *is* no longer, or perhaps never *was*, except in the retrospection of thought. (13; original emphasis)

14 He also contrasts the social experiments informing *Lucinde* with Hegel's view of marriage:

We should not understand the "substantiality of marriage" to mean anything other, ultimately, than the "intellectual and moral" attribution, for the two sexes, of their respective roles, which is to say that these roles are subject to a *relève* – the suppression, retention, elevation, spiritualization and humanization within a living unity that actively produces meaning, of the natural difference of the sexes. (Lacoue-Labarthe, IMP 66)

15 Freud received for his fiftieth birthday a medallion with his own bust on one side, and on the other Œdipus and the Sphinx, with the legend in Sophocles's Greek "he who knew the famous riddles and was a most powerful man." See Armstrong 52.

16 See Nancy in *The Pleasure of Drawing*: "Beautiful form – that is, *drawing* [...] [in the] sense of what *draws itself* – opens a revelation. Revelation is quite different from the appearance of something that was hidden. It is, rather, the appearance of what was never hidden" (105; original emphasis).

17 On Venus's unexpected appearance in Lacoue-Labarthe's text, Marta B. Helfer comments:

is this Aphrodite, this tutelary goddess of aesthetics, the *necessary* figure for the scandal of the æsthetic? Does this figure perhaps repeat or mime a little too programmatically the Hegelian, "phallogocentric" identification of woman with the sensuous, the fictional, the narcissistic – that is, the hypersubjective, which is to say, the scandalous? (112)

18 See Antoine Berman's study of German Romantic thought through the lens of translation. He writes:

through *Bildung* an individual, a people, a nation, but also a language, a literature, a work of art in general are formed and thus acquire a form, a *Bild. Bildung* is always a movement toward a form, *one's own form* – which is to say that, in the beginning, every being is deprived of *its* form. (Berman 43–44; original emphases)

19 Hegel §753.

20 The topos of finding one's argument against Hegel already legislated for in his works appears in Michel Foucault:

to really escape Hegel presupposes […] taking the measure of how far the recourse we have against him is also, again, perhaps one more trick that he plays on us and which, after it has gone its course, we find him waiting, immobile and elsewhere. (75)

21 Lacoue-Labarthe, "The Agony of Religion" 66–67.

22 Ibid. 67.

23 See Derrida.

bibliography

Armstrong, Richard H. *A Compulsion for Antiquity: Freud and the Ancient World*. Ithaca, NY: Cornell UP, 2005. Print.

Berman, Antoine. *The Experience of the Foreign: Culture and Translation in Romantic Germany*. Trans. S. Heyvaert. Albany: SUNY P, 2004. Print.

Derrida, Jacques. *Le Toucher, Jean-Luc Nancy*. Paris: Galilée, 2000; *On Touching, Jean-Luc Nancy*. Trans. Christine Irizarry. Stanford: Stanford UP, 2005. Print.

Foucault, Michel. *L'Ordre du discours*. Paris: Gallimard, 1971. Print.

Hegel, G.W.F. *The Phenomenology of Spirit*. Trans. Terry Pinkard. Cambridge: Cambridge UP, 2018. Print.

Heikkilä, Martta. "Art/Æsthetics." *The Nancy Dictionary*. Ed. Peter Gratton and Marie-Ève Morin. Edinburgh: Edinburgh UP, 2015. 26–28. Print.

Helfer, Marta B. *Rereading Romanticism*. Amsterdam: Rodopi, 2000. Print.

James, Ian. "Art." *The Fragmentary Demand: An Introduction to the Philosophy of Jean-Luc Nancy*. Stanford: Stanford UP, 2006. 202–30. Print.

Lacoue-Labarthe, Philippe. "The Agony of Religion." *Ending and Unending Agony*. Trans. Hannes Opelz. New York: Fordham UP, 2015. Print.

Lacoue-Labarthe, Philippe. "L'imprésentable." *Poétique* 21 (1975): 53–95; Trans. by Thomas Trezise as "The Unpresentable" in *The Subject of Philosophy*. Minneapolis: Minnesota UP, 1993. 116–58. Print.

Lacoue-Labarthe, Philippe, and Jean-Luc Nancy. *L'Absolu littéraire: Théorie de la littérature du romantisme allemand*. Paris: Le Seuil, 1978. Trans. by Philippe Barnard and Cheryl Lester as *The Literary Absolute: The Theory of Literature in German Romanticism*. Albany: SUNY P, 1988. Print.

McKeane, John. *Philippe Lacoue-Labarthe (Un)timely Meditations*. Oxford: Legenda, 2015. Print.

Nancy, Jean-Luc. *Demande: Littérature et philosophie*. Paris: Galilée, 2015. Trans. by Robert Bononno as *Expectation: Philosophy, Literature*. New York: Fordham UP, 2017. Print.

Nancy, Jean-Luc. *Les Muses*. Paris: Galilée, 2001. Trans. by Peggy Kamuf as *The Muses*. Stanford: Stanford UP, 1997. Print.

Nancy, Jean-Luc. *The Pleasure of Drawing*. Trans. Philip Armstrong. New York: Fordham UP, 2013. Print.

Rancière, Jacques. *Æsthetics and its Discontents*. Trans. Steven Corcoran. Cambridge: Polity, 2004. Print.

The Corporeality of Existence

For T., for J.-L. N.

This paper will, in its successive steps and movements, revolve around one single question, a question that might, at first sight, come across as somewhat irrelevant or even impertinent within the context of philosophical or academic discourse. How romantic is Jean-Luc Nancy? Or: is there a specifically Nancyan sense of romance? There were times when I thought there were more relevant questions to ask, like: what kind of ontology is implied in Nancy's work? Or to what extent is Nancy re-treating religion?[1] But I am increasingly convinced that the question of love, or indeed more specifically of *romance*, is the most intimate inspiration of Nancy's work, the key unlocking all other keys.[2] The theme of love has always played an important role in his work, from the early essay "Shattered Love" ("L'amour en éclats," 1986) to his later works on the body and pleasure. In this paper, I will touch upon a number of these texts, but I will more particularly refer to two of Nancy's more recent works, the recently translated work *Sexistence* (2021, published in French in 2017 and *Expectation: Philosophy, Literature* (2018, published in French in 2015 as *Demande: Littérature et philosophie*).[3]

The question of romance, that is, the question of passionate interaction, of intrigue, of writing, of dramatization. This quite heterogeneous web of associations already implies a number of age-old philosophical issues: the relation between love and thinking; the relation between love and literature; and, subsequently,

aukje van rooden

JEAN-LUC NANCY, A ROMANTIC PHILOSOPHER?
on romance, love, and literature

between philosophy and literature; the issue of the relation itself. The knot uniting these issues under the single heading of "romance" has been most firmly tied about two centuries ago, in the late eighteenth-century movement of early German, i.e., Jena, Romanticism, that significant moment in intellectual history where the barriers between philosophy and literature were broken down and where, quite generally put, the sense of the world was conceived of as a matter of *romanticization*.

Although Nancy himself would be reluctant to call himself a Romantic philosopher in this

This is an Open Access article distributed under the terms of the Creative Commons Attribution-NonCommercial-NoDerivatives License (http://creativecommons.org/licenses/by-nc-nd/4.0/), which permits non-commercial re-use, distribution, and reproduction in any medium, provided the original work is properly cited, and is not altered, transformed, or built upon in any way.

historical sense of the word, this is exactly what I want to argue here: I want to show that Nancy's philosophy of love – and by extension his philosophical thinking *tout court* – should be placed in the tradition of German Romanticism, rather than in that of, for instance, phenomenology, ontology, or philosophy proper. This claim is massive in its depth and scope and can impossibly be explored here in an exhaustive way. Instead, I will flesh out this perspective by advancing four successive hypotheses that enable to mark the contours of what I call Nancy's romanticism. With this exploration, I hope to do three things at once: firstly, to underscore what I take to be the core or pulse of Nancy's thinking: the issue of romance; secondly, to investigate to what extent this romantic pulse might be traced back to the Romantic tradition; and, thirdly, to emphasize why Nancy's romantic thinking is relevant for us today.

let love in

Let me start with the relation between philosophy and love. In a sense to speak of philosophy is always to speak of its relation to love, or rather, of philosophy *as* a relation of love, a love relation. After all, its etymology prevents philosophy from being *unrelated* to love, to the desire or love of wisdom, truth, or thinking, irrespective of the exact meanings attributed to these words. But, as Nancy has pointed out in "Shattered Love," the whole point is to understand what this love relation consists of. If philosophy is to be understood as the love of thinking, then, Nancy holds, "perhaps *only in spite of all philosophies*," that is, only insofar as philosophy is *something else than* philosophy, since what we call "philosophy" has "betrayed" this love ("Shattered Love" 84).

But if philosophy is the betrayer of its own essence, cheats on its own love, it is, according to Nancy, notoriously so, compulsively, and this holds for all philosophies. Philosophy cannot but betray its essence. Or as Nancy puts it: "If thinking is love, that would mean (insofar as thinking is confused with philosophy) that thinking misses its own essence –

that is misses by essence its own essence" ("Shattered Love" 90–91). Predominantly being "lovers" of the possessive type, philosophers usually attempt to "master" what offers itself to thought, to "privilege," "hierarchize," and "exclude" (83) within the "mastery of a triumphant doctrine" (85). According to Nancy, "thinking" should in fact be the opposite of such an attempt to master or possess. Indeed, as befits a love relation, thinking should consist of the exposition to what exceeds it, of "a reticence that lets the singular moments of this experience offer and arrange themselves" (83).

The point, then, for Nancy – and this is my first hypothesis – is not to make room for love in philosophical thinking, but to think love in such a way that thinking itself becomes loving, that it takes place in a loving way, as an "act" of love. Indeed, Nancy asserts: "'love' […] would name the *act* of thinking as much or as more than it would its *nature*" ("Shattered Love" 84; my italics). But if thinking is an act of love, what does this love consist of? According to what philosophical tradition or model do we have to understand it? Although Nancy, in "Shattered Love," traverses virtually the whole Western tradition, to align himself perhaps mostly with the Heideggerian idea of Care (*Sorge*), I believe it is in his 2008 conference for children, his *petite conférence sur l'amour*, that he has found the most powerful and also most outspoken formulation of this love: namely, in terms of a *passionate romantic* love, in the ordinary sense of the word, the whimsical love that strikes uninvitedly, the love that cannot but be expressed at the risk of changing everything.

The central figure in this conference on love is the famous child's play of plucking the petals of a daisy while singing the rhyme "he loves me, he loves me not" or "she loves me, she loves me not." Picking one petal of the flower for each phrase, the phrase uttered on picking the last one supposedly expresses the nature of the love at stake. Tellingly for his exposé, the French rhyme referred to by Nancy differs in a crucial respect from the English one – a difference that is passed over in silence by the translator. Whereas the English rhyme – but as far as I can tell also those in most other languages – speak of a binary "yes" or "no" (they love me, they love me not), the – perhaps typically French, but at least typically Nancyan – love is a whole spectrum of loves, a proliferation of different forms and intensities. The French rhyme taken by Nancy as a reference does not indicate *whether* there is love, but *to what extent*. It does not say "I love you, I love you not," but says "I love you a little, a lot, passionately, madly, not at all" (*je t'aime un peu, beaucoup, passionnément, à la folie, pas du tout*).[4]

This proliferation of love(s) was already anticipated by the title of Nancy's early essay "Shattered Love," *l'amour en éclats*, suggesting love to be shattering, bursting, scattering. The figure of the child's play, however, also enables an important and crucial *assessment* of the gradations of love. In the end – and this is my second hypothesis – , for Nancy a relation is only one of love when it is *passionate*. The first two varieties "I love you a little, a lot" cannot be love according to Nancy because "the emphasis is entirely on me" ("Love" 70). Indeed, measured by *my* preferences, I like you a little, or a lot, better than him or her. Conversely, in the case of madness or *un amour à la folie*, the emphasis is entirely on the other. Where loving "a little, a lot" is too little to be called love, loving madly is too much to be called love: "Love is thrilling, and it can make you want to do anything. But in the end it can also ask too much of the other person and of yourself" (77–78). "At the extreme," Nancy remarks, "it's even possible for two people to destroy each other" (77).

The urge to rethink love in philosophy stressed in the essay "Shattered Love," is now presented in its most acute form. Stretched between the poles of self-absorption and destruction, love is for Nancy the most lively expression of what it means to *be*, together, in co-existence.[5] If he wants to open or re-open thinking to love, to think lovingly, this is because the forgetfulness of love proper to philosophy is in the end nothing else than a forgetfulness of being. "[L]ove is missing from

philosophical ontology" (89), Nancy therefore concludes "Shattered Love," reading the Heideggerian history of the forgetfulness of being in terms of philosophy's blind spot for this law of love (which, in the end, is also the law of philosophy itself).[6]

This law of love is that of a necessary transcendence or transgression, of an "extreme movement beyond the self" (Nancy, "Shattered Love" 86). This is also why passionate love can only be unquantifiable. As Nancy has it: "'I love you' is absolute. We must say 'I love you,' period" ("Love" 69). The law of love – and we all know this – is to be blown away, to be knocked off your feet, in an unanticipated manner. In Nancy's words: "[i]n love, we are two [and] from the moment we are two, everything changes" (70).[7] *Everything changes*, without reserve, and without end. The inevitable option of this one petal of passion, of this one touch by passionate love thus disengages the whole economy of successive, classifiable gradations,[8] making the love affair not so much a binary affair of loving and not loving, but a *rhythmic*, syncopating one, never guaranteed and therefore to be renewed all the time, both stopping and setting in motion the whole proliferation of intensities of love.[9]

Although setting everything in motion, not much is needed for love to strike as Nancy argues in "Shattered Love":

> As soon as there is love, the slightest act of love, the slightest spark, there is this ontological fissure that cuts across and that disconnects the elements of the subject proper – the fibers of its heart. One hour of love is enough, one kiss alone, provided that it is out of love – and can there, in truth, be any other kind? (96)

So love may well be beyond measure, it certainly doesn't lack concreteness. What counts in love, or *as* love, is not the ideal or the eternal, but is always *concrete* (sometimes also called "discrete" by Nancy). It is, as Derrida had aptly put it in *On Touching – Jean-Luc Nancy*, a matter of "exorbitant exactitude" (26). Not surprisingly then, and in line with

Derrida's characterization of Nancy's work as a philosophy of the *touch*, love exemplarily manifests itself for Nancy in the *caress*, which he takes to be the "gesture of love": "The caress teaches us that what counts in love is the presence of the other, the touch of the other, and, in a certain sense, nothing (of the) other (*rien d'autre*)" ("Love" 75).

In his recent book *Sexistence* (2017), Nancy (inevitably I would say[10]) takes his work on love and the touch to a point that some would perhaps consider most unromantic: he suggests to consider *sex* to be the truth of love. Sensationalist as this claim might seem, *Sexistence* is in my view a work of invaluable importance, and unprecedented both in the philosophical tradition and, for reasons that will become clear, in Nancy's oeuvre. Although Nancy considers love and sex to be "almost similar" (*Sexistence* 158; all translations are mine), his point is not to take them as completely synonymous.[11] Rather, Nancy considers sex as that what *in* love makes up, in a paradigmatic way, its ontological disposition. In his 2001 essay "The 'There Is' of Sexual Relation," Nancy already described this specific ontological disposition as a non-substantial one. Insofar a sexual relation is to be considered a relation, this relation "is" not, according to Nancy; it does not have any permanence or substance, since sex is not there before or independently of the act: "If relation is pursued from the angle of a 'something,' we can say that here is no relation *of* the sexual, or that the sexual does not relate anything" ("The 'There Is' of Sexual Relation" 5). Not only can the sexual act be dispersed over an unlimited series of looks, hints, advances, and retreats, it is also never really "there," which is to say that it designates "that which is not any thing [...] but happens between things" (6).[12]

Indeed, we can see how all three characteristics attributed to the passionate romantic love relation are intensified in sexual intercourse: firstly, the *lack of permanence* of this always to be renewed relation; secondly, the *immeasurability* of unreserved passionate exposition; and, thirdly, the material *concreteness* of the loving touch. By situating sex at the heart of his view on love, Nancy also dissociates his thinking of love more clearly from competing models like that of divine, parental, or marital love. Furthermore, the perhaps still somewhat rosy picture of the crushing nature of passionate love given in his conference for children, now more explicitly includes the physicality, the *eros* and *jouissance* of love-making.

making love (with language)

The next step is to link this view on romantic, passionate love with Romanticism. What makes *Sexistence* and Nancy's earlier texts on love Romantic in the historical sense of the word – and in my view also particularly interesting – , is the key role attributed to *language*. As is well known, the register used by Nancy to describe the love relation is predominately one of the physical body, of touch, and *jouissance*. But on closer inspection – and this is my third hypothesis – , Nancy considers the most exemplary gestures of love to be *expressions of language*. Or rather, if the caress is the paradigmatic gesture of love, as we saw earlier, it seems that Nancy takes *caressing by means of language* as the caress par excellence. Caressing by means of language, that is, being touched by language, touching language. In what way exactly, then, are we to relate touch, language, and love? And in what sense can this way be called Romantic?

Let me start with the most basic and most exemplary form of love's linguistic expression: the sentence "I love you." Love, Nancy already claimed in "Shattered Love," is not expressed by the word or concept "love," but by this avowal or expression: "[L]ove's name is not 'love,' which would be a substance or a faculty, but it is this sentence, the 'I love you' just as one says 'the cogito'" (100). The specific nominalist status is of importance here. This sentence does not describe a love I already feel, nor does it perform what we can call a standard performative speech act. It is according to Nancy a statement that opens the self to the other, and that expresses – if anything – an engagement with this opening.[13]

Paradigmatically, then, the linguistic expression "I love you" lacks, or rather exceeds, every possible informative content; it is an address at the limit of speech, an excessive form of speech at the basis of which is nothing else than the desire to exceed ourselves in an exposition to one another. This was also one of the key claims alleged by Nancy in his seminal work *Being Singular Plural* (1996), written ten years after "Shattered Love." The singular plurality of our relation, Nancy asserted here, is not expressed by "the representation of something that is real" but by "what is real in the representation – its effectiveness and its efficacy. (The paradigm for this is 'I love you' or, perhaps more originally, 'I am addressing myself to you')" (*Being Singular Plural* 58). More basically, this fundamental ontological status of the phrase "I love you" is also asserted by Nancy in his conference on love: "In a certain sense 'I love you' says it all, everything is contained in it. When we say 'I love you' we say everything" (66). Or inversely: "As long as we haven't said 'I love you' we haven't said anything" (84).[14]

Both in *Sexistence* and in the essay "Exclamations" (*Expectation: Philosophy, Literature*) Nancy pushes this claim to its extreme when he presents sexual exclamations to be the ultimate form of such an address at the limit of speech. Most literarily, these exclamations are language *à bout du souffle*, bursting of sense according to Nancy.[15] By taking these sexual exclamations as paradigmatic, Nancy does not hint at the peculiar, private language of lovers, but at language *as such*, or, better still, at the *heart* of language, at what makes it tick so to say:

> The speaking being [is] the desiring being [...] This is perfectly clear when I say "I love you, I long for you." But in the end this holds for every true utterance that somehow exceeds the mere informative (for instance "hello" or "goodbye" or even a whole philosophical treatise, a novel or a poem, or a conversation). (*Sexistence* 47)

So it doesn't matter if it is a single word, a silence even, or a whole narrative or book, when expressed out of the love to exceed ourselves – and what else is expression after all? – , these are all gestural significations, modes of touching language.

Set against a somewhat dramatized historical background, the *way* in which language touches, however, has changed according to Nancy and this is where his philosophical project overlaps with that of the eighteenth-century Jena Romantics. Nancy, in *Sexistence* and elsewhere, understands this background in terms of what Hölderlin had called the "flight of the gods" and what Nancy himself in *Expectation: Philosophy, Literature* calls the absence of a "metalanguage" (57).[16] In this situation, we need to "think afresh [...] how we address ourselves to ourselves" (Nancy, *Sexistence* 63). The most important point to consider in this respect is that both language and sex have entered, after the "flight of the gods," what Nancy calls a "regime of infinitude": "Language and sex entered a regime of infinitude at the moment their sacred character had disappeared, that is to say, at the moment when sense is no longer given as an original depot in speech and in semen" (53–54).[17]

Whereas love and language – that is, also loving language, exposing language – once had a well-defined meaning and goal (that is, transmitting the divine or cosmic order that was also the very source of their sense), they are now liberated from meaning and end, literally end-less, directionless, and motivated by nothing else than their own movement and circulation. Importantly, this liberated, infinite movement of sense is for Nancy, just like for the Jena Romantics, not so much a *desacralization* of our world, but rather a disclosure of its very truth, which is indeed that of being motivated or moved by nothing else than its own movement or circulation, by "*l'élan ou la poussée du sens*" as Nancy has it (*Sexistence* 54), by the vigour or impetus of sense. Already in *Being Singular Plural* Nancy had described this as "just another sort of 'Copernican Revolution'": social being no longer revolving around something else, but "revolving around itself or turning on itself [or also *turning on* itself]" (57).

What Nancy takes from the Romantic tradition, then, is, firstly, the idea that this self-excitement happens in and through language, through ways of speaking and writing, and, secondly, that it is in the end perhaps *nothing but* this happening or "passing," this passage or movement of thinking. Indeed, the Romantic's hope for such a new Copernican revolution was what Novalis famously called a *romantization* of the world: the appeal to exposing ourselves anew, for the first time, or again and again as if for the first time, to its original sense, to the sense that originates from – or rather *is* – the everyday world itself, expressed with new élan, in our common language, the *lingua romana*.[18] In Nancy's romantic vocabulary the world's self-exiting movement is called the *pulse*, the *pulsation* or *drive*. Indeed, as Nancy asserts, this pulse has been, in a variety of forms, the central motive of modern thought:

> [...] Kant opens an epoch where Reason has to consider itself as *Trieb*, pulse, impetus [*poussée*], tension and desire moving towards an "unconditioned" that in the end proves to consist of nothing else than its own push. Called "will" by Schopenhauer, and later by Nietzsche, then appearing as "drive" with Freud – after having passed through the "labour power" of Marx and the "leap" of Kierkegaard. Definitely also through the parallel "differences" of Deleuze and Derrida – differenciation and differance that share at least the involvement of a tension, a pulse and a pulsation.[19]
> (*Sexistence* 31)

In a sense, Nancy's oeuvre aspires nothing else than continuing this train of modern thought, pushing it further, in unforeseen directions. Yet, even if Nancy would rightly claim that post-Kantian philosophy *as such* is a thinking of this self-exciting movement or pulse, it is with Jena Romanticism that it becomes an overtly *relational*, *plural*, and *linguistic* affair.[20]

To be sure, the Jena Romantics wanted to generate a form of thinking and writing that was grafted on the infinite "energy" or "chemistry" of connection, interaction, and exchange – of what they called "sympoesy" or "symphilosophy."[21] Moreover, as Nancy also stressed on a number of occasions, Jena Romanticism designates the moment in the history of philosophy when philosophical thinking is presented as a *literary* affair (cf. *The Literary Absolute*). Especially in their short-lived journal *Athenaeum* (1798–1800), the Jena Romantics experimented with a variety of philosophical-literary and dialogical forms of writing, many-voiced collections of fragments, letters, and conversations – all of which included, perhaps for the first time in philosophical history, the voices of women. More specifically, the moving force of what Nancy calls "*l'élan ou la poussée du sens*," is what the Jena Romantics called the *Witz* – the witty remark or thoughtful match, the spark or *je ne sais quoi* of thinking, that what *makes sense* but is itself irretrievable. Indeed, in his book-length study of Jena Romanticism, co-authored with Philippe Lacoue-Labarthe, Nancy takes the Romantic *Witz* as the life-force of Romantic thinking, being "not merely a 'form' or a 'genre,'" but "a spiritual faculty, a type of spirit" that "can seize upon and bring to light new, unforeseen, and, in short, creative relations" (Lacoue-Labarthe and Nancy 53).

The link between *Witz* and love imposes itself here. Not surprisingly, then, analyses of the *Witz* were at the centre of Nancy's early writings.[22] In one of the earliest of these writings, entitled "Menstruum Universale" (1978), Nancy suggests – tentatively, but clearly anticipating his most recent work on love and *sexistence* – that the logic of *Witz* should be compared to the logic of non-reproductive love-making. In a footnote to his definition of *Witz*, Nancy advances that "once again, and in many different ways, we find the union of the sexes which obeys in every respect the 'logic' of *Witz*" – teasingly concluding: "This aspect of the sexuality of *Witz*, [...] will not be developed here" (*The Birth to Presence* 416n3). Tellingly, it is this very essay that is republished as the programmatic prologue to Nancy's 2018 book *Expectation: Philosophy*,

Literature. Containing a large collection of philosophical-literary texts written by Nancy over the past thirty-five years, this volume stages, as Jean-Michel Rabaté remarks in his preface, "a courtship between philosophy and literature that has never been presented with such wit, grace and finesse" (xii–xiii) and encloses in many respects the Romantic philosophical itinerary of Nancy's that I am trying to sketch here.[23]

resuscitating the romantic heart

Although the Jena Romantics are amongst Nancy's earliest and most important sources of inspiration, Nancy is reluctant to call himself their inheritor and references to Jena Romanticism are virtually absent in his later works on love, sense, or *sexistence*. The trouble with the Jena Romantics – highlighted by Nancy – is that they, too, somehow betrayed the love of thinking. By wanting to contain it, and idealize it into a work that would famously be "complete in itself like a hedgehog" (Athenaeum fragment 206 (Firchow 1971)), they have absolutized the non-economy of love's passionate proliferation in the form of a complete return to the self, "the torn borders folded back into the sweetness of microcosmic self-enclosure. Exposition itself ends up as introjection, return to self" (Nancy, "Art, a Fragment" 660). Having tried to turn unreserved exposition into complete self-enclosure, the Jena Romantics have perhaps even reached the opposite of love, that is, the opposite of being, a work of death, "[converting] its interruption, noncompletion, and in-finitude – into finish" (125).[24]

Certainly, we could understand the Romantic project in terms of a necessary failure, resulting from an ambiguity at the heart of Romanticism, of a thinking that somehow, perhaps out of "naiveté" (Lacoue-Labarthe and Nancy 17), will always miss its own opportunity, that cannot but eclipse its own "unthought possibility" (Hoffman-Schwarz 202). This is what Maurice Blanchot suggests in his essay on "The Athenaeum," where he describes this unthought possibility as "the

non-romantic essence of romanticism" (357). Critically inheriting Jena Romanticism would then be to embrace the fundamental ambiguity or aporia of Romanticism, in which the whole and the fragment, the work and its unworking, the finite and the infinite hold each other captive in a never-ending oscillation.

Nancy at times also seems to endorse this view by stressing equivocality, fragmentation, and dissolution as the main heritage of the Jena Romantics. The reason why Nancy is, in my view – in his heart – , *more* romantic than his contemporaries, is that he eventually takes another route. This is my fourth and final hypothesis. What Nancy takes from the Romantic moment is not the break, disruption, or *inoperativity*,[25] but – in it or behind it – the love, energy, pulse, and passion. Rather than ascribing Romanticism's failure to a necessarily unworking, non-romantic heart of Romanticism, Nancy speaks of the "*petrified*" heart of Romanticism (*Expectation* 20), that is, a heart that stopped beating, that stopped opening itself to what exceeds it. We should therefore perhaps say that Nancy does not aim at pursuing the *unromantic* heart of Romanticism, like Blanchot and others do, but rather at *defrosting* the heart of Romantic thought, re-opening it, resuscitating it. Not by revealing a hidden, alien core, but by *stimulating* it.[26] Or, as Nancy puts it in plainly Romantic terms in *Sexistence* by "alchemy, magic, chemistry, fortuitous processes, manoeuvres or encounters, by combinations and re-combinations, mutations – whatever" (119).

This is exactly – including the uncomfortable feeling of "whatever" – what makes this work unprecedented in the clarity of its attempt. The pulse used by Nancy to resuscitate the Romantic heart of thinking, the heart of Romantic thinking, is, to be sure, a plainly *romanticized*, dramatized, fictionalized language.[27] More so, and also more convincingly so, than in his earlier works, Nancy extends, interrupts, or rather *relays* philosophical discourse by fragments and portions from popular novels, poems, cinematic dialogues. He crosses and combines ages and places, genders and voices, from Lucretia to Céline, from Pasolini to Audre Lorde – shifting from masculine to feminine voices, from the singular to the plural – letting a stammering poetic rhythm or experimental blogpost take over where his philosophical discourse risks to enclose itself upon itself, or where it gets out of breath.

With increasing pertinence, Nancy's oeuvre shows that we need a new way of thinking, a new way of addressing ourselves to ourselves, a way that helps philosophy's petrified heart to open up and fall in love, again, anew. In doing so, Nancy's work shows that what matters is not so much its propositional content, but the fact that his texts are themselves performative acts of touching, texts that address us, act upon us, rather than communicate something to us. I have suggested to call this way "romantic," because it draws its motivation from a reflection on relationality, love, and passion. And because it involves, in line with the historical moment of Romanticism, an appeal to connect philosophy, in a fundamental way, to what since then is usually called "literature" – not the non-positional tenderly touching literary-philosophical style that we have gradually become used to, but a more excessive, exorbitant one, as unsettling as the unexpectedly uttered phrase "I love you."

echo by jean-luc nancy

Aukje van Rooden leaves me speechless: she has brought something to light, the extent of which at least, but probably even its precise existence, I did not know myself. I mean to say that I have often taken recourse (like others, admittedly) to the phrase "I love you" as an example of a statement that is at the same time performative as well as void – thus, performing a void (but a void can be filled …) – and by the same token does not make for an "example" but rather constitutes the borderline-case of the address: not a call but a statement, a declaration that declares itself overwhelmed by what it declares. Aukje van Rooden, in her final note, is right to cite the interview where I express my desire to write, not "about" sex, but "motivated" by sex (the

original French expression I used at the time escapes me, but she translates it as "motivated" … I would say "mobilized" (*mobilisé*), "pushed" (*poussé*)) – for I think that 'I love you' is in a way sexual realization (*performance*) itself: crossing the uncrossable distance …

But, at the same time, for a very long time now, I have also thought that the gesture of philosophy is less one of knowing or even understanding than a gesture of love: philosophy means saying, or wants to say, "I love you" to being, reality or existence – precisely because it experiences the strangeness, indeed resistance or even hostility, of this reality.

What can really (*vraiment*) be said to be? Perhaps what really is, is such only if I love it. So, if I give it a place or a role that is as indispensable as it is impossible.

It seems to be that any philosophy is an attempt at not contenting oneself with saying "I love you," making this realization (*performance*) on the edge of language really real (*réellement performante*).

In fact, I will certainly have to come back to this. If I can … For Aukje van Rooden rightly points towards the genre of fiction, which exceeds philosophy precisely because fiction performs a declaration of love (it gives existence to another). Reciprocally, "I love you" turns out or confesses itself to be fiction (not, of course, philosophy or true knowledge), but according to a faith that makes it real …

Yet, not everyone who wants to has the voice (or the way) of fiction …

disclosure statement

No potential conflict of interest was reported by the author.

notes

1 Cf. Bram Ieven, Aukje van Rooden, Marc Schuilenburg, and Sjoerd van Tuinen, eds, *De nieuwe Franse filosofie: Denkers en thema's voor de 21ᵉ eeuw* [The New French Philosophy: Thinkers and Themes for the 21st Century] (Amsterdam:

Boom, 2011); and Alena Alexandrova, Ignaas Devisch, Laurens ten Kate, and Aukje van Rooden, eds, *Re-treating Religion. Deconstructing Christianity with Jean-Luc Nancy* (New York: Fordham UP, 2012).

2 In many respects, this claim follows naturally from Derrida's influential portrayal of Nancy as a philosopher of the *touch* (*On Touching – Jean-Luc Nancy*). Albeit highly rewarding, this approach cannot but – and from Derrida's perspective of course also needs to – address the possible risks of what the latter would call a metaphysics of presence or immediacy. I believe that a characterization of Nancy as a romantic rather than a haptocentric thinker, more clearly situates Nancy's work within a framework that defies any metaphysics of immediate presence, drawing, as we will see, not only from the phenomenological tradition, but also from a thorough reflection on the thinking of *energeia* and of language.

3 The shift from "littérature *et* philosophie" to "philosophy, literature" – that is, from literature and philosophy as two distinguishable category genres to a presentation of the two in an interrupted continuity – is telling, as is perhaps the inversion of the order.

4 Not only the rhyme, but also the flower seems to slightly differ between languages and cultures. In France, one plucks the *marguerite* (*Chrysanthemum leucanthemum*), but for instance in The Netherlands and Germany it is the *madelief* or *Gänseblume* (*Bellis perennis*). They are related, but the latter is much smaller. In English both flowers are called *daisy*, but in American-English it refers to the *Chrysanthemum leucanthemum* and in British-English to the *Bellis perennis*.

5 "Is there life more lively than in the love-relation? [*Est-il vie plus vivante que l'amoureux rapport?*]," Nancy asks elsewhere. "Lettre à Descartes." 4 September 2018, Stockholm (unpublished).

6 For a similar claim, see also Abbott 146.

7 This is also what makes love at the same time a matter of desire and of loss. Speaking of love and pleasure in his interview with Erik Meganck and Evelien Van Beeck, Nancy remarks: "Instead of meeting the other or myself in pleasure, I lose myself in it, as well as the other. Pleasure is therefore the *locus*, the register, of loss, of the *perte totale*" ("Jean-Luc Nancy over seks en wetenschap" 347; my translation).

8 In "Shattered Love," Nancy had already presented love as an unsettling of economic laws, as "that which brings an end to the dichotomy between the love in which I lose myself without reserve and the love in which I recuperate myself" (96).

9 Love shares this incalculable syncopation with poetry according to Nancy. See the essays "The Poets Calculation" and "Narrative, Narration, Recitative" in *Expectation: Philosophy, Literature*.

10 In retrospective, one can discern the trajectory leading to this point from, amongst others, *Corpus* [1992], "The 'There Is' of Sexual Relation" [2001], and other texts on pleasure and the body (collected in English in *Corpus II: Writings on Sexuality* (New York: Fordham UP, 2013)), to *Coming* (with Adèle van Reeth (New York: Fordham UP, 2017); translation of *Jouissance* (Paris: Plon, 2014)).

11 Cf. also "Love is stimulated by sex, like sex is aroused by love [...] The one is the truth or the virtue of the other" (Nancy, *Sexistence* 158).

12 Nancy's essay draws from Lacan's famous (interrelated) claims that "there is no sexual relation" and that "*jouissance* is impossible." I will not elaborate on Nancy's reading of Lacan or Lacanian psychoanalysis, since the intention of Nancy's essay is not to explore these statements within the tradition of psychoanalytic theory, but to investigate what exactly one is saying, ontologically, when making these claims. In this respect, the notion of the "there is" (*il y a*) of the title is less a reference to Lacan than to Levinas, and perhaps via Levinas to Blanchot. To say that sex "is" "nowhere" and can be dispersed over a possibly unlimited series of acts or events is of course also to say that it is "everywhere," always at stake, as Nancy suggests in *Coming* "Perhaps it begins very, very far from the sexual act itself" (Nancy and van Reeth 20).

13 This is why Nancy calls the phrase "I love you" the "promise" to relate oneself to an other, a promise that is itself already a form of relating, if not the ultimate form of relating – because nothing else than that:

> Love [...] always arrives in the promise and as the promise. It is thus that it touches and that it traverses. For one does not know what one says when one says "I love you," and one does not say anything, but one knows that one says it and that it is its

law, absolutely: instantly, one is shared and traversed by that which does not fix itself in any subject or in any signification. ("Shattered Love" 101)

The passage continues:

if one more proof or account were necessary: the same holds true when one hears "I love you" said by an other whom one does not love and whose expectations will not be met. Despite everything, it cannot be that one is not traversed by something that, while not love itself, is nonetheless the way in which its promise touches us. (101)

14 The expression of the singular plurality of existence investigated by Nancy in *Being Singular Plural* in terms of the "I love you" or "I am addressing myself to you" is that of the *symbol*. There is no room to elaborate this line of argumentation here, but it would be very well possible to investigate Nancy's romanticism as well as its sources in the German Romantic tradition in terms of the symbolic.

15 Quoting Paul Celan in "The 'There Is' of Sexual Relation," Nancy already remarked that "[t]he kiss, at night, *burns sense into language* [(s')imprime une brûlure de sens]" (16).

16 This was already the main point in his 2000 text "'One day the gods withdrew ...' (Literature/Philosophy)" (inserted in *Expectation: Philosophy, Literature*) but is in an interesting way reiterated in *Sexistence*. The first version of this 2000 text, called "Entre-deux," was published in *La Magazine Littéraire* no. 392, November 2000, before being published as *"Un jour, les dieux se retirent ... " (Littérature/philosophie: entre-deux)* (Bordeaux: William Blake, 2001). Cf. also Nancy, "Éros est revenu au-devant de la scène lorsque Dieu est mort." Here we see how Nancy's work on Christianity intertwines with his work on love and language and Collins is right in noting that Nancy's work on love, mainly "Shattered Love," "can be seen as a prefiguring of his later deconstruction of Christianity project" (Collins 309). In the same vein, it would be interesting to reread Augustine's *deus interior intimo meo, superior summon meo*, often quoted by Nancy, as an expression of amorous or sexual interaction.

17 On the regime of infinitude and on the relation between sex and language, see also Nancy, "Sexistence" and "Aux bords de l'intime."

18 In Novalis' words:

The world must be made Romantic. In that way one can find the original meaning [den ursprünchlichen Sinn] again [...] This operation is as yet quite unknown. By endowing the commonplace with a higher meaning, the ordinary with mysterious respect, the known with the dignity of the unknown, the finite with the appearance of the infinite, I am making it Romantic. – The operation for the higher, unknown mystical, infinite is the converse – this undergoes a logarithmic change through this connection – it takes on an ordinary form of expression. Romantic philosophy. *Lingua romana.* Raising and lowering by turns. (151).

19 To this philosophical-historical overview, we can also add Spinoza's *conatus* explained by Nancy in terms of love and desire, or rather of a "desire of the subject or desire as subject, and here I even dare to say: being as desire" (*La pensée dérobée* 90; my translation).

20 As well as perhaps a reflexive one, as is stressed by Nancy in his interview with Florian Pennanech, "Undoubtedly, Romanticism was the first moment in Europe's development when there was a self-awareness of that pulsation" ("Le souci poétique").

21 Exemplary in this respect are the Athenaeum fragments 112 and 375, and Ideas 23 (Firchow 1971). Moreover, the Jena Romantics oftentimes put their energetic thinking in terms of love, e.g., in Ideas fragments 83, 103, and 104.

22 Amongst the earliest texts of Nancy's on Jena Romanticism are the translation of and introduction to Jean Paul's "Sur le Witz" (with A.M. Lang). *Poétique* 15 (1973); "Le dialogue des genres" (with Ph. Lacoue-Labarthe). *Poetique* 21 (1975); "Menstruum Universale." *SubStance* 21 (1978 [1976]); *L'Absolu litteraire: Theorie de la litterature du romantisme allemande* (with Ph. Lacoue-Labarthe) (Paris: Seuil, 1978); the translation of and introduction to Brentano's "Entretien sur le romantisme" (with A.M. Lang and Ph. Lacoue-Labarthe). *Po&sie* 8 (1979).

23 Also for Rabaté, then, the Romantic *Witz* is what most clearly characterizes the genre, form or spirit of Nancy's texts. Although Rabaté stresses the key role of Romantic *Witz* in the

Nancyan courtship between philosophy and literature, he, somewhat surprisingly, does not so much present Nancy as an heir of Romanticism, but as an heir of Paul Valéry, and, consequently, of symbolism. As argued above, this asks for a reflection on the role of the "symbol" in Nancy's work, which should undoubtedly also draw from the typically Romantic preference of the symbolic over the allegoric. On Nancy's reiteration of the Romantic theme of the *Witz*, see also Rabaté, "'Wet the Ropes'" and Kollias, "Kant with Lacan, Freud with Romanticism."

24 In *The Literary Absolute*, Nancy and Lacoue-Labarthe interpret the Romantics in a similar vein as Heidegger had interpreted Schelling in *Schelling's Treatise on the Essence of Freedom*, that is, as one of the last metaphysics, still under the spell of some form of idealism. I want to suggest that this Heideggerian (or Schellingean) lens perhaps leads them to too hastily denounce Romanticism as a form of "eidesthetics," while overlooking – or not choosing to follow – the romantic focus on *energeia* described by them as "the second Schlegelian path" that is, according to them, however only "a single element lost in the ensemble of the fragments" (Lacoue-Labarthe and Nancy 56–57):

> The second, Schlegelian path might be indicated by *Athenaeum* fragment 375 as the path leading toward "energy" or toward "the energetic man," defined by the "infinitely flexible ... universal power through which the whole man shapes himself," well beyond the "genius" who "shapes a work." Energy extends to the limit of the work and of the system; its "infinite flexibility," linked to "an incalculable number of projects," effects an infinite fragmentation of work and system [...] The fragment on energy, however, is unique, a single element lost in the ensemble of the *Fragments*. (56–57)

25 This is what Simon Critchley calls "unworking Romanticism."

26 Nancy hints at this in his interview with Florian Pennanech, "The romantic desire was denounced and revived at the same time: we had to be wary of falling again in its trap and we needed to give it a fresh impetus, to find a new incentive [*resort*]" ("Le souci poétique").

27 This does not mean that Nancy has entered the domain of novelistic or fiction writing. Or he does so only, as he himself would assert, when "fiction is not limited to the invented character of a story [but when] invention is taken to be nothing but the outer face of speech edging its way to the extreme where it will designate itself as being exceeded" (Nancy, *Sexistence* 169). We could perhaps also call this kind of writing "intrigue" or "intriguing writing" as Nancy himself does in his Preface "L'intrigue littéraire de Levinas" to Emmanuel Levinas, *Œuvres 3: Eros, littérature et philosophie: essais romanesques et poétiques, notes philosophiques sur le thème d'éros* ("L'intrigue littéraire" 14). In an interview preceding the publication, and even the writing process, of *Sexistence*, Nancy said that although he had the plan to take up the theme of sex, he had not yet found the right way of writing about it:

> I do say that the question of sex remains absent in philosophy, but I cannot solve this by employing an objectifying discourse. This might work when talking *about* sex, but what I am looking for is in fact a writing that is *motivated by* [*gemotiveerd door, engagé par*] the question of sex. ("Jean-Luc Nancy over seks en wetenschap" 344; my translation)

bibliography

Abbott, Mathew. "On Not Loving Everyone: Comments on Jean-Luc Nancy's 'L'Amour en éclats' [Shattered Love]." *On the Love of Commentary*. Spec. issue of *Glossator: Practice and Theory of the Commentary* 5 (2011): 139–62. Print.

Blanchot, Maurice. "The Athenaeum." *The Infinite Conversation*. Minneapolis: U of Minnesota P, 1993. 351–59. Print. Translation of "Athenaeum." *L'Entretien infini*. Paris: Gallimard, 1969. 515–27. Print.

Collins, Ashuk. "Being Exposed to Love: The Death of God in Jean-Luc Marion and Jean-Luc Nancy." *International Journal of the Philosophy of Religion* 80 (2016): 297–319. Print.

Critchley, Simon. "Lecture 2: Unworking Romanticism." *Very Little ... Almost Nothing: Death, Philosophy, Literature*. London: Routledge, 1997. 99–165. Print.

Derrida, Jacques. *On Touching – Jean-Luc Nancy*. Stanford: Stanford UP, 2005. Print. Translation of *Le toucher, Jean-Luc Nancy*. Paris: Galilée, 2000. Print.

Firchow, Peter, ed. *Friedrich Schlegel's Lucinde and the Fragments*. Minneapolis: U of Minnesota P, 1971. Print.

Hoffman-Schwarz, Daniel. "Romantics/Romanticism." *The Nancy Dictionary*. Ed. Peter Gratton and Marie-Eve Morin. Edinburgh: Edinburgh UP, 2015. 199–202. Print.

Kollias, Hector. "Kant with Lacan, Freud with Romanticism: Jean-Luc Nancy and the Syncope of Form." *Oxford Literary Review* 27.1 (2012): 45–65. Print.

Lacoue-Labarthe, Philippe, and Jean-Luc Nancy. *The Literary Absolute: The Theory of Literature in German Romanticism*. New York: State U of New York P, 1998. Print. Translation of *L'Absolu littéraire: Théorie de la littérature du romantisme allemande*. Paris: Seuil, 1978. Print.

Nancy, Jean-Luc. "Art, a Fragment." *The Sense of the World*. Minneapolis: U of Minnesota P, 1997. Print. Translation of "L'art, fragment." *Lignes*, 1993. Print.

Nancy, Jean-Luc. "Aux bords de l'intime: Entretien avec Michael Foessel." *Esprit* 7 (2017): 155–62. Print.

Nancy, Jean-Luc. *Being Singular Plural*. Stanford: Stanford UP, 2000. Print. Translation of *Être singulier pluriel*. Paris: Galilée, 1996. Print.

Nancy, Jean-Luc. *Corpus*. Paris: Métaillé, 2006 [1992]. Print.

Nancy, Jean-Luc. *Corpus II: Writings on Sexuality*. New York: Fordham UP, 2013. Print.

Nancy, Jean-Luc. "'Éros est revenue au-devant de la scène lorsque Dieu est mort': entretien avec Nicolas Dutent." *L'Humanité* 11 May 2018. Web. 18 May 2021. <https://www.humanite.fr/jean-luc-nancy-eros-est-revenu-au-devant-de-la-scene-lorsque-dieu-est-mort-655114>.

Nancy, Jean-Luc. *Expectation: Philosophy, Literature*. New York: Fordham UP, 2018. Print. Translation of *Demande: Littérature et philosophie*. Paris: Gallilée, 2015. Print.

Nancy, Jean-Luc. "Jean-Luc Nancy over seks en wetenschap: interview met Erik Meganck en Evelien Van Beeck." *Tijdschrift voor filosofie* 79 (2017): 343–52. Print.

Nancy, Jean-Luc. *La pensée dérobée*. Paris: Galilée, 2001. Print.

Nancy, Jean-Luc. "Le souci poétique: entretien avec Florian Pennanech." *fabula-LhT* 10 (2012). Web. 18 May 2021. <http://www.fabula.org/lht/10/nancy.html>.

Nancy, Jean-Luc. "L'intrigue littéraire de Levinas." Emmanuel Levinas, *Œuvres 3: Eros, littérature et philosophie: essais romanesques et poétiques, notes philosophiques sur le thème d'éros*. Ed. Jean-Luc Nancy and Danielle Cohen-Levinas. Paris: Bernard Grattes/IMEC, 2013. 9–30. Print.

Nancy, Jean-Luc. "Love." *God, Justice, Love, Beauty: Four Little Dialogues*. New York: Fordham UP, 2011. 63–96. Print. Translation of *Je t'aime, un peu beaucoup, passionnément ... : Petite conférence sur l'amour*. Montrouge: Bayard, 2008. Print.

Nancy, Jean-Luc. "Menstruum Universale." *The Birth to Presence*. Stanford: Stanford UP, 1993. Print. Reprint of "Menstruum Universale (Literary Dissolution)." *SubStance* 21.6 (1978): 21–35 and "Menstruum Universale." *Aléa* 1 (1981). Print.

Nancy, Jean-Luc. "'One day the gods withdrew ...' (Literature/Philosophy: In-Between) [2000]." *Expectation: Philosophy, Literature*. New York: Fordham UP, 2018. 25–30. Print. Translation of *"Un jour, les dieux se retirent ... " (Littérature/philosophie: entre-deux)*. Bordeaux: William Blake, 2001. Print.

Nancy, Jean-Luc. "Sexistence." *Diacritics* 43.4 (2015): 110–18. Print.

Nancy, Jean-Luc. *Sexistence*. New York: Fordham UP, 2021. Print. Translation of *Sexistence*. Paris: Galilée, 2017. Print.

Nancy, Jean-Luc. "Shattered Love." *The Inoperative Community*. Minneapolis: U of Minnesota P, 1991. 82–109. Print. Translation of "L'amour en éclats." *Aléa* 7 (1986): 59–91. Print.

Nancy, Jean-Luc. "The 'There Is' of Sexual Relation." *Corpus II: Writings on Sexuality*. New York: Fordham UP, 2013. Print. Translation of *L'"il y a" du rapport sexuel*. Paris: Galilée, 2001. Print.

Nancy, Jean-Luc, and Adèle van Reeth. *Coming*. New York: Fordham UP, 2016. Print. Translation of *Jouissance*. Paris: Plon, 2014. Print.

Novalis. "On Romanticism." Stephen Prickett, ed. *European Romanticism: A Reader.* London: Bloomsbury, 2014. 151. Print. Translated from Novalis. *Schriften. Historische Kritische Ausgabe.* Vol. 2. 1981. 545. Print.

Rabaté, Jean-Michel. "'Wet the Ropes': Poetics of Sense, from Paul Valéry to Jean-Luc Nancy." Introduction to Jean-Luc Nancy. *Expectation: Philosophy, Literature.* New York: Fordham UP, 2018. ix–xx. Print.

I introduction

Two small books, light in their weight but heavy in their common gravity, confront one another: *Corpus* (Jean-Luc Nancy) and *Ethics of the Spread Body* (Emmanuel Falque). Written more than twenty years apart from one another, both put an experience into language. The former – *Corpus* – precedes the author's own arresting experience of the transplanted heart, related in "The Intruder," and attempts to speak "starting from the body."[1] The latter – *Ethics of the Spread Body* – follows an experience in palliative care, this time not from the side of the patient, but that of the team of carers.[2] Better still, the concept of the spread body (*corps épandu*), which first appeared in *The Wedding Feast of the Lamb*, comes from a corporeal and medical experience in the world of surgery and anaesthesia as well. In short, there is something that intersects, if not meets, in experiences that are certainly different, but that both try to speak of our true corporeality, underneath the abstraction of the "lived-experience of the flesh" or the "ownmost body" (*corps propre*) (*Leib*) that phenomenology never ceases to deploy, whilst the materiality of the body (*Körper*), in illness at least, cannot be forgotten.

So it goes, and in an identical reaction or an identical leap, at the opening of *Corpus* and *Ethics of the Spread Body*. Starting with *Corpus*: *Hoc est enim corpus* – "this is indeed a body."

> Instantly, always, it is a *foreign body* that demonstrates itself, a *monster* impossible to swallow [...] And all thoughts of the "ownmost body" (*corps propre*), laborious

emmanuel falque

translated by marie chabbert and nikolaas deketelaere

SPREAD BODY AND EXPOSED BODY
dialogue with jean-luc nancy

> efforts at reappropriating what we used to consider, impatiently, as "objectified" or "reified," all such thoughts about the ownmost body are comparably contorted: they amount only to *the expulsion of what we desired*. (5; my emphasis, trans. mod.)

Ethics of the Spread Body, then:

> The human body always remains animal, even manipulable, in the medical context – as the clinical or reclining (*klinein*) body, on the hospital bed more so than anywhere else. However, whereas we once feared the positivism of the body-object; we will today rather, and by way of a backlash, fear the excess of concern (*soin*) taken in, or attention paid to, the body-subject. For, by dint

of holding forth on the "carnal lived-experience" of the patient (*leiblichkeit*), we have nevertheless forgotten their bodily mass (*körperlichkeit*). (18)

An identical aim, itself double, thus innervates these two works – *Corpus* and *Ethics of the Spread Body*. (a) *First aim*: not, or no longer, remaining stuck in the singular repetition of the body-subject (*corps sujet*) or the ownmost body (*corps propre*). For by dint of saying "I am my body" ("*je suis mon corps*"), in contemporary phenomenology especially, I do not know – or rather, I end up forgetting – that one day my body "will get me" (*m'aura*). The experience of disease, and even more so that of the reception of something absolutely foreign in oneself (the intruder of the transplanted heart), certainly suffices to make evident and to make known that *I perhaps "follow" my body* (*je "suis" peut-être mon corps*). However, we then understand it here, in a way that is surely strange, even in French, where I walk, even run after my body – *following it* (*à sa suite*), for it goes its own way ("*suis*" of the verb *suivre*, to follow); rather than it being fit (*habitable*) for the way of understanding in which it would be my dwelling ("*suis*" of the verb *être*, to be). I *have* a body, or rather I "follow" ("*suis*") it, all the more so because it governs and precedes me (*suivre*, to follow); rather than it being the appropriate site of my lived experience in need of hospitality (*être*, to be).[3]

(b) *Second aim*: returning to Christianity as a particular determination of the body according to an urgency that is first of all cultural – never mind the lure of the single carnal lived experience (the proper) or the invasion of the virtual (the projected). Christianity, "deconstructed or not," establishes itself on a single word that makes of corporeality, even its objectivation or its "this" ("*ceci*"), the source of the West in all its articulations: "*Hoc est corpus meum*," Nancy emphasises,

we come from a culture where this cult phrase will have been tirelessly uttered by millions of people officiating in millions of rites. Everyone in this culture, Christian or

otherwise, (re)cognizes it [...] It is our *Om mani padne ...* , our *Allah ill'Allah*, our *Schema Israel*.

In the same way, and from my own perspective this time – even if the Christian, as Nancy says, gives to this word the "*value of a real consecration* (God's *body* is *there*)" (*Corpus* 3; my emphasis, trans. mod.) – the issue at stake in philosophy, but also in the theology of today, is to envisage the meaning, *including the cultural one*, of this phrase, probably the condition for God himself to continue addressing himself to man (*l'homme*). Without the "words (*mots*) of the body" (recognition in language), which are not exactly the "ills (*maux*) of the body" (the ordeal of suffering or disease), the God become body could today neither articulate nor give himself to man. If the *hoc est corpus meum* – this is my body – no longer makes sense in our time, it is not certain that Christianity can still inhabit our culture, unless it falsely sets itself up as counterculture.

Christianity is not, for the believer and even less so for the philosopher, a simple matter of certitude, be it negative or positive. It is also a question of culture and not merely of faith, of a *vision for all* and not merely of a *privilege for oneself*. There is not, on the one hand, "those that see," and, on the other, "those that do not see" – whether it is a question of phenomenology or theology. It is first of all through an "in common," to speak in line with Nancy, or in a "community of being," to speak in line with Merleau-Ponty, that the Christian message must introduce itself or at least take shape. Against the illusion of the leap, or against the wrong or misunderstood separation of orders (order of the flesh, order of the spirit, order of charity), I will advocate here the "tilling" or "overlaying" of the disciplines of philosophy and theology, but this time first from a cultural point of view. Although I have operated it in the other direction as well, by accepting the point of view of what is revealed; it is precisely Jean-Luc Nancy whom I've learned this from, who himself cited it many years ago – it is on a basis provided by Nancy that I have forged the distinction that is important to me today between the "believable" (*croyable*) (adherence to faith) and the "credible" (*credible*) (comprehension of faith): "Arriving, thus, and certainly, at some form of confessionalism," suggests *The Wedding Feast of the Lamb*, there where the Eucharist must also, and first of all, be understood as "a matter of culture" (§8),

> we had better take care, however, that the *hoc est corpus meum* is not solely the domain of Christianity. As I said, the Eucharistic dogma is not only "believable" (by giving faith), it is also "credible" (with a universalisable rationality) – in which the present works maintains the pretention of addressing itself *to all*.[4] (43; trans. mod.)

Whether one is a Christian or not, and perhaps all the more so when one is a Christian than when one isn't, we can and must read Nancy. For, in principle, the "deconstruction" and "dis-enclosure" of Christianity are in no way an attack, hence it has led Martin Heidegger, more or less explicitly, towards a form of paganism or neutrality. It is, on the contrary, a matter of making evident the internal process of *deconstruction* inherent to Christianity itself, and to make emerge from this and in its *dis-enclosure* (*déclosion*) a kind of "extra-Christian" space that would be "something different from the space of a transfigured Christian thinking," that would be "an exterior or outside of Christianity itself" (Manchev 172–73). Far from recuperating (Christianity), or being recuperated (by Christianity), Nancy's thought must remain thus: an outside (*dehors*) of Christianity that certainly interrogates the cultural ground of Christianity, but at the same time stands out (*hors*) from it, not in order to cleverly or violently rid itself of it, but to think oneself "before" Christianity. It is not a question of incomplete possibilities of Christianity, or of a transfigured or otherwise dressed Christian thinking; but of being human today on the basis of the alterity and the foreign element that Christianity has introduced:

the thesis of the dis-enclosure is radical: it is not merely a question of undertaking a deconstruction of Christianity [...], but additionally to conceive of Christianity as such as deconstruction [...] Christianity "as such" is (on the contrary) not the principal question. Thinking religion, from a point of view that is philosophical, historical, anthropological, sociological or political, is certainly a task of the highest importance. But, beyond that, thinking is confronted with the metacritical imperative: thinking thinking itself, its own becoming and movement. To experience the experience (*faire l'expérience de l'expérience*) of thinking. (Manchev 170)

As I have shown elsewhere, to say that "there is no drama of atheist humanism," is of course not to say that Christianity is doing better today than it was yesterday, nor even that its future is assured when the horizon seems blocked to many. Believing that it could be that easy would probably amount to keeping one's eyes shut, and to stand in an overhang that makes us leave behind our common humanity would amount to properly refusing to enter into dialogue. To the contrary, however, it simply entails suggesting that "times have changed": what Henri de Lubac rightly accomplished in his era – *The Drama of Atheist Humanism* (1950) – , we need to articulate and think *today* as well, but in a *different way*. Today, not believing in God, and even not invoking God, is not or no longer necessarily being against God. Not all "non-theism" is necessarily an "a-theism" or "anti-theism," emphasises Maurice Merleau-Ponty in his inaugural lecture at the Collège de France, entitled *In Praise of Philosophy*. In a phrase directed precisely to de Lubac's approach, he says: "one misses the point of philosophy when one defines it as atheism. This is philosophy as it is *seen by the theologian*" (Merleau-Ponty, *In Praise of Philosophy* 46; my emphasis, trans. mod.).[5]

To reread Nancy today, or rather to think "with" or "on the basis of" him, is thus to think the body, for sure – whether it be spread-out (my position) or exposed (Nancy's) – , but also to think it insofar as it is rooted in a so-called Christian "culture," which we cannot legitimately avoid interrogating. What is an issue for atheism (not ignoring the Christian culture from which it stems), is also an issue for Christianity (interrogating the body so as to avoid enclosing it, today, in a straightforward conceptuality of the past). *The Wedding Feast of the Lamb* responds to *Ethics of the Spread Body*, like *The Deconstruction of Christianity* responds to *Corpus*. In both cases it is a matter of setting up a dialogue, between different works, between "Christianity" (*christianité*) and "corporeality," but according to different points of view and inverse endpoints: on the one hand, starting from something credible that may still become believable (my perspective), and, on the other, starting from something credible in which it has become properly unbelievable to believe (Nancy). However, in both cases there is an identical point of departure, or a common pedestal: the "credibility" of Christianity as such – and here of the statement "this is my body" (*hoc est enim corpus meum*) – , i.e., its cultural importance, whether one stands "inside" (myself) or "outside" of it (Nancy). There is thus debate (*débat*) but no combat (*combat*), except in the precise sense of a *loving struggle* (*combat amoureux*): "In the field of essential thinking," emphasises Martin Heidegger, "all refutation is foolish. Strife among thinkers is the 'loving struggle' concerning the matter itself" (256; trans. mod.).[6]

II the foreign body

"How, then, are we to touch upon the body, rather than signify it or making it signify?" At least as concerns the excesses of signification (phenomenology) and interpretation (hermeneutics), this declaration from *Corpus* (9), leads us – or returns us, I would say – to what I have elsewhere called the "true body," or better, the "shock of the body," in that it is or sometimes becomes "foreign" to myself:

It is a shock of the body, what the philosopher sometimes forgets by dint of either

referring himself to a phenomenon that is always ready to show itself or by thinking too often that it can always signify. The *a priori* of manifestation in phenomenology, like that of interpretation in hermeneutics, has destroyed *in ovo* the fright of the exposed body, at least in that it is always believed able to be received, whilst to the contrary, and most often, it is but "unassimilable matter" that repels us. (Falque, *Ethics of the Spread Body* 15)

From *Corpus* to *Ethics of the Spread Body*, there is an identical intention, even though the ways of resolution might be different.

That same intention can be read, first of all, in a search for a body that is truly of the body. Nancy's entire perspective, in *Corpus* as well as in "The Intruder," indeed boils down to recognising that what might at first appear to me as "my ownmost body," i.e., "own" (*propre*) or "mine," most often articulates itself to me as a "foreign body" – "of the body" (*hoc est corpus*) more so than "my body" (*corpus meum*): "If my own heart was failing me," the philosopher asks himself, "to what degree was it 'mine,' my 'own' organ? Was it even an organ?" (*Corpus* 162). The experience of the transplant brings to experience (*fait vivre*) what is foreign (*l'étranger*) in me, or rather lets it be experienced in me – an "intruder that is no longer in me," to follow the confession of the post-scriptum to the French edition of *L'Intrus* a few years later, but "the intruder that I have become" (47). Where we could have wrongly believed in an incorporation, not just carnal but also psychical, by force of carrying or assimilating the organ; the confession is made that it becomes less who I am than that I do not become who it is, not so much that it is appropriated by me than that I am not it in being assimilated to it. It is not the other that becomes mine, but me that becomes other, or "of the other," for myself: "That 'the body' *names the Stranger absolutely*, is an idea we've pursued to its successful conclusion," *Corpus* confesses (9; my emphasis, trans. mod.).

However, what seems at least of the order of an experience of the extra-ordinary, in the sense that it exits from the ordinary; in what way does the presence of the stranger as such in the "grafted body" say something other, but to a lesser extent, than what is ordinary in corporeality? In other words, is there not also in the transplant what constitutes the most common aspect of our corporeality – the impossibility of recognising my own body as "mine," to the point that it sometimes becomes, to me and for myself, foreign? "Must one thus render everything subjective in order to recognise oneself in one's identity?" I asked in "Résistence de la présence":

> There is, indeed, the beautiful description of the phantom limb as an absent part of the body that we nevertheless feel (*ressent*) (Merleau-Ponty).[7] However, there is also the numbness or at least local anaesthesia in that part of the body that we no longer feel (my perspective). To *the absence of the body felt as present* (the phantom limb related to the ownmost body), I oppose *the presence of the body experienced* (*éprouvé*) *as absent* (the tumour or the anesthetised body experienced (*vécus*) as totally foreign (*étranger*) to oneself). It will not do to always refer the "foreign body" (*corps étranger*) to the "ownmost body" (*corps propre*), or the "body" to the "flesh." Turned on its head, relating the flesh (*Leib*) to the body (*Körper*), or *experiencing* (*éprouver*) the "*ownmost body*" also as a "*foreign body*" – in the French sense of the unassimilable and non-incorporable – , this is, in my opinion, the common experience of the sufferer in illness and the insomniac in health. Both suffer (*subissent*) the same weight of materiality, in the mode of reclining, on the one hand, and in the mode of standing upright, on the other. (114–15)

"One cannot reduce the body."[8] This is what the two approaches considered here hold most in common. To say that the body is "irreducible" and "uncompressible" is to recognise it for others, of course, but also for oneself, my own body (*propre corps*) as foreign (*étranger*), or as "a" stranger ("*un*" *étranger*). Not "my other self" (*alter ego*), but an "other than myself" (*ego alter*): "*Corpus ego* has no

propriety, no 'ego-ness' (still less any 'egotism')," for "ego-ness is [still] a [...] signification" (Nancy, *Corpus* 26).

III outside-sense

This body, that of *Corpus*, certainly, but also that of *Ethics of the Spread Body*, does not maintain itself in signification – breaking definitively with all the lures of philosophical idealism, but also with a certain form of "descriptivity of the flesh" (*Leib*) or a "hypertrophy of interpretation" (*Verstehen*). Phenomenology and hermeneutics are partly related and are here questioned in their constant and implicit searching for the sensible, or rather how they remain stuck in what I have called the *a priori of phenomenality*. If it is appropriate to return to "the pure, and, so to speak, still mute experience," to follow Husserl in his *Cartesian Meditations*, one wonders why, and to what extent, it must still and always "be made to utter its own sense with no adulteration" (77; trans. mod.). Otherwise put, below (*en deçà*) sense, but also below non-sense, there is what I call "the extra-phenomenal" (*Hors phénomène*) and what Nancy calls "a-significance":

> I would prefer to take hysteria as the body's becoming totally parasitical upon the incorporeality of sense, to the point that it mutes incorporeality, thereby showing, in its stead, a piece, a zone, of *a*-significance [...] At the outset, there is no signification, translation, or interpretation: there is this *limit*, this edge, this contour, this extremity, this outline of exposition [...] This alone can close or release space for "interpretations." (*Corpus* 23; trans. mod.)

Let's say it outright: we find "a-significance" in Nancy, like we find the "outside" in Blanchot, the "*Il y a*" in Levinas, "Chaos" in Nietzsche and the "heterogenous" in Bataille; or that which I have called, for my part, the "extra-phenomenal." No longer the "possibility of the impossibility of the phenomenon," which still leaves in place the horizon of signification, even in a phenomenology of the night (the act of suffering, for example, still requires us to be sufficiently alive in order to feel it); but "the impossibility of the possibility of the phenomenon," this time in a night of phenomenology (the very impossibility of suffering, the very conditions of the taking place of the event having disappeared with the trauma that suppresses any horizon, and thus the very possibility of appearing or taking place). "To speak of the night of phenomenology is not to speak of non-appearance in the possible horizon of appearing but of the suppression of appearing itself – the very conditions of appearance," I write in "The Extra-Phenomenal":

> If the possibility of appearing itself were to disappear, then it is not "non-manifestation" which would be in question but, rather, the non-possibility of "manifesting." In contrast to the *possibility of the impossibility of the phenomenon* – the non-appearance of a phenomenon that could appear or that remains withdrawn – there exists (or rather doesn't) the *impossibility of the possibility of the phenomenon*. (9–10)

In the frame of this "outside-sense," Nancy's "exposed body," though it nevertheless figures in the title of the present essay, does not give out unto an exposition that would be a manifestation, or even an expression, rather the contrary. Like the spread body, it is not here to manifest, yet neither to hide; but rather to "self-pose" itself (*s'"auto-poser"*) in its very existence: "*Exposed*, therefore: but this does not mean putting something on view that would have previously been hidden or shut in" (Nancy, *Corpus* 35).

IV expansion and exposition

"Spread body," on the one hand, "exposed body," on the other: such is thus, not the opposition, but the common ground of the inquiry; on which, as I will show, a differentiation nevertheless outlines itself concerning the means of transcription ("describing" (*décrire*) and "writing" (*écrire*)) and its aim (possibly "theological" or "a-theological"). The gap between the two is all the more distinct because a same

groundswell cuts across *Corpus* and *Ethics of the Spread Body*, and thus the difference cannot be made evident but on the basis of a common belonging. So, what about the "spread body," on the one hand, and the "exposed body," on the other? Spreading-oneself-out (*s'épandre*) and exposing oneself (*s'exposer*), are they the same thing? To be there *in situ*, on an operating table, on a hospital bed, asleep or on the cross; is that the same as the exposed body, the body showing-its-skin (*ex-peausé*) – I will come back to this – , not in the sense of a manifestation, but at least in the sense of an outside of my ownmost body that has become strange to me?

Starting with the spread body. "Between the *extended body* (corps étendu) (Descartes) and the lived body (*corps vécu*) (Husserl)," as I noted by way of the opening to *Ethics of the Spread Body*,

> there is thus and by way of hypothesis a third type of body – which I am calling here the *spread body* (corps épandu) – a kind of border zone or intermediate body between the objective body and the subjective body. Extended, the body on the hospital bed is first of all as an animal, or an ever-manipulable object. Lived, however, that same body is envisioned (*visé*) as human, surrounded by proper care in a shared community in search of a sensible world (*monde sensé*). Between the two, or rather, in this between, what I have called the "spread body" emerges – extended in its materiality and lived in its intentionality [...] For, by dint of holding forth on the "carnal lived-experience" ("*vécu charnel*") of the patient (*leiblichkeit*), we have nevertheless forgotten their bodily mass (*körperlichkeit*). (17–18)

The "spread body" is thus for me a concept, like the "exposed body" in Nancy. Better still, the expansion of the body seeks something other, or an other-than (*un autrement*), that is not simply "body" (*Körper*) nor simply "flesh" (*Leib*). Whether it is in palliative care, or by way of the experience of the transplant of the intruder, what is observed (*le constat*) is the same, even though the lived experiences (*les vécus*) certainly differ. In a play on words that surely only works in French: the "ills" (*maux*) of the body never let themselves be reduced to the "words" (*mots*) of the body (Falque, *Ethics of the Spread Body* 29–33). In suffering, the body is "fall," "disaster," "weight," "its own weight of water and bone" – "'the body' is our anxiety stripped bare" (Nancy, *Corpus* 7; trans. mod.). Here, the homology of *Ethics of the Spread Body* and *Corpus* thus requires that the "ills" (*maux*) of the body be said with the "words" (*mots*) of language, a discontinuation of the gap of the "re-presented," which, according to Nancy, makes the body "constructed" rather than "described" (*décrit*), or better, "constructed" rather than "written" (*écrit*): "The body: that's how we invented it [...] It's our old culture's latest, most worked over, sifted, refined, dismantled, and reconstructed product" (*Corpus* 5–7).

Let it be clear here. According to Nancy, there are thus two types of bodies: no longer "flesh" (*Leib*) and "body" (*Körper*), as in phenomenology; but "constructed body" and "written" or "ex-scribed" body – I will return to this. For the "spread body" and the "exposed body" search for different things, or the same thing differently. Neither is it simply a third term, but rather what we could call, in French, an "extra-terminal" (*Hors terme*) – in the triple sense where, in French, it is not a middle between two extremes, nor a word of language sufficient for signifying, nor what would have an end or a goal as if one day we'd have gotten on top of it. On my account, the body is "extra-terminal" in virtue of the fact that it does not connect, does not signify, neither completes nor accomplishes.

"Describing before constructing," is what *Ethics of the Spread Body* seeks to do. "Writing," or rather, "ex-scribing" rather than "representing," is what *Corpus* aims for. To describe the body, at least as concerns palliative care, is to accept to hear and to see what articulates itself and lives itself out on a hospital bed – the so-called "clinical" body in that it is reclining. So it goes with the "words" used by nursing teams to transmit, or rather to passing along, the "ills" observed or even experienced during treatment: "nausea," "vomiting," "asthenia," "soiled," "redness," "headache," "convulsions," "pulmonary aspiration," "ulcers," "embedded tumour," "swollen tongue," "pus," "infection," "obstruction," "secretions," etc. (Falque, *Ethics of the Spread Body* 34–38). Here, the description struggles with, or at least warns us against, signification and interpretation. The expansion or spreading-out of the body is the "reclining" (*klinein*), neither extended as reduced to the state of a thing, nor lived as experiencing what is own rather than foreign.

In the experience of palliative care, of course, but also asleep or on the cross, the spread body is "*spread-out* on the hospital bed" – "thing" or "animal" nailed to the bed like one is also nailed to the cross. However, it is also "envisioned" (*visé*) or "experienced" (*vécu*) by the other as human, and this is its originality. In my view, it is less the materiality of the body that constitutes its humanity, than our way of intending it: "the 'spread body,' between the extended body of Descartes and the lived body of Husserl," as I have already noted elsewhere,

> preserves extension's resistance and lived experience's intentionality. It is at the same time "body" in its absolutely irreducible materiality and "flesh" in its lived experience, yet the synthesis of which is impossible. The anesthetised, sleepy, or crucified body, appears and appears to itself first of all as "body" (*Körper*) in an organicity sometimes so invasive and suffering that one must silence the pain that it causes, and subsequently as "flesh" (*Leib*) in the way of envisioning that I myself, or someone else, unceasingly assign to it (the way the physician, for example, envisions the human body he is operating on). ("Le fou désincarné" 333)

Moving onto the exposed body. Nancy's "exposed body," meanwhile, is not "described" (*se "décrit"*), it is rather "written" (*s'"écrit"*) or "ex-scribed" (*s'"ex-crit"*). To be written or ex-scribed, rather than described – that is what *Corpus* aims at:

I am addressed *to* my body *from my body* – or rather, the writing "I" is being sent from bodies to bodies [...] "Writing" remains a deceptive word. Anything so addressed to the body-outside is *exscribed*, as I try to write it, right alongside this outside, or as this outside. (19)

To start from the body as one writes by one's body. It is not thinking that guides the body, but the body that guides thinking; this is what constitutes the exposed body. Bodies – and perhaps even more so, the skin, I will return to this – , are "written bodies – incised, engraved, tattooed, scarred" (11). Coming to us in the body that ex-scribes itself is not "exposition" in the sense of what is manifested, but the "showing-of-skin" (*ex-peau-sition*), in the sense of being traumatised (*marqué à vif*), even marked for life (*marqué à vie*). I do not leave my skin, just like I will never leave my flesh, and it is from this "outside" that I perceive my flesh as the flesh of the other. The body exposes itself in its skin – or rather, shows-its-skin (*s'ex-peause*), skin-show (*Expeausition*) (33) – less according to a mode of phenomenalisation, than of definitive inscription. The body is text, not because it makes sense, but because it traces and subsists in its traces.

Thus, in *Corpus*, but also in *Ethics of the Spread Body*, there is an emergence of bodies, or rather "bodily tissues" (*des "chairs"*), that exhibit themselves each day to those who know how to see them – or, rather, that one cannot not see, but nevertheless recognising that that they are camouflaged under the representations of the body:

in a quarter or third of the world very few bodies circulate (only flesh, skin, faces, muscles – bodies that are more or less hidden: in hospitals, cemeteries, factories, beds from time to time), while everywhere else in the world bodies multiply more and more, the body endlessly multiplied (frequently starved, beaten, murdered, restless, sometimes even laughing or dancing). (Nancy, *Corpus* 9)

Rather than speaking about the body, we should speak of the "flesh" (*la chair*), or

rather "bodily tissues" (*des chairs*) – but in the common French sense of the word, as I explained in *Ethics of the Spread Body*. There is, of course, the "flesh" (*la chair*) of phenomenology (*Leib*), or the "body" (*le corps*) of scientific objectivity (*Körper*); but there is also the "flesh" (*la chair*), or the "bodily tissues" (*les chairs*), of which we are made up – not simply the "meat" or "butchery" (Deleuze), but the "shreds" in which we can still discern our common humanity: "Between flesh and body, between the lived experience of the body and its extension, between *Leib* and *Körper*," as I noted in *Ethics of the Spread Body*,

one would thus have to return to the "flesh" or rather the flesh of many. The plural "flesh" or bodily tissues are here understood as those shreds of the body that are impossible to separate from myself, tumours that are not me and even so progressively invade me; they flood me in invasive fashion and soon become me *entirely*. In medicine one speaks of "flesh" being cicatrized, in cooking of "flesh" being "firmed up," in prisons of "flesh" that is tortured, or in war of "flesh" being crushed as "cannon fodder" (*chairs à canon*). Between *Leib* and *Körper*, between body as subject and body as object, stands *caro* (in Latin), *Fleisch* (in German), *flesh* (in English), which one had better retrieve today, including in palliative care, which is directly exposed to it. (60–61)

However, the "bodily tissues" have in a way, to follow Nancy here, "given way" underneath the "bodies." Or rather, let's say that the construction of the body (*hoc est corpus meum*) has killed its exposition. Everything here is a matter of determination – of culture, first of all, and of manifestation and exhibition, subsequently. (a) As far as culture is concerned, first of all, it is clear that in *Corpus*, as well as in *Ethics of the Spread Body*, the constructed body is certainly not the lived body (*Leib*), but neither is it the manifested body (epiphany). It is the merit of Nancy that he breaks, and definitively so, with all antecedents or "pre-"s – whether the pre-reflexive or the pre-linguistical (*pré-langagier*) – as if an originary corporeality has but to "prepare" what it isn't: thought or language. (b) As far as manifestation or exhibition is concerned, then, if the body is "exposed," to put it in the word of *Corpus*, that does not mean that the exposition signifies some "intimacy that is extracted from its withdrawal, and carried outside, put on display." In which case, "the body would be an exposition of the 'self,' in the sense of a translation, an interpretation, or a staging" (Nancy, *Corpus* 33; trans. mod.). There is not an inside and an outside, and the body is not the outside of an inside, an inside we call soul, flesh or spirit. The *exposed body* does not articulate a model of expressivity, always remaining in the construction or at least in the sensible; it rather articulates a model of self-positing (*auto-position*), by which it presents itself there in reality without signifying anything, if not the fact of maintaining itself (*se tenir*) in being, and thus of existing:

> Exposition, here, is the very being (what's called "existing"). Or better yet: where the being, as a subject, has for its essence self-positing; self-positing here is exposition itself, in and of itself, in essence and structure. *Auto = ex = body*. The body is the being-exposed of being. (*Corpus* 35)

As in *Ethics of the Spread Body*, the "nausea," "redness," "headache" or "convulsion," we find here, and this time in *Corpus*, what I call the "true body": not its representation (*Körper* or *hoc est corpus*), nor the flesh (*Leib* or *corpus meum*); but its exposition, not so much as exhibition or expression, but as the "there" (*là*) of its properties by way of which it is also said to exist "within itself":

> Its members – phallus and cephale – its parts – cells, membranes, tissues, excrescences, parasites – its teguments, its sweating, features, colors, all its local colors [...] Decomposition everywhere, not confined to a pure and unexposed *self* (death), but spreading *all the way to the worst rotting*, yes, spreads even there. (*Corpus* 35; trans. mod.)

We understand, then, and easily – I have announced it – why Nancy articulates the "exposed" (*exposé*) body as the "showing-of-skin" (*ex-peau-sé*), in a play on words that only works in French. The features mentioned here – "cells, membranes, tissues, teguments, sweating, ... " – are those of the skin (*peau*), i.e., of what is seen as exposed, but without the surface here being the recovery of an interiority. Neither "caress" (Levinas), which does not know what it is looking for, nor "skin-ego" (Anzieu), that would define me as such; for Nancy, the skin is rather the "outside of the body," which, of course, exposes me to others, but also sometimes makes me a stranger to myself (not being "comfortable in one's own skin," as they say). It is here not merely a matter of a "biological concept" – and in this the "exposed body" diverges from the "spread body," which is probably more biological – it is rather the site of an "ex-appropriation."

V this is my body

Should we then end with the "this is my body" – *hoc est corpus meum*? This is the great question that a reader so imbued with theology or the Christian tradition cannot but ask himself. For, as I indicated in the introduction, "credible" Christianity is as important, if not more so, as "believable" Christianity, in that its articulation in culture forms the condition for its extension in faith: one cannot but ask oneself whether phrases like "this is my body" or the act of "transubstantiation," for example, have today been surpassed once and for all, unless they are assigned a content that no longer has anything to do with the act of theologising. As I announced in the introduction: it is no longer, or at least not merely, *Ethics of the Spread Body* confronting *Corpus*; but also *The Wedding Feast of the Lamb* confronting *The Deconstruction of Christianity*. For, precisely in this work, "transubstantiation," "incorporation" and "institution" are all variations of one of its chapters, which is entitled, precisely, "This Is My Body."[9]

At the very least, and already in *Corpus*, it is clear where the dialogue with Christianity, if not engaged in fully, at least serves as a point of departure for discussing corporeality: *hoc est corpus meum* – "this is my body" as the central formula, not just of a religion, but also of what makes up so-called "representative" thinking, or the thought "of representation," of the West. Hence, without any violence, it is a matter of "de-theologising," not against Christianity – deconstruction is here in no way a destruction – but to let open-up (*éclore*), or dis-enclose (*déclore*), another or new form of corporeality. Like Nietzsche's *Zarathustra*, of which one wonders if Nancy is here claiming the paternity, it is a matter of deploying "possible forms of the body" that have not yet been produced nor engendered by culture.

The construct is therefore prosecuted, confronted with the described or rather what "exscribes itself." For, if there is an obsession at the beginning of *Corpus*, it is less with the body itself (*corpus*) or my ownmost body (*corpus meum*), than with the loss of the "this" (*hoc*) that is (*fait*) my body: "*Hoc est enim* ... challenges, allays all our doubts about appearances, conferring, on the real, the true final touch of its pure Idea: its reality, its existence." That is, the text continues, "how we invented the body" (Nancy, *Corpus* 5; trans. mod.). The "body of *that* (God, or the absolute, if you prefer)," the "'that' *has a body*" and the "'that' *is* a body (and so we might think that 'that' is *the* body, absolutely)" (3), constitutes the essence of Christianity (*christianité*), and thus of the West in its entirety, in the *hoc est corpus meum* – that is to say, the "This is my body." We can thus say that the opening of *Corpus* is harsh, to say the least, for those who believe it, or believe it still.

When it comes to "transubstantiation," perhaps it would be better (though not in my opinion) to rid oneself of it (*s'en defaire*) than to re-establish it (*refaire*) differently. The act of "transubstantiation" would belong to a bygone and outdated world, caught in the representation to which the showing of skin (*expeausition*) is opposed. What is coming

"now that the world of bodies comes," *Corpus* explains,

> is not at all what a weak discourse about appearance and spectacle would have us presume (a world of appearances, simulacra, and phantasms, lacking flesh and presence). This kind of weak discourse is only a Christian discourse on transubstantiation, but a hollowed-out substance (and also Christianity, no doubt ...). (39; trans. mod.)

The reference is nevertheless important enough to require emphasis. Nancy is criticising, not so much the transubstantiation as such, not even the "this is my body" as such, but the cultural effects they have produced, and the way in which what was first of all corporeality has subsequently become represented. The simulacrum of the body, or "flesh without presence," *Corpus* emphasises, is not the "transubstantiation," but the transubstantiation "lacking substance (and also Christianity, no doubt ...)."

There we have everything. It is probably less Christianity itself that is rejected, or detheologised, by Nancy, than the act by which Christianity as such has let itself be emptied out, or exhausted, of its flesh (*chair*) or bodily tissues (*chairs*), and thus of its substance. The transubstantiation, as well in the sense of the quasi-transfusion of bodies, or exchange of substances, in a true kind of "bodily contact" (*corps à corps*).[10] Such is, for us today, the meaning of the "wondrous exchange" of bodies, to use a phrase of Irenaeus, by which my life is shared in the act, including the Christian one, of "transubstantiating," and not merely projected in an objectivised world or enclosed in my ego-ness:

> The bread is consecrated bread, his body branched into ours so that we "become one body"; the wine is consecrated, his blood flowing in our veins. To be nourished with his body can and should be understood as a kind of organic transplant – a sharing of powers (the body) by which I live through his true corporal power, in the way of a community of life, even a transfusion of blood: "It is no longer I who live, but it is Christ who lives in me"

(Gal. 2:20). (*The Wedding Feast of the Lamb* 109)

* * *

Where Christianity has come to deliver the teaching of a "real presence" of the body *from* the body, the discourse *on* the body in the "this is my body" has made a copy of it in the mode of the represented, even virtual – a designated body rather than a shared body. The appearance of the body, objectifying the bread as body or the wine as blood in an address (*hoc est corpus meum*), has forgotten what Nancy calls "the flesh and blood," nor merely symbolised or represented, but as that which "forms body" (*font corps*), or "the body." We will find neither realism nor symbolism there, but a new way of writing, or of "writing oneself out" (*s'écrire*), "from the body." To address oneself to my body "from my body," and to say "it is from my body that *I have* my body as a stranger to me – expropriated" (Nancy, *Corpus* 19), is not simply to make the body a new point of departure in the place of the soul – as Martin Heidegger may have put it, incorrectly, concerning Nietzsche – ; it is rather "to write oneself out" or to "ex-scribe oneself," in the sense where the trace of the body is the body as such, as it is also in the so-called "body of writing": "Anything so addressed to the body-outside is *exscribed*, as I try to write it, right along this outside, or as this outside" (*Corpus* 19).

Hiding behind the "*hoc est corpus meum*" there is a quarrel that, at this point, and to conclude, it would be appropriate to re-examine. For, though the debate here is philosophical, it also has its roots in a theological controversy. "What the mouth of the faithful receives," asked King Charles the Bald in the ninth century of the theologians of the time, is it "figurative" (*in figura*) or "real" (*in re*)? We know what happens in the terrible debate between, on one side, Paschasius Radbertus and Lanfranc (realism), and, on the other, Ratramnus and Berengar of Tours (symbolism). Though the outcome certainly matters – the victory of realism over symbolism, though mainly in the Catholic context – ,

only the philosophical aim counts for the purposes of this essay.[11]

"This is my body" – *hoc est corpus meum* – has it not indeed lost its cultural consistency by dint of being represented? If the true "obsession" is that of always finding a "this" (*hoc*) in order to "presentify the Absent" and to avoid sinking into an "anxiety without end," would it not be the case that the body, within Christianity itself, allowed itself to be reified? Should not force be thought of as body, and not merely the body as force? Substance as "act of being" (Aquinas), or rather, as "agitating force" (Leibniz), or "substantial link" (Blondel); does that not say more than objectification, and representation as well?[12] Such is the path I have sought to go down, in a time of a "deconstructed" Christianity, but of which the dis-enclosure will consist less in searching another form of corporeality outside of the tradition, than in articulating it at the heart of the latter as a "this is my body," less represented than actually experienced (*expérimenté*): to conclude, we should say with Jean-Luc Nancy that "the body's neither substance, phenomenon, flesh, nor signification. Just being-exscribed" (*Corpus* 19).

echo by jean-luc nancy

Spread (*épandu*), exposed – extended (*étendu*) in any case the body spreads us out (*nous étale*): it withdraws us from the assumption and subsumption in an interiority gathered up on itself.

In fact, it is perhaps above all a question of an effect in the order of representation and a certain diffuse ideological consciousness: we had become accustomed to thinking in words like "soul" or "spirit," even "subject" or "person" (which have always had quite distinct technical meanings); a kind of immaterial entity supposed to constitute the identity of a human being and, moreover, depicted as immortal when operating a religious register.

In reality, this depiction was the projection of what we can today call the singularity of an existence. One could say that it was a popular version of what philosophy had thought of as the meaning of an individual existence without, however, stopping at the singular distinction of each existence. With Judeo-Christianity – and, no doubt, with a lateral Roman contribution, that of the legal subject – this distinction became essential because it is to each person that the so-called Word of God is addressed.

This means that existence is grasped on the basis of an address, an interpellation. The call (*l'appel*) comes from the outside. The outside implies an "inside" that is "inside" only insofar as it is turned to the outside. In a way, spiritual interiority immediately turns out to be exteriority as susceptibility for or possibility of receiving a call or encountering another in general.

The body is the other – as the separation from the child's body shows ... "This is my body" means: I am here (*là*). Or: there is an "I am here (*là*)" every time that this is a body.

disclosure statement

No potential conflict of interest was reported by the author.

notes

1 The two essays by Nancy that Falque is referring to were published together in English in a volume referred to here as *Corpus* (2008). However, in French, they are published separately as *Corpus* (1992) and *L'Intrus* (2000) – Trans.

2 An English translation is available, though it is merely a preparatory essay to this work: see my "Toward an Ethics of the Spread Body." [For clarity, the title of Falque's *Éthique du corps épandu* is translated in the text; however, the reference is always to the French edition – Trans.]

3 See Falque, *Éthique du corps épandu* 38–40.

4 On this "tilling" and "overlaying" of philosophy and theology, rather than a leap, see Falque, *Crossing the Rubicon* §17 ("On 'Tilling' or Overlaying") and §19 ("From the Threshold to the Leap").

5 For a commentary on this passage and my own position, see Falque, *The Metamorphosis of Finitude*,

chapter 3 ("Is There a Drama of Atheist Humanism?"), 30–40 (especially §11 ("Atheism From the Theologian's Viewpoint"), 33–36).

6 I return to this point in my *The Loving Struggle* (Heidegger's phrase is cited as epigraph to the book).

7 See Merleau-Ponty, *Phenomenology of Perception* 93–94:

> The man with one leg feels the missing limb in the same way as I feel keenly the existence of a friend who is, nevertheless, not before my eyes; he has not lost it because he continues to allow for it, just as Proust can recognize the death of his grandmother, yet without losing her, as long as he can keep her on the horizon of his life.

8 See my "Peut-on réduire le corps?"

9 See Falque, *The Wedding Feast of the Lamb* 199–217.

10 In French, *corps à corps* (literally, "body-to-body") refers to a fistfight, some kind of hand-to-hand combat – Trans.

11 For a development of this debate, see my *The Wedding Feast of the Lamb* §27 ("The Dispute over Meat"), 188–95.

12 See my *The Wedding Feast of the Lamb* §29 ("Transubstantiation"), 200–05.

bibliography

Falque, Emmanuel. *Crossing the Rubicon: The Borderlands of Philosophy and Theology*. Trans. Reuben Shank. New York: Fordham UP, 2016. Print.

Falque, Emmanuel. "The Extra-Phenomenal." Trans. Luke McCracken. *Diakrisis Yearbook of Theology and Philosophy* 1 (2018): 9–28. Print.

Falque, Emmanuel. "Le fou désincarné." *Descartes et la phénoménologie*. Ed. D. Pardelle and C. Riquier. Paris: Hermann, 2018. 315–38. Print.

Falque, Emmanuel. *The Loving Struggle: Phenomenological and Theological Disputes*. Trans. Bradley B. Onishi and Lucas McCracken. London: Rowman, 2018. Print.

Falque, Emmanuel. *The Metamorphosis of Finitude: An Essay on Birth and Resurrection*. Trans. George Hughes. New York: Fordham UP, 2012. Print.

Falque, Emmanuel. "Peut-on réduire le corps?" *Epoché*. Ed. S. Bancalari. *Archivio di Filosofia* 83.1–2 (2015): 91–107. Print.

Falque, Emmanuel. "Résistence de la presence." *Archivo di Filosofia* 86.2 (2018): 101–23. Print.

Falque, Emmanuel. "Toward an Ethics of the Spread Body." *Somatic Desire: Recovering Corporeality in Contemporary Thought*. Ed. Sarah Horton, Stephen Mendelsohn, Christine Rojcewicz, and Richard Kearney. Lanham: Lexington, 2019. 91–116. Print.

Falque, Emmanuel. *The Wedding Feast of the Lamb: Eros, the Body, and the Eucharist*. Trans. George Hughes. New York: Fordham UP, 2016. Print.

Falque, Emmanuel, and Sabine Fos-Falque. *Éthique du corps épandu suivi de Une chair épandue sur le divan*. Paris: Cerf, 2018. Print.

Heidegger, Martin. *Pathmarks*. Ed. William McNeill. Cambridge: Cambridge UP, 1998. Print.

Husserl, Edmund. *Cartesian Meditations: An Introduction to Phenomenology*. Trans. Dorian Cairns. The Hague: Martinus Nijhoff, 1960. Print.

de Lubac, Henri. *The Drama of Atheist Humanism*. Trans. Edith M. Riley, Anne Englund Nash, and Mark Sebanc. San Francisco: Ignatius, 1995. Print.

Manchev, Boyan. "Jean-Luc Nancy, La déconstruction du christianisme." *Critique* 718 (2007/3): 169–82. Print.

Merleau-Ponty, Maurice. *In Praise of Philosophy and Other Essays*. Trans. John Wild and James Edie John. Evanston: Northwestern UP, 1970. Print.

Merleau-Ponty, Maurice. *Phenomenology of Perception*. Trans. Colin Smith. London: Routledge, 1962. Print.

Nancy, Jean-Luc. *Corpus*. Trans. Richard A. Rand. New York: Fordham UP, 2008. Print.

Nancy, Jean-Luc. *L'Intrus*, nouvelle édition augmentee. Paris: Galilée, 2010. Print.

The broader context of my engagement with Jean-Luc Nancy's thought in this article is formed by the rise, more than a decade ago, of new realist movements in continental philosophy, more specifically the speculative realism of Quentin Meillassoux and the object-oriented philosophy of Graham Harman and Levi Bryant. Despite vast differences between these two types of new realism, and also between individual positions within each broader type, what unites the new realist movement is a common enemy, variously named correlationism (by speculative realists) or the philosophies of access (by object-oriented ontologists), two labels that are supposed to encompass philosophies from Kant onward: transcendental idealism, German idealism, phenomenology, hermeneutics, deconstruction.[1]

The basic tenets of correlationism are easy enough to explain: correlationism would assert the unsurpassability of the correlation between thinking and being and reject any Absolute, that is, any "real" that is not already reduced to its relation or its givenness to a consciousness or an intentional power more broadly construed that has the ability to make sense of this given. Correlationists deny knowledge – or, in its stronger version, even the thinkability – of anything that is not correlated to the human being's thinking or sense-making power. In the words of Harman, for correlationism, "everything is reduced to a question of human access to the world, and non-human relations are abandoned to the natural sciences" (*Prince of Networks* 156). Correlationists, then, study the human being's mode of access to what appears, but as a result, they have to limit the validity of their knowledge-claims to what exists insofar as it is accessed.

marie-eve morin

AN ONTOLOGY FOR OUR TIMES

Since they cannot step out of their mode of access, they cannot "compare the world as it is 'in itself' to the world as it is 'for us,' and thereby distinguish what is a function of our relation to the world from what belongs to the world alone" (Meillassoux, *After Finitude* 3). New realists seek to shake philosophy out of its "critical slumber" – its focus on finitude and the limits of thought – and renew the philosophical concern for the Absolute, for things in themselves, for what is *not* in any way for us.

If the new realists seek to counter the correlationism they think is pervasive in current continental philosophy, it is not so much, or at least not only, because it is misguided. Indeed,

Meillassoux insists that the arguments in favour of correlationism appear to be obvious and indefeasible. Rather it is because it has pernicious effects. It is "incapable of confronting" or "actively limits the capacities of philosophy" to confront the events of our times, such as "the ecological crisis, the forward march of neuroscience, the increasingly splintered interpretations of basic physics, and the ongoing breach of the divide between human and machine" (Bryant, Srnicek, and Harman 3).[2] This incapacity would be the result of three related features of correlationism: (i) correlationism is anti-science; (ii) correlationism, by limiting the power of reason, leads to fideism; and (iii) correlationism is anthropocentric.

In this article, I want to focus on the third point.[3] Correlationism would be anthropocentric because it reduces everything that exists to its being encountered by or given to human beings. The form of anthropocentrism found in correlationism would be based on human exceptionalism.[4] If humans occupy the centre of the universe, and consequently the centre of our theorizing, it is because they are singled out in some way or other in the great chain of being. In its most general formulation, we can say that correlationism radically singles out the human being as the privileged site of the disclosure of Being. Things are not worthy of concern in themselves since, unlike us humans, they are incapable of entering into meaningful relations with their environment. They only become worthy of concerns once they are within the circuit of human thinking or manipulation. As a result, everything that exists – that is, everything that is given, since for a correlationist only something that is given can be said to exist – is reduced to the same, namely, to being a correlate or an object.

flat ontology against anthropocentrism

The new realists of the object-oriented sort will want to overcome this anthropocentrism by developing a radically egalitarian or flat ontology, that is, an ontology that undoes the privilege of the human being as the centre of the universe and the only agent of meaningful encounters. There are two ways in which object-oriented ontologists seek to flatten their ontology or to create a "democracy of objects," to borrow Levi Bryant's term. The first one, followed by Harman and Bryant, is to assert that within the domain of entities or objects there is no privileged entity or class of entities: everything that is an object is equally an object or everything that is real is equally real, no matter its size, properties, and so on. The result is not only that relations between humans or between humans and non-human objects cannot be privileged, since the human is an object like any other, but more generally that no infra-, supra-, or mega-object – particles, God, the world as supercontainer/ultimate unifier – can serve as the ground, cause, or explanation for any other object. The second path to a flat ontology, followed by the early Latour and Tristan Garcia, asserts that there is only one kind of entity or that being is said only in one way. Anything that is, which means, anything that has an effect, is an object or is real in the exact same way. Whereas the former ontologies are not so flat after all,[5] since they still differentiate between an object and its spatial locations and temporal instantiations as well as between that object and all of its potential relations, the latter entails an ontological monism that runs the risk of unduly multiplying real entities: not only is the apple an object, but so is the apple in this light, the apple on the desk, the apple at 3:34 p.m. on Tuesday, the apple and my neighbour's bulldog, and so on.[6] We have a "democracy of objects" that is much more populous and unruly than in the first case.

Despite the multiplication of objects, object-oriented ontologies are bound to feel reductive – or even "eliminative" – to some. I am, after all, reduced to being an object like everything else.[7] Of course, such ontological equalization was exactly what was sought, and the fact that it feels so foreign and disorienting shows how anthropocentric our familiar ontologies have always been. Yet there is another way to "flatten" our ontologies, from the top rather that from the bottom so to speak. This consists in attributing to other living beings, to inanimate things, or even to matter itself, characteristics that are normally reserved only for human beings: thought, agency, feelings. Such an ontology does indeed ontologically equalize all beings and remove the human being from the centre. Paradoxically, it also runs the risk of reaffirming the special character of the human. Why else would we in our decentring procedure, elect to attribute a *human* predicate to all things?[8] In such an anthropomorphic universe, the human being is still making the world – and each thing in the world – in his own image: "all things do x *like humans do.*"

Yet, in order to overcome anthropocentrism, it is not necessary to reject anthropomorphism wholesale. Indeed, anthropocentrism might be most effectively avoided with a small dose of anthropomorphism, or what Steven Shaviro calls, in *The Universe of Things*, "a cautious anthropomorphism." Indeed, Shaviro claims that if he attributes feelings to stones, for example, it is "precisely in order to get away from the pernicious dualism that would insist that human beings alone (or at most, human beings together with some animals) have feelings, while everything else does not" (61).[9] This attribution of a capacity for thought or feeling to everything that exist, animals, plants, minerals, artefacts, and so on, must, however, come with a dislocation of our concept of thinking and feeling from its conscious and intentional mode in human beings. Without such a dislocating we would be guilty of a reckless anthropomorphism that, in the words of Meillassoux, "consists in the illusion of seeing in every reality (even inorganic reality) subjective traits the experience of which is in fact entirely human, merely varying their degree (an equally human act of imagination)."[10] If thought is limited to its rationalist or intentionalist definition, then of course only humans think and attributing thought to other entities seems to be an undue projection of our subjective mode of being onto the rest of what exists. In rejecting this anthropomorphism wholesale, Meillassoux would, according to Shaviro, end up smuggling

anthropocentrism back into his philosophy (see *Universe* 125). For Meillassoux, all there is to thought is what thought is for us. Thought is exceptional to human beings. We could say that for Meillassoux humans are still in some way at the centre; it is just that the centre is bad and the Real has to be sought as far away from the centre as possible. Meillassoux's philosophy would seek to evade the gravitational pull of the human centre and find an escape from thought in thought.[11]

Now that I have sketched with broad stroke the complex matrix in which new ontologies are situated – a matrix that contains the four axes of flatness, anthropocentrism, human exceptionalism, and anthropomorphism – I want to turn to Jean-Luc Nancy's ontology and ask where it fits within this complex matrix. To anticipate, I do think that Nancy offers us a kind of flat ontology, but one that does not lead to the erasure of all differences. Nancy's ontology, I intend to show, avoids reckless anthropomorphism, even while claiming that the stone, too, is free, as well as a pernicious anthropocentrism, even while also reserving a special role for the human in the creation and destruction of the "sense of the world."

jean-luc nancy's ontology

Before we can assess Nancy's ontology in terms of the matrix outlined above, it is necessary to first lay down the basic tenets of this ontology. In the simplest terms, Being, for Nancy, means *Setzung*, position or positioning. An essence doesn't exist or it exists only when it is positioned. This is how Nancy reads the positive formulation of the Kantian thesis that is also discussed by Heidegger in *Basic Problems of Phenomenology*: "Being is absolute position of a thing."[12] Nancy paraphrases this claim in the following way:

> Being is neither substance nor cause of the thing, rather, it is a being-the-thing in which the verb "to be" has a transitive value of "positioning," but one in which the "positioning" is based on and caused

by nothing else but *Dasein,* being-there, being thrown down, given over, abandoned, offered up by existence. ("Of Being-in-Common" 2)

An essence doesn't exist, or rather its existence consists in its taking place, its arrival or coming to presence "here and now."[13] Reading Kant's thesis through Heidegger's deconstruction of metaphysics, Nancy will understand existence – the *fact* that there is such and such, rather than *what* there is as such – as abandoned being. The latter expression has a double meaning. First, Being is abandoned or left behind as a cause or ground, or a condition of possibility that would precede what is and serve to explain why what is is. In other words, the answer to the fundamental question of metaphysics, "why are there beings rather than nothing?," is not to be sought in the antecedence of Being, or of what Heidegger sometimes calls Beingness. The answer already lies in the question: "Since there is something, and not everything, it is because this thing is in abandonment, it is because everything is abandoned" (Nancy, *Birth* 43). This is the second sense of abandonment: the cause or ground of the thing withdraws into the thing itself.

It is this abandonment as deliverance from foundation and release into existence that Nancy calls "freedom" (*Experience* 92–95, 114–15). At this point, Nancy goes beyond the Heideggerian formulation of the abandonment as *es gibt,* which according to him is the formulation of a *Verlassenheit/Vergessenheit* that also calls for a guarding/sheltering or a reminiscing. To the Heideggerian *es gibt,* Nancy will oppose *il y a,* the abandonment of beings to the *y,* to the spacing of a place (*Impératif* 145).[14] In this *il y a,* the ontological difference is cancelled both as a difference between two realities, Being and beings, and as the abandonment of beings by Being *Birth* – as the withdrawal and reserve of Being. There is no difference anymore between existence and the existent. Or, to be more precise, the existent's "reality" is

nothing other than the putting into play of its own existence right at, or in the midst of, its existence itself (Nancy, *Creation* 71–73, 102–03).[15]

The notion of creation *ex nihilo* is another way of thematizing this same abandonment. To say that the world – beings as a whole – is "created" out of nothing does not mean that it is produced by a very powerful Demiurge on the basis of a pre-existing nothing. In such a case, not only would God pre-exist the world, but the nothing would be a pre-given substrate out of which the world is made. To truly think of a creation *ex nihilo,* we must not only get rid of the idea of a God-Maker, we must also undo the *nihil* insofar as it functions as underlying, pre-given substrate. Ultimately, what needs to be emptied out or deconstructed is the very place of the transcendent principle that would provide ground and reason for the world, a place that can be occupied by a God-Maker, by the "Man" of humanism, or by the "Nothing" of nihilism. This is why Nancy can claim that atheism is still Christian and enjoin us to

> keep the place empty, or better still, perhaps, to ensure that there shall be no more place for an instance or for a question of a "reason given" ["*raison rendue*"], of foundation, origin, and end. *Let there be no more place for God – and in this way, let an opening [...] open.* (*Adoration* 33)

The deconstruction of the very idea of transcendent principle leaves us with – though such a negative, melancholic way of speaking as if we had lost something betrays the incompleteness of our deconstruction – the world in its proper sense: "nothing but that which grows [*rien que cela qui croît*] (*creo, cresco*), lacking any growth principle" (Nancy, *Dis-Enclosure* 24; see also *Being* 16). What the abandonment of Being ultimately underlines is an expenditure without reserve, and hence a certain availability or abundance of what is. Indeed, while *abandonner* has the connotation of a withdrawing or leaving behind, and hence of a neglecting or not caring for, *être à l'abandon* does not only have this connotation of destituteness but also points to a certain freedom, availability, or even overabundance of what is. It is in this sense that we speak of an overgrown garden as a garden *à l'abandon* (Nancy, *Birth* 36–37).

At this point, our cursory description of Nancy's notion of being or existence as positioning might give the impression that Nancy deconstructs what Derrida calls the metaphysics of presence – the attempt to ground what is as a whole in something that is first and that is pre-eminently present – only to reinstate it at the level of particular individual entities, each harbouring the principle of its own presence within itself. Yet this would miss, I think, an essential feature of Nancy's ontology.

We began by saying that Nancy appropriates Kant's thesis according to which existence is not a predicate of the thing but its position or positioning (*Setzung*). What was not mentioned is how Nancy transforms this thesis or raises to the second power by stating that community is not a predicate of existence but the position of existence, or the position of position. This means that for the thing to be – where being has the transitive value of positioning – it must be *with* other things. In other words, existence is always in common and always implicates more than one thing in their mutual ex-position, com-position, and dis-position. Positioning then is always from the start modulated by the prefixes ex-, com-, dis-. As Nancy writes,

> In existence and as existence, position [...] never posits *an* instance of existence as *a* distinct thing, independent, related to the unity and unicity of its essence [...] In the positing, essence is *offered or given*. That is, essence is ex-posed to being, or to existing, outside of being as mere subsistence, or as immanence. ("Of Being-in-Common" 3)

Each thing, each one, or each singularity, insofar as it exists, does not have the structure of substantial presence, but is offered, abandoned, exposed. The question is: by what and to what is it offered or abandoned? The answer is: nothing other than itself. Yet it is important not to misunderstand this "self" by which and to which each thing is abandoned,

lest we fall back into a thinking of substantial presence. As Nancy points out, *soi* is what we call in French a *cas régime*. It has "no nominative case, but is always declined" (Nancy, "Of Being-in-Common" 3). Philosophically, this grammatical point means that *soi* is never a subject that remains the same across all alterations or that folds all exteriority into itself and appropriates all otherness for itself. Here we can see how Nancy appropriates Derrida's thinking of differance to radicalize or aggravate Hegel's thinking of the self until it caves in ("Of Being-in-Common" 3). The self is never merely itself as a pure point of presence but, insofar as it is or exists (transitively), is present *to* itself. Being "to-itself" or "toward-itself" (*à-soi*) denotes for Nancy the movement of existence so that there is no present self at the origin or end of this movement. Rather, the self is an effect of the movement toward an exteriority that the self can never fully reappropriate or reflect back into itself. This inappropriable exteriority is not some other thing out there, but the limit upon which the self is exposed – to itself and to others, to itself as an other – and which properly belongs neither to the inside nor to the outside (Nancy, *Birth* 154–55; *Being* 40–41, 95–96). This limit *is* no positive thing that can be given in the form of presence, yet it allows that there be things (Nancy, *Experience* 69).

Existence as exposition or exposure on the limit is a crucial feature of Nancy's ontology. The limit is not only the place where I am exposed to others, to what lies outside of me. It is not only the place of the in-common. It is also the place where each existent feels itself existing because it feels itself from the outside and as an outside. If community is not added after the fact to the existent or the self, it is because the self already holds its own self as an "otherness," "in such a way that no essence, no subject, no place can present *this otherness in itself* – either as the proper selfness of an other, or an 'Other,' or a common being (life or substance)" (Nancy, *Birth* 154–55). The movement of exposition at the limit is only possible, according to Nancy, because there is already a spacing, or a nothing, at the heart of the thing itself. Without this nothing at the heart of the thing that spaces the thing out "in itself," turns it toward the outside, and exposes it unto its limit, the thing would collapse into itself and would not quite succeed in coming to presence. In other words, without this nothing/spacing that opens up the thing *to* ... itself and others, there is no spacing *between* things but only a black hole:

> a total absence of exteriority, a nonextension concentrated in itself, not something impenetrable, but rather its excess, the impenetrable *mixed with* the impenetrable, infinite intussusception, the *proper* devouring itself, all the way to the void at its center – in truth deeper, even, than the center, deeper than any trace of spacing (which the "center" still retains), in an abyss where the hole absorbs even its own edges. (Nancy, *Corpus* 75)

Substantial presence is, according to Nancy, such a black hole: a hole that is the absolute negation of *ex*-position or presence-*to* insofar as it does not even have edges upon which it would be in contact with an exteriority.

It is in terms of this exposition unto the limit or edge that Nancy understands the finitude of what exists, of each singularity. Such finitude is not a limitation imposed on a being by the fact that there happens to be other things outside of it that press against it. The finite being exists at its limits or is affected by its end, not as something external imposed on it, but as something that is originary, and it is only in such auto-hetero-affection that it exists as the being that it is. At the same time, since the finite being does not cease to be exposed at its limits, its exposition is endlessly repeated and therefore never finished once and for all. Finitude therefore will itself be the true infinite: "the good infinite or the actual infinite – it is infinity in the actuality of the act itself insofar as it is the act of exceeding itself" (Nancy, *Corpus II* 15). The finite being is not infinite in the sense that it would go on indefinitely without beginning or end; rather it has no *proper* beginning or end; at no point can it be properly complete or finished. This absence of proper

completion is not a lack: in every instant, each finite being is fully exposed, without holding anything back, without leaving anything to be actualized later. Again, it is worth emphasizing that Nancy is not falling prey to a metaphysics of presence. If each finite being is *fully* offered, this does not mean that it stands in full presence; rather it always remains in the movement of a coming to presence, a movement without grounding – present – arche or telos. In Nancy's words:

> The coming is infinite: it does not get finished with coming; it is finite: it is offered up in the instant. But that which takes place "in the instant" – in this distancing of time "within" itself – is neither the stasis nor the stance of the present instant, but its instability, the inconclusiveness of its coming – and of the "going" that corresponds to that coming. The coming into presence takes place precisely as nonarrival of presence. (*Sense* 35; see *Experience* 159)

To be finite is never to cease to "arrive" to the world and hence never to cease to be exposed to all there is. It is also in this sense that Nancy will be able to say that a finite being is absolute. Not in the sense that it has no exteriority and is absolved from contact with any exteriority at its limit or edge. Such an absolute would be an essential contradiction, since not only would it have to be separated from its outside by a limit, but this limit itself would have to be without relation to its outside, the enclosure itself would have to be enclosed (Nancy, *Inoperative* 4). This is the black described above. For Nancy, the absoluteness of a singularity is the withdrawal of its essence as cause or ground, "in the fact of existence, in its singularity, in the material intensity of its coming," and freedom "is the philosophical name of this absoluteness" (*Experience* 109).

a flat ontology?

Even after only this cursory introduction to Nancy's ontology, we can see how what Nancy proposes can be considered to be flat ontology. Every "one," every singularity, insofar as it comes to presence and in this coming is caught up in the movement of exposure, exists. Existence does not come in degrees. It is said of each thing equally without being thought metaphysically as an underlying principle that would be diffracted in every "one" that exists. Rather, in its freedom, existence means nothing more than the creation of the world as the "explosion of presence in the originary multiplicity of its partition" (Nancy, *Being* 2–3; trans. mod.). Hence, to speak of *the* world can be misleading. No world provides an overarching horizon or a super container that would unify this multiplicity into a whole.[16] "That there is no whole (or *the* whole)," Nancy writes,

> is not the definition of a lack or the indication that something has been taken away, because there was no whole before there was not-the-whole [*pas-de-tout*]. It indicates, rather, that all that there is (for there is indeed all that there is) does not totalize itself, even though it is the whole [*le tout*]. (*Corpus II* 9; trans. mod.; see *Creation* 109)

The lack of totalization means, positively, that there is each singular being, each with all the others singularly. Nancy's ontology is one of the irreducibility of singular beings.

We can go even further if we point out that the Nancean "logic" of existence as exposition unto and at the limit knows neither hierarchy nor individuality so that when Nancy speaks of singularities he does not have in mind just individual human beings or individual things. Every "one" – stone, cat, community, book, thought, feeling, city, and so on – exists. In this sense, Nancy's ontology seems flatter than Harman and closer to Latour's or Garcia's: it is an ontology of the events, strokes (*touches*), or flashes (*éclats*) of being, rather than of already individualized entities. Indeed, the famous phrase "being singular plural" not only means that there is always a plurality of singularities but that a singularity is always itself a plurality of singular events, strokes, or flashes of existence and that as a result singularities are not identifiable in themselves but rather obtain their "identity" in their

movement of disentanglement and differentiation from/with (*d'avec*) other singularities (see Nancy, *Being* 12, 32, 65–66, 152–53).

Here, Nancy's ontology seems to fall prey to a form of reductionism, which Harman calls "overmining." Rather than undermining objects by locating their true being in some underlying matter or particles, overmining, Harman tells us,

> happens whenever a philosophy tells us that an object is nothing more than how it appears to the observer; or an arbitrary bundling of immediately perceived qualities; or when it tells us that there are only "events," not underlying substances; or that objects are real only insofar as they perceive or affect other things. In all these cases, objects are treated as a useless hypothesis, a false depth lying beneath the immediate givens of consciousness or the concrete events of the world. ("Road" 172)

Of course, Nancy does not reduce existence to what appears to consciousness, but because singularities have no depth or no hidden interior of their own, "no individual character outside their mutual touching and weighing," they are reducible to a series of relational events (Harman, "Interface" 100). If the singular character of each thing is completely determined by its relations, then singularities are merely effects of relations rather than entities in their own right. Because nothing determinate exists prior to or independently of relations, nothing would exist but relations. For Harman, such a "continuum of relational structure without individual zones" does not essentially differ from "the monism of a whole without parts" ("I Am" 787). As a result, Nancy's ontology would ultimately not be an ontology of the plurality of singularities, or, in Harman's vocabulary, of determinate objects, but an ontology of an indeterminate in-itself. Having removed what exists from its reliance on an indeterminate material substance as well as a transcendent principle, Nancy's creation of the world sought to affirm the plurality of what exists. Yet by defining what exists in terms of relational events, it goes too far and leaves us with a big mixture of relations without independent relata, without determinate parts.[17]

This lack of determinacy, Harman thinks, comes to the fore when Nancy speaks of the thing as "whatever," of *quelque chose*, something, or of *n'importe quoi*, anything at all, as *quelconque*, as anything whatsoever (see *Birth* 173–74). Hence when Nancy writes that "*some* thing is free to be a stone, a tree, a ball, Pierre, a nail, salt, Jacques, a number, a trace, a lioness, a marguerite" (*Birth* 186), Harman takes this to mean that "there is no Pierre, no salt, and no lioness before they touch one another. The in-itself is a unified *whatever*" ("Interface" 100–01). The thing would be "whatever" – read: an undifferentiated in-itself – before it enters in relation with other things and through these relations gets determined as this or that. But such a unified in-itself is exactly what Nancy's thinking of freedom has undermined. To say that the thing is free to be salt, Pierre, or a lioness, is not to say that it is some undifferentiated mass or glob, but rather to say the coming to presence of some thing is "unfettered by any attachment to or foundation in a substance or a negation of substance" (Nancy, *Birth* 177). The indeterminacy of the *some* of something, or of the *whatever* of anything whatsoever, is "not a privation, nor is it a poverty," but "its most characteristic affirmation, with the compaction, the concretion, wherein the thing 'reifies' itself, properly speaking" (Nancy, *Birth* 174). Indeed, *quelconque*, from the Latin *qualis* and *cumque*, does mean a certain indeterminacy with regard to the *quality* or kind, the "what" of the thing, but for Nancy this indeterminateness is also the material concretion of the thing as existent. As Nancy writes, "'Whatever' is the indeterminateness of being in what is posited and exposed within the strict, determined concretion of a singular thing, and the indeterminateness of its singular existence" (*Birth* 174). The whateverness of the thing is both its "conceptual" indeterminacy (its lack of essential determinations) and its concretion (its determinacy: *this* tree).

For Harman, singular beings can only be rescued from ontological overmining or undermining if they are withdrawn from their relations, that is, if they are "deep." Now it is true that for Nancy things are not "deep" if by that we mean that they have a hidden interior in which they would conceal their ownmost truth, locked away from any interactions or encounters. Yet the fact that each singularity is essentially "with" all others does not mean that it is nothing outside of its relation. Harman seems to equivocate between two different claims: there is nothing prior to relations, and there is nothing but relations. While the first claim is true of Nancy's ontology, the second is not. There is nothing prior to relations – not even a substrate we could call prime matter or even "the nothing" – because existence for Nancy denotes not the presence of the thing by itself or in itself, but the coming of what is *to* itself and others. What is primordial then are neither self-identical things (in Harman's vocabulary: determinate non-relational objects) nor relations within an indeterminate, undifferentiated glob, but rather the spacing or opening of the to-itself. As Nancy writes:

> Thought rigorously, it is not a matter of "other" or of "relation." Rather, it is a matter of a diaresis or a dissection of the "self" that precedes not only every relation to something other but also every identity of the self. In this diaresis, the other *is* already the same, but this "being" isn't confusion, still less a fusion: it is the being-other of the self in as much as neither "self" nor "other," nor some relation between them can be given to them as an origin. (*Finite* 7; trans. mod.)

Existence as the movement of the *to* or *toward* is a function of the diaresis of the "self": the self is rent and affected with otherness, exteriority or spacing at its core. This diaresis also means that the existent is turned toward the outside and exposed on its limit that both separates and joins it from other things. Nancy's ontology is not one of pure relations without relata; yet each relatum is not constituted by an inside that would remain unaffected by its relations.

Rather the "inside" of each self is always felt on the outside or through some exteriority. If it is indeed the case that there is no singularity in-itself, no singularity that would have its own identity within itself prior to its exposition to and contact with other singularities, we must also remember that exposition, contact, and weight all imply an interruption or a resistance, and hence a certain identity or ipseity of the singular beings. The "inside" is an effect, not an illusion. This is how we should read Nancy's claim that the question of the "with" ultimately means "never any identities, always identifications" (*Being* 66; trans. mod.).

The charge of "overmining" is not the only one that can be levelled against Nancy's ontology. Another apparent consequence of the apparent lack of depth or internal structure of singularities is that anything – including any set of things – is itself a singularity. This worry plagues object-oriented ontologies that, following Badiou, take set theory as their model: any one is a set, any set is a one. This formalism means that this apple, this apple and my desk, as well as this apple and my neighbour's bulldog are all equally "singular objects" or sets. While this model allows us to theorize pure multiplicity without original or final "One," it does not give us any means of resisting general equivalence. This is an important worry since according to Nancy the problem of our times is not so much metaphysics – the necessity to undo metaphysical principles – but nihilism. The issue at stake is: how to undo metaphysical principles without falling into the general equivalence of all things where any thing or set of things equals any other thing or set of things and hence is exchangeable for any other thing or set of things? How to escape the indefinite circle of a "*tout se vaut*"? How to think the exceptional value of each singularity in its concreteness without enclosing it in itself? How to ensure that the deconstruction of all metaphysical principles leads to a genuine thinking of plurality, one that does justice to the plurality of existents in their co-ex-istence? The multiplicity that formalism allows us to conceptualize is not, in Nancy's framework, a genuine plurality.

Nancy can escape the formalism of ontologies based on set theoretical models because for him the "with" does not concern abstract sets of "ones" that build further ones, but always material, worldly events. "A singularity," he writes, "is always a body, and all bodies are singularities (the bodies, their states, their movements, their transformations)" (Nancy, *Being* 18).[18] A pebble, a cell, a community, a book, even a thought – not the abstract thought content, but the material event of the thought, which, as Nancy says, weighs and as such "affects us with a perceptible pressure or inclination" (*Gravity* 76) – all these are material events and not formal units. Any identifiable "one" – and there are "identifiable ones": this pebble, this community, this thought – is not constituted as a "one" merely through the formal process of "counting as one" but rather constitutes itself as "one" through a plurality of internal events and external relations, which gives it its own recognizable style. Such movement of singularization or identification – or rather of self-identification, since it is not a question of an external process that identifies what counts as one – prevents the absolute enclosure of *any* singularity, including infra- and supra-individual ones, since it never leads to the sublation of the internal and external edges upon which the singularity is exposed to itself and others. Furthermore, such a movement takes place in the world, or as the world itself, the "real" world, as we call it.

still too much anthropomorphism?

At this point, I hope to have convincingly showed how Nancy provides us with a sort of flat ontology, but one that has a different character than Harman's and Bryant's as well as Latour's and or Garcia's. I also hope that it has become clear that Nancy's ontology does effect a decentring of the human. This does not directly address the question of the role of anthropomorphism in this decentring. Nancy recognizes that the question of the existence of the world, not as the context of the existence of human being, but as the proliferation of differences among beings, is a difficult one. It is not so much a question of extending the kind of being of the human to all other beings through a sort of reckless anthromorphization, but of understanding how other beings also display modes of existence that are not reducible to their being there for human beings, taken into the circuit of human existence and illuminated by it. Humans and things equally exist, in the technical sense given by Nancy to the term existence as being-*to*.

Speaking of the stone, Nancy will claim that "it is difficult to reduce 'the stone in the stone' to a 'pure' immanence; or we must say that 'immanence' is also and in a way 'to itself'" (*Finite* 322n14). In other words, if the stone *is* (transitively) and is not merely there to be understood or manipulated by human beings, then its being has, however minimally, the same structure of self-relation or of being-to-itself that was described above. If the stone did not have a minimal spacing at the heart of itself that turned it inside out and exposed it to itself and others, how, Nancy wonders, "could its hardness *feel* hard?" (*Finite* 322n14). *Comment sa dureté se ferait-elle sentir dure?* How could the stone make its hardness be felt? Or more literally: how could its hardness make itself feel hard? It is because the stone is not a mass closed in upon itself – a point without extension, a black hole – but is stretched out and exposed at its limits, that it can be encountered in its resistance and impenetrability. Such an encounter between exteriorities is more primordial than the sentient or conscious encounter with the hardness of the stone as such. The stone first makes itself feel hard through its exposure *to* rather than being felt as hard by a sentient being.

By attributing a minimal form of existence as being-to-itself to the stone, Nancy seems to have endowed to the stone an occult power of making itself feel hard. Is Nancy's ontology then a form of animism or panpsychism, where stones have souls, feelings, and agency? Isn't Nancy guilty of improperly anthropomorphizing "the Real" at this point? Nancy responds to this worry in *The Sense of the World*:

One need not fear that I am proposing here an animism or a panpsychism. It is not a matter of endowing the stone with an interiority [...] For the differance of the to-itself, in accordance with which sense opens, is inscribed right at the "in itself." (*Sense* 61–62; trans. mod.)

Nancy is not proposing an animism or panpsychism because he has decoupled existence as being-to not only from intentional consciousness, but more generally from the interiority or unity of sentient life. At the same time, we could argue that Nancy is proposing a kind of animism or panpsychism, provided we remember his definition of soul: "The soul is the body's difference from itself, the relation to the outside that the body is for itself" (*Corpus* 126). The soul here is not a principle of animation, life, unity, interiority but rather of the body's diaresis and exposure.

Though Nancy's meditations on the stone are doubtless one of the most puzzling parts of his corpus, I think it is fair to say that their goal is to turn our attention away from our lived experiences toward what Nancy calls the sense of world. We have until now avoided the notion of sense, which is without a doubt the keystone of Nancy's thinking. In reality, throughout we have been speaking of nothing but sense under the notion of existence as being-to. If I refrained from using this term, it is because it is often too closely associated with phenomenology, for which sense is inextricably linked to appearing, and hence to an instance to which appearing is given (be it transcendental consciousness or Dasein or the lived body). For Nancy, on the contrary, sense is not tied to intentionality, interiority, or life, but to spacing and exteriority, or to what Derrida calls a "technical supplement."[19]

still too much human exceptionalism?

Sense-making, then, is not a human activity but one of all singularities, living and inorganic, infra- and supra-individual. Yet, in his ontology, Nancy does reserve a special role for the human being in the creation of the world. The world, as we mentioned above, is a com-position or dis-position of a multiplicity of singularities – of worlds – exposed to themselves and to each other. It is the play of a plurality of edges that open right in the middle of, *à même*, the world. *Mondialisation* or world-forming points to this com-position of world(s): we, singularities, are ex-posed, and through our exposure form a world at our outer edges. We articulate ourselves and each other. This articulation is not a human or even a human-centred activity.

Yet, in *Being Singular Plural*, Nancy explains the relation between the human being and other singular beings in the world in the following way: humans are "those who expose *as such* sharing and circulation by saying 'we,' by *saying we to themselves* in all possible senses of that expression, and by saying we for the totality of all being" (3; trans. mod.). World is existence, sense, exposition; the human existent is exposed to and in turn exposes this exposition by saying "we" for all beings and for each one, one by one. Nancy explains this redoubling of exposition in the following terms:

> Humans are the exposer [*l'exposant*, also the exponent] of the world; they are neither its end nor its ground – the world [that is, the exposing of singularities to themselves and each other] is what is exposed by and to humans [*l'exposé de l'homme*]; it is neither their environment, nor their representation. (*Being* 18; trans. mod.)

This exponential characteristic of human beings also means that humans, and humans alone, are potentially also the unexposer of the exposing. To exist, for us humans, is to engage in, to be responsive to, and responsible for, existence as exposition.[20] As a result, human existing takes on the active connotation of a "deciding to exist" because it is always possible for the existents that we are to close off not exposition itself – indeed we cannot

not be in-common, we cannot not ex-ist or expose ourselves – but the exposing of exposition. Our existence as decision is the responsibility for the freedom of the world, understood as the ungrounded diffraction or dissemination of singularities that articulate "the" world. Hence, when Nancy ends the second section of *The Creation of the World* by affirming that "it is for us to decide for *ourselves* [*c'est à nous de* nous *décider*]" (74), the *nous* in favour of which we are to decide cannot be the self-enclosed human subject, individual, or collective.

The decision of existence is the decision to inhabit the world in such a way that the world can really form a world: an ungrounded, untotalizable plurality of existents, co-articulating themselves with and against each other. This puts demands on us insofar as, in our exponential character, we are the exposer of the plural exposition of singularities. Being the exposer in this way does not give us power over the plurality of beings that form the world, but it does make us responsible for how we relate to this plurality not only at the practical level but also at the level of thought and discourse. It singles the human out in a way but without falling into exceptionalism. As a result, Nancy's ontological discourse does not completely depoliticize human existence by absolving us of our responsibility for the unworlding of the world in which we nevertheless always remain exposed. Indeed, if we were merely objects like any other objects, or vitally material like any other vitally material thing, then our ontology would not have the resources to account for the humans' role in the destruction of the sense of the world. It would leave us powerless but also blameless.

conclusion

Speculative realism was heralded as a new philosophical movement capable of confronting the problems of our times by allowing us to think what post-Kantian philosophies were supposedly unable or unwilling to think: the real or the outside, what is not in any way for us. Yet if Nancy is right and the problem of our times is not so much metaphysics as nihilism, then it is not enough to decentre the human, flatten our ontology, and claim that there are only objects and that all objects exist equally. Rather, from this perspective, flat ontologies are heir to the deconstruction of metaphysics and perfectly compatible with a thinking of general equivalence. Ontological discourse about the world can act to cover over the plural exposition of singularities that form the sense of the world by grounding the world metaphysically in an *arche* or *telos* that subsumes or sublates the multiple edges that open right at world-singularities. It can also do so, however, by flattening all modes of beings and reducing all differences between singularities in ways that render them equivalent and exchangeable. To overcome this general equivalence, what is needed is not merely a non-metaphysical, non-human-centric thinking of being, but, much more importantly, a material and plural thinking of singularities and their absolute value. Within this thinking, it is also possible to reserve a role for the human without re-centring sense or value onto the human. This allows us to account for the potentially destructive participation of the human in the sense of world, both at the level of actions and at the level of discourse, including ontological discourse. In sum, in attempting to situate Nancy's ontology within the matrix formed by flatness, anthropocentrism, human exceptionalism, and anthropomorphism in the context of the "realist turn" in continental philosophy, I hope to have shown how Nancy provides the tools to move toward a thinking that is truly up to the demands of our times.

echo by jean-luc nancy

Here, as with other texts written in English, I am embarrassed – and this text's length and density makes me even more afraid of missing important aspects. Nevertheless, I perceive its accuracy and richness – both in information

and analytical ability – , for which I thank Marie-Eve Morin very much, who has undertaken to confront me with proposals or philosophical discourses I remain quite ignorant of due to my English.

If I may add something, it would be a remark about the word "flat," which plays such an important role here. It makes one think that we are opposing ourselves to "deep" or "inflated" (as we say "having a flat tyre").

My first reaction is to ask, when speaking of "flat ontology," what we are to make of an idea like the following from Nietzsche: "Those Greeks were superficial – *out of profundity!*" (*The Gay Science* §4). This statement means that the taste for beautiful appearances, the taste for form in the broadest sense (including Plato's *idéa*) comes from a sense of the difficulty, even the danger, that depth can represent. Without elaborating a commentary on Nietzsche, I'd like to emphasize the following, which belongs to his thinking as what provides it direction: depth (*profondeur*) always risks revealing itself to be without ground (*fond*).

The revelation of the "without ground" and its threat is nothing other than a collar of the "death of God." If God – supreme being, the supreme ontological guarantor – is dead, then far from simply being rid of him, we are facing an abyss. Rid of all "sufficient reason," we cannot simply enjoy the beautiful appearances so as to forget the abyss. Everything Nietzsche's Madman says goes in this direction.

I understand very well that "flat ontology" does not suggest a game of beautiful appearances. It does not say, like Nietzsche once again, that "we have art in order not to die of the truth."

Nor is that what I would like to say. I would rather like to point out that this abyssal depth – precisely because it is abyssal – is not a depth inviting us to take into account differences of degree (and thus differences in value) between supposed heights or depressions. Differences in nature are not necessarily differences of degree: human language is not more elevated than this or that mode of animal communication.

It is true that these differences in value have been manipulated a lot. Reducing them to their functional or structural distinctions, however, does not imply a mere levelling (flat) of values, but rather an opening towards other evaluations, that are themselves changing and transformable.

disclosure statement

No potential conflict of interest was reported by the author.

notes

1 If they avoid calling their enemy idealist, it is so as to prevent the pointless rejoinder of the Kantian or the phenomenologist that their position is not a form of subjective idealism. See Meillassoux, "Time Without Becoming" 4.

2 See also Sparrow 19 and Shaviro 1. Here I leave aside the claim that it leads to Nazism as Tim Morton claims:

> Correlationism itself only works if there is some kind of phobia of illusion. So one trajectory of correlationism culminates in Nazism. Correlationism itself is a breeding ground for Nazism, because in order to escape its paradoxes one might retreat still further into an extreme form of anthropocentrism. (224)

Because we are afraid of getting things wrong or of being led by an illusion, we close the circle of the correlation tighter and tighter: not the human but Dasein, not Dasein but German Dasein, and so on. Here I share Peter Gratton's sentiment: "This is perhaps a good time to call for a moratorium for the moral blackmail that either one agrees with a given position or one accedes to 'Nazism'" (237–38n37).

3 For a thorough engagement with the first point also in relation to Nancy's ontology, see Ian James, *The Technique of Thought*, especially chapter 2. In this book, James seeks to connect post-deconstructive thinkers such as Nancy to scientific thinking in order to develop a "post-Continental naturalism."

4 Human exceptionalism serves as justification for anthropocentrism, but the two claims are distinct. It is possible to imagine an anthropocentric theory that would be (weakly) justified merely by the fact that it is done (contingently) by a human (the theorist) without claiming that the human alone is in a special position within the universe, granting it the privilege of theory (or experience, or truth).

5 As Levi Bryant comes to acknowledge on his blog Larval Subjects. See the post, "I Guess My Ontology Ain't So Flat."

6 On the difference between the two kinds of flatness, and between Harman and Garcia in particular, see Graham Harman, "Tristan Garcia and the Thing-in-Itself."

7 For a critical engagement with Harman and objectification from a feminist phenomenological perspective, see Anna Mudde.

8 Of course, another possibility is radical eliminativism, where we affirm a universe in which anything that appears remotely special to the human is radically eliminated. Pick the thing that is the most foreign to being human (the thing that obviously does not make human beings special or distinct in any way) and assert that that is what all things – including humans – are at bottom ontologically reducible to.

9 See also Bennett 99: "A touch of anthropomorphism, then, can catalyze a sensibility that finds a world filled not with ontologically distinct categories of beings (subjects and objects) but with variously composed materialities that form confederations."

10 "Iteration, Reiteration, Repetition: A Speculative Analysis of the Meaningless Sign." Talk pronounced at the Freie University in Berlin in June 2012.

11 To use Jeffrey Cohen's terminology, we could say that Meillassoux's philosophy goes too far in that rather than being disanthropocentric, it ends up being squarely misanthropic. See Cohen a.o. 25, 63.

12 See Kant A592/B620–A603/B631 and Heidegger §7.

13 Let us dissipate two potential misunderstandings of Nancy's gloss right from the start: first,

the reader of Heidegger will notice the slippage from Being to existence to Dasein. This slippage or equivocation is not innocent and, as I will discuss below, is an essential feature of Nancy's ontology. Second, when we say that an essence does not exist (or is nothing), we do not mean that ideas, abstract entities, or thoughts do not exist. Yet they exist only insofar as they are not mere significations but are always also exscribed in contact with a material body (lip, pen, neuron, keyboard).

14 An abridged version of the chapter from which I am quoting is translated as "Abandoned Being" in *The Birth to Presence*, but the paragraph I am referring to is omitted.

15 For a more detailed reading of the relation between Nancy and Heidegger on the abandonment of Being, see Morin, "'We Must Become'" 23–30.

16 Through a different route, then, Nancy arrives at a position similar to that of new realist Markus Gabriel, who, in *Why the World Does Not Exist*, argues that, while everything else in the world exists or is real, the world itself does not exist because it is impossible to take on an external perspective on the world as a whole – indeed, if one were to take on such a perspective, it would itself be situated *in* the world and hence not all-encompassing.

17 Ian James also addresses Harman's reading of Nancy's whatever in his review of Shaviro's *Universe of Things*. The context is the encounter between Whitehead's process philosophy and Harman's object-oriented ontology staged by Shaviro's book. As James shows, the central debate in Continental philosophy ought not to be one between correlationist and "realist" or "materialist" philosophies but rather between philosophies of relations and "isolationist" philosophies of substance. It is within this context, between Whitehead and Shaviro, that the originality of Nancy's ontology can be located. Ultimately for James this also aligns Nancy with the ontic structural realism of Ladyman and Ross, a claim he develops later in chapter 2 of his *Technique of Thought*.

18 Such bodies however should not be too quickly assimilated to the lived body of phenomenology. They are material, but always remain dislocated, *partes extra partes*, without organic or lived

unity, shot through with opacity and foreignness. On the relation between Nancy's bodily ontology and phenomenologies of the lived body, see Morin, "*Corps propre*."

19 For an engagement of Nancy that puts the category of sense at the centre, see James, *Technique of Thought*, chapter 2, esp. 60–64. Though James does understand sense as material and matter as a principle of differentiation, his reading somewhat underplays the differance *at the heart* of things. The thing (as an "instance of material differentiation") is not only constituted by its relation (contact and separation), but also by difference, opening, or spacing in its self (or as itself).

20 On the relation between the decision of existence and the freedom of the world, see Morin, "'We Must Become'" 34–38.

bibliography

works by jean-luc nancy

Adoration: The Deconstruction of Christianity II. Trans. John McKeane. New York: Fordham UP, 2012. Print.

Being Singular Plural. Trans. Robert D. Richardson and Anne E. O'Byrne. Stanford: Stanford UP, 2000. Print.

The Birth to Presence. Trans. Brian Holmes et al. Stanford: Stanford UP, 1993. Print.

Corpus. Trans. Richard A. Rand. New York: Fordham UP, 2008. Print.

Corpus II: Writings on Sexuality. Trans. Anne E. O'Byrne. New York: Fordham UP, 2013. Print.

The Creation of the World or *Globalization*. Trans. François Raffoul and David Pettigrew. Albany: SUNY P, 2007. Print.

Dis-Enclosure: The Deconstruction of Christianity. Trans. Bettina Bergo, Gabriel Malenfant, and Michael B. Smith. New York: Fordham UP, 2008. Print.

The Experience of Freedom. Trans. Bridget McDonald. Stanford: Stanford UP, 1993. Print.

A Finite Thinking. Ed. Simon Sparks. Stanford: Stanford UP, 2003. Print.

The Gravity of Thought. Trans. François Raffoul and Gregory Recco. New York: Humanities, 1997. Print.

The Inoperative Community. Ed. Peter Connor. Minneapolis: U of Minnesota P, 1991. Print.

L'impératif catégorique. Paris: Flammarion, 1983. Print.

"Of Being-in-Common." *Community at Loose Ends*. Ed. The Miami Theory Collective. Minneapolis: U of Minnesota P, 1991. Print.

The Sense of the World. Trans. Jeffrey S. Librett. Minneapolis: U of Minnesota P, 1997. Print.

other works

Bennett, Jane. *Vibrant Matter: A Political Ecology of Things*. Durham: Duke UP, 2010. Print.

Bryant, Levi. *The Democracy of Objects*. Ann Arbor: Open Humanities, 2011. Print.

Bryant, Levi. "I Guess My Ontology Ain't So Flat." *Larval Subjects* 14 Feb. 2013. Web. <https://larvalsubjects.wordpress.com/2013/02/14/i-guess-my-ontology-aint-so-flat/>.

Bryant, Levi, Nick Srnicek, and Graham Harman, eds. *The Speculative Turn: Continental Materialism and Realism*. Prahran, Vic.: re.press, 2011. Print.

Cohen, Jeffrey Jerome. *Stone: An Ecology of the Inhuman*. Minneapolis: U of Minnesota P, 2015. Print.

Gabriel, Markus. *Why the World Does Not Exist*. Trans. Gregory Moss. Cambridge: Polity, 2015. Print.

Garcia, Tristan. *Form and Object: A Treatise on Things*. Trans. Mark Allan Ohm and Jon Coburn. Edinburgh: Edinburgh UP, 2014. Print.

Gratton, Peter. *Speculative Realism: Problems and Prospects*. London: Bloomsbury, 2014. Print.

Harman, Graham. "I am Also of the Opinion that Materialism Must Be Destroyed." *Environment and Planning D: Society and Space* 28 (2010): 772–90. Print.

Harman, Graham. "On Interface: Nancy's Weights and Masses." *Jean-Luc Nancy and Plural Thinking: Expositions of World, Ontology, Politics, and Sense*. Ed. Peter Gratton and Marie-Eve Morin. Albany: SUNY P, 2012. Print.

Harman, Graham. *Prince of Networks: Bruno Latour and Metaphysics*. Prahran, Vic.: re.press, 2014. Print.

Harman, Graham. "The Road to Objects." *Continent* 1.3 (2011): 171–79. Print.

Harman, Graham. "Tristan Garcia and the Thing-in-Itself." *Parrhesia* 16 (2013): 26–34. Print.

Heidegger, Martin. *Basic Problems of Phenomenology*. Trans. A. Hofstadter. Bloomington: Indiana UP, 1988. Print.

James, Ian. *The Technique of Thought: Nancy, Laruelle, Malabou, and Stiegler After Naturalism*. Minneapolis: U of Minnesota P, 2019. Print.

James, Ian. "The Touch of Things." Rev. of *The Universe of Things: On Speculative Realism* by Steven Shaviro. *Cultural Critique* 97 (2017): 203–27. Print.

Kant, Immanuel. *Critique of Pure Reason*. Trans. P. Guyer and A.W. Wood. Cambridge: Cambridge UP, 1998. Print.

Meillassoux, Quentin. *After Finitude: An Essay on the Necessity of Contingency*. London: Bloomsbury, 2009. Print.

Meillassoux, Quentin. "Iteration, Reiteration, Repetition: A Speculative Analysis of the Meaningless Sign." Talk pronounced at the Freie University, Berlin, June 2012.

Meillassoux, Quentin. "Time Without Becoming." Lecture given at Middlesex University, London, 8 May 2008. Web. <https://speculativeheresy.files.wordpress.com/2008/07/3729-time_without_becoming.pdf?>.

Morin, Marie-Eve. "*Corps propre* or *corpus corporum*: Unity and Dislocation in the Theories of Embodiment of Merleau-Ponty and Jean-Luc Nancy." *Chiasmi International* 18 (2016): 333–51. Print.

Morin, Marie-Eve. "'We Must Become What We Are': Jean-Luc Nancy's Ontology as Ethos and Praxis." *Nancy and the Political*. Ed. Sanja Dejanovic. Edinburgh: Edinburgh UP, 2015. Print.

Morton, Timothy. *Realist Magic: Objects, Ontology, Causality*. Ann Arbor: Open Humanities, 2013. Print.

Mudde, Anna. "Being (with) Objects." *Continental Realism and its Discontents*. Ed. Marie-Eve Morin. Edinburgh: Edinburgh UP, 2017. Print.

Shaviro, Steven. *The Universe of Things: On Speculative Realism*. Minneapolis: U of Minnesota P, 2014. Print.

Sparrow, Tom. *The End of Phenomenology: Metaphysics and the New Realism*. Edinburgh: Edinburgh UP, 2014. Print.

Affectivity, sense, and affects: it is on the basis of these three terms that I would like to begin a reflection on emotions that will be speculative; such a reflection would on the one hand think about the limits of what philosophical conceptuality can know, divulge, or reveal about emotions, and on the other hand, it would interpret the affective life in an experimental way in relation to biological thinking. Such speculative thinking, situated at the limits of both philosophy and biological knowledge, will pose the question of emotions in the context of an interrogation of limits in general: the limits that separate the biological organism from its environment and from other organisms, but also the limits that separate human beings from animals, as well as those, both ontological and epistemological, that separate speculative philosophy from science or natural science from the humanities.

Since its origin, of course, philosophy has questioned emotions: Plato, Aristotle, Descartes, Spinoza, Hobbes, and Hume have all given us theories of emotion. In the limited framework of this discussion, I do not propose to revisit these theories or to go through this complex and diverse philosophical history. Rather, I should like to begin with a recapitulation of basic definitions. Since the discourse engaged with here is primarily a French one, it might be useful first to consult the *Petit Robert*, which tells us that the French word "affect" means: "To touch (sb) by an impression, an action on the organism or the psyche." From this definition the meaning of "affectivité" follows in a consistent manner: "affectivity" means, and I quote, "an aptitude to be affected by pleasure or pain," or it means "the whole of affective life." And

ian james

AFFECTIVITY, SENSE, AND AFFECTS
emotions as an articulation of biological life

therefore affect is an "elementary affective state," i.e., the experience of a simple impression or sensation, for example, of pleasure or pain, an experience which, becoming more complex or richer, we call an emotion or feeling. In all these definitions the experience of touch, and therefore of feeling and sensation, remains primordial. The evidence of this primordial role played by touch in affectivity or in the experience of affects and emotions is underlined not only by dictionary definitions but also by the usual linguistic usage. When we feel emotions, we say we are "touched" by this or that. There is therefore no affect or emotion without a touch of some kind, without a sensing, a feeling, or a sensation. It could be added that there is no affect or emotion without a sense understood as meaning or instance of intelligibility, however basic. The impression on the organism which constitutes the experience of being affected by something will always and without exception have some sense for the affected organism, even, and perhaps above all, when this sense remains below any possibility of linguistic meaning and below any operation of understanding or cognition that might be called superior or rational.

In this context it is not possible for a philosophical or speculative reflection on emotions to ignore the bodily, and therefore biological, dimension of affective life. But this poses a problem. On the one hand, affects and emotions are part of the qualia of experience; they refer to the phenomenal aspect of our experience, which can only be accessed through subjective introspection. It is well known that philosophy tends to question emotions from the perspective of first-person experience. On the other hand, biology, as a science which aims to be objective, determines the existence of organisms as objects of knowledge from the outside and in the third person. If we really want to philosophically take into account the bodily dimension of emotions, that is, if we want to take into account affectivity, and therefore the touch and feeling which constitute it primarily as such, we need a way of thinking which will bring together the phenomenal and qualitative perspective which is said in the first person and the biological and quantitative perspective which is said in the third person. We would need, if you like, a naturalistic thought that would put the philosophy that questions phenomenal experience and the science that determines objective existence in a certain relationship of continuity.

One cannot speak of a naturalism of emotions without first referring to Spinoza and his famous definition of affects towards the end of the third part of the *Ethics*. But this definition either underscores or makes more complex the problem of the qualitative and the quantitative that has been alluded to. Here is the definition given by Spinoza:

The affect that is said to be a passion of the soul is a confused idea by which the mind affirms a greater or lesser force of the existence of its own body or of some part of it than before, and whose presence determines the mind to think this rather than that. (155; trans. mod.)

This formulation is entirely consistent with a naturalistic perspective insofar as it does not pose an ontological separation or distinction between the biological body on the one hand and the soul or mind on the other. All that exists is one and the same physical corporeal and mental reality that precedes the body–mind distinction. So Spinoza affirms a psychophysical monism. But this single reality translates for us as body and mind, two distinct perspectives which are in a parallel or isomorphic relationship with each other. The mind in this context is thus above all not autonomous with respect to the "force of existence of its own body" which is affirmed by affect, hence the whole Spinozist discourse on the impossibility of repressing affect; this is the "servitude" he discusses in the fourth part of the *Ethics*. On the one hand, this definition tells us that affects, affirming the existence of bodily forces, are in a certain way the basis of the life of the mind and of human consciousness, that is to say, the basis of phenomenal experience. The mind is constituted by its idea of the body and one is conscious of the body through the consciousness of its changes. So it is affects that constitute, at its base, the mind. On the other hand, it is possible that in this Spinozist definition of affects, we have not left the point of view of the first person at all. In the context of the psychophysical parallelism which defines affects as a confused idea of mind affirming the flow of a corporeal force of existence, it is quite possible that one nevertheless remains entirely within the domain of experience as lived in the first person and in the perspective of a qualitative apprehension of existence: it is always a question of the qualia of experience. So even if the body here is thought metaphysically in an ontological continuity with consciousness and with the life of the mind, it is not thought phenomenologically in continuity with the perspective of the biological body determined as an object and in the third person, that is to say, according to the point of view proper to scientific knowledge. The flow of the forces of the body and affects in Spinoza, and the conatus of which this flow is the expression, is not accessible, I would say, by way of biological science.

This problem has been bequeathed to the philosophical tradition that was inherited from Spinoza. I am thinking here above all of Nietzsche and the Nietzschean theory of force and affects as taken up by Gilles Deleuze in his writings of the 1960s (see Deleuze, *Nietzsche et la philosophie* and *Différence et répétition*). Even if one acknowledges that Deleuze's thought aspires to be a metaphysics that would be adequate to modern science, and acknowledging also that contemporary philosophers such as Keith Ansell-Pearson, Manuel DeLanda, and John Protevi, for example, have put Deleuze's thought in continuity with biology and with complexity theory in particular, I would say that this problem persists (see Ansell-Pearson, *Viroid Life*; *Germinal Life*; DeLanda; Protevi). All these thinkers find a parallelism between scientific thought and Deleuze's thought (the problematic question of parallelism is always at the forefront), but the fact remains that forces and affects in Deleuze, as in Spinoza and Nietzsche, are always related to an immanent experience or a qualitative dimension of bodily existence and experience, a dimension that is not susceptible to objective and quantitative scientific determination.

If we leave the European philosophical tradition to engage the Anglo-American tradition as it developed during the twentieth century, the problem arises in another but no less irreducible way. From a general point of view, it can be seen that Anglo-American philosophy of mind and psychology tended, during the twentieth century, to ignore emotions. However, towards the end of the century, around the year 2000 and up to the present day, there has been a strong revival of interest in theories of emotions in Europe and the United States. There is, for example, what is known as affect

theory, which brings together a very wide range and multiplicity of perspectives from cognitive science, neurology, evolutionary biology, but also from the humanities. This field is very vast and it is not possible to do any justice to it in the limited framework of this argument.

What is important is the fact that, as has been underlined here and as is recognised in the field of "affect theory," any theory or philosophy of affects must take into account the bodily and therefore biological dimension of emotions. But at the same time theory must also take into account the dimension of affects or emotions which cannot be reduced to physiology. The multi- and interdisciplinary character of affect theory clearly meets this requirement. However, it should be asked whether the difficulty of the psychophysical parallelism identified in Spinoza nevertheless remains problematic in this context.

As for naturalism, and this is of particular interest to us here, the Anglo-American tradition offers a radical solution to the problem of qualitative experience and its determination or in-determination by science. The trajectory of this tradition can be traced from its roots in American pragmatism, that of John Dewey for example, to its beginning and its subsequent evolution in the philosophies of Wilfred Sellars, Willard van Orman Quine, David Lewis, and the neuro-philosophy of Paul and Patricia Churchland. The characteristic feature of this tradition is the desire to place philosophy in a relationship of continuity with natural science and thus to confer on scientific knowledge the ultimate authority in determining reality. It is science, therefore, which in principle has exclusive authority in all matters concerning ontology and epistemology. What results from this philosophical valorisation of science is a tendency to want to eliminate everything that resists empirical or scientific determination. Nowhere is this tendency more visible than in the eliminativist materialism of Paul and Patricia Churchland.

The central thesis of eliminativist materialism is that all reality is physical and that all our preconceived ideas about inner and qualitative experience constitute a naive psychology that will eventually be replaced by neuroscience. So indeed emotions, memories, and consciousness itself, do not exist as such. We will need other, more scientific categories that will designate entities that can be determined empirically. Here is a quote from Paul Churchland:

> If they are ultimately physical, inner qualities should be accessible epistemologically not only from the first-person or "subjective" point of view; they should also be accessible from one or more objective points of view, from some instrument that could scan brain activity for example. (227)

So from this point of view the problem of emotions does not ultimately arise. The category of emotion would belong to a naive psychology that would be eliminated altogether in favour of a determination of a nervous or neurological activity that is perfectly measurable under experimental conditions. The question of the qualitative dimension of emotions would be removed, but at the price of removing the qualitative dimension of existence in general, i.e., of consciousness and of first-person experience.

This extreme naturalistic position is obviously not sufficient as a theory or philosophy of affects and emotions. For to eliminate in this context is not simply to theorise elimination as such but rather to repress. A fundamental and irreducible dimension of experience is repressed on the sole pretext, which is not very philosophical, that it is not accessible to objective or quantitative science. Even if sensing, feeling, and affectivity are not measurable or quantifiable, it is no less certain that we sense and feel and that affects and emotions have an undeniable existence and reality. From the beginning, it should be remembered, the task here has been to find a way of thinking that would bring together the phenomenal point of view and the biological point of view, that is to say, the first- and third-person perspectives.

What is needed, therefore, is another approach to biology, a biological thought that is not so brutally materialistic and reductive with regard to the existence of living organisms. What is needed is a biological way of thinking that would be more sensitive to the specificity of living things and to their interactions with their environment. The resources for such thinking are not found in the American naturalist tradition but rather in the French tradition of historical epistemology and more particularly in the biological philosophy of Georges Canguilhem. Canguilhem, as is well established, is known for his influence on Michel Foucault, on the development of French structuralism during the 1960s, and on Althusser's reinterpretation of Marx in particular. But it is much less recognised in the Anglo-Saxon tradition of the philosophy of science. The late Jean Gayon, who was Professor of Philosophy and History of Science at the Sorbonne, has noted that Canguilhem's biological thought is not very unified but rather scattered in various publications written over several decades, which probably explains the difficulty of its reception outside France. In an article on the question of individuality in Canguilhem's biological philosophy, Gayon emphasises the relational character of his understanding of living organisms. In Canguilhem's view, "individuals," Gayon emphasises, "should not be conceived of as beings but as relations" (308). From the biological point of view, he continues, while quoting Canguilhem directly: "individuals are beings that have needs, and therefore constitute 'an absolute and irreducible reference system' in a given environment [...] the ontology of life must be subordinated to the axiology of life" (320). This remark should be remembered because it underlines that vague notions of matter or physical substance, i.e., the levels of explanation to which biology tends to reduce the existence and activity of living things, are not at all sufficient to take into account the specificity of life. More fundamental to the biological organism are values, or rather value relationships, which define the living as living.

The following quotation, taken from an essay entitled "The Living and its Environment" and dating from the 1950s, explains this Canguilhemist perspective more clearly:

From the biological point of view, one must understand that the relationship between the organism and the environment is the same as that between the parts and the whole of an organism. The individuality of the living does not stop at its ectodermic borders any more than it begins at the cell. The biological relationship between the being and its milieu is a functional relationship, and thereby a mobile one; its terms successively changing roles. The cell is a milieu for intracellular elements; it itself lives in an interior milieu, which is sometimes on the scale of the organ and sometimes of the organism; the organism itself lives in a milieu that, in a certain fashion, is to the organism what the organism is to its components. (Canguilhem, *La Connaissance de la vie* 144; *Knowledge of Life* 111)

Canguilhem presents us here with a model of biological individuation according to which there are only relationships, that is to say relationships among relationships and so on, without a background of substance which underlies the relational structure thus posed. So there are various biochemical processes and their relationships to molecular microstructures which in turn form intracellular structures. Such intracellular structures function in relation to cells, those of the cells in relation to organs, those of the organs in relation to those of the organism, and the structures of the organism function in relation to the surrounding environment. But the essential point here is that the organism at all its levels of organisation is constituted by these functional relationships. It is not a question of relationships between elements or substances that already exist, but rather of elements that exist only in these relationships or thanks to the reference system constituted from these relationships.

The relationship in Canguilhem is always a "relation to"; a relation between a specific point in a structure which, when put in relation, constitutes a living being as such in its interiority and exteriority. But, and this is the decisive point, this "relation to" is always, as a functional relationship, a relationship of "sense." The system of functional relations that

constitutes the living organism at all its levels is always a system that makes sense, or more precisely is a sense. Canguilhem defines "sense" here in the following terms:

> From the biological and psychological point of view, a sense is an appreciation of values in relation to a need. And for the one who experiences as lives it, a need is an irreducible, and thereby absolute, system of reference. (*La Connaissance de la vie* 154; *Knowledge of Life* 120)

Therefore, functional biological relations as "relations to" constitute the biological organism as a centre of reference for these relationships and as a "sense." And sense in this context is to be understood axiologically as a system of reference that is experienced in a way that individuates the organism as an autonomous and discrete value. It is in this context that Canguilhem notes or affirms that "the being of an organism is its sense" (*La Connaissance de la vie* 147; *Knowledge of Life* 113).

And it is here that we can return to the question of affectivity, of sensing, and feeling and to the possibility of touch, which underlies any affection, affect, or emotion. For if, for Canguilhem, sense has an ontological significance in his understanding of the living, and if sense is always a "relation to" that is constitutive of the organism as such, it is also possible to understand this "relation to" of sense as a mode of touch, and in terms of a fundamental affectivity operating at all levels of biological organisation. That is to say, the most elementary biochemical processes, the interactions of cells and organs, and the organism's sensible and intelligible interactions with the environment, all can be understood as an economy of touch and of affectivity. Thus sense and its "relation to," considered as touch and fundamental affectivity, articulate all biological life, that is to say all the so-called "internal" structuring of the organism as well as its apprehension of, and its interactions with, the world around it. From this we can speculatively argue that what we call affects or emotions are only a continuation or prolongation of this touch and fundamental affectivity which constitutes the living organism.

This is not to say, of course, that amoebas, viruses, or bacteria have or feel emotions. It is to suggest, however, that affects and emotions, being a continuation or prolongation of an affectivity proper to the most elementary biochemical processes, are not fundamentally different from the sensing and feeling experienced by the simplest biological organisms. It is only a difference in degree and of relational complexity. From this a no less speculative hypothesis can be put forward, namely, that consciousness too is a continuation or extension of this fundamental biological affectivity. To sense, to feel, and to feel that one feels, would be in this context the condition for any intentional directedness of consciousness. We would therefore be completely with Spinoza in affirming that it is affects and affectivity in general that constitute, at its base, the mind or the conscious life.

But here there is no longer any parallelism between the physical and the psychic. From this point of view, considering affects, emotions, and consciousness as a continuation or extension of the "relations to" of sense that organise biological life as such, requires a reconfiguration of the dividing lines that have separated qualitative experience from quantitative determination. For qualitative or phenomenal experience on the one hand, and quantitatively determined biological elements on the other, are no longer considered in parallel but in direct continuity. It was suggested somewhat polemically at the beginning of this discussion that Spinoza's psychophysical parallelism gave, despite its monistic metaphysics, a definition of affects which was oriented according to qualitative experience and the first-person perspective. It was also proposed that this strong orientation towards the qualitative dimension of immanent existence was prolonged in Deleuzian metaphysics. Starting from Canguilhem's biological thought, and interpreting both "physical" structures and "psychic" sensing or feeling as "relations to" of sense, it is no longer possible to separate the quantitative from the qualitative, the objective determination from the phenomenal subjective experience.

And it is here that we must refer to the pre-eminent contemporary thinker of sense, touch, and thus of the fundamental affectivity of existence in general, that is to say, Jean-Luc Nancy. For Nancy, like Canguilhem, confers on the term sense an ontological significance, albeit in a broader perspective that goes beyond biology. Let us recall that in *Le Sens du monde*, Nancy also underlines the relational character of sense: "There is sense only in a relation to some 'outside' or 'elsewhere' to which sense consists in relating" (*Le Sens du monde* 17; *The Sense of the World* 7). And just as Canguilhem insists that the biological organism is its sense, Nancy for his part insists that the relations and sharing of sense that constitute existing entities or singularities make or rather *are* the world: "Thus, world is not only correlative of sense, it is structured as sense, and conversely, sense is structured as world" (18; 7–8). Or also: "the world no longer has sense, but it is sense" (19; 8). This reference to Nancy opens up the possibility of placing physical, geophysical, biophysical, and psychophysical relations in an ontological continuity with each other. By crossing Canguilhem's biological thought and Nancy's thought of sense, we arrive at a naturalistic perspective which situates the psychic life of living beings, their sensations, their affects, their emotions, as well as their awareness of the world and of themselves, in a direct continuity with physical life. This opening onto a novel naturalism has been developed further elsewhere (James, *The Technique of Thought*).

The reconfiguration proposed here of the dividing lines that separate the psychic and the physical, the biological body and the emotional body, is not without consequences for other configurations of lines and limits. Not separating the qualitative dimension of existence from its quantitative determination also has implications for the way we distinguish between fields of knowledge or cognition, for example, the relationship of philosophy or the humanities to the so-called "hard" natural sciences. And not to separate the relations of sense that physically organise the biological organism and at the same time condition the

THE PULSE OF SENSE

psychic possibility of sensing, feeling, of having emotions, and, finally, of thinking, this forces us to reconceive the distinction between animal and human life. For, if we know, since Darwin at least, that human life is in biological continuity with animal life, this thought of affectivity, sense, and affects also makes it clear to us that emotions, as an articulation of biological life and as the basis of consciousness, are fundamental qualities of sensible experience for both human beings and animals. From a qualitative point of view there is nothing essential to distinguish between the two. From the emotional life of elementary organisms to the rich and complex emotional life of mammals (including humans), birds, and, who knows, reptiles, it is only a question of differences in degree, complexity, and relational articulation.

echo by jean-luc nancy

First of all, Ian James gives me great pleasure by reminding me that I am a former student of Canguilhem, whose teaching meant a lot to me. Because of him, I did a year of biology as part of the scientific training then required for the *aggrégation* in philosophy.

Actually, this memory touches – yes, it touches! – on an important component of my intellectual framework: an attention to what is alive (without "vitalism") that meets – paradoxically – the Heideggerian meaning of ek-sistence and what I would call, simplifying, a meta-Christian sense of incarnation. This framework also ties into Derrida's "life death."

I am therefore in complete agreement with this paper, which for me also opens reflection in the direction of the Freudian "It" and "drive," two names for an arch-primitive community of the living …

disclosure statement

No potential conflict of interest was reported by the author.

bibliography

Ansell-Pearson, K. *Germinal Life: The Difference and Repetition of Deleuze.* London: Routledge, 1999. Print.

Ansell-Pearson, K. *Viroid Life: Perspectives on Nietzsche and the Transhuman Condition.* London: Routledge, 1997. Print.

Canguilhem, G. *Knowledge of Life.* Trans. Stefanos Geroulanos and Daniela Ginsburg. New York: Fordham UP, 2008. Print.

Canguilhem, G. "Le Vivant et son milieu." *La Connaissance de la vie.* Paris: Vrin, 1965. Print.

Churchland, P. "The Rediscovery of Light." *The Journal of Philosophy* 93.5 (1996): 211–28. Print.

DeLanda, M. *Intensive Science and Virtual Philosophy.* London: Bloomsbury, 2002. Print.

Deleuze, G. *Différence et répétition.* Paris: Presses Universitaires de France, 1968. Print.

Deleuze, G. *Nietzsche et la philosophie.* Paris: Presses Universitaires de France, 1962. Print.

Gayon, J. "The Concept of Individuality in Canguilhem's Philosophy of Biology." *Journal of the History of Biology* 31.3 (1998): 305–25. Print.

James, I. *The Technique of Thought: Post-continental Naturalism in Nancy, Laruelle, Malabou and Stiegler.* Minneapolis: Minnesota UP, 2019. Print.

Nancy, J.-L. *Le Sens du monde.* Paris: Galilée, 1993. Print.

Nancy, J.-L. *The Sense of the World.* Trans. J.S. Librett. Minneapolis: U of Minnesota P, 1997. Print.

Protevi, J. *Life, War, Earth: Deleuze and the Sciences.* Minneapolis: U of Minnesota P, 2013. Print.

Spinoza, B. *Ethics Proved in Geometrical Order.* Trans. Michael Silverthorne and Mathew J. Kisner. Cambridge: Cambridge UP, 2018. Print.

The Emancipation of Christianity

introduction

In Nancy's recent work on Christianity's deconstruction, one can notice a certain hesitation in the metaphors Nancy uses to describe what is happening to Christianity: either one can understand the process of this auto-deconstruction as a metamorphosis, which seems to imply that an older form of the "same" phenomenon takes on a new shape, or this process is to be seen as a mutation, in which the new form only ever takes place at the expense of the old phenomenon (*Adoration* 32, 50, 55, 80, 111n7). Metamorphosis, then, seems to be a slow process and seems to imply a step forward, whereas mutation might be understood more as a leap, an instant change in which the newer form of a culture has nothing to do whatsoever with the older form. This article will seek to exploit this hesitation on Nancy's part and relate it to Derrida's critique of Nancy in his magnificent *On Touching* (2002).

joeri schrijvers

METAMORPHOSIS OR MUTATION?
jean-luc nancy and the deconstruction of christianity

the end of metaphysics: from a principle for the world to a world without principle

Nancy's deconstruction of Christianity squares with his phenomenological ontology of "being-with" in the very precise sense that Christianity has, from time immemorial, according to Nancy at least, always been exposed both to metaphysical structures and that which remained outside of it. In this way, Christianity, for Nancy, occupies an exceptional and paradigmatic place: although it is metaphysical to its very core, it simultaneously has sown the seeds of its (own) overcoming. Nancy is quite

clear on this: for him, Christianity and "monotheism [oppose], as much as [they comfort] the reign of the principle" (*Dis-Enclosure* 24).

The deconstruction of Christianity is, however, not to be taken as a provocation; it is not against Christianity as a virulent atheism would be: Nancy rather asks how Christianity can still make sense in a culture which is no longer Christian; that is, a culture that no longer *shares* all Christian presuppositions (*Dis-Enclosure* 141–43)? The deconstruction of Christianity is thus a comportment toward what one can call the relics and the remainder of the Christian culture. It is, according to Nancy, precisely from out of Christianity's vanishing that a thought of the world or of our being-with might appear, for "already in the most classical metaphysical representations of [...] God, nothing else was at stake, in the end, than the world itself" (*Creation* 41). The attempt to grasp the world within one, single worldview or to comprehend the totality of beings from out of a highest being or principle will, when faded away, give way to the thought of the world without principle, without sufficient reason or any given – it will make us face the sheer presence of "world." If all historical highest beings – God, nature, reason, history – have functioned as a way of filling in the gaps by, for instance, explaining that which could not and cannot be explained – i.e., the existence of the world – then the deconstruction of Christianity aims to attend to the nothingness, the void or the gap left after the flight of the gods. Nancy's rather straightforward response to Marion is in this regard perhaps worth pointing out already: "[Marion's] proposition does not emerge yet out of a 'self-giving' (and of 'self-showing' of the phenomenon, whereas I propose here, simply, that nothing gives *itself* and that *nothing* shows *itself* – and that is what is" (*Creation* 123n24). Nancy's thought, therefore, must be seen as an attempt to cope with a world *without givenness*, without any principle *being given*, and to stick to the world *as* it (now) worlds considered from the fact *that* it worlds (and that it is only the world which worlds). This "worlding of the world" is *ours*: it is not regulated by something or someone "out there" nor is it regulated and controlled by an ideal somewhere "in" the world. Hence what can be called Nancy's axiom: "we who are no more than us in a world, which is itself no more than the world" (*Being Singular Plural* 17)). Here Nancy joins a trend in contemporary French phenomenology: what is being investigated is not this or that phenomenon, this or that appearance; it concerns rather a phenomenology to the second degree for which what matters is not that which appears but the appearing of appearance itself, considered as an event. For Nancy, this event is the event of world.

It is in *this* world that Christianity is auto-deconstructing. And it is important to note that for Nancy Christianity vanishes in a quasi-automatic way. Such an *auto-deconstruction* only ever occurs if the (metaphysical) system of Christianity "has contained its fatal agent within itself ever since its conception," as Reiner Schürmann wrote (197). Such a *"fatal agent,"* for Nancy, seems to be whatever givenness has been posed, presupposed or otherwise taken for granted: from the very moment that the presupposition is made that God is the foundation and ultimate unification of the world (ontotheology) or that such a unification is left to the transcendental postulates (Kant and modernity), it must be stated that such a "presupposition also contains the principle of its own deposition" (*Creation* 71). The Christian community, too, has been (mis)-guided by the reign of the principle, by metaphysics: this community, too, was "thought as bound by a transcendent or mystical bond and the bond itself as a reunion lifted into a unity" (Nancy, "The Confronted Community" 28). Christianity was perhaps the greatest idea of community to date: it imagined a communion of saints and sinners, of the living and the dead. This bond was then conceived as a "way": all are on their way to God. In a sense, everything is on its way to God. And here is Nancy's caveat: nothing remains outside of this history of salvation, nothing is outside the givenness (or creation) of this God. Yet we can witness a deconstruction of this narrative: one might say that what remained outside of this narrative, what perhaps was repressed, is now resurfacing as reflux.

Concretely, this means that Christianity will break under the pressure of the separations and the divisions that constituted it in the first place. One can therefore understand Nancy's project as trying to expose and disassemble those *"internal divisions"* within Christianity which will eventually cause the disintegration of its assembly and be the death of it. Nancy mentions several examples of these divisions. One can, for instance, think of the Christian quarrel over, on the one hand, the prohibition of images and the right to represent the sacred on the other. Derrida has noted another division: the portrayal of the Gospel of Jesus as touching and touched by human beings and Jesus' own prohibition of any such touch (100–03). Nancy added that it is precisely this paradox of Christianity – the paradox connecting *"hoc est corpus meum"* and *"noli me tangere"* – is at issue (*Noli me tangere* 14). Most important is, however, the division between a Christianity that lets itself be reduced to metaphysics and a Christianity that precisely resists such a reduction.

what is metaphysics? marion and kant

Jean-Luc Marion begins his exposition of ontotheology with the claim that concepts too can function as idols, as "the making available of the divine" (9) in that it produces a "concept that makes a claim to equivalence with God" (13). Marion thinks of the Greeks: the idea of the Good (Plato), the divine self-thinking (Aristotle), and of the One (Plotinus) (cf. 10). Then Marion discusses Aquinas' five ways to prove the existence of God, and comments that:

> the question of the existence of God is posed less before the proof than at its end, when it is no longer a question of simply establishing that some concept can be called *God* [...] but more radically that that concept or that being coincides with God himself. (ibid.)

Here Marion hints at the devastation that took place in the transition to modernity, when the consensus that this being indeed has to be called God is lost. Marion's answer is as unsettling as it is correct: "the consensus of 'all' is replaced by the idiomatic phrase 'by [God] I mean [...]'" (11). Nancy will add the *"Jemeingötterung"* brought to us by American soap operas (*Dis-Enclosure* 116; "Mon Dieu!" 271–78). Understood in this way, the transition from modernity to postmodernity might hint at an even more profound loss. For, just as Marion describes the transition from the Middle Ages to modernity as the loss of consensus in

matters divine, the transition from modernity to postmodernity could be described as the loss of consensus of precisely those postulates that Kant used to redefine the limits of knowledge at the dawn of modernity. So, for instance, whereas the modern *subject* was that instance that remained the same despite the variations of its lived experiences, the postmodern subject is shattered, schizophrenic, and, according to Levinas and Marion, in a permanent state of alteration rather than remaining the same (Levinas, *Totality and Infinity* 36). Whereas the postulate of the *world* was, for Kant, used to assure the unity and the coherence of the world amidst all the subject's diverse experiences, postmodernity's plurality presupposes a multitude of worlds that altogether seem to forbid the thought of a unity underlying all these different worlds. Whereas the postulate of *God*'s existence assured the coincidence of virtue and happiness, it now sometimes seems as if happiness is what is to be obtained at all costs, and perhaps especially that of virtue.

For Marion, the concept then prescribes for God his being: God *has to be* the cause that causes everything else without itself being caused. For Heidegger and Nietzsche (and in a certain sense Nancy), the principle, because of its unifying tendencies, prescribes for the world its being. In the mechanical and mathematical universe that issued from the thoughts of Descartes and Kant, this means that the piece of wax has to be the *res extensa* that this mathematical worldview prescribes for it. And yet, the fact that, for instance, the smell of this particular piece of wax can also serve as a sort of Proustean reminder of days spent with my grandmother is thereby forgotten or, who knows, repressed.

what is metaphysics ii: nietzsche and heidegger

The response to the problem has mainly consisted in identifying this or that figure as responsible for the beginning of metaphysics – was it Suarez or rather Duns Scotus? Such a response, obviously, always runs the risk of being less concerned with ontotheology than with safeguarding other thinkers from precisely this problem. Fréderic Nef's rather blunt response has been to regard ontotheology as inexistent or as such nowhere to be found in the history of thinking (224). This latter thesis has provoked Jean-Yves Lacoste to respond that it "at the least has proven that [ontotheology] is not omnipresent in the history of philosophy" (*Danger* 18n1). It could also be, in a third response that we claim as our own, inexistent in the sense somewhat of a fathom, a ghost, or illusion. In this case, ontotheology is but a "thought-experiment"; yet one that is particularly hard to avoid and its ghostly existence might have more traction in reality than we would like to admit.

For Heidegger, the end of metaphysics has given rise to technology and, through technology, to nihilism. Let us begin, then, with the nihilism that we all know and we all experience. This is the nihilism which, for Lacoste, "is associated with the mathematization of being in its totality" (*Theological Thinking* 79). In effect, one of Heidegger's insights which seems particularly true a good sixty years later, is that "the quantitative becomes a special quality and thus a remarkable kind of greatness" (*Question Concerning Technology* 135): the quantitative becomes its own kind of quality and perhaps the only one we can still think. Nancy, moreover, has almost word for word repeated this observation when speaking of "the conversion of quantity into quality" (*Fukushima* 34).

What separates Nancy's deconstruction of Christianity from a great many Christian theologians is his recognition that today's culture, its metaphysics, its nihilism and its atheism, is (still) a *Christian* one. Far from opposing nihilism and Christianity, as is often fashionable in theological circles, Nancy writes that "Christianity is accomplished in nihilism and as nihilism" (*Dis-Enclosure* 147). The Christian religion, precisely because of its historical and worldly dimensions, tends to evaporate in that very world and, in the process, let the question of world, and how to deal with it, evaporate into nihilism just as well. Christianity

is not what saves us from nihilism, it is its accomplice.

First, then, we should note what Heidegger regards as the distinctive "element" in which Nietzsche's nihilism arises: Nietzsche is "the first to pose the thoughtful question[:] is the man of today in his metaphysical nature ready to assume dominion over the earth?" (*Thinking* 65). Can humanity take up its responsibility for the earth without the back-up of the principle? One has to know very little of Nietzsche's fate to come to the conclusion that it is likely Heidegger would have responded in the negative. The contemporary debates about global warming might perhaps again testify to this.

Yet, this possibility of an "*Erdregierung*" faces us as a task (and perhaps not only one of thinking) once the *causa sui*, or whatever we called the highest being, stopped securing and safeguarding (the being of) all other beings. What remains after Nietzsche, according to the Heideggerian plot, is a situation in which all beings value, rank and categorize all other beings with no other standard than this valuing itself. This is how what is "best" and "better" gets increasingly confused with what is "more," or how, in contemporary capitalism, the highest good is confused with the greatest amount of riches.

In his course on thinking, Heidegger focused on the relation of such valuing to the present, rather than its relation to the past or the future. The will to power, one might say, only ever wants the present. It wants the present because that which appears here and now, before us, can and will be controlled and dominated in its very appearing. Phenomenologically, the appearing of appearances will be reduced to what can be contained objectively of this appearance here before me. It is no coincidence that what can be thus contained are above all mathematical and geometrical features: what can be counted, ranked and categorized.

If Nietzsche, for Heidegger, has somewhat of an exceptional position, it is that he envisioned the possibility of a transition, to a higher "man" or to a new age. This transition, as Heidegger sums it up, is contained in Nietzsche's call to

THE PULSE OF SENSE

save ourselves from revenge and resentment, from *Rache*.

What does this *Rache* do? What does it want? This revenge, Heidegger will argue, reduces "being" to "beings," the event of "appearing" (verbally) to this appearance (nominally) and finally it ascertains that "pure presence," in its highest and "best" form should be "the presence that persists, the abiding present, the steadily standing 'now'" (*Thinking?* 102). All this is familiar: it is from this that Derrida's logocentrism and "metaphysics of presence" takes its cue. What is less familiar is what this *Rache* rages against, what it does not want.

The will to power rages against the past, for the past is that which this will to power cannot change and over which it cannot exercise domination – "everything passes except the past," as a Belgian journalist once wrote. "Faced with what 'was,' willing no longer has anything to say" (Heidegger, *Thinking?* 92). In a certain sense, the will rages against the fact (or the event) that "being" was present (or: presences) even when it cannot be reduced to "beings" or this presence here: the will rages against the past as that which exceeds its claim to power, it suffers from not being able to alter and control the "coming and going" of beings and of being, which, if well understood, extends to the present as well as the future. Metaphysics and ontotheology are not, as a secular thinker would have it, a refusal of God and the divine, they are rather a *rage against time*. It is for this reason that time, itself, will be reduced to "the now" from Aristotle onward. Here thinking has decided that "a being is more being when it is most present" (Heidegger, *Thinking?* 101). The otherworldliness or *Hinterweltelei* of which Nietzsche spoke is thus first of all the invention of a realm without time. At the end of metaphysics, once being is unhinged from God and from all timelessness, it appears all the more clearly that we have to be readied to think the event of time and of world. It is here that Nancy's thought of a mutation in our culture leaps into the unknown and the speculative: Nancy seems to think that one is

able to leave this old Christian metaphysics behind in one stroke and that what we are facing today is an *entirely new* situation with no ties to our past whatsoever.

Heidegger's examples of the nihilism in our culture have been met with furrowed brows: the typewriter (which prevents us from thinking), abbreviations (which prevent us supposedly from "dwelling in language") and newspapers (they prevent us looking beyond the present). Yet three other examples deserve our attention here to see how this metaphysical nihilism, in our time also, rages against the time being granted to us. The first example clarifies what Heidegger intends here: "Today's reckoning in sports [with] tenths of seconds, in [...] physics even with millionth of seconds [...] such reckoning is [...] the surest way to lose essential time" (*Thinking?* 101). Time, then, becomes something to count on, something certain to be always and already there. It is what other texts of Heidegger would call a "tranquillization": this counting "began [when] man suddenly became restless because he had no more time" (*Thinking?* 105). A second example of this handling of time Heidegger significantly observes in the Christian tradition, namely in the question of remorse and repentance. These, obviously, share a relation to the past similar to that of vengeance. Just as vengeance, so too remorse does not want what is now in the past to have happened at all. Heidegger is claiming that through the Christian forgiveness of sins, remorse is caught up just as well in some sort of instrumentalization and safeguarding of time (*Thinking?* 105). It is perhaps to such a thing that the medieval commerce in "indulgences" testifies. A third characteristic of this metaphysical rage against time is to be noted in the transposition Nietzsche forges between the features of the Absolute and what now is known as the modern subject. Heidegger traces Nietzsche's concept of the will to Schelling's notion of primal being as willing: this "will" that needs to be seen as eternal, self-affirming and independent of time, for instance (*Thinking?* 90–91). This means: the subject erects itself as that which has to be, and forcefully wants to be, itself always and everywhere. This subject allows for no change (hence the rage against time), no dependency for its being on "Being" (hence what we now call its forgetting of otherness). Although Nancy's thinking of the event seems to track such a granting and givenness of time, many passages in his thought imply that to take into account such granting, one can do entirely without the metaphysical tradition. Hence, again, our question: is it a metamorphosis or a mutation of culture which we are facing?

what is the deconstruction of christianity?

This brings us to a first definition of metaphysics and of the deconstruction of Christianity: the securing of the principle and the want of a hold over being. In short: metaphysics, in its (post)modern guise wants to prescribe for the world its being. Hence Nancy's attempt to think the world as world and as no more than world – *ex nihilo* and *from scratch* as it were. Nancy and Heidegger share a similar diagnosis of the current state of the world. With the recent publication of the *Schwarze Hefte* in mind, it is quite clear too that Heidegger would have seen in nihilism a Christian phenomenon. Where Heidegger and Nancy differ is in their respective response to this global crisis.

In an oft overlooked passage, Nancy in effect writes that this want of a hold is the form a deconstruction of Christianity most often takes: the nostalgic longing for and return to a "pure" origin of Christianity, not yet tainted with metaphysical – scholastic or modern – impurities (*Dis-Enclosure* 39). One can observe this quite often in Christianity and in theological circles, for instance, in the quest for a historical Jesus or in the longing for a Christianity not yet corrupted by dogmatics, etc. One sees this just as well in politics and in all sorts of nationalisms: the desire to unify the "people" through a return to a Golden Age in which the people were not yet divided and it could, in principle, repulse all others and otherness. This makes plain that

Heidegger, too, might have succumbed to such a form of metaphysics: his attempt to return to a "pure" thinking in a "purely Greek" manner might testify to this. In sum, it is this version that the deconstruction of Christianity, conceived as a cultural compound, today most often takes.

Nancy's account of Christianity's deconstruction differs from this version in that it assumes that there will never have been such an origin. From the very start, not to say "in the beginning," there was mixture, intertwining and confusion between "Christianity" and its pagan predecessors. In this regard, there is no "essence" of Christianity if this were to mean that Christianity is isolated from all cultural and contextual developments. It is such a mixture of, say, paganism and Christianity that is the starting-point of Nancy's conception of a deconstruction of Christianity: Christianity is both within and without metaphysics or "the reign of the principle." It is such a Christianity that Nancy today sees evaporating in, again, an entirely new context: the historical and worldly dimensions of Christianity are such that Christianity in the end can be substituted for a thought of world. It is this beginning, this new dawn which for Nancy, it seems, needs to be constructed from scratch.

a share of being: being between us

One could call Nancy's position a more "existential" version of Derrida's *différance* stripped of an ultimate signification. Nancy is envisioning the event of being as the arrival of a surprise which surpasses our anticipations and representations. Being is what happens in however minute an occasion, but always according to the logic of the "with." The meaning of being, then, cannot occur "for one alone": this is Nancy's version of what Levinas called the "intersubjective curvature of space."

A few examples: one can indeed have a phenomenological intuition of a table and reduce what is commonly understood as a table to it being a plateau with four legs. Yet, for this intuition to be true, it will need to be confirmed by an other – can you see the table in the same way? Yet this other too, for this confirmation, is dependent upon the "institution" (Merleau-Ponty) of entire realms of cultural meanings and signification – if we were to put a table before the inhabitants of the Stone Age, for example, it is quite likely that they would not know how to use this object.

Nancy gives the example of the Cartesian *cogito*: I can doubt the existence of others, I can even doubt the existence of a world out there, but I cannot doubt the very fact that it is I who doubts. Descartes' conclusion is that since I think, I must also be: I am not sure that there are others at all, I am sure only of the fact that I exist. Nancy comments: for such a solipsistic phrase to be true, it must presuppose that others, namely "each one of Descartes' readers" (*Being Singular Plural* 31) must also be able to understand this solitude of the Cartesian *cogito*, and so confirm this solipsism (all the while rendering it inoperative).

Being then, for Nancy, is that which is always and already shared: it is what takes place between us, and of which no one can lay hold, like all meanings, even that of the solipsistic *cogito* is dependent on others for confirmation. In this sense, one might compare Nancy's envisioning of being with the way in which a *deck of cards* is distributed among its players: though all players share in the same deck of cards, the deck of cards itself is not appropriated once and for all by the players, and although the players share in the same set, the hands of all players are each time different. The set of cards "is" nowhere else than in its being shared among all of the players.

It is this "with," this "compound" that Nancy tries to make sense of: Nancy is trying to understand how there is an address and a salutation to the other in all that is said, both transcendentally, i.e., how – to use Nancy's terminology – being-with-other-beings constitutes the very being of "my" being and of all beings, and temporally, i.e., how being and existence is made up of each time different encounters, by our dwelling in different groups, by our attending to and tarrying with happenings each time anew. Nancy thus describes the ontology of being-with as a world-wide web of relationships

in which all are dependent upon all, supplement one another and in which no relation takes precedence over another *to the point of eclipsing all essence (substance, ousia, etc.)*. It is here that I would like to diverge from Nancy's position.

the deconstruction of christianity: a muted incarnation

Nancy's thought of the world emerges out of the progressive disappearance – the auto-deconstruction – of Christianity and of its ontotheological variations. Apart from this historical reason for a deconstruction of Christianity, one can also point to more philosophical reasons for engaging in such an enterprise. These reasons also follow from Nancy's thought that there is a displacement proper to Christianity, a displacement that will expose its secret resources off which it, until now, has fed (*Dis-Enclosure* 34). These philosophical reasons can also be elucidated by means of Nancy's take on the doctrine of the Incarnation, for the secret resource that Nancy is pointing to turns out to be precisely his account of the intertwining of the transcendental and the empirical. Such a conception seeks to understand just how the intelligible *dwells in* the sensible. It is the awareness that at times the transcendental is not the condition of possibility of the empirical at all, but rather the other way around, how the empirical serves as the condition of possibility of the transcendental in such a way that it is the transcendental itself which *takes on body*, or *becomes flesh*. Nancy notes that the Christian account of the Incarnation was nothing but a foreshadowing of his account of *spacing* as the intertwining of the empirical – the fact that beings take place in space and time – and the transcendental realm – "spacing" as the condition of possibility for anything to take place at all. This "spacing" then, the creation of the "with one another of all beings" (cf. Nancy, *Creation* 73), borders on being a-historical: it is that which escapes history, the symbolic order and all narratives but makes them nevertheless possible.

It is, thus, for Nancy a matter of advancing the "spacing" of the world as a *factum brutum* which exceeds the theological account of the Incarnation. For, whereas in theology it is the latter which justifies the former, for Nancy the former in fact is the condition of possibility of the latter to the point that it becomes but an illustration of the former. For Nancy (as perhaps for Derrida), such theological short-cuts are begging the question, if only because they miss the "rather troubling [...] duality" of "the spacing *within* the Incarnation" (Derrida 262) – of the mute matter which crosses (theological) intelligibility. The problem, as we will see shortly with the help of Derrida, is to understand just how this excess of the incarnational spacing towards Christianity's understanding of the Incarnation can be assessed *in* and *from within* a Christian culture, or, to use Nancy's words: how one can tear oneself out of tradition from within tradition or overcome Christian culture from within that very culture (cf. *Dis-Enclosure* 65)? Note, in passing, that this is the very way in which Heidegger posed the question of overcoming metaphysics: it is not so much a stepping outside of metaphysics as if one could simply decide to choose to, as it were, change terrains, it is rather a question of stepping back from metaphysics through questioning it from within (*Identität* 41).

It is, according to Nancy, from out of Christianity's vanishing that a thought of the world might appear: it is a comportment of *transcending without a Transcendent*, without anywhere or anyone to transcend to, except for the gap that is the world. This, however, is no sheer atheism. Such atheism does not attain the rank of a world without principle: Nancy indeed seeks to counter current atheism that can be as dogmatic as the religion it seeks to overthrow. For Nancy, atheism "close[s]" as much as it "forms" the horizon of the contemporary world (*Dis-Enclosure* 18). Its stress on finitude and its denial of infinity in fact is according to Nancy but one more way *not* to deal with the world that has been transmitted to us – if only because it seeks to dismiss and disregard the "bad infinity" of consumerism

and general equivalence where $n + 1$ products are awaiting purchase. For Nancy, on the other hand, if atheism *forms* a horizon – and finitude conditions as it were all thought of infinity –, it is on the contrary necessary to liberate ourselves from such (modern) limitations on all thinking of infinity and world. To be more precise: the task of thinking is to restore infinity and restore it in such a manner that it takes up the dimension of world. This means that the existence and event of world itself, however finite, knows not of any borders and limitations that thought has given the world: the world, simply, does not fit into the conceptual schemes that modern and metaphysical significations have constructed for this very world. However finite this world and its beings may be, this finitude itself, Nancy argues, is endless and infinite (*Sense of the World* 29–33): its finitude goes all the way up and all the way down and stretches from the past towards our future and beyond – the future of others and other generations. But all this, for Nancy, means that this world does not stop making *sense* and is always and already *meaning*ful, and it is this happening of sense that needs to be thought.

Nancy's interest in Christianity, its theology and its religion, is only indirect, that is, only insofar as it is the Christian religion that has delivered us into this situation in which there no longer subsist any horizons for the world. This is, in fact, what his play on the verbs *fermer* and *former* in relation to the horizon here indicates: atheism can close and form a horizon as much as a religious return to one or the other Golden Age does. Both atheism and a return to theism, then, close the horizon, whereas, in fact and in reality, there is no such horizon for the thinking of world: the absence of any horizon (of a golden age as much as a determined telos) is precisely what is real.

Yet this alterity within the world, its opening onto sense, and this shared event of being and world that can never be at the disposal of one (highest) being (or disposed to a highest being), cannot be elucidated without an enquiry into our Christian provenance.

Nancy's concept of "provenance" is important to his deconstruction of Christianity. "Provenance," he writes, "is never simply a past; it informs the present, produces new effects therein without ceasing to have its own effects" (*Dis-Enclosure* 30).

This provenance, then, should teach us not only under which pressure Christianity breaks but also how the exhaustion and possible extinction of Christianity might give way to a confrontation with that which "comes to the West and Christianity from beyond themselves, what comes toward us from the depths of our tradition as more archaic than Christianity" (Nancy, *Dis-Enclosure* 143). It is the release of what Derrida has called "the paganism within Christianity" and what Nancy names the "paradoxical fulfilment of Christianity in its own exhaustion" (*Dis-Enclosure* 71).

This intertwining of Christianity's fulfilment and its exhaustion is, for Nancy, only possible because at the heart of Christianity there is an internal divide which causes it to disrupt from within. Christianity is at a crossroad, or rather, it *is* this crossroad. In this way, Christianity for Nancy, due to its essential intertwining of "flesh" and "word" in its teaching of the Incarnation, will have been the prefiguration of an ontological intertwining of materiality and meaning that extends to all things. Christianity values matter as well as meaning and logos: its "system" will have put us on the track of an ontology of "the with," where the one is always with the other, where there is no word that cannot become flesh and no flesh that is not already fused with meaning(s) and (metaphysical) signification(s). For Nancy, the "essence" of Christianity is such, however, that it will have given way to the existence of multiple incarnations – where every incarnation (of meaning) *touches* other meanings in such a way that there will never have been a *pure* origin or telos (of Christianity or of anything else). This multiplicity is what Nancy calls the *singular plural* – there is not one form of Christianity that would not be related to all other forms of this phenomenon, just as all these other forms make for the idea and concept one has of this one form of Christianity that one could call "one's own."

enttheologisierung vs. secularization

This is the second definition of the deconstruction of Christianity that Nancy has in mind: "After" Christianity, the relics of this religion encounter a context that is alien to it: Christianity would then dissolve in this context like sugar in coffee. If you like: this second form of Christianity's deconstruction is a *caffe latte*, whereas the first form would constitute a *cappucino* rather, where the two layers, namely Christianity and its surrounding context, would remain separated.

Between these two forms, there are lines of communication though. And it is these that are of interest here. Christianity for Nancy one recalls is both inside and outside metaphysics. Once outside of metaphysics – the second form of deconstruction – Christianity delivers to us something more archaic than Christianity. Nancy will conceive of this phenomenon as *Enttheologisierung*. Yet when still within metaphysics, if one can put it thusly, Christianity does dispatch onto culture "durable sediments" and transmits features of the Christian narrative to this culture (Nancy, *Dis-Enclosure* 37). These, for Nancy, are the phenomena of liberty, fraternity and equality through which the Enlightenment retains the best of Christianity; *Enttheologisierung* translates the feature of a *creatio ex nihilo* that enables and forces us now to form a world from the ground up as it were.

The auto-deconstruction of Christianity in this way entails the detheologization of the world. This concept shows Nancy at his most innovative, since he carefully distinguishes this deconstruction from one more "secularization of the theological" (cf. *Creation* 44, 51). Detheologization aims to think the "sense" of Christianity's deconstruction. Sense might be interpreted here as "direction," as to where exactly this auto-deconstruction is heading. For this, it is important to understand contemporary culture as one that is "no longer" Christian but also as one that is not, for all that, "unchristian." It is such a situation that makes for the originality if not novelty of the contemporary relation and to which a great many contemporary theologies fail to relate. For this situation forbids the classical thesis of *Löwith*, for instance, for whom the (post)modern era was but a secular version of what religion once had to offer. The deconstruction of Christianity aims at a "detheologization" and not at a "secularization" of the theological, since this latter option would entail that all happenings within our culture would, in one way or another, still be Christian, e.g., *human rights*. "*Secularizing the theological*" would indeed mean not only that all events within the world could be answered for and recuperated by theology but also that there could be something like a permanent presence or essential core to Christianity that could in principle be transmitted from one culture to another without this core being altered or contaminated by such a transmission. There would, then, be nothing that would not be Christian. This is the critique that Derrida will level against Nancy: all these secular translations will one day be retranslated and then everything would remain the same. One wonders whether this is not exactly our situation today. We would, for Derrida, be dealing with a *metamorphosis* of a Christian culture rather than a *mutation* as Nancy thinks.

Nancy does not deny that certain of these secularizing tendencies do take place, as is indicated already by the "durable sediments" Christianity has given our culture. He does, however, deny that these translations will always lead to the greater benefit and glory of Christianity. On the contrary, *these secular translations are able to run their own course and at times even depart from Christianity*. In this way, these translations can create a cultural situation where questions arise that can no longer be answered by Christianity or theology and for which the old Christian answer would simply be unfit. One might think here of the contemporary indifference toward religion, the existence of which, in the Catholic teachings at least, is simply denied.[1] Secular translations of religion can therefore create the space

wherein a deconstruction of Christianity can occur. With this, Nancy is close to *Hans Blumenberg* who argued that the "legitimacy" or "novelty" of modernity was precisely that it moves beyond Christianity and introduced humanity to new questions and situations (through science and technology, for example) for which the Christian tradition contained no answer, very much like Christianity itself, and its question of the "sense" and "direction" of history, outstripped the Greek thought of cyclical time (65–75).

Nancy's deconstruction of Christianity then aims to describe a sort of tipping-point: a situation in which we move from secular translations of Christianity (human rights, eschatologies without eschaton) to a situation of complete *Enttheologisierung*. Whereas "secularization" means that Christianity changes or is changing but that these changes (still) happen in the (same) "Christian situation," detheologization conveys the situation in which Christianity *is* changed (by something other than itself). The question, of course, is: is it true? Is it an accurate description of our context?

The proof, then, would be in the pudding: are there phenomena in the contemporary world which, whilst deriving from the Christian tradition, are now, qua signification, completely devoid of any Christian resonance? Is Christianity over and done with when it comes to delivering sediments to contemporary culture? It is in effect noteworthy that Nancy seeks to give a sense to infinity again: "Our culture has dedicated itself to another reduction. [One] called this 'the thinking of suspicion' – namely suspicion of any form of the absolute, the ideal, the unconditional. These three words themselves inevitably provoke suspicion. And yet *they are necessary*" (*Adoration* 70). Even in a post-Christian world, one is in need of the absolute and the unconditional.

Nancy in effect argues that capitalism is part and parcel of the Christian heritage. We know that for Nancy both capitalism and nihilism are the inevitable outcome of Christianity, for the one God, supposedly, gives way to both nihil-ism (nothing has any value) and to capitalism (everything has the same value, quantifiable through money): "this monovalence of value [...] hardly behaves otherwise than as the apparent nonreligious transcription of the monoculture whose monotheistic conception it carried" (*Dis-Enclosure* 31). These, then, are the two infinities of the day: either the bad infinity of consumerism or – which is basically the same – the "infinitely nothing" of nihilism which cannot value any product of any worth at all. One will have to see whether the "infinite finitude" of Nancy's deconstruction is able to counter these first two versions of infinity.

derrida's critique of nancy

We have come across three forms of the deconstruction of Christianity: the first one wants a hold on a disappearing cultural context through a return to the "pure origins"; the second one, stressed by Derrida, argues for the fact that whatever the fate of religion in our days what we are witnessing now is the secularization of any and all theological themes (even if all these translations can be retranslated and serve as a back-up for the first form); the third form, finally, favoured by Nancy, argues that we have come to a tipping-point and a complete *Enttheologisierung* is our fate. This tipping-point, it seems, is the difference between a metamorphosis or a mutation of a Christian culture.

It is here that we must focus on Derrida's critique of Nancy. One can imagine Derrida pondering these forms and imagine him asking: is it true that Christianity will in the long run disappear? Is this not only a postulation, an illusion or even wishful thinking on the part of Nancy who quite rightly passes for an atheist? And even if it is bound to disappear, how will we know when exactly it has disappeared? And if it has disappeared is there really not a chance that it will return? And just how are we able to fix the boundaries between a Christian and a post-Christian era?

These are rather simple questions, but the fact of the matter is that Derrida, in *On Touching*, develops a devastating critique about Nancy's rather synchronic and monolithic account of Christianity. One might argue that Derrida's *On Touching* is to Nancy what his *Violence and Metaphysics* was to Levinas. At one point, for instance, Derrida mentions the presence of some "destructive effects" in Nancy's works. Nancy, according to Derrida, might very well be "one of those post-war eschatological inflations which excoriate themselves in the desperate call for a new era" (269 both quotes). These destructive effects show themselves on several occasions: Derrida's main worry is with the fact that at crucial stages of his deconstruction Nancy seems to omit a deconstructive spirit and erects dualistic (for lack of a better word) alternatives that allow for no lines of communications at all. This is especially clear when it comes to Nancy's thinking of the compound that is Christianity: *either* it is the possibility of a destruction of world that is coming to us *or* it is the creation of a new world *ex nihilo*; *either* it is the sin and evil of "closing in on [one]self" (*Adoration* 53) through one or the other (religious, political) identity *or* it is the adoration of an openness to "the Outside"; *either* it is the faith of a reason that so adores *or* it is the particular *beliefs* of all sorts of "religion"; *either* it is in effect an attempt to remain with these (dogmatic and institutional) forms of religion and Christianity *or* it is Nancy's own *paganism without paganism* that salutes the sheer happening of being and "divinizes" the passing of each and every one of us; *either* the banal *Jemeingötterung* – the "oh *my* God's" of American sitcoms – *or* the name of God who is nowhere else than in our greeting one another – the German *gruß Gott* is a nice example, since "God" here is but in our "hello and goodbyes."

All of a sudden it seems as if all lines of communication between these alternatives are *closed* and Nancy's form of deconstruction is a one-way street awkwardly close to most of the classic secularization theories. Consider, for instance, the following quote:

> The world has lost its capacity to "form a world": it seems only to have gained that

capacity of proliferating [...] the "unworld" (*immonde*) which, *until now* [...] has never in history impacted the totality of the orb to such an extent. Everything takes place as if the world affected and permeated itself with a death drive that soon would have nothing else to destroy than the world itself [...] The fact that the world is destroying itself is not a hypothesis. (Nancy, *Creation* 34 and 35)

It is this strange mixture of hope and apocalypticism that for Derrida forms one of the destructive effects within Nancy's thought, for it implies an absolute rupture between our era or the one to come and earlier metaphysical times. The point, according to Derrida, is that these indications of temporality are such that one has to ponder whether the postulation of such an absolute cleft between our age and the previous ones is philosophically valid at all – in the end Nancy is not the first philosopher to proclaim the end and the fulfilment of its history. In short, Derrida's thought of "destructive effects" seems to indicate that Nancy is not so much working out of the (post)-Christian tradition, from within, that is, but that Nancy is rather positing himself outside of that very tradition, out of metaphysics as it were, observing and representing and thus repeating that tradition in precisely the very way he wanted to avoid.

The question for Derrida is whether or not a peculiar form of metaphysics is returning in Nancy's work. Metaphysics means here simply the possibility of the pure gaze, perceiving what it perceives in a clear and distinct manner, touching whatever it touches upon in manners unmediated and untainted by history, interpretative manoeuvres or (con)-texts. Derrida's argument in this regard is quite complex, but it runs, if one turns to the language of phenomenology, something like this: even though one wants to escape the logic of immediacy or of intuitive fulfilment of intentionality by pointing to whatever resists such fulfilment – what remains absent or does not give itself – this resistance itself will, in turn, give way to effects and illusions of immediacy. Let us listen to Derrida: "[The]

dehiscence of the outside and the other comes to inscribe an irreparable disorganization, a spacing that dislocates, a non-coincidence (which *also* yields the chance effects of full intuition, the fortune of immediacy effects) wherever Husserl speaks of 'coincidence'" (181). In other words: even if one believes in the interruption (or mediation) by the other or by otherness, chances still are that this will "produce an *illusory* belief in immediacy of contact" (253).

For Derrida it would be to such a metaphysics that we all fall prey, and Nancy is no exception: "for [...] it can moreover *always* happen – we have to insist on it – that the intuitionistic [...] logic of immediacy shows itself to be irrepressible [...] not only here and there in Nancy's text, but massively elsewhere" (129). Such an "intuitive" metaphysics, then, would give rise to a realist naiveté – as if one can touch without remainder or residue upon that which obstructs, hinders and resists the immediate grasping of all touching – we know we have no immediate grasp on reality but yet we turn this knowledge into just such a grasp of reality; I know my view of reality is not *the* view on reality but will nonetheless consider it such.[2]

To be sure, for Derrida, it is not a matter of denying this dehiscence, but of respecting the fact both that this dehiscence *will* be denied – turn into realism, declaring and prescribing what is real – and that one will have to reckon with this fact which is an "archi-facticity" precisely as "contingency" (187) – thus, "real." To put it in phenomenological terms again: it is not only a matter "to reintroduce a priori what is constituted into what is constituting" (Levinas, *Totality and Infinity* 147) or to understand how the one constituting is always already constituted by that which he or she constitutes, it is also, and above all, a matter of knowing *just how* this occurs.

One more example of such a destructive effect, although not mentioned by Derrida, is Nancy's rigid distinction between faith and belief. Nancy asks, for example, "whether faith has ever, in truth, been confused with belief" (*Dis-Enclosure* 12)? Faith, for Nancy,

THE PULSE OF SENSE

is *ex nihilo*, it is not a belief in something particular. Faith is a faith in nothing, in the world or at least in the event of world, whereas belief is the pretence to know everything about, for instance, the world in and through one or other proposition or dogma. Yet here Nancy neglects that faith only ever arises out of a belief system that is already there, that is "instituted" to use Merleau-Ponty's words again and that so constitutes a cultural context on which all autonomous constitutions are ultimately dependent.

Another example. One finds, in Derrida's *On Touching*, quite a revealing comment on the two short-hands the two thinkers use to designate the gesture of deconstruction. Whereas Derrida's "if there is any" [*s'il y en a*] is widely known and discussed, Nancy's "there is no 'the'" [*il n'y a pas le/la ...*] is not (Derrida 287–88). And yet, the difference here, however minute, is of utmost importance. Imagine a conversation in which someone says "all politicians are bad." The response, obviously, is that not all politicians are the same and that, thus, there is no such thing as "the" politician – in general. Derrida's short-hand, though, will not say that there is no such thing – as the politician, as hospitality. For speech, communication, interactions, crossings between you and me, between us, to occur at all, it is necessary, Derrida suggests, that both of us, and all of us, *do* have a concept, an essence, of that which is understood as "the" politician, otherwise a response to such a statement would not even be possible. In other words: one cannot do without representations, essences, concepts, etc. *Il faut généraliser* – one must generalize. In Derrida's words: "Nancy knows that one has to use cunning, make deals, and negotiate with it [since] the definite or defining article is already engaged or required by the discourse that disputes it" (287).

This imperative is what is left open in Derrida's "if there is any" and what Nancy seems to forget. Derrida's "if there is any" leaves room for more interpretations: since we sometimes must generalize, however violent towards this other here and that being there, however

impossible in the face of this singular existence and the plurality out there, we will have to recognize a sort of soothing of concepts to reality, a sort of aspiring of the concept towards the purity of that which it designates, an existence of ideality and signification. For if Derrida mentions time and again that a pure hospitality is forever presupposed, his "if there is any" such hospitality, indicates not only, and simply, that one, of course, cannot speak of this general and absolute hospitality without taking all the concrete and empirical forms of hospitalities into account, but *simultaneously* admits that one will need to speak of a general form of hospitality from the moment onward that – *s'il y en a* – there is, was or will have been such a concrete hospitality. This is why Derrida explains his short-hand in the following way: "'If there is any' does not say there is none" (288). Derrida, then, notes the difference between his "if there is any" and Nancy's "there is not 'the'": if the former turns *to a conditional* – hence it can also be read: since, whenever and if there is such a thing as an act of hospitality – the latter turns to a negative modality – there is no such thing as Hospitality. Consider the difference, then, between "a good politician, if there is any" (Derrida) and "there is no such thing as a good politician" (Nancy): the former speaks in a provisional manner – while it is highly unlikely that any such one thing will occur, one cannot exclude the fact that it might occur either – the latter speaks in a negative and almost dogmatic manner: even if there would be such a thing, one cannot and may not conclude to the fact that this would be a general thing, a group of people that could be comprehended through an essence. Nancy is already in denial of any factuality: there cannot be, and never will be "the" ... Derrida's response to this, however, is that were it not for such an essence gathered from the diverse forms of politicians or hospitalities, one would not even be able to recognize the fact that "a" good politician has come along or "an" act of hospitality has occurred *as much as* it is through these concrete extant acts that one gathers an essence and ideality of these acts.

The point is that Nancy, and his tendency to dislocate the possibility of concepts and essences of all sorts, seems to reduce philosophical discourse to the singularities of all sorts of empirical events to the point of eclipsing essence. It is to forget, as Levinas has argued, that "to the ineffable ideality of the substrate there responds an echo of the world in which significations are said" – in the world, one always and already speaks *of* something *to* someone (*Otherwise than Being* 189n21).[3] What seems to be lacking in Nancy's account of the world thus seems to be a phenomenology of language, of the echo between the signification of the word and the world in which signifiers are *always already* used, of the fact that language is, at any rate, always the speaking of some*thing* to someone. It is then worth pondering that if we want to speak of the appearing of appearing it is perhaps not all that bad to start with simple appearances – from the thing to the world as it were.

The irrepressibility of essence we are advancing here because of the noted return of metaphysics and some sort of "essentiality" and ideality implies that Nancy's thought of the world in some sort of way *posits* a point outside the world which, even in his case, functions as the postulation of a sort of givenness, a concept(ion), albeit the givenness of nothing. Nancy's mistake on essence and on metaphysics – not its eclipse but its haunting, like a ghost – should shed light on just how to proceed here for what Nancy's deconstruction of Christianity omits is the back and forth between concrete beliefs and a faith of the deconstructive sort. If we are to follow Derrida, and deem Nancy too hopeful when it comes to a point "after" Christianity – not to say naive and idealistic (*Fukushima* 64) – it is because this empty space, this anarchic event of world into which we are thrown, will *always* be occupied anew, even if it "*must not be occupied*" (*Adoration* 33). It is this that Heidegger (and Derrida) knew all too well (*Question Concerning Technology* 69): the first form of deconstruction always gets the better from the second and third one. It is about this domestication and occupation, and how (not) to avoid it, about

why, when and how the anarchic happening always and already turns into a principled authoritative happening in which one religious observance or political identity takes precedence over others (or, more simply, where *a* view on humanity becomes *the* view on humanity) and why the deconstruction of Christianity despite everything *most often* takes the form of a cry for a lost supposedly pure origin that Nancy remains all too silent.

If we may come back to our title, then, it is clear that no matter how much one wishes for a mutation of our culture, it is a metamorphosis that is happening. If the novelty of world-forming never seems to occur *ex nihilo*, but only ever through a transformation of the old, then it is exactly from Christianism to Christianism, from ontotheology to ontotheology and from foundationalism to foundationalism that we are proceeding. This would not be a somewhat utopian mutation but rather a metamorphosis that calls nonetheless for thinking. We, and Nancy, would do well to realize that, when it comes to the fate of religion in the West, this need not be a bad thing. The compound that our Christian culture still is, would show us then that we are neither secularized properly nor properly Christian. Perhaps it is this between that we would need to think today.

echo by jean-luc nancy

As with all texts in English, my reading is hesitant and allows me to grasp the text in its entirety and movement only poorly. I nevertheless think I do perceive the precision of the analysis and discern the core of the Derridean criticism which reproaches me for believing to exceed metaphysics – and Christianity – as well as thinking a "utopian mutation" instead a transformation from within.

It seems to me this debate can go on indefinitely. I can recognize everything Derrida has criticized me for – but I nevertheless do not think that I am quietly calling upon a lost pure origin or a "new beginning" *ex nihilo*. I rather think that the debate itself is wrong. It corresponds to a state of our culture in which,

THE PULSE OF SENSE 183

in fact, we were inclined towards radical loss and inauguration, and it was right to point the naivety – itself ultra-metaphysical – of this attitude.

But I have precisely always tried to say that Christianity – in virtue of the very fact that it deconstructs itself – indicates within itself, below itself, an unassignable anteriority that is not a matter of joining. Perhaps this anteriority is to be found precisely in the end of the origins as they had been represented by all religions up to this point. That is to say, with Christianity (or the becoming-modern of the world), the necessity of thinking the *ex nihilo* as that which does not constitute an origin, that which happens and keeps on happening, announces itself. It so happens that humanity comes to think the world comes from nowhere and that it can come to end up nowhere. No beginning, no end, but incessant resurgence of ... nothing.

I admit that this has, without a doubt, remained too implicit in what I have written. To me, it was so obvious as to be evident without needing to state it ... (this has happened to me more than once).

Perhaps this becomes clearer if we consider what Joeri Schrijvers says about another aspect of the *ex nihilo*: the difference between faith and belief. Of course, all faith is affirmed and is nourished or at least fostered by the beliefs of a given time and place. If I ask "Did Shakespeare, who is said to have been a Catholic, have faith?," I cannot expect an answer in which the statements of Christian dogma are reinterpreted as they are in Hegel. However, my question concerns the strength of Shakespeare's adherence, in particular his freedom from self-interested motives that any belief may contain.

If there is faith, an act of faith, there is something that remains irreducible to the socio-psychological representations of a belief. There is a real trust, a real abandonment to the complete unknown of the supposed "object" of faith. It is neither an object nor a subject. It is an act, or perhaps rather a gesture. That which makes faithful – less according to the observance of an oath than

according to a force that nothing guarantees. No cultural or psychological context takes this into account. It comes out of the "nothing" that "I" am outside any historical, psychological, cultural determination. Faith is characteristic of the human being insofar as it is "outside of itself." Judeo-Christianity has made a distinct trait out of it, linked to the covenant or to divine grace. But this explicitation goes beyond the explanation! I am going to leave it at that because I would have to write an entire book. I hope others will!

disclosure statement

No potential conflict of interest was reported by the author.

notes

1 See, for instance, *Gaudium et Spes*, no. 41, "[The Church] knows that man is constantly worked upon by God's spirit, and hence can never be altogether indifferent to the problems of religion."

2 This is also the reason why one should not underestimate the fact that Derrida points to the very same reproach as the one he, once, famously criticized Levinas for: empiricism. The question of empiricism and realism pops up regularly in *On Touching*, see page 46 on Nancy's "absolute realism," also pages 116–17 and above all page 287 on why Nancy risks to hand philosophy's discourse over to "the most irresponsible empiricism."

3 Derrida has, moreover, commended a similar thought to Nancy when saying that still "there are so many questions to be asked about the history of the *idea* [...] and about the irrepressible and undeniable constitution of ideality [...] and the obscure trafficking between sense, common sense and the senses" (117).

bibliography

Blumenberg, H. *The Legitimacy of the Modern Age*. Trans. R. Wallace. Cambridge, MA: MIT P, 1985. Print.

Derrida, J. *On Touching – Jean-Luc Nancy*. Trans. C. Irizarray. Stanford: Stanford UP, 2005. Print.

Heidegger, M. *Identität und Differenz*. Pfüllingen: Neske, 1976. Print.

Heidegger, M. *The Question Concerning Technology*. Trans. W. Lovitt. San Francisco: Harper, 1977. Print.

Heidegger, M. *What is Called Thinking?* Trans. J.G. Gray. London: Harper Perennial, 2004. Print.

Lacoste, J.-Y. *Être en danger*. Paris: Cerf, 2011. Print.

Lacoste, J.-Y. *From Theology to Theological Thinking*. Trans. W. Hackett. Charlottesville: The U of Virginia P, 2014. Print.

Levinas, E. *Otherwise than Being, or Beyond Essence*. Trans. A. Lingis. Pittsburgh: Duquesne UP, 2000. Print.

Levinas, E. *Totality and Infinity. An Essay on Exteriority*. Trans. A. Lingis. Pittsburgh: Duquesne UP, 2000. Print.

Marion, J.-L. *The Idol and Distance. Five Studies*. Trans. T. Carlson. New York: Fordham UP, 2001. Print.

Nancy, J.-L. *Adoration. The Deconstruction of Christianity II*. Trans. J. McKeane. New York: Fordham UP, 2012. Print.

Nancy, J.-L. *After Fukushima. The Equivalence of Catastrophes*. Trans. C. Mandell. New York: Fordham UP, 2015. Print.

Nancy, J.-L. *Being Singular Plural*. Trans. R. Richardson et al. Stanford: Stanford UP, 2000. Print.

Nancy, J.-L. "The Confronted Community." *The Obsessions of Georges Bataille. Community and Communication*. Ed. A. Mitchell. New York: SUNY P, 2009. 19–30. Print.

Nancy, J.-L. *The Creation of the World* or *Globalization*. Trans. F. Raffoul et al. Albany: SUNY P, 2007. Print.

Nancy, J.-L. *Dis-Enclosure. The Deconstruction of Christianity I*. Trans. B. Bergo et al. New York: Fordham UP, 2008. Print.

Nancy, J.-L. "Mon Dieu!" *Dieu en tant que Dieu. La question philosophique*. Ed. P. Capelle-Dumont. Paris: Cerf, 2012. 271–78. Print.

Nancy, J.-L. *Noli me tangere. On the Raising of the Body*. Trans. S. Clift et al. New York: Fordham UP, 2008. Print.

Nancy, J.-L. *The Sense of the World*. Trans. J. Librett. Minnesota: Minnesota UP, 1997. Print.

Nef, F. *Qu'est-ce que la métaphysique*. Paris: Gallimard, 2004. Print.

Schürmann, R. *Heidegger on Being and Acting. From Principles to Anarchy*. Bloomington: Indiana UP, 1987. Print.

As Jacques Derrida wrote to his Japanese friend: "What deconstruction is not? everything of course! What is deconstruction? nothing of course!" (*Psyche II* 6) I will start by saying the same thing about "desecularisation."[1] It is what happens, a present event, without ever becoming an established fact. It cannot be established because it cannot be defined. The meaning – a verb rather than a noun here – of desecularisation appears when reading secularisation as if it were placed under deconstruction. This reading then becomes the dis-enclosing of secularisation understood as a linear history. Secularisation does not culminate in a definite factual state but will end endlessly. By bringing desecularisation "into play" with other notions – like secularisation, deconstruction, dis-enclosure, and desacralisation – , its meaning will become apparent, even if – or precisely because – all these terms do not bear definition. They are not clear and distinct ideas. However, proximity will produce sense.

The notions presented above will frustrate the more traditional approaches in metaphysics. Belonging to the differential register, they do not obey the epistemological accounting that aims at *adaequatio rei et intellectus*. Sense is the arrival of world, advent. There is no other world, no world that is other than this world, where the truth about this world is hidden – and accessible through the correct Cartesian strategies. There is, however, the other *of* the world (Nancy, *Dis-Enclosure* 10). Where the world is enclosed, sense cannot arrive. An enclosed world can never be the event of sense. This other of the world cannot be dialectically recuperated as an "other-than." The irreducibility of this alterity is

erik meganck

DESECULARISATION
thinking secularisation beyond metaphysics

often neglected, ignored, or even denied in the models by which secularisation is theorised. Hence, there is a need for "desecularisation" to understand the present, its provenance and its possibilities.

The exploration of a provocative term like desecularisation will only find favour with those who at least acknowledge the sense of the "end"[2] of metaphysics as the event of a *mutation* (as Jean-Luc Nancy likes to call it[3]) and have at least considered Nietzsche's autopsy of God. There are several reasons for this condition. First, without this recognition, any talk of desecularisation remains idle and should be rejected as a purely speculative mind game, in the same way as the work of

Nietzsche, Heidegger, Derrida, and Nancy is rejected by most metaphysicians and by analytic philosophers. Second, metaphysics in its current form still abhors any thought that resists its programme and modern aspirations. This resistance has been called a "step back" (Heidegger) or deconstruction (Derrida). Third, and following from the two former reasons, it should be kept in mind that a thoughtful understanding of the aforementioned mutation may well require a different approach than the methodological one that prefers those concepts, models, and theories that hitherto served metaphysics well. This means letting go of the "tried and tested," an adventure that is still considered subversive by those who do not accept the notion of the "end" of metaphysics and mistake the experience of the death of God for a shallow atheist proposition. The exposition that follows will only make sense within this "post-metaphysical" framework.

Why not, then, speak of "the post-secular"? This has become a recognised scientific concept in the philosophy and sociology of religion, as well as in theology.[4] Though seemingly "objective" in the way the human sciences prefer their concepts, it is strongly connected to another one – often without any explicit model of where this connection is developed – , namely: "reconfessionalisation." The fact that there exist many positions vis-à-vis both concepts, separately or together, does not diminish the connection. It simply means that the prefix "post-" is not without its problems – other problems than those that are produced by that other prefix "de-." Instead of the prefix "post-" that has marked or contaminated modernity, metaphysics, Christianity, and secularism, I am opting here to explore the hermeneutic potential of that other one, "de-," that I borrow from Heidegger's *De-struktion*, Derrida's *deconstruction*, and Nancy's *déclosion*. I do not thereby mean to imply that the one prefix would solve the problems that the other one poses or cannot solve. Indeed, if there is something that could be called "desecularisation," it is not a solution, nor a theory or model. It is rather a name that appears where and when secularisation runs

up against its own "ends" and where all sorts of hidden strategies, that are supposed to keep the secularisation thesis pure and radical, come to light. In this way, the terminological consideration turns into a philosophical position.

I will read desecularisation, radical secularisation (or nihilism), deconstruction, dis-enclosure, and desacralisation as "hermeneutic grounds" instead of metaphysical or scientific concepts or theories that find themselves compelled to obey rather severe demarcation criteria and rigid deductive potential.[5] By this I mean to say that I do not consider them mutually exclusive or competing theoretical alternatives, but partly overlapping potent cultural experiences and perspectives that can communicate in a non-dialectical yet dialogical manner. Hermeneutic grounds never contradict each other and cannot falsify one another, nor can they prove something or be proven themselves. This presupposes abandoning the (anachronistic but all too present) ambition of one definitive and total explanation, i.e., following Heidegger's "step back."[6] But it also means that I cannot offer a clear-cut definition of desecularisation, which is why it is so important to confront this term in its philosophical proximity to others, like secularisation, deconstruction, dis-enclosure, and desacralisation. This confrontation of hermeneutic grounds is supposed to yield insight rather than the falsification of all but one. There is no philosophical institution that decides between hermeneutic grounds. Thought itself makes them grow or peter out. Therefore, desecularisation cannot be the *Aufhebung* of cultural Christianity and secularisation; nor the synthesis of radical secularisation, deconstruction, and desacralisation.

Moreover, and this is of major importance, this hermeneutic approach implies that the secularisation thesis cannot be considered wrong. The secularisation thesis itself is not abolished or falsified; its explanatory potency is simply observed to be fading.[7] The same goes for the relation between secularisation and desecularisation. Whereas secularisation as a political ideology has acquired an almost militant rhetorical impact, I present desecularisation in a modest register. Therefore, secularisation and desecularisation are not treated as each other's opposites, the latter being the antithetic reaction to the former. Desecularisation turns secularisation from a metaphysical explanation and a modern philosophy of history into a hermeneutic ground or a currently promising and heuristically fertile cultural perspective. Desecularisation figures as the slope across which secularisation glides from a metaphysical *erklärende* position into a hermeneutical *verstehende* ground. This way, secularisation becomes an interesting cultural perspective that explains many things without proving anything. It is not a hard fact or principle allowing for stringent deductions, nor does it tell the State how to relate to the Church. It is not purely coincidental that in France, the prototype of laicism,[8] non-believers like Marcel Gauchet advocate a re-introduction of religions in the public debate. Still, this plea is not an argument in favour of desecularisation, nor is desecularisation the ground for Gauchet's plea. The plea belongs to desecularisation inasmuch as it does not contradict secularisation but questions its absolute theoretical validity and remorseless socio-political implications.

Finally, I want to conclude this introduction on a theological note. Since it has become more or less unanimously accepted that secularisation belongs to the very history of Christianity and is not a pagan attack from "without," scholars have often referred to the Christ hymn that Paul recites in his letter to the Philippians (Phil. 2.6–9). The emptying, incarnating, and humiliating in the first part of the *kenosis*-hymn was accepted as the historical inclination that justified the promotion of secularisation to the ultimate label of history. Leaving all other theological nuances aside, it is perhaps striking how these same scholars shamelessly leave out the subsequent verses where the hymn talks of exaltation. The humiliation also being at the same time an exaltation has all too often been neglected by secularisation theories. Desecularisation points to the humiliation being at the same time also the exaltation, without these two movements being separated and then logically united in an economy of salvation or any other sacred strategy. It would therefore be wrong to identify secularisation with the first movement, i.e., the humiliation, and desecularisation with the second, i.e., the exaltation. But the elaboration of all this would take us beyond the scope of this (philosophical) article.

* * *

The popularity of the classical strong secularisation thesis is waning.[9] To start with, secularisation did not turn out to be a universal phenomenon accompanying the systematic and inevitable modernisation of the whole world. Therefore, any attempt at identifying secularisation with History is premature – and often ideologically motivated.[10] Furthermore, some, like Hans Blumenberg, suspect this thesis of being a strategic scientific tool to keep modernity within the Christian tradition instead of granting it a historical and cultural autonomy (see *The Legitimacy of the Modern Age*), whereas Karl Löwith explicitly calls secularisation an inherent part of the history of Christianity (see *Meaning in History*). A strong proponent of "desecularisation" as an alternative to or even refutation of secularisation is Peter Berger, formerly a fervent advocate of the secularisation thesis. He considers secularisation a typical Western, modern phenomenon that certainly does not apply to the whole world and at all times (Berger 9). This, however, is not the way I understand desecularisation here, favouring John Caputo's version instead (*On Religion* 56–66) – which I will discuss later on.

Not only is there disagreement about the explanatory radius of the term "secularisation," also its formal status or position is unclear. The secularisation thesis has, according to some like Caputo, become a "grand narrative" (as coined by Jean-François Lyotard), a priori overarching history (Caputo and Vattimo, *After the Death of God* 82). Even apart from the adequacy of the thesis, this Hegelian streak renders it less valid nowadays than it seemed half a century ago. To this, others like Gianni Vattimo reply that Christianity itself perhaps once was a grand narrative, but its own nihilist inclination defies such overarching (*The Transparent Society* 2–10). I suspect that this, in the line of Wilhelm Dilthey, means that Christianity is the ultimate motive (and motif?) of the dissolution of the system of grand narratives (see Dilthey).[11] So, according to Vattimo, secularisation is what prevents secularisation becoming a grand narrative. Among many others, like Caputo and Vattimo, René Girard does not place secularisation outside the history of Christianity but considers it a faulty self-interpretation of modern Christian culture. To the extent that Girard is right, it becomes all the more difficult to continue accepting the secularisation thesis as an absolute explanation or model for the history of Christianity (Girard 23–47).

The suggestion that secularisation might not be the "natural" model for the history of Christianity and the place of religion in modern society is precisely what desecularisation brings into view. If it is difficult to define "secularisation," it is impossible to define "desecularisation." Both terms relate to each other as metaphysics does to deconstruction. Desecularisation is a name for what always has accompanied the formulation of all secularisation models and kept them away from their "fulfilment" as in a delay.[12] I want to make it clear from the very start here – and will elaborate later on – that desecularisation can in no way be thought of as either the alternative, successor, or falsification of secularisation.

Actually, desecularisation *is* secularisation in terms of taking the "step back." In this sense, "de-" does carry the connotation of "undoing." It "undoes" the historical determination of secularisation without promoting it to an ahistoric eternity, to the one and total History of Being itself. Indeed, it works the other way around since such eternity or infinity is actually dissolving into endlessness. It also neutralises the ideological purport of secularisation. The contention that secularisation is supposed to be the ultimate orientation of history suffers from socio-political ideology. Secularisation is determined as a qualification, even the definition of history. If there is such a thing as history, in the sense that events take

place according to a certain logic – which post-modern thought rejects – , this logic does not have to be secularisation. Inasmuch as secularisation implies the reduction of the event of the world to a historical logic that only allows for one index, it rests on the modern presupposition of Being as progress. Secularisation produces the notion of a history and the possibility of understanding the meaning of events through their historical position, thereby denying meaning to anything in the shape of singular events. This is indeed a "self-image" of modernity as the outcome and realisation of a consistent cumulative process.

If the present is marked by secularisation, that does not imply that secularisation is the only way of (re-)connecting this present with a past and a future. Therefore, it would be futile to look for a beginning of or an end to secularisation. The modern notion of history as progress implies an archaeology and a teleology in history. This is why desecularisation belongs at least to post-modernity.

Unlike desecularisation, secularisation enjoys the aura of science. It remained a theological (canonical, ecclesiastical) notion for a long time until sociology picked it up and it became, step by step (again, sometimes ideologically motivated), a name for history itself. Secularisation is still the "official" scientific label of modern historical orientation. Since a successor has not (yet) arrived, we will have to wear out modernity, with science and technology as our main "mind map." Until further notice – which is yet another way of saying "During post-modernity" or "As long as metaphysics finds itself under deconstruction" – , we still tend to consider the spontaneous reference to science and technology as evident, even to the extent that one may tend to forsake as meaningless the questions that fall outside their scope (e.g., philosophical questions about science that do not legitimate science as the only valid intellectual paradigm). Narratives other than science and technology – which, by the way, are usually not considered narratives but explanations – have to justify themselves in public discourse or at least confess to utter modesty by forsaking any claim to truth on the grounds that they lack a very specific methodology and therefore do not provide certainty. After all, post-modernity is actually still modernity, it is just modernity conscious of the fact that it will never completely fulfil its own "original" ambitions.

Despite this scientific aura, secularisation is nevertheless contaminated by ideology, as mentioned earlier. It has become a socio-political argument that can only explain the run of history in one direction: as progress, i.e., emancipation from primitive – pre-modern, religious, romantic – thought. Looking back, one sees of course why the notion of secularisation makes sense. But it seems exaggerated to claim that each and every one of the historical events called upon to support the secularisation thesis allow for an *ex post* prediction about the current state or position of religion in the public sphere. This consideration is supposed to make acceptable the possibility that this state or position is not a necessary outcome of history as a linear process of secularisation but rather an essentially contingent one on a whole spectrum of possibilities. As Heidegger has said, metaphysics has exhausted its possibilities since the death of God (*Basic Writings* 374–77; *Off the Beaten Track* 157). Therefore, an alternative to or extension of secularisation is not to be expected.

Here, I will instead be looking for Heideggerian "winks," signs of hope and optimism, in philosophy. I will read the "end" of secularisation in the same vein as Heidegger and Derrida read the "end" of metaphysics.[13] Subsequently, I will situate what I am calling "desecularisation" vis-à-vis radical secularisation (Vattimo), deconstruction and dis-enclosure (Derrida and Nancy), and desacralisation (Girard).

the "end" of secularisation

Heidegger refers to late modernity as

a stage of Western metaphysics that is in all likelihood its final stage, since metaphysics, through Nietzsche, has deprived itself of its own essential possibility in certain respects, and therefore to that extent other

possibilities of metaphysics can no longer become apparent. (*Off the Beaten Track* 157 – see also *Basic Writings* 374–77)

He seems to be talking about certain exhaustion: metaphysics is losing or leaving behind what has the character of a potency. Perhaps the secularisation thesis has likewise exhausted its explanatory potential. The often heard call for a neutral politics, for a completely privatised religion or "philosophy of life," marks that exhaustion – especially since this call for neutrality is itself a philosophical option that is staged as a "natural (or, in this case, historical) law." The shift from option to law or fact becomes visible in desecularisation: secularisation only demonstrates and confirms the alleged fact of the implosion of transcendence, the marginalisation of religion, and theology's becoming applied social, moral, or political philosophy; desecularisation, meanwhile, denounces the rhetorical nature of the formulations of secularisation theories – without condemning it. Desecularisation condemns, first, the suppression of this rhetorical nature, and second, the subsequent installation of another – allegedly rational – absolute principle or Highest Being. Again, desecularisation is secularisation confessing rather than supressing its rhetorical operation. There is nothing wrong with rhetoric, except when it is presented as rational. Then it becomes bad sophism.

A philosophical line that runs, roughly, from Nietzsche through Heidegger to Derrida and Nancy is called "the critique of metaphysics." Yet, this tradition does not prepare the actual abolition of metaphysics – which is why I prefer "critique" to "criticism."[14] Rather, it proclaims the destruction (Heidegger), deconstruction (Derrida), dissolution (Vattimo), or dis-enclosure (Nancy) of metaphysics as belonging to its very own history – with "history" understood as destiny (Heidegger, Vattimo) or eventuality (Derrida). This dissolution does not destroy metaphysics but shows the untenability of modernity's self-proclaimed project or essential possibility, namely, the total scientific explanation and technological control of reality.[15] Its "end" is not just a temporal category, in that it is historically marked, but also a spatial one, in that it brings the limits of metaphysical explanation into view. Discerning this spatial aspect of secularisation entails its relative, not absolute, suitability as definition of history. Metaphysics "ends" when and where it becomes apparent that its foundations are not eternal and objective structures but rather the effects of an eventuality that remains unseen and even unheard-of from the very moment these foundations were decided upon.

As it is, secularisation closes off and encloses Christianity as a history and a territory. As a history, it denies the significance of anything coming from "without" in the sense of an "advent." Secularisation precludes any "fresh" approach to Christianity, any future Christianity that is not the product of secularisation as its official historical vector. Advent, in its philosophical sense, can then only be experienced as the ritual or ceremonial repetition of the one original event of incarnation that instituted the definitive nihilist inclination of history. As a territory, it rids the world of all alterity, of any "outside" where the meaning of the world would reside, insofar as it is not in turn the effect of secularisation. One symptom of this enclosure is a particular interpretation of the historical and global role of the *Universal Declaration of Human Rights*. The term "universal" implies territorial enclosure, whilst the contention that it constitutes the historical achievement and full meaning of Christianity entails historical enclosure: Christianity has no further meaning to offer the world, neither in space nor in time. It is over, and the imperative that says it should be thus, is called secularism. This secularism is opened-up or dis-enclosed in desecularisation. *Dis-Enclosure* is the title of Nancy's first volume on the *Deconstruction of Christianity*. It is precisely about the opening of the world, or rather: about the world-as-opening. "Opening" should be read as a verb in the present continuous tense, not as a spatial determination.

Nancy's *déclosion* or dis-enclosure is not a programme aiming at the restauration of pre-modern theocracy or the installation of postmodern one. Again, the "end" of secularisation does not entail the beginning of something "new" like desecularisation that is barely more than the negation of the former. It is through dis-enclosure that we are able to understand the philosophical meaning of monotheism and its atheist inclination (see my "Toward a Divine Atheism" and "In God's Name"). Monotheism is not the opposite of polytheism, it is not the transition from "many" to "one" – that would be henotheism – , but rather the affirmation that nothing in this world can be identified with God or as divine. Monotheism is therefore a critique of any enclosure of the world. In fact, "Christianity designates nothing other, essentially (that is to say simply, infinitely simply: through an inaccessible simplicity), than the demand to open in this world an alterity or an unconditional alienation" (Nancy, *Dis-Enclosure* 10). God might be the name of what keeps the world open, of what turns extrapolation into advent, of what perverts a neat and clear end into an "endless ending" (see my "Opening the World").

The sense of the world is in the first place *umsonst* and therefore divine, adorable – to use the term employed by Nancy (see *Adoration*). The sense of the world does not belong to that world. This has been convincingly demonstrated by Heidegger as well as Wittgenstein (as I explain in my "World without End"). Since it would be easier to have nothing instead of something, Christians believe that creation happened out of love, that which radically defies the natural path of least resistance. Indeed, when monotheism asserts that nothing in the world can be God, secularisation is auto-destructive since it rules out anything that does not belong to the world, anything that is *in* but not *of* this world. It resembles a law of entropy in that the vector of secularisation can never be reversed. One day, all transcendence will be – or, in its ideological connotation, should be – dissolved and there will be nothing left to secularise. Since desecularisation rejects this entropic interpretation, it also saves secularisation from philosophical suicide.

So, the "end" of metaphysics is not the beginning of something else. The "end" of metaphysics is the "beginning" of deconstruction, which is metaphysics itself but with its hidden maintenance tools – what Derrida calls "transcendental signifieds" – becoming visible as such, and therefore removable. Metaphysics resembles an old magician, still performing on stage but simultaneously revealing how his magic tricks work. The public is still in awe, not because of the tricks; rather they are in awe that the magician could ever have made them believe it really was magic.

Thinking metaphysically means preferring clear and distinct ideas over poetic maunderings, concepts over metaphors, logic over rhetoric, pure origin over opaque provenance. Analytic schools are still trying to "clean up" thought, thereby often criticising speculative discourses in metaphysics without recognising their own resort to presuppositions that resist analysis. Deconstruction is where metaphysics has to admit to itself that it is indeed the effect of a decision based on groundless preferences that it erroneously considered self-evident or otherwise objective.

This claim to objectivity no longer holds, which is how the "end" of secularisation belongs to the "end" of metaphysics: in secularisation as a "theory of history," the subjective meaning of the genitive appears from behind the objective meaning that is typical of metaphysics. The latter presupposes an objective history that is adequately represented in the theory that is secularisation. The former meaning disturbs this objective one by pointing out that the theory belongs to a history instead of merely theorising it objectively from an ahistorical point of view. Modernity displays a tendency for considering all previous thought as imperfect due to its historicity, limited steps on the path towards full rational explanation. It is important to note that the secularisation thesis belongs to modernity and that modernity is "ending."[16] The historicity of the modern theory of history denies the objective nature and absolute truth of secularisation. More precisely, it denounces this nature and truth as typical of a certain period of thought, namely, modern metaphysics.

If secularisation can be considered a theory that stems from a historical-eventual decision, then it will be acceptable to consider the "end" of that decision, in the sense of the temporal and spatial limits of an explanation that is not absolutely objective but rather eventual. The disclosure of the decision motivates the dis-enclosure of secularisation. The "end" of the decision that involves secularisation does not recant or replace that decision. Metaphysics, and secularisation with it, "end" when they are shown to be the effects of a decision. It is perfectly feasible, if not probable, that they will never completely disappear. The "end" is endless to the extent that there is no reason to predict its end. Thought beyond metaphysics can – and according to some, like Heidegger, will – only arrive in an event that cannot be deduced from current thought. Extrapolation and calculation of this "other thought" is impossible, since extrapolation and calculation belong to metaphysical thought. To calculate thought beyond metaphysics would still be metaphysics. Thinking metaphysically, holding on to scientific thought as the access to absolute and final truth, is therefore the most efficient way to prevent a new dawn of thought. Even if such a dawn never arrives, thinking metaphysically is at least the most efficient way to keep metaphysics going against the grain of its "end."

If the line beginning with Nietzsche and running up to Nancy, through Heidegger and then Derrida, is the one along which the "end" of metaphysics becomes visible, then the only correct way of "reading the signs of the times" is to stop thinking metaphysically about secularisation. Then secularisation evolves from the (ideologically enhanced) description of the objective inclination of history towards a powerful but particular perspective on the history of Christianity. To those signs of the times belong radical secularisation, deconstruction, and desacralisation. I will now explore how each of these relates to desecularisation.

radical secularisation

To Vattimo, the contingency of history becomes visible through secularisation – or as he calls it, "weakening."[17] Weak thought acknowledges the dissolution of metaphysical and religious transcendence and considers the nihilist tendency that has become apparent in late-modernity to be an event that can be qualified as ethically positive. A history that throughout eternity is referred to an absolute Origin, by epistemological strategies like dialectics, has dissolved into an irreducible plurality of (hi)stories without any central coordination or transcendent reference (Vattimo, *The Transparent Society* 7).

Following a line through Löwith and Dilthey, Vattimo discovers that it is Christianity (*caritas*) that motivates weakening (*pietas*) and this is what he calls "secularisation." Christian love is motivated by the kenotic movement of God, his self-emptying, whereby it inspires the dissolution of moral systems and epistemological structures. In short, Christian destiny is nihilist. God is no longer a substance that resides in transcendence. God has left transcendence behind and has dissolved into a reality that, paraphrasing Nietzsche, no longer consists of facts but of nothing but interpretations – which is also an interpretation. In fact, secularisation divulges the ultimate meaning of Christianity, the Good Message proclaims that there are only messages. When transcendence implodes, the epistemological levers that can promote interpretations to facts are no longer available. This is Vattimo's epistemo-theological understanding of secularisation.

Vattimo draws our attention to the decreasing ability of metaphysical principles and norms to ground rigid epistemological and moral systems. This is indeed what Nietzsche meant by his autopsy of (the moral and cultural) God. The institution that allowed metaphysics to promote interpretations to facts has reached its destitution. Paradoxically enough, the death of God kills atheism as well. The philosophically strong arguments in favour of atheism have faded together with all other absolute principles. The "deliverance" of the Biblical God is an unintended effect of this Dario Antiseri probably stresses this too strongly (101–03). Free from the shackles of metaphysics, (re)thinking God in faith became an intellectually acceptable challenge.[18]

Nevertheless, as we have seen, this is an effect that Vattimo wants to avoid. In such reappearance, he would probably recognise the apocalyptic "leap" that leads man away from reality, from this worldly flux of interpretations into a *Hinterwelt* that has always been supposed to be more true than this world. This "leap" into pre-modern faith is meant to be the "positive" compensation for the "negative" loss of certainties. Metaphysics is – tragically enough to some – no longer considered capable of solving the fundamental problems of human existence and this existential vacuum generates a tendency to turn to traditional faith to supply the same anchorage as metaphysics used to. But that would be the denial of nihilism and therefore a betrayal of secularisation, according to Vattimo.

If secularisation is nihilist, then there is no legitimate expectancy of something beyond, like a dialectically provoked desecularisation. Nihilist secularisation has to be the final word in historiography since it cannot itself be secularised. After all, Vattimo asks us rhetorically, who would want to weaken the motivating force behind it, namely, charity? Nevertheless, his notion of a secularisation exempt from secularisation seems highly arbitrary. Only *pietas* can understand secularisation as destined. Perhaps, Caputo, like Derrida, therefore offers a more fertile – non-ontological – perspective since, unlike Vattimo, he does not consider secularisation "the end of the story" (i.e., on the basis of the dangerous idea that secularisation can itself not be secularised or, in my terms, on the ground of the impossibility of desecularisation).

Once secularisation is no longer a scientific fact but rather functions as a hermeneutic ground, like weakening, should it not allow for desecularisation as what contaminates the concept of secularisation and prevents it from acquiring scientific status as factual truth? Is not Vattimo betraying his own basic intuitions when he identifies secularisation with *caritas* and then declares *caritas* exempt from secularisation? In doing so, he turns charity, secularisation, and weakening into the epistemo-theological levers his weak thought precisely pretended to dissolve. Perhaps this is what Caputo has in mind when he says that he suspects that Vattimo's secularisation itself needs secularising (Caputo and Vattimo, *After the Death of God* 83ff.): secularisation, too, needs to be thought through, discussed, interpreted, secularised.

Could desecularisation then start off as the secularisation of secularisation – thereby avoiding the false prophecy of a desecularisation that arrives from "beyond" as something completely new and different? Vattimo's only way out of this difficulty seems to be the retort that it is Christianity's destiny itself that led to it. In his view, the self-emptying of God means Christianity's voluntary self-delivery to philosophy on the strict condition that this be a nihilist hermeneutics. It is the Christian message itself that turns God into a cultural event, an ethical and social field boarded by charity, that is watched over by philosophy – a *pietas* that echoes Heidegger's *an-denkende Gelassenheit*. But here's the *petitio principii* again, since it is Christianity *as interpreted by* the nihilist hermeneutics of weakening that is supposed to *lead up to* the nihilist hermeneutics of weakening.

The *petitio principii* – which need not be an argument for or against *pietas* – hides yet another serious problem that nihilism cannot solve. The nihilist interpretation of Christianity thrives on a very partial interpretation of the biblical notion of *kenosis*, as I already mentioned. In fact, nihilism ignores the "second movement" in *kenosis* that is an inextricable part of it. In Paul's letter to the Philippians, the ancient Christ hymn rhymes "humbled" with "exalted" (Authorised King James version) or "emptied" with "raised high" (Jerusalem Bible). Without attempting any justification, Vattimo only retains the first movement and then recognises this as the ultimate motif of the history of Christianity that has to be a nihilist secularisation. Such arbitrary reading

of a theological key term is philosophically hard to accept.

Vattimo considers secularisation the progressive extinction of the nostalgic desincarnation reflex. Referring moral and socio-political habits and customs to eternity instead of the present goes against the historical grain as read by weak thought or *pietas*. Pre-modernity is obsessed with the sacred nature of God, which is precisely what God leaves behind in his return as late-modern nihilist hermeneutics. Vattimo contends that we should welcome this opportunity for unshackling ourselves from a violent transcendence that has oppressed humanity for so many centuries. Secularisation, or the dissolution of transcendence, be it philosophical or theological, is to him a morally positive event. It does not need to be applauded – nor regretted, by the way – for it belongs to destiny, but it does need humanity's collaboration. If man understands the morally positive effect of secularisation, namely, the diminution of violence in the world, then he will experience this evolution as an appeal. This is how Vattimo understands Girard's "desacralisation." Secularisation is the (hi)story of emancipation from the strangleholds of an always arbitrary transcendence.[19]

desacralisation

In line with his disconnection of incarnation and desincarnation, Vattimo identifies desacralisation with secularisation, which is a mistake according to René Girard. Even worse, the latter thinks this identification may well be dangerous. Girard considers it naive in that it ignores the threat of an apocalyptic outburst of "original" violence. This violence is implied in the hermeneutic experience of mimetic desire as inherent to the human condition – rather along the lines of the so-called social contract theories, especially Hobbes'. To desire what the other desires – or owns – will provoke envy and a subsequent threat of violence. This threat is curbed and the violence is repressed by culture and its social institutions. Girard discovers a significant relation between the "given fact" of culture and this –

perhaps hypothetical – violence. Why is it, he asks, that no society seems able to keep its internal violence under control without regularly expelling what he calls "the scapegoat"? Indeed, it seems a historical constant: whenever a society labours under a major crisis, a minority (whether religious, political, or economic) gets the blame. Moreover, it is always a vulnerable – at least according to our social standards – and innocent – at least as far as the internal tension is concerned – minority. Girard tries to reconstruct this reflex, studying myth as well as religion and art. Instead of treating these expulsions as accidental, he discerns a pattern, considering them all variations on a recurrent theme.[20] This pattern, called "the scapegoat," will show the way toward differentiating between secularisation and desacralisation; a difference that goes unnoticed by Vattimo.

In order to relieve its internal tensions, every society will select a scapegoat and literally put the blame on it. By murdering or expelling the scapegoat, society will assume that the tension has disappeared together with its cause. They will remember the expelled victim with gratitude since, instead of being the cause of violence, the scapegoat has become the cause of peace.

The scapegoat mechanism hides more than one paradox. First, the victim gets the blame although he is actually innocent. There is no reason at all why this or that specific segment of society should be singled out as "guilty" of causing the crisis. But the tendency to blame "the other" is just as universal as envy. Second, once it is removed (ritually killed or expelled), everyone agrees that there be peace since the cause of violence has gone. They realise that they own this peace to the slaughter. Therefore, they now revere the scapegoat as the cause of peace. The allegedly guilty victim becomes the holy patron of society. This, says Girard, is the meaning of *sacri-ficium*: slaughtering and revering are two sides of the same coin, two vectors of one and the same logic. The scapegoat is not made holy as a sort of compensation for the sacrifice, because that would imply a recognition of the scapegoat's innocence.

In order to keep the peace, law and order are installed to prevent the outbreak of mimetically motivated violence. This hierarchy – literally, holy order – is actually a derived form of violence, namely, repression, curbing original violence. But this derived form of violence, however severe, is unable to curb once and for all the original violence. Over and over again, societies will "solve" their crises by applying the mechanism of the scapegoat, from exile to plain genocide. This is, Girard contends, because people still have not understood the anthropological message of Christ.[21] That message can be summarised thus: violence is human, love is divine.

Christ never wearies of urging his disciples to see how the scapegoat mechanism works. And in the end, he asks his Father to forgive his murderers, since they indeed do not know what they have done (Luke 23.34). So, in fact, did those who killed the moral-cultural God in Nietzsche's famous parable (§125 of *Die fröhliche Wissenshaft*). In both cases, humanity is supposed to take its time in coming to understand the ultimate meaning of the message that is handed down to it. But whereas Nietzsche was satisfied with a hundred years – more or less coinciding with the breakthrough of post-modern thought in France after Nietzsche's prophesy – , Girard hopes that two thousand years will finally suffice to get the message through, or at least its anthropological purport.

By explaining the mechanism of violence, Christ wants to deliver the world from violence precisely by attributing all violence to the world itself. This way humanity will be able to see God as he really is: the source of charity. Life in peace is only possible if humanity recognises the violence in itself instead of projecting it onto the other. When humanity believes that there is no source of violence outside itself, it will accept the transcendent source of love. It will then realise that it needs to turn to that source in order to curb the violence in itself instead of turning to derived violence and the scapegoat mechanism in an attempt at curbing the unduly allocated and misunderstood original violence.

Girard calls the effect of Christ's message, its inscription in human culture, "desacralisation." It is the kenotic process of leaving religious power behind, of taking a distance from the violent source of religion and culture. It is the refusal to accept the challenges of those who mock him (Matthew 27.39–44; Mark 15.29–32; Luke 23.35–39) and to take revenge against his prosecutors, murderers, and traitors. Desacralisation not only delivers heaven from violence, since it is shown to belong to the world, but also glorifies divine love, as the transcendent source of all true peace and love. Perhaps desecularisation here indicates that *kenosis* is not the mere abolition of transcendence but the intrinsic reference of incarnation to this divine love.

God's omnipotence must not be measured by the rod of cosmic power, which is rather typical of natural religion. As theologians like Hans Urs von Balthasar point out, it is precisely *kenosis*, leaving cosmic power behind, that evidences a sovereignty that lies beyond the worldly opposition between power and weakness (29–34). In a non-dialectical and non-economical way, the utter weakness displayed in the event of the passion demonstrates power, the humiliation carries glory in it. This is why Balthasar will warn us against thinking of *kenosis* as the one essence of God, as the dialectically or eventually purified meaning of Christianity, like Vattimo does.

By identifying secularisation and desacralisation, Vattimo considers the former as warranting the diminution of violence. The reference to the divine source of love is absent from his nihilism. Girard disagrees. According to him, the aforementioned identification does not resolve but rather hides the problem of violence. Desacralisation facilitates the diminution of violence whereas the same cannot be said about secularisation. Girard understands secularisation as the transition from a religious to a secular (economic) culture and therefore also the transition from religious to economic violence, namely, competition. There is not less, only other violence. The systematic socio-economic excommunication of minorities only mirrors the inability of socio-political hierarchy that curbs original violence. The solution does not lie in the abolition of social order and religion, at least as long as we do not recognise the violence in ourselves. If nihilism is the ultimate meaning of Christianity, as Vattimo contends, it has to pass through the recognition of the difference between desacralisation and secularisation. Even then, it will have to be a biblical nihilism that not only recognises *kenosis* but also glory as an integral part of what Paul calls "the mind of Christ" (Phil. 2.5) when introducing the *kenosis*-hymn we discussed – a passage that Vattimo (arbitrarily and therefore violently) leaves out.

The almost-nothing – "that" whereof the Samaritan becomes "neighbour" – is not bluntly just what it is, but paradoxically harbours an incomprehensible greatness in that it urges us to suspend our egocentric projects and surrender to it. This notion of greatness-in-weakness is typical of Paul. His theology is indeed scandalous in the ears of the Jews (religion) and an absurdity in the eyes of the Greek (metaphysics). There is nothing dialectic and therefore nothing strategic or economic in Paul's theology. Incarnation, *kenosis*, passion, etc. are not investment funds that have glory and eternal bliss as their dividend. Weakness does not cause greatness.[22]

Philosophical nihilism in the style of Vattimo obviously misses the hermeneutic subtleties of the biblical ("meontological") meaning of the "almost-nothing." Stripped of all labels, conventions, socio-economic, political, juridical definitions and positions, the almost-nothing becomes the pure mirror of inalienable dignity, the glorious threshold of nullity. This biblical nihilism is expressed in Christian charity and lies hidden as a silent premise at the heart of many philosophies as well as Western culture. It is the silent core of Kant's ethics, without any rational ground. Precisely this dignity was erased by the great fascist regimes, products of modernity. Here we see how modern secularisation is "overdone" desacralisation: obscuring the divine source of love, the love that warrants the inalienability of human dignity, allows for man to be submitted to his own ideologically absolute creations, be they political or economic.

Desecularisation resists the identification of secularisation and desacralisation. The difference between desacralisation and secularisation is not a thing, a process, a concept, a theory, an explanation. One cannot add desecularisation to desacralisation and arrive at secularisation as the supposedly complete history of Christianity. Any other dialectic operation will equally fail. The above difference can be understood along the biblical, but equally philosophically valid, difference between a closed and an open world. Secularisation, as we have seen, always tends towards the enclosure of the world – the more radical, the more explicit. Desacralisation empties heaven of everything but divine love. Heaven, however, does not refer to another world. It refers to this world when and where two or more are gathered in God's name, i.e., in charity (Matthew 18.20). That is the difference. When two or three are gathered, there is society, morals, solidarity. The difference hides in the name. This name can only mark an opening. There is nothing charitable about enclosure, on the contrary – and this may also be read politically. Charity – receiving, even welcoming the other *as other* – , presupposes an open world, philosophical hospitality.

When secularisation becomes history, its paradigm remains metaphysical in the traditional sense. We have seen how even radical models of secularisation can hide a massive metaphysical core. Any alterity is always matched against what is established as identity. Between any two entities, a relation of identity or opposition needs to be established. This is where the identification of secularisation and desacralisation becomes a mistake. It presupposes two complementary worlds and declares one of them redundant, namely, the sacred as opposed to the profane. But the result is still a firm identity: this world as the true world. That is precisely what Nietzsche denounced in his fourth chapter of *The Twilight of the Idols*: "How the 'true word' finally became a fable." It is not just the *Hinterwelt* that has become a fable, but the notion of true world itself. And, I presume, a world that has no longer the ambition to enclose itself in any form of determination as the only true world, e.g., a scientific one, allows for alterity and openness. In this sense, the difference between secularisation and desacralisation can only be thought by desecularisation.

deconstruction and dis-enclosure

Of course, replacing secularisation with desecularisation in order to realise a scientific shift that would allow for God's comeback, even explain and justify it, would be the wrong "strategy." Desecularisation is as such a confusing term since it hints at a dependence upon and at the same time in the same way a distance from secularisation, rather than its rejection. The prefix "de-" has to be read in the same register as Derrida's *déconstruction* and Nancy's *déclosion*. Desecularisation "accompanies" secularisation as long as the latter functions as a paradigmatic term. It does not explain anything, on the contrary, it complicates and disturbs the clearly oppositional structure of the themes that secularisation pretends to explain, like the relations between Church and State, believing and knowing, theology and philosophy, private and public; or it questions the interpretation of the official discourse on human rights as the ultimate meaning and destiny of Christianity and therefore as a historical, factual enclosure. This complication and disturbance is partly due to the dissolution of the exclusive truth-claim of (human) science, in this case sociology, history, and theology.

Just as deconstruction is not the opposite of metaphysics and dis-enclosure not the opposite of system, desecularisation is neither the opposite of secularisation. As the opposite of secularisation, desecularisation would spell the linear accumulation of the socio-political purport of religion. In that case, the history of parts of Europe and the United States would fall under the law of secularisation whereas other parts and continents would fall under the opposite law. As its successor, desecularisation would just reverse the linear dynamics of this purport. Neither model makes sufficient sense. The division of the geographical or historical world in two separate parts that each obeys an opposite secularising law is too superficial. No oppositional scheme can work here.

Nevertheless, all too often, differential thinking is hauled back into metaphysics and stretched onto the rigid grid of oppositional logic. It happens to deconstruction (see deconstruct*ivism*) and it also happens to desecularisation (see, for example, Berger's *The Desecularisation of the World*). The motive behind this is the metaphysical aspiration to a complete explanation. If secularisation generally fails to meet this ambition, traditional thought will not deconstruct it but will add a complement to it in order to remedy its lack of explanatory reach. This is the first step toward a dialectic reconciliation between secularisation and desecularisation – a reconciliation that will, of course, eventually prove incomplete and therefore in need of a complementary theory, forever delaying full and final truth.

Desecularisation accompanies secularisation and will disappear together with it – if the secularisation model will indeed ever totally disappear. This joint venture has to be understood in the palliative register. Desecularisation does not want secularisation theory to be "euthanised" or abolished, nor can it predict when the theory will "die" or lose all of its explanatory potential. When secularisation stops meaning anything, desecularisation will simultaneously lose its epistemic legitimacy. Desecularisation has no meaning, makes no sense separate from secularisation. It is not even a theory; it is the contamination of a theory by its own "partiality," caducity, and mortality.

Desecularisation frustrates the exclusive focus on secularisation as a linear process and renders our thought unable to continue ignoring what becomes visible at the "end" of secularisation. The fact that secularisation is actually an article of faith that has drawn support from sociological data, and has been defended with a sometimes religious ardour that has escaped the attention of many philosophers and theologians who bluntly accepted secularisation as the definite and ultimate label of history. Many philosophers and scientists, however, already demonstrate their disinclination to submit to the ideological purport of secularisation and their intellectual fair-mindedness in recognising the cultural significance of religion – at least as an indestructible cultural theme or a legitimate socio-political item.

Desecularisation could also be the name of a first glimpse at what is to come. What is to come is itself not desecularisation. The experience that what is coming can be seen through or despite secularisation, is simply *called* desecularisation here. So, it cannot be the successor of secularisation but might be a name for tendencies that remained outside the explanatory reach of the secularisation thesis. Post-secular thought is not a philosophical period that comes after what could be called – by Charles Taylor – "the secular age" but is rather the thoughtful attitude that realises that secularisation was just one way of looking at reality, a way that is not declared wrong but has had its time as an explanatory monopoly.

To Caputo, secularisation, like desecularisation, belongs to the contingency of history. They are processes that come and go. But, and this is crucial, he never asserts their mutual exclusivity, so they can happen simultaneously. He holds secularisation to be the objective reduction of religion to something else (politics, economy, sexuality, etc.) (Caputo, *On Religion* 59–60). Desecularisation takes the role of a "true" faith that is not submitted to epistemological laws, as in "truth without Knowledge" (115) – hence the importance of the Derridean "indecidability" in Caputo's theology (128). Caputo's God avoids this objective reduction that is typical of modernity. Desecularisation allows for secularisation to keep on petering out, possibly endlessly, as well as for God to come back even if and when secularisation is not completely abolished yet. The reappearance of God in public discourse does not contradict nor is it contradicted by secularisation as long as it is not "radicalised."

The lesson desecularisation has learnt from differential thought is that it has to be co-existent with secularisation, since the latter is not "wrong" or "over." Therefore, it cannot pretend to be its replacement. Also, the rather popular idea that secularisation is perfectly capable of adequately describing a history that is confined to a strictly delineated space and time – i.e., the "West," "old Europe," or *Abendland* – but that the widening of the geographical and historical scope demands a complement, neglects the fundamental problem of the secularisation thesis.

Perhaps this neglect reappears in the paradoxical problem that John Milbank discerns – namely, why post-modernity rejects, together with every modern aim and aspiration, the notion of the one and only History and yet holds on to secularism (see "The End of Enlightenment"). As I have shown, desecularisation deconstructs this secularism by removing or undoing the "historical absolute" that hides beneath the modern notion of progress (evolution, growth, accumulation, etc.). This way, desecularisation belongs to metaphysics under deconstruction and joins in the movement that is captured by this "de-," a movement that was already prepared by Heidegger's "step back."

conclusion

The confrontation or dialogue between desecularisation and the other notions that belong to current thought proved fruitful. Their proximity has revealed the following: the necessity to secularise secularisation itself, the importance of differentiating between secularisation and desacralisation, the rightful belonging of desecularisation to the events of deconstruction and disenclosure at the "end" of metaphysics, and the need for ideological disinvestment of secularisation.

Desecularisation cannot be reduced to these other marks or hermeneutical grounds that make up the present. This impossibility of a reduction to already existing tendencies suggests the philosophical legitimacy of desecularisation as a mark of the present – without, of course, exhausting its meaning and potential. Desecularisation stands on its own but remains rather unintelligible without the other notions that are presented in this article.

echo by jean-luc nancy

I must admit that I am doubly embarrassed: first, this text is in English, and secondly, it handles notions that I am unfamiliar with and amongst which I find it difficult to situate myself (desecularisation, radical secularisation, etc.).

Secularisation has always struck me as a ramshackle concept. As Blumenberg asked Schmitt: What is it about? What kind of displacement or transformation? I will add that Schmitt was at least partly mistaken in saying that our political concepts are secularised theological concepts. For the latter – especially ecclesiological truths – were themselves already religious recoveries of concepts, or rather of forms, that were basically borrowed from Rome or left behind by Rome after its collapse. The state of complete cultural dissolution that had its beginning then is that not a single category issuing from this history seems salient: sacred, myth, holiness; are these operational concepts? I wouldn't know. I do not doubt that the rich analyses put forward by Erik Meganck are very interesting, but it strikes me that we are before an unknown such that we cannot introduce our instruments of intending or measuring into it. But this is itself already a new situation and perhaps rich in unexpectedness – unexpected such that no term can penetrate, neither god, nor sacred, nor salvation, etc.

So, here I am, very embarrassed. I can of course tell that our world is lacking myths; but what is without myth is first of all the "tautegory" (Schelling) of a world, that is to say that our world does not articulate itself – or that it only articulates itself in the language of technoscience. Another discourse can only be born from another world – and maybe there won't be another world. At least, today, it is in this impoverishment that we are required to exist. This, perhaps, is teaching us something that we cannot measure.

disclosure statement

No potential conflict of interest was reported by the author.

notes

1 See also Meganck, "Ratio *est* Fides" 162–63.

2 The brackets will show that this end is not to be read in the usual way, as denoting how something is definitely over at a definitive moment. The "end" is an event that could continue forever, as in an endless ending. It evokes the experience of a dissolution that is at the same time a salvation and not a loss. It has been called deconstruction. During its "end," metaphysics is under deconstruction. Under deconstruction, metaphysics can only endlessly end.

3

> Nous sommes [...] nous sommes là dans un moment qui, je crois, n'est pas du tout un moment de crise, c'est un moment de mutation complète et cette mutation est aussi forcément une mutation du temps, une mutation de la temporalité dans laquelle nous sommes; et notre «maintenant» aujourd'hui est je crois un maintenant qui nous fait signe, justement, vers l'ambiguïté du signe de l'appel ou de la promesse qui ouvre à l'avenir. (Nancy, "Le présent du temps" 30)

This article is the transcription of a video conference, recorded on 23 October 2014 and repeated, at my invitation, at the Institute of Philosophy in Louvain on 1 March 2016.

4 Twenty years ago, Phillip Blond edited *Post-Secular Philosophy. Between Philosophy and Theology* (London: Routledge, 1998). Recently, this notion was honoured with a real textbook by Justin Beaumont, *The Routledge Handbook of Postsecularity* (London: Routledge, 2018).

5 I found the notion of hermeneutic ground in Vattimo's "Toward an Ontology of Decline." He never elaborated on this, though I think it is very useful, especially if inspired by a Heideggerian understanding of Gadamer's notion of horizon in *Truth and Method*.

6

> For us, the character of the conversation with the history of thinking is no longer Aufhebung (elevation), but the step back. Elevation leads to the heightening and gathering area of truth posited as absolute, truth in the sense of the completely developed certainty of self-knowing knowledge. The step back points to the realm which until now has been skipped over, and from which the essence of truth becomes first of all worthy of thought. (Heidegger, *Identity and Difference* 49)

7 One can compare this, perhaps, to Lyotard's hermeneutic ground: the "end of the grand narratives." This end does not imply the disappearance of the great historical ideologies that are still familiar to us all, but just establishes its vanishing potency.

8 In the term "laicism," it is the suffix "-ism" that points at an ideological trait. It has moved from explanation to obligation. Instead of describing the problematic relation between State and Church, laicism holds that State and Church should be separated, ever more than is actually the case.

9 This strong version of the secularisation thesis is defended by the "Four Horsemen": Richard Dawkins, Tom Harris, Daniel Dennett, and Christopher Hitchens. Here, religion is depicted as a primitive and untrue form of knowledge that needs to be replaced by science. A less rigid or strong position would hold religion to be untrue, but valid as poetic or therapeutic discourse.

10 Secularisation became ideological when it justified the ignoring of certain insights or phenomena that could contradict or at least temper the claim to absolute and objective validity of the secularisation paradigm and its thesis or theses. Because these phenomena failed to establish this thesis or support this paradigm, they were

epistemologically condemned to philosophical and theological excommunication. Whatever would be capable of disturbing the explanatory potential of secularisation was ideologically reduced to marginal disturbance, nostalgic spasm or re-confessional reflex. Indeed, arguments that tended to "sidestep" secularisation were accused of ideological strategy, namely, conservative interests or even ultramontanism. That secularisation is hereby identified with the progressive run of history is made clear by those who indignantly exclaim "How is this possible in 2020!" when someone dares to have doubts or reserves about "expanding" abortion or euthanasia legislation. This is where political debate turns secularisation into ideology and strategy: when thoughtfulness is considered a symptom of thoughtless adherence to alleged religious dogma.

11 This way, Lyotard's proclamation of the "end" of the "grands récits" (see *The Postmodern Condition*) can be read as the confirmation of Löwith's doubts about secularisation, about the thesis that progress is an absolute historical imperative.

12 According to Derrida, such forms of delay are not temporary or secondary, but they mark the impossibility of the fulfilment due to an endless process of reference – endless since there is no mechanism or institution that is able to allow this process to debouch into pure eternal spiritual ideas.

13 For a more extensive elaboration of the problem of "end," see my "Is Metaphoricity Threatening or Saving Thought?"

14 Whereas criticism seems to presuppose an external point of view from where something is criticised, critique is concerned with a "rerun" or retake to enable one to see where and how things went awry.

15 Some will argue that science does not aim at total explanation, because totality is not really a scientific notion. Science aspires to a new explanation when a current one is not or no longer adequate. But when I include modern philosophy as the legitimation of science, the totalisation aim remains valid.

16 Secularisation theories exclusively belong to modernity, are typical of modernity. This does not imply the contention that secularisation itself exclusively belongs to modernity. Only its theorisation does. Some even consider creation as a first secularisation "event."

17 See my "*Philosophia Amica Theologiae*" and "God Returns as Nihilist Caritas."

18 The impact of Derrida on anglophone philosophers of religion around the year 2000 revealed the same "hope." Thinkers like John Caputo, Kevin Hart, Merold Westphal, and Richard Kearney enlisted "deconstruction as a chastening fire through which Christianity must go for its own sake" (Joy 41 – see also Caputo, *The Prayers and Tears of Jacques Derrida*; Hart; Westphal; and Kearney).

19 Vattimo's arbitrary nature of metaphysics is not quite the same as its decision-character in Derrida or Heidegger's elaboration of the notion of "clearing." In fact, Heidegger and Derrida consider metaphysics to be a history or the effect of an eventuality, within this decision or clearing, each theory can be seen as a convergence of "prepared" and "arbitrary"; while Vattimo only considers the arbitrariness of each theory. As far as metaphysics as such is concerned, he follows Heidegger in that he accepts its historico-destinal character.

20 As in music, a theme is not meant to be heard, it serves as a basic guideline when composing music. It also enables one to recognise "tunes." In the same vein, the original scene of the sacrifice never really took place in history, but serves as an abstract prototype of all the historical, mythical, and aesthetic (e.g., literature) variations.

21 At this point, Girard supposedly loses his scientific credibility. I think this is unfair, because Girard insists on only considering the *anthropological* meaning of Christianity, not articles of faith. The anthropological meaning of Christ's message results from a literary study of the Gospel.

22 This accords with Caputo's analysis in *The Weakness of God*.

bibliography

Antiseri, D. *The Weak Thought and Its Strength*. Aldershot: Ashgate, 1996. Print.

Balthasar, H.U. von. *Mysterium Paschale: The Mystery of Easter*. San Francisco: Ignatius, 1990. Print.

Berger, P., ed. *The Desecularisation of the World: Resurgent Religion and World Politics*. Grand Rapids: Eerdmans, 1991. Print.

Blumenberg, H. *The Legitimacy of the Modern Age*. Cambridge, MA: MIT P, 1983. Print.

Caputo, J. *On Religion*. New York: Routledge, 2001. Print.

Caputo, J. *The Prayers and Tears of Jacques Derrida: Religion Without Religion*. Bloomington: Indiana UP, 1997. Print.

Caputo, J. *The Weakness of God: A Theology of the Event*. Bloomington: Indiana UP, 2006. Print.

Caputo, J., and G. Vattimo. *After the Death of God*. New York: Columbia UP, 2007. Print.

Derrida, J. *Psyche. Inventions of the Other II*. Stanford: Stanford UP, 2008. Print.

Dilthey, W. *Introduction to Human Sciences*. Princeton: Princeton UP, 1989. Print.

Gadamer, H.-G. *Truth and Method*. London: Continuum, 2004. Print.

Girard, R., et al. *Christianity, Truth, and Weakening Faith*. New York: Columbia UP, 2010. Print.

Hart, K. *The Trespass of the Sign. Deconstruction, Theology, and Philosophy*. New York: Fordham UP, 2000. Print.

Heidegger, M. *Basic Writings*. London: Routledge, 1978. Print.

Heidegger, M. *Identity and Difference*. New York: Harper, 1969. Print.

Heidegger, M. *Off the Beaten Track*. Cambridge: Cambridge UP, 2002. Print.

Joy, M., ed. *Continental Philosophy and Philosophy of Religion* (Handbook of Contemporary Philosophy of Religion, 4). New York: Springer, 2011. Print.

Kearney, R. *The God Who May Be: A Hermeneutics of Religion*. Bloomington: Indiana UP, 2001. Print.

Löwith, K. *Meaning in History: The Theological Implications of the Philosophy of History*. Chicago: U of Chicago P, 1949. Print.

Lyotard, J.-F. *The Postmodern Condition. A Report on Knowledge*. Minneapolis: U of Minnesota P, 1984. Print.

Meganck, E. "God Returns as Nihilist Caritas. Secularization according to Gianni Vattimo." *Sophia. International Journal of Philosophy and Traditions* 54.3 (2015): 363–79. Print.

Meganck, E. "In God's Name." *Acta Comparanda* XXXI (2020): 5–17. Print.

Meganck, E. "Is Metaphoricity Threatening or Saving Thought?" *Metaphors in Philosophy*. Ed. W. Van Herck et al. Brussels: ASP, 2013. Print.

Meganck, E. "Opening the World. A Spiritual Reading of Jean-Luc Nancy." *Frate Francesco* 83.2 (2017): 469–78. Print.

Meganck, E. "*Philosophia Amica Theologiae*. Gianni Vattimo's 'Weak Faith' and Theological Difference." *Modern Theology* 31.3 (2015): 377–402. Print.

Meganck, E. "Ratio *est* Fides. Contemporary Philosophy as Virtuous Thought." *International Journal of Philosophy and Theology* 77.3 (2020): 154–70. Print.

Meganck, E. "Toward a Divine Atheism: Philosophical Polytheism and Religious Monotheism." *Acta Comparanda* XXIX (2018): 129–42. Print.

Meganck, E. "'World without End.' From Hyperreligious Theism to Religious Atheism." *Journal for Continental Philosophy of Religion* 3.1 (2021): 65–89. Print.

Milbank, J. "The End of Enlightenment: Post-modern or Post-secular?" *The Debate on Modernity*. Ed. C. Geffré and J.-P. Jossua. London: SCM, 1992. Print.

Nancy, J.-L. *Adoration: The Deconstruction of Christianity II*. New York: Fordham UP, 2013. Print.

Nancy, J.-L. *Dis-Enclosure: The Deconstruction of Christianity*. New York: Fordham UP, 2008. Print.

Nancy, J.-L. "Le présent du temps." *Eidos* 24 (2016): 15–32. Print.

Vattimo, G. "Toward an Ontology of Decline." *Recoding Metaphysics. The New Italian Philosophy*. Ed. G. Borradori. Evanston: Northwestern UP, 1988. Print.

Vattimo, G. *The Transparent Society*. Baltimore: Johns Hopkins UP, 1992. Print.

Westphal, M. *Towards a Post-modern Christian Faith: Overcoming Ontotheology*. New York: Fordham UP, 2001. Print.

1 introduction

The modern Western world is about to fulfill its secularization: that was the common description of the current era, from the 1960s toward the end of the last century. The protests against this development of a successful, fully achieved secular society that would also mark the "end of history," were considered to be the last scraps of sectarian religious groups refusing to reduce the world to human existence and its activities and possibilities, in favor of their God.

In the meantime, in large parts of the world, supermarkets are open on all Sundays. Nevertheless, few people today, the twenty-first century being underway for two decades, would still speak of a "secularized" world. Christianity and in a broader sense the monotheistic religions have not disappeared at all. That does not mean that the orthodox mass of believers would suddenly have been exploded, nor that churches, mosques and synagogues are fuller than in 1990. It seems to be a much more complex intertwining of secularity and religion – an entanglement that was actually always there, that had never disappeared as secularism has; not in the modern, Western world, and not at all in the world outside the West.

This global, continuous intertwining complexity of a complicity of religion and secularity is thus not a recent whim of history, which would temporarily damage the achievements of the Enlightenment. On the contrary, the current discomfort and the current uncertainty about the self-evidence of both secularity

laurens ten kate

RAISING DEATH
resurrection between christianity and modernity – a dialogue with jean-luc nancy's noli me tangere[1]

and religion seems to be very old. They guide the history of monotheistic traditions from the outset.

In this context, Jean-Luc Nancy poses the question whether monotheism actually needs a God, and if so, what kind of God? Does monotheism need the existence of God or does it flourish at the death of God? Nancy raises such questions from his first works to his most recent studies on Christianity.

The innovative aspect of Nancy's thinking lies in the fact that he links the analysis of secularization with its roots. According to him,

This is an Open Access article distributed under the terms of the Creative Commons Attribution-NonCommercial-NoDerivatives License (http://creativecommons.org/licenses/by-nc-nd/4.0/), which permits non-commercial re-use, distribution, and reproduction in any medium, provided the original work is properly cited, and is not altered, transformed, or built upon in any way.

these roots lie, among others, in Christianity and in the strange God of Christianity. In this sense Nancy is a "radical secularist": he confronts the paradigm of secularization with its roots (*radices*, Latin) to break it open in this way and to provide it with new meanings after critical questioning. In parallel fashion, he confronts the theology of Christianity with its roots, that already, from its earliest history onward, announce a certain secularization.

In this article, I will further elaborate on Nancy's questions regarding the relationship between religion and modern secularity, as they underlie his project of a "Deconstruction of Christianity."[2] Deconstruction is not destruction. Deconstruction challenges the claim to the "naturality" of concepts, convictions, beliefs, desires, as well as of developments, histories, conditions. This claim dominant in modernity is rooted in a double assumption: that of the obvious and that of the essence. Deconstruction calls for de-naturalization, and searches for the absurd, unexpected and unthought elements in a tradition, a text, an oeuvre, an event, a generally shared opinion, et cetera. Moreover, deconstruction is not so much a technique, a method, an approach; deconstruction is an event, it "happens," for instance, *within* Christianity. Nancy's project is not so much a deconstruction of the Christian religion as such, but an exploration of the deconstructive elements that this religion contains, elements that can also be found in the other monotheistic religions.

After a brief introduction to Nancy's project, I elaborate on one of the themes central to the deconstruction of Christianity: that of resurrection. I discuss parts of Nancy's essay *Noli me tangere*[3] and provide it with interpretation and commentary. In doing so, I will comment on Nancy's thesis that the "truth" of resurrection is a parabolic truth, and that therefore the resurrection story, and in fact the whole story of Christ's life and death, as laid down in the four gospels, is a parable. In dialogue with Nancy, I then develop my own vision of the resurrection, in which death is given a central meaning in a paradoxical way. In this concentration on death, the resurrection appears in a new, modern-secular perspective. This deconstruction of the resurrection leads to the conclusion that it is not so much a life after death, but a life in death. The resurrection of Christ – of the mortal, earthly, vulnerable God – is an affirmation of life here and now, of the humanity and physicality of that life: a "yes" to the world.

2 the return of religion?

The phenomenon of our time usually referred to as the "return of religion" to the socio-political scene or as the development into a post-secular society, is complicated and ambiguous. Is it a return of what was temporarily lost? Or rather an ongoing tension between religion and secularity, a tension that is in a way productive, since in it religion and secularity are mutually transformed? This is the way Charles Taylor phrases it in his *A Secular Age*.[4] Unlike many of his contemporaries, Nancy is not at ease with the term "return of religion," nor with the concept of the post-secular.

However, Nancy refrains from any defense of secularization by proclaiming the "end of religion," as contemporary atheist thinkers like Michel Onfray (*Atheist Manifesto*) or Richard Dawkins (*The God Delusion*) do. He also finds a certain synthesis of secularism and religion in a post-secular society, as Jürgen Habermas (*Between Naturalism and Religion*) sees it, unfruitful. Instead, Nancy wants to get rid of a general understanding of religion. He proposes to concentrate on certain historical religious configurations – *assemblages* (assemblies) he calls them – and in particular that configuration that has given a stamp to the Western European world: the monotheistic traditions. These configurations have never disappeared in modernity, so it is pointless to speak of a "return" of them. He then tries not to understand monotheism and secularity as opposed philosophies of life that would follow each other in history. Like Taylor, he holds that they originate from the same source and are intertwined from the outset. In *Dis-Enclosure* and in *Adoration* he investigates the possibilities and consequences of this insight.

3 deconstructions of christianity

The first preparations for Nancy's explorations in the borderland between Christianity and modernity can already be found in his early work. There he is interested in the hybrid and mostly de-institutionalized ways in which religion appears in the late twentieth and twenty-first centuries. This is the case in his reflections on "divine places," or in his discussion with Nietzsche, Heidegger and Bataille about the role of the "sacred" in the secular world (see Nancy, "Of Divine Places"). Secondly, these indications can be found in his approach to art and literature and to the political-religious myths of the twentieth century (Nancy and Lacoue-Labarthe; Nancy, "Myth Interrupted"). More explicit announcements of Nancy's project of a deconstruction of monotheism can be found – all in footnotes – in *The Sense of the World* (55n50), twice in *Being Singular Plural* (16n20, 60n52) and in *La pensée dérobée* (155).

Though not referring to a deconstruction of Christianity explicitly, all these publications contain the theoretical preliminary work for the two more detailed and concentrated studies, one about creation, the other about resurrection: *The Creation of the World* and the aforementioned *Noli me tangere*.

In *Noli me tangere*, which contains an analysis of John 20.11–18 (containing the famous "do not touch me!" (Noli me tangere) in verse 17, the words that Jesus speaks to Mary Magdalene after his resurrection) as well as of the ways in which this scene has been resumed in painting, Nancy draws attention to a fundamental dimension of "withdrawal" in the appearance of Christ at the empty tomb. He goes so far as to state that this is not so much about a resurrection from the dead, but that death itself would "rise" and claim its place in life. Not death is conquered in favor of a "life after death," but death itself, and with it the dead, assert themselves in the resurrection, Nancy suggests. According to him, resurrection is not about eternal life as liberation from the limitations of death and mortality, as Christianity proclaimed it in its later, medieval phases. It is not about eternal life, but about the intertwining of life and death *in* life, something that was much later determined by Martin Heidegger as *Sein zum Tode* (being toward death).

It is important to analyze this focus on life in the here and now as a possibly secular feature of the Christian religion. There lies one of Nancy's ambitions: in the end, Christianity should be read against the grain, as a form of atheism.[5] Seen this way the incarnation, that is, the humanization of God and his death on the cross, is a secular element in Christianity, but also the resurrection: the emancipation of death within life. The combination of Good Friday and Easter is an indication of a certain secular impulse that makes Christianity what it is: an essentially modern religion.[6]

4 earthly resurrection, immanent transcendence

Having said that, the resurrection of Christ is the truth of Christianity: the main nourishment for a belief in a life after death and thus in the possibility of conquering death and leaving it behind. This belief has been preached and spread by Christianity from the first centuries of its history onward. It does so on the basis of the short account with which all synoptic gospels conclude: Christ was buried by friends after his humiliation and crucifixion, but after three days the grave is empty. It seems as if the monotheistic religions find their main attraction in this belief: human life on earth is important, but is only fulfilled in another, next life.[7] The gnostic and apocalyptic position is then quickly taken: life in another world, life in another time are what matters. This life here and now is in darkness. Hans Blumenberg considers this the *Weltverneinung* (world denial) of monotheism and analyzes it as its unmodern aspect, and even presents it as the constant threat and delegitimization of modern culture.[8]

THE PULSE OF SENSE

But does the short story about the empty grave necessarily lead to a belief in the victory over mortality? Nancy doubts this in the programmatic first chapter of *Noli me tangere*. According to him, the resurrection has little to do with a return to life after death. Christ does not return again, but he disappears, he just leaves (*partance*). His appearance is that of a disappearance, and his departure is a departure as a dead person. That is why Mary Magdalene, who first discovers the empty tomb, cannot touch Christ. "Christ does not want to be held back, for he is leaving [...] To touch him or hold him back would be to adhere to immediate presence [...]" (Nancy, *Noli me tangere* 15).

Nancy concentrates on this departure, and according to him it is only in departing that Christ is present. Hence, the appearance at the empty grave is an appearance between presence and absence, between life and death, in which these two extremes become intertwined. Christ lives as a dead man, and his "life" consists of constant dying. As he is coming, he has already left, which means that his "coming" consists of a constant departure. Nancy's book must address a departure from the outset, already at his "departure point": yes, the book itself must be a departure.

This departure, which I previously referred to as a dynamic of withdrawal, is applied to a theology of the resurrection, which must shed light on life in death (and vice versa), not life after death. According to Nancy, the touch (*touche* in French, *tangere* in Latin) follows this dynamic, because it is not just "grip," "grasping" or "appropriating," but also and above all the opposite: the fleeting contact that passes before it can become substantial.[9] The touch must be thought beyond any form of clinging; her presence is never immediate, but it is midway between presence and absence.

> To touch him or hold him back would be to adhere to immediate presence, and just as this would be to believe in touching (to believe in the presence of the present), it would be to miss the element of the departing according to which the touch and

presence come to us. (Nancy, *Noli me tangere* 15)

Nancy then continues with the remarkable proposition that, understood this way, the resurrection acquires its "nonreligious," that is, I would add, modern meaning.

But where does Christ go now? Back to the grave? Between which poles does the oscillation move? Between life and death, I just stated. In the text of John this oscillation is portrayed because Christ's departure is described as "ascending to the Father." The body that is raised, that wants to be touched without being held, that simple, human, mortal, body that has just died, stands up to "toward the Father" (John 20.17). But is this ascent a departure from earthly life and from the human state? A gesture of *Weltverneinung*? By no means. John hurries to assure the reader that Christ's Father is also the Father (the God) of humans. Whoever ascends to the Father, leaves to the God who is the God of those who have not conquered death – and will never conquer it. The Father is the God of mortals. Whoever stands up to return to this Father does nothing but raise the mortal human body here and now, on the earth: "[...] the 'Father' is none other than the absent and the removed [...] He [Christ] is departing for the absent, for the distant" (Nancy, *Noli me tangere* 17). However, this "absent," "distant" Father is not transcendent nor elsewhere:

> If he could say "Who has seen me has seen the Father," then the latter is not an other, nor is he elsewhere. He is, here and now, what is not seen and what nonetheless shines with glory, what is not in the light but behind it.[10] (*Noli me tangere* 17)

As a consequence, Nancy rightly emphasizes the importance of the physicality of the resurrection: hence the subtitle of the book, *On the Raising of the Body*. The "glory" of the resurrected body, as the Christian imagery has so often expressed it, is not some kind of spiritualization or deification. It only points in the direction of the vulnerable, earthly, dead body that stands up and "shines" as such. Nancy therefore speaks of two bodies at the end of his analysis:

> Two bodies, the one of glory, the other of flesh, are distinguished in this departure, and in it they belong, partially but mutually, to each other. The one is the raising of the other; the other is the death of the one. (*Noli me tangere* 47)

John's emphasis on the earthly nature of the Father is not only reflected in Nancy's focus on the *body* in his deconstruction of the resurrection. In Matthew's version of the resurrection this is expressed in a similar way with regard to Christ. Matthew finishes his gospel with the promise given by Christ: "I am with you, every day, until the completion of the world" (Matthew 28.20). Christ says that all power is given in heaven *and on earth* (Matthew 28.18). When he leaves for the "heavenly Father," that means that he, as someone who is transcendent – he transcends ordinary life – does so *within* the immanent world. He is dead, he is absent in full presence, among us, "with us," with and among all humans, as if heaven were nothing but an opening, an interruption *into* the world from within that world. Heaven is like an event: the event of an appearance that is simultaneously disappearance. In other words, heaven is opened by the resurrection, not just that of Christ on Easter morning, but time and again, as an eternal revelation. Nancy formulates this as follows, referring to John 18.36:

> What "is not of this world" is not elsewhere: it is the opening in the world, the separation, the parting and the raising. Thus "revelation" is not the sudden appearance of a celestial glory. To the contrary, it consists in the departure of the body raised into glory. It is in absenting, in going absent, that there is revelation [...] (*Noli me tangere* 48)

5 resurrection from or of death?

The resurrection stories in the synoptic gospels are very short. John's version covers the two final chapters of his text and is therefore the longest. They are modest epilogues that seem to fall outside the main line of the story. That main line consists of the Passion Story which forms the long and extended center of the narrative. Consistently, all four gospels work their way toward one point: the cross. John literally goes the furthest by putting these words into Christ's mouth when he actually dies on the cross: "It is fulfilled" (John 19.30). The apotheosis seems to take place on the cross; what does that strange "encore" of the resurrection do after such a tragic culmination? Certainly, in contract with the enormous weight given to the doctrine of the resurrection in later Christianity, it seems rather of secondary value in the original texts of the gospels.

This epilogue character of the resurrection indicates that it does not undo death on the cross, but rather accompanies and intensifies this central event. An epilogue does not add a new theme to a story, but it interprets and resumes what has happened before. What has happened is [...] the death of God in his Son. This holiest of all deaths cannot and should not simply be undone in a hypostasis in which life, preferably an eternal, henceforth immortal life would triumph. This death must be taken seriously. Maybe she tells something about life.

> The resurrection is not a return to life. It is the glory at the heart of death: a dark glory, whose illumination merges with the darkness of the tomb. Rather than the continuum of life passing through death, it is a matter of the discontinuity of another life in or of death. (Nancy, *Noli me tangere* 17)

The death of God on the cross as a theological theme is mirrored here in death as an anthropological and ethical theme: as a constitutive albeit paradoxical element of human life. The death that "lives on," that "survives" in the resurrected Christ is, as such, a critical, aporetic counterforce to a life that is self-sufficient and that ignores its constant vanishing point. "Die in order to live" is a key trope in the religious language and experience of the monotheistic traditions.

Nancy's rather provocative thesis seems to have good grounds, so far, and not just because the essential coherence of death and life is strongly emphasized by all four evangelists. The good grounds can already be found in the proper vocabulary of the evangelists, of the book of Acts and of the *Corpus Paulinum*. After all, a "resurrection from/out of death" (*anastasis ek thanatou*) is never indicated, but the expression is mostly: resurrection of the dead (*anastasis tōn nekrōn*), where the "of" is a subjective genitive. The dead rise, and they rise as dead. Even when the variation "resurrection out of the dead" (*anastasis ek nekrōn*) is used, this does not mean "resurrection from the realm of the dead," as it is often interpreted too easily. It can at most simply indicate that the resurrection comes from the dead – that they are the ones who set it in motion.

> Death is not "vanquished" here, in the sense religion all too hastily wants to give this word. It is immeasurably expanded, shielded from the limitation of being a mere demise. The empty tomb un-limits death in the departing of the dead. (Nancy, *Noli me tangere* 16)

The resurrection of death is the death that rises in life. Nancy tries to sharpen this thesis by pointing out the parabolic nature of the resurrection story, and of the gospel in a broader sense.

6 resurrection as parable

Nancy opens his book with a prologue about the meaning of the parable in the gospels. The aforementioned first chapter begins with the thesis that the resurrection story, and in particular John's version, is a parable: the concluding parable of the longer parables that are actually the four gospels.

> One episode from the Gospel of John gives a particularly good example of this sudden appearance within which a vanishing played out [*se joue*]. It is not a parable spoken by Jesus; it is a scene from the general parable that his life and his mission make up. (Nancy, *Noli me tangere* 11)

Why is Christ's entire life and death a parable? And why do parables form such an important narrative genre in the synoptic text traditions? Because in the parable a type of truth presents itself that has little to do with the closed forms of truth of the metaphysical traditions – truth as substance or essence – or of logical traditions – truth as an adequation of reason and reality: as an adequate statement. The truth of the parable is neither of these, nor is it true. She is parabolic because she plays a game with herself: a game that always seeks a place between true and false.

This play with truth and untruth follows the same structure of withdrawal as that of the resurrection itself. Truth is only true when it loses itself, gives it away, sacrifices itself. The truth must retreat in order to be what it is: it must "die in order to live," and "live as a dying person." This awkward "scandal" (*skandalon*), as Paul calls the event of loss that is the cross (Galatians 5.11), brings coming and disappearance, presence and absence together.

We also see this in an equally parabolic legend (not even a biblical one), that of Christ's encounter with Veronica, in which he gives away his "true face" to Veronica's sweat cloth. The resurrected Christ appears here, even before he has physically died, already as the "relinquished" Christ. His death has already taken place in the gift of himself, during his walk up the hill of Golgotha toward the cross. To be "true," Christ must not keep his truth with him, but must give it away to the other, to Veronica.[11] Between the image itself (Christ's face) and the recipient of the image that has become in turn the holy image (the cloth, kept in many churches in Europe as relic), the truth resides: that is the "scandalous" equation of copy and original, which according to Nancy is articulated in every parable, and in a general way in the parable of Christ's life, death and resurrection. The image is no longer secondary, unreal, fiction (as one can say: "This was only imaginary" or "I only imagined it"), but together with the original it forms the space of truth. "The parable is thus not to be situated in the relation of the 'figure' to the 'proper,' or in the relation of 'appearance' to 'reality,' or in the mimetic relation [...]" (Nancy, *Noli me tangere* 7).

Truth, also and precisely that of resurrection, is in this sense a dynamic, relational and in a certain sense excessive event, rather than a static state of affairs (Nancy, *Noli me tangere* 8). It is not of the order of being that rests within itself and enjoys its untouchable truth. On the contrary, truth is constantly touched by its "other," the untrue, and in this game the truth gives itself away to that other, in order to be true again, in a different mode: true *in* the reception by the other. In sum, this is not a classical ontological truth. It is a "modal ontology" of truth, as Boyan Manchev has developed it in dialogue with Nancy's work: no *ens* nor *ratio*, but *modus*.[12] The truth as a mode, as it is active in the parable, always changes, as in an infinite modulation: in the musical technique of modulation, keys, often associated with certain motifs and melodic lines, keep coming back, but appear in a different form and combination each time. Their "being" exists in their interaction with themselves and with other motives. In the interspace between all these modes the truth takes place, as in the story of the resurrection between the modes of death and life, of disappearance and appearance.

If parabolic truth is a game between giver and recipient, where she must give up her claim to truth, if she is an event that changes every time, as if in a structure of modulation, is there still a difference between this game of truth and the content, the "message" of the parable itself? We have discovered in our reading of the resurrection story that precisely this difference between form and content is at stake. Ultimately, we must note that the main character in the parabolic narrative, such as the risen Christ in the verses of John, himself has a parabolic status: he appears as the disappearing, and his disappearance (departure) is at the same time his presence, his coming. He himself becomes the embodiment of the game of truth: he is, as it were, the "sudden appearance within which a vanishing is played out," as I cited Nancy above.

In other words, Christianity, read from its trope of the resurrection, distances itself from what Nancy calls *croyance* (belief), and opens itself up to the instability that has been given with every parabolic tradition: that of a *foi* (faith) in which the believer loses him- or herself, because the truth of this faith abides between appearance and disappearance, between life and death. In this sense it is a non-religious faith, that does not give "solace," that precludes reassuring identification: the end of religion.

> Would this not be what distinguishes faith from belief, without possible reconciliation of the two? While belief sets down or assumes a sameness of the other with which it identifies itself and in which it takes solace (he is good, he will save me), faith lets itself be addressed by a disconcerting appeal through the other, thrown into a listening that I myself do not know. (Nancy, *Noli me tangere* 10)

In his analysis of the parable as the basic structure of the gospel, Nancy also takes a personal critical interpretation of the common idea that the parable can only be "heard" by those who "have ears to hear," "eyes to see." Nancy refers here to the passages in Matthew 13, in which Christ is asked by his disciples why he speaks in parables. Nancy interprets the words that Christ quotes from Isaiah: "You will listen well, but you will understand nothing, and you will look well, but you will have no insight" (Matthew 13.14) as follows. The truth of the parable arises only in the act of listening, in the dynamics between giver/narrator and receiver/hearer, as mentioned above with reference to the Veronica legend.

> [...] the parable might be expected to open their eyes, informing them of a proper meaning through its figurative system. But Jesus says nothing of the sort. To the contrary, he says that, for those who hear them, parables fulfill the words of Isaiah: "By hearing, ye shall hear, and shall not understand; and seeing ye shall see and shall not perceive." (Nancy, *Noli me tangere* 5)

That explains Nancy's emphasis on listening: a believing, insecure listening whereby the person who has faith is decentered, and by this does not achieve "proper meaning" but is, in a way, lost. This decentering consists in the fact that in the interplay of parabolic truth neither the narrator nor the listener knows what they are doing; they are not in command of the content of what is told/heard. This content remains untouchable, like Christ himself in the resurrection verses in John 20.

To conclude, my analyses indicate that Christianity's holy texts point at something other than life after death. The resurrection portrays a different relation between life and death: that of death in life, that is, a vanishing point around which all life would revolve and from which that life would derive its sense. This strange death is more than physical death – it is daily present as "life," as the absent in and of life – and it brings death back to the earthly, mortal body: no victory over the death in an eternal spiritual life. It is this death that Nancy spots in the resurrection.[13]

Nancy calls this death-in-life, as we saw, the "nonreligious" dimension of the Christian resurrection discourse, which he then analyzes as a parabolic discourse. It is death itself, and with it the dead, who rise without giving up their point of disappearance, their death. A rehabilitation of mortality? Yes and no. Of course, this parabolic truth of the story cannot be the final message of it. True to her game of truth, the text not only "plays" with the idea of appearing in disappearance, as Nancy suggests, but also with that of "appearing again after having disappeared": of a life after death. In order to be parable, the parable must leave the reader/hearer in the dark and allow multiple interpretation options to resonate. This is true of almost all biblical parables.[14] As soon as one reading method becomes evident, the vanishing point on which all appearances are focused, disappears itself. We can, however, conclude that the truth that Nancy detects in the text triggers the less obvious interpretation: that in which the text appears to deconstruct itself by articulating a fundamental paradox. The traditional Christian reading makes identification with the figure of Christ possible in view of salvation and redemption; this reading attempts to "touch" Christ, so to speak, as Mary demands: "He will redeem me!" The deconstructive reading places the reader before an enigma never to be solved: no identification is possible. Only in this way can Nancy pinpoint the ancient evangelical traditions as traditions that deconstruct themselves, and open themselves toward a modern, secular rephrasing.

7 resurrection in a modern novel – epilogue

This is also why Nancy can state that the Christian parable opens the way to modern literature and art. *Noli me tangere* "is attempting to clear the way, however slightly, for this hypothesis" (Nancy, *Noli me tangere* 8). It should be noted that Nancy does not seem to have the ambition, at least not in *Noli me tangere*, to substantiate this hypothesis, for his only example of modern literature is Maurice Blanchot's novel *Thomas the Obscure* (1999).

With Blanchot, Nancy conducts a dialogue from his first publications onward. In *Dis-Enclosure* we find a short chapter about the theme of the resurrection in Blanchot's stories: "Blanchot's Resurrection." That is remarkable, since this writer is known for his strong interest in the possible meaning of death, dying and mortality in his work. Using a particular phrase from *Thomas the Obscure*, Nancy shows how in this novel almost literally the notion of risen death in the resurrection parable is being re-articulated in a modern narrative, while maintaining the words and names of the biblical narrative. In the passage in question, the main character, Thomas, is compared to Lazarus, the protagonist of that other resurrection story in the Gospel of John (John 11): "He walked, the only true Lazarus, whose very death was resurrected" (Blanchot 74).

Parallel to his approach to the resurrection story, Nancy searches here for the connection between resurrection and death:

> The resurrection in question does not escape death, nor recover from it, nor dialecticize it. On the contrary, it constitutes the extremity and the truth of the phenomenon of dying. It goes into death not to pass through it but, sinking irremissibly into it, to resuscitate death itself. To resuscitate death is entirely different from resuscitating the dead. ("Blanchot's Resurrection" 89)

Then, Nancy applies Blanchot's vision of death as a central feature of human life in his exegesis of Lazarus's revival – thereby deconstructively reading the old verses of John 11 into secular modernity. The "truth" of Lazarus's resurrection "resides in the simultaneity of death and a life within it that does not come back to life, but that makes death live qua death. Or yet again: the true Lazarus lives his dying as he dies his living" (Nancy, "Blanchot's Resurrection" 91–92).

In the biblical story, Christ comes too late to save Lazarus from dying. He has other activities, and although he knows that Lazarus is sick, he stays away "two days" (11.6). When he finally arrives, Lazarus has died; Christ can only announce his resurrection. "Your brother will stand up" (11.23), he tells Martha; the words "from death" or "from the dead," although the reader expects them, are not added. Martha thinks Christ is talking about the end of time ("the last day"; 11.24), but the latter corrects it, and draws the resurrection into the here and now: "I am the resurrection and the life" (11.25). As strange as Nancy's proclamation of resurrected death may seem, the "life" that Christ embodies here ("I am [...]") is the experience of the night that the "dark," "obscure" Thomas in Blanchot's novel wants to enlighten: live your death, die your life. But the night cannot be illuminated unless it is turned into a day. Death cannot be lived unless it is turned into a life again. Christianity demands the impossible from us. Perhaps it is herein that it finds its challenging actuality.

echo by jean-luc nancy

With the precaution I have to take whenever I read a text written in English – a reading that is for me uncertain and incomplete – , I can say that Laurens ten Kate takes the reflections on the Christian resurrection I sketched out a step further. Indeed, it seemed impossible to me to leave this representation at the heart of the Christian message a mere fantastical projection of an afterlife. This project certainly exists, it is shared by some and has its authorizing texts in the Gospels. The latter, however, carry a message that, it should be noted, places little emphasis on the "return to life" – as is evident above all in the resurrection of Lazarus, i.e., in one of the three resurrections and within the Gospels the one operated by Jesus (after all, that isn't much, all the more so since two of them are each only to be found in one of the four authors -- this requires interpretation, but I am not going to attempt it here). But the resurrection that takes place on or from Jesus himself, without any thaumaturgy, there are many signs of the absence of the arisen in his very presence. It is not someone who is brought back to life again – as one can be revived after a terrible accident – , but someone who lives differently. Who lives "here" elsewhere than "here." Which precisely raises the question of the being-here.

The way in which Laurens ten Kate understands this other life – as the life of death or as death in life – seems to me to be carrying the meaning of this "message" further (as well as the very fact that this is a message, *angelon*). I am struck by a connection that I had not made at the time of writing the book he is basing himself on. It is a connection to the famous passage from the *Phenomenology of Spirit* where Hegel writes that the spirit does not recoil before death but dwells within it. (It is certain that Hegel is thinking of Jesus at the tomb.) This dwelling, Hegel adds, is the magical force that converts the negative into being. The spring of the (all too) famous *Aufhebung* is given here as "magic." What does this word mean? Since it cannot be explained in the Hegelian context (it's a *hapax* in the *Phenomenology*), it must be understood as mysterious in the strongest sense (i.e., what is illuminated by itself).

We would of course have to reread the latter passage analyzing the resurrection – shortly before we come to "absolute knowledge." That has no place here either; I only want to point out that this is an essential stage in the deconstruction of Christianity: the egress from "survivalist" representation and at the same time the return – or new

arrival – to mystery in excess of signification.

As a thank you, I offer Laurens ten Kate this little Hegelian exercise ...

disclosure statement

No potential conflict of interest was reported by the author.

notes

1 An early version of this study was published in Dutch in *Tijdschrift voor Theologie* (Journal of Theology) 53.1 (2013): 26–43.

2 For a recent overview and detailed commentary on this project, see Ten Kate et al.

3 Jean-Luc Nancy, *Noli me tangere: Essai sur la levée du corps* (Paris, 2003). Five years later it appeared in an English translation: *Noli me tangere: On the Raising of the Body*. In the following, I will refer to the English edition. For scripture passages I basically follow the edition used by the translator of *Noli me tangere*: *The Authorized King James Version* (Oxford, 1997).

4 Taylor develops this insight throughout *A Secular Age*, whenever he distinguishes between political and social secularity as the secularization of the public sphere, psychological secularity (the need to believe in a God gradually decreases), and what he coins as secularity 3: new relations between immanence and transcendence, new "conditions of belief" that mark the modern world.

5 See, e.g., *Dis-Enclosure*, "Atheism and Monotheism" 14–28.

6 The question of whether these secular traces have found their way into Christianity (and in a broader sense in all monotheistic religions) despite the global socio-political success of this religion (a success that has been possible through submission, the hierarchy, the violence, exclusion, fear, discipline, moral overdetermination of life, etc.), or *thanks* to this success, is the challenge for further research. Nancy's project also only indirectly meets this demand.

7 Islam has also put the belief in the hereafter in a massively central position, albeit on the basis of other text traditions not related to the figure of Christ. Only Judaism is for the most part silent about life after death. The belief in this is limited here to a confidence that God will take care of his *people* – not of the individual soul – even after death.

8 See Blumenberg, in particular Part II, chapters 1 and 2. For my discussion of Blumenberg's analyses of world denial in relation with the Christian legacy in modernity, involving also Nancy's deconstructions of Christianity, see "To World or not to World."

9 On the notion of "passing by," see my analysis in *Re-treating Religion*, "God Passing By: Presence and Absence in Monotheism and Atheism" 132–44.

10 Nancy quotes John 14.9.

11 See also my analysis in "De afgestane Christus." In Dutch, there is the wordplay with *opstaan* (to resurrect) and *afstaan* (to relinquish, to yield) – of course untranslatable. The name Veronica is usually traced back to the Latin *vera* and the Greek *icon*: "the true image." This etymology from two different linguistic regions is no more than a corruption of a later date; the name must actually be traced to *berenikè*, Greek for "bearer of victory."

12 See Ten Kate et al., *Re-treating Religion*, "The Ontology of Creation: The Onto-Aisthetics of Jean-Luc Nancy" 261–74, in particular 266–67 and 271–72. Manchev bases his search for a "modal ontology" on, among other things, Nancy's views on Christian themes such as *creatio ex nihilo*, incarnation, and death and resurrection, as elaborated in *Corpus*. For Nancy, the body that stands up in its mortality is pre-eminently modular: it changes its mode every time and is never "substance." But it is precisely that

modular body that God has chosen for himself to be "truly God, truly human" (*vere deus vere homo* as Christian theology has formulated in dogmatic form): God gives up and loses his divine status in order to "modify" himself into a human being "in Christ." "God made himself body [...] consisting entirely of modalizing, or modification, rather than substance [...] God modalized or modified himself, but his self in itself is only the extension and indefinite expansion of modes" (Nancy, *Corpus* 61).

13 In this sense Nancy contrasts the Christian experience of death with that of mythical antiquity as well as with "other" cultures, such as so-called natural religions, or with religions based on reincarnation such as Hinduism:

> The Greco-Roman world was the world of mortal mankind. Death was irreparable there; and whether one tried to think about it in terms of glory or in terms of deliverance, it was still the incompatible other of life. Other cultures always have affirmed death as another life, foreign yet close by, strange yet compatible in various ways [...] Christianity, reinterpreting an aspect of Judaism, proposed death as the truth of life and opened up in life itself, the difference of death. (Nancy, *Adoration* 23)

This genealogy of ways in which death is experienced also has consequences for our conception of "eternal life"; the opposition between "in" life and "outside" or "beyond" life is deconstructed here:

> Eternal life is not life indefinitely extended, but life withdrawn from time in the very course of time. Considering the life of ancient mankind [the Greco-Roman world – LtK] was a life measured by its time, and the life of other cultures was a life in constant relationship to the life of the dead, Christian life lives, in time, what is outside of time. (Nancy, *Adoration* 23)

See also my analysis in "De wereld tussen ja en nee. Monotheïsme als modern problem bij Assmann, Nancy en Blumenberg" (The World between Yes and No: Monotheism as a Modern Problem in Assmann, Nancy and Blumenberg).

14 Think of Luke 15.11–32, the famous parable of the "lost son." In it, the narrator, Christ, deliberately leaves in the dark who this son is after all who takes off with the "life" of his father (usually translated with "legacy" or "possession," but that is not stated in Greek), give everything away ("wasted"?) and then return to the father. An excessive party is the father's response to this disappearance action, because "this son of mine was dead and has come to life again" (Luke 15.24). Is this son the prototype of the "sinner" and the "publican," with whom Christ "eats," as the prelude to this parable – to the anger of the Pharisees and scribes? (Luke 15.2). Is he the derailed criminal who nevertheless receives forgiveness? Or does the "death" he sought have Christological implications? Is the son perhaps Christ himself? The parable does not reveal anything.

bibliography

Blanchot, Maurice. *Thomas the Obscure.* Ed. George Quasha. *The Station Hill Blanchot Reader: Fiction & Literary Essays.* Barrytown, NY: Station Hill, 1999. Print.

Blumenberg, Hans. *The Legitimacy of the Modern Age.* Cambridge, MA: MIT P, 1983. Print.

Dawkins, Richard. *The God Delusion.* Boston: TransWorld, 2006. Print.

Habermas, Jürgen. *Between Naturalism and Religion: Philosophical Essays.* Cambridge: Polity, 2008. Print.

Kate, Laurens ten. "De afgestane Christus. Over ware beelden als gevonden voorwerpen" (The Relinquished Christ: About True Images as Articles Found). *Veronica.* Ed. Robert Zandvliet and Harry Haarsma. Schiedam: Ketel Factory, 2012. 1–5. Print.

Kate, Laurens ten. "De wereld tussen ja en nee. Monotheïsme als modern problem bij Assmann, Nancy en Blumenberg" (The World between Yes and No: Monotheism as a Modern Problem in Assmann, Nancy and Blumenberg). *Tijdschrift voor Filosofie* 73 (2011): 9–45. Print.

Kate, Laurens ten. "To World or not to World: An Axial Genealogy of Secular Life." *Radical Secularization: An Inquiry into the Religious Roots of Secular Culture.* Ed. S. Latré, W. Van Herck, and G. Vanheeswijck. New York: Bloomsbury Academic, 2014. 207–30. Print.

Kate, Laurens ten, A. Alexandrova, A. van Rooden, and I. Devisch, eds. *Re-treating Religion: Deconstructing Christianity with Jean-Luc Nancy.* New York: Fordham UP, 2012. Print.

Nancy, Jean-Luc. *Adoration: The Deconstruction of Christianity II.* New York: Fordham UP, 2012. Print.

Nancy, Jean-Luc. *Being Singular Plural.* Stanford: Stanford UP, 2000. Print.

Nancy, Jean-Luc. "Blanchot's Resurrection." *Dis-Enclosure: The Deconstruction of Christianity.* New York: Fordham UP, 2007. Print.

Nancy, Jean-Luc. *Corpus.* New York: Fordham UP, 2008. Print.

Nancy, Jean-Luc. *The Creation of the World, or Globalization.* Albany: SUNY P, 2007. Print.

Nancy, Jean-Luc. *La pensée dérobée.* Paris: Galilée, 2001. Print.

Nancy, Jean-Luc. "Myth Interrupted." *The Inoperative Community.* Minneapolis: U of Minnesota P, 1991. 43–70. Print.

Nancy, Jean-Luc. *Noli me tangere: On the Raising of the Body.* New York: Fordham UP, 2008. Print.

Nancy, Jean-Luc. "Of Divine Places." *The Inoperative Community.* Minneapolis: U of Minnesota P, 1991. 110–51. Print.

Nancy, Jean-Luc. *The Sense of the World.* Minneapolis: U of Minnesota P, 1997. Print.

Nancy, Jean-Luc, and Philippe Lacoue-Labarthe. "The Nazi Myth." *Critical Inquiry* 16 (1990): 291–312. Print.

Onfray, Michel. *Atheist Manifesto: The Case against Christianity, Judaism and Islam.* New York: Skyhorse, 2014. Print.

Taylor, Charles. *A Secular Age.* Boston: Belknap/Harvard UP, 2007. Print.

"*How 'to talk religion'? Of religion? Singularly of religion, today?*" Derrida asks at the opening of "Faith and Knowledge." "*How dare we speak of it in the singular without fear and trembling, this very day? And so briefly and so quickly? Who would be so imprudent as to claim that the issue here is both identifiable and new?*" (42).[1] At a time when religious fundamentalisms of all traditions and on all continents fight for the monopoly of religious truth, no definition seems as uncertain as that of religion. To be sure, the definitions proposed by Edward Burnett Tylor, William James and Emile Durkheim in the nineteenth and early twentieth centuries, which all revolve around the notion of transcendent belief, never received a universal consensus. These have, nevertheless, been used in social sciences for more than a century and still constitute the theoretical ground on which secularism – and more generally any socio-political consideration of the religious – rests in the modern West. Over the past few decades, however, manifestations of the religious across the world have come as a challenge to these – overall widely accepted – definitions.

Globalisation and the emergence of New Age spirituality in Western countries, in particular, have raised the question of whether non-theistic devotion and ritual practices detached from supernatural belief can be described as *religious*. To this day, specialists remain divided on the question of whether Shintoism, Taoism, Buddhism and other non-Western forms of spirituality which globalisation has

marie chabbert

THE ETERNAL RETURN OF RELIGION
jean-luc nancy on faith in the singular-plural

brought under the spotlight should be considered as religions, philosophical traditions or lifestyles.[2] As for spiritual approaches to environmentalism, vegetarianism and mindfulness developing at a fast pace across the West, governmental agencies such as the French Interministerial Mission of Vigilance and Combat against Sectarian Aberrations are still to settle on whether these should be considered religious, sectarian or strictly profane.[3] In *Islam Faced with the Death of God* [*L'Islam face à la mort de Dieu*], philosopher Abdennour Bidar suggests that they might be

---

This is an Open Access article distributed under the terms of the Creative Commons Attribution-NonCommercial-NoDerivatives License (http://creativecommons.org/licenses/by-nc-nd/4.0/), which permits non-commercial re-use, distribution, and reproduction in any medium, provided the original work is properly cited, and is not altered, transformed, or built upon in any way.

neither but rather testify to Westerners' "fundamental spiritual dissatisfaction" (9) and longing for "a spiritual future somewhere beyond the ancient Divine and the present Nothingness, beyond the belief of some and the atheism of others" (37).[4] Reformist currents of the three Abrahamic religions as well as recent work in the anthropology and the philosophy of religion however also contributed to challenging the idea that transcendent belief is *conditio sine qua non* of religion.[5] Religious leaders and believers increasingly describe religion in terms of "lived experience" and "reflective faith," arguably in reaction to the pressing need to distinguish religion from what is often presented – legitimately so or not – as its terrorist caricature; to sort the religious wheat from the chaff, as it were.

Far from confirming the traditional understanding of religion, then, the so-called "return of religion" at the forefront of international preoccupations – which belied the widely held belief in the pending disappearance of religion from the modern world – has blurred the boundaries of what was hitherto understood as religion. It has reshuffled the deck indeed, to the point that one may wonder not only whether it is justified to speak of current manifestations of religion across the world in terms of a *return*, but also whether it is necessary to keep speaking of religion *in the singular*, that is to say, by referring to a universal structure of religiosity distinct from politics, economics, art, and so on. That is the relativistic question over which contemporary philosophical, anthropological and sociological analysis of religion keeps stumbling. In *Philosophy and the Turn to Religion*, Hent de Vries observes that religion "No longer [is] identifiable as a clearly demarcated field of research" (1), a tendency to which many scholars have contributed by re-evaluating the demarcation between theology and philosophy, revelation and reason, the sacred and the profane, in other words, between religion and its *other*. Exemplary studies include John Milbank's *Theology and Social Theory*, Moshe Halbertal and Avishai Margalit's *Idolatry*, Talal Asad's *Genealogies of Religion* and Jean-Luc Marion's

Being Given, among other works from the so-called "theological turn of French phenomenology" (Janicaud). Yet, as anthropologist Michael Scott warns, because religion tends to become "a 'floating signifier,' a symbol emptied by a surfeit of possible and seemingly contradictory meanings [...], [b]ecause 'religion' has the semantic capacity to capture aspects of almost anything, the concept threatens in many analytical contexts to disappear altogether" (860).

Why would that be an issue? Talal Asad calls for such a disappearance on the basis that considering religion as a determinate sphere of human reality is ethnocentric since it requires a transcendent divine relatively detachable from this-worldly matters (27–54). If this corresponds to Abrahamic religions – Christianity in particular, on which definitions of religion were modelled – , this contradicts immanent forms of spirituality, which do not conceive of religion as a separate institution. As Derrida observes in "Faith and Knowledge,"

> There has not always been, [...] nor is there always and everywhere, nor will there always and everywhere [...] be *something*, a thing that is *one and identifiable*, identical with itself, which, whether religious or irreligious, all agree to call "religion." (72–73)

This issue is most pertinent to secularism, a political principle which depends on the definition of religion as a determinate anthropological category. The secular separation of religion from the public sphere in order to guarantee the neutrality of the State and the freedom of consciousness fails to accommodate the variety of immanent spiritualities found across cultures and throughout history. No wonder Asad's anti-essentialist position received wide attention and acclaim among anthropologists. "And yet, one tells oneself, **one must still respond**," Derrida suggests (73). If essentialist definitions of religion may well be ethnocentric and, ultimately, unviable, according to Derrida, **"one still must respond**. And without waiting" (75). In today's world of rampant religious violence, relativism remains weak in the face of the practical exigencies of peaceful coexistence: refusing to speak of religion in the singular does not make existing religious claims and violence any less real. Scholars and political leaders *must* be able to speak of – and better still, respectively study and organise their countries' relation to – something that "is happening and so badly" (75).

In line with Derrida, I believe that the contemporary necessity to be more inclusive of the variety of spiritual experiences found across the world should not resolve itself in the dissolution of the concept of religion. One must be able to *respond* to the questions that the return of religion raises for us today. Not by falling into old traps, that is to say, by depicting the religious as a category *sui generis* overlooking the particularities of determinate historical religions (de Vries 3), but rather by attending to both its undeniable diversity and unshakeable singularity, *simultaneously*. It is out of this conviction that the present paper has been written, in order to outline one way in which one can still speak of religion in the singular today while taking into account the plurality of an issue that is, as Derrida rightly notes, both identifiable and new (9). To this end, I propose to think with Jean-Luc Nancy. This may seem surprising, considering that Nancy states at the opening of *Dis-Enclosure* that "The much discussed 'return of the religious,' which denotes a real phenomenon, deserves no more attention than any other 'return'" (1). Does this mean that, for him, the "return of religion" is not worth considering, and that those questions which drive my paper are not worth asking? Absolutely not. In what follows, I demonstrate that Nancy's point is far subtler, even providing us with new resources to think religion in the singular-plural today.

the return of the same

The first thing to note is that Nancy indexes the value and significance of the "return of religion" today to the logic of the return itself, a logic which he examines in "The Forgetting of Philosophy." He observes that the latter depends on the interruption of a given state of equilibrium – a crisis – which is eventually overcome so that the lost equilibrium is found again. This means that the "return" comes with "two major implications. On the one hand, the crisis is deemed merely superficial, and, on the other hand, the return of some deep meaning must be understood as the return of the identical" (Nancy, "The Forgetting of Philosophy" 17). The logic of the return thus inscribes itself within a philosophical tradition which considers the principle of identity as the highest principle of thought, a tradition which Heidegger studies in *Identity and Difference* under the name of "ontotheology" (44). Ever since the first Greek philosophers, Heidegger observes, metaphysics has focused on identity and its correlates not only to the detriment of difference, but also to the point that difference has only ever been considered in its difference *from* identity. In other words, what matters to the Western eye is always identity first, then, Heidegger stresses, "what differs in the difference" (70). Yet even in that case, difference is usually considered as a superficial challenge to the status quo soon to give way to the return of a reinforced sense of identity. This is what Hegel theorised as dialectics. In the *Phenomenology of Spirit*, Hegel proposes that a subject's sense of self-identity benefits from an exposure to negation (19). By extrapolating this dialectical logic to an approach to history, he contributed to presenting crises as minor challenges to the status quo giving access to higher degrees of identity. When considering the effects of crises, Western scholars are thus tempted to focus on what *returns*, rather than on what dramatically changed. Such is the case of the philosophical, anthropological or sociological studies evaluating the long-term effects of the death of God on religion in the West. These have so far focused on the crisis, followed by a resurgence, of past religious fervour – *the return of the Same* – rather than on the multiple changes in religiosity and its perception to which I have alluded. More precisely, these studies shed light on a dialectical re-centring on what is deemed essential in the traditional definition of religion, namely, transcendent belief, following trajectories which I respectively designate as *post-secular* and *postsecular*.[6]

On the one hand, the recent upsurge of fundamentalist currents in most religious traditions, from Islam to Protestantism, Judaism and Hinduism, is interpreted as the return of a devotion to transcendent beliefs which proponents of the "secularisation thesis" thought condemned to disappear. Much like the Freudian "return of the repressed," whose violence is proportional to that of the repressive gesture,[7] however, this return manifests as "a religious and hyperreligious upheaval or surrection," as Nancy puts it in *Dis-Enclosure* (3). Secularism is violently rejected – a rupture symbolised by the hyphen in the term postsecular – in favour of the return, not simply *of* religion as it used to be understood before the rise of atheism, but *to a purer* version of religion. The latter, which comes down to an uncompromising reading of the dogma, even implies a rejection of the former. Salafism is an emblematic example with its pursuit of the supposedly lost pure religiosity of the first generations of Muslims. When coupled with Jihadism, this search for purity justifies the destruction of any "infidel," whether atheist, of another religion than Islam or even Muslim but non-Salafi. Yet nothing guarantees that the fundamentalist interpretation of the Quran proposed by Salafism has anything to do with that of the first generations of Muslims, or that such a reading is "purer" than any other, whatever this means.

Fortunately, not all manifestations of the return of religion in the contemporary world prove so violent. Some are the result of efforts made by reformist currents at work within Abrahamic religions as well as by philosophers of religion to make space for religion in the secular age.[8] Like post-secularism, however, this trajectory, which I refer to as "postsecular," relies on a dialectical logic in that it attempts to *save* the perceived essence of religion, that is, the possibility of transcendent belief. To do so, the reformist currents and thinkers of this trajectory do not hesitate to transform, adapt, multiply and disseminate

concepts such as the sacred, the divine, and their traditional sources so that they fit in a world dominated by the death of God. Contrary to what Michael Scott suggests, then, stretching the semantic capacity of religion does not necessarily end in the dissolution of the concept. Rather, I contend that such a gesture simultaneously re-centres on what is deemed most essential in religion while universalising it, an approach that is at least as ethnocentric as any approach to religion in the singular. I suspect that Jean-Luc Marion's radicalisation of the phenomenological method developed by Husserl and Heidegger is exemplary of such a postsecular trajectory. According to Marion, whereas phenomenology is committed to exploring the thing in itself "while avoiding forging hypotheses, both on the relationship that links the phenomenon with the being *of whom* it is a phenomenon, and on the relationship that ties it with the I *for whom* it is a phenomenon," as Lyotard's definition goes (7),[9] Husserl and Heidegger indexed the phenomenon and its appearance to the intentional horizon and the subject who "receives" the phenomenon, thereby failing to think the phenomenon *as it appears*. As Marion explains in *Being Given*, "the giving intuition does not yet authorize an absolutely unconditioned apparition, nor therefore the freedom of the phenomenon giving itself on its own basis" (185). He therefore proposes to re-centre phenomenology on unconditional phenomenality, that is to say, on *revelation* for, he writes, "the phenomenon, which happens as an event, takes on the figure of the revealed" (Marion, "L'événement, le phénomène et le révélé" 24).[10] I argue that, by granting revelation such a primary phenomenological value, Marion participates in a postsecular return of religion. His radicalisation of phenomenology re-inscribes the possibility of revelation at the heart of every phenomenon, thereby guaranteeing its relevance in the modern secular world.[11]

Whether post-secular or postsecular, then, there does seem to be a twofold return of religion in the contemporary world. What Nancy suggests, however, is that "it is not certain that an interpretation in terms of 'return' [...]

is sufficient, provided that thought is not too lazy" ("The Forgetting of Philosophy" 13). The definitional crisis evoked in the first section supports this claim: religion today, or at least our Western perception of it, does show signs of an irreversible change for which the ever-growing body of literature on the "return of religion" does not account. Nancy goes so far as to argue that the "return" on which Western scholars have been focusing over the past few decades consists less in a spontaneous return *of* religion than in an artificial fear-driven return *to* religion in reaction to these changes. As he remarks in "The Forgetting of Philosophy," "All the modern problematics of difference attract the protestations of the thinkers of the return, who see in them a destruction or frustration of identity" (64). Out of fear of the unknown, proponents of the "return of religion" would artificially minimise the contemporary transformations of the religious in favour of the comforting – but simplistic – return to identity. Besides, given that identity is a determining principle of Western thought, one could suggest that this return *to* religion, which is but a retreat to identity, partakes of what Derrida calls "globalatinisation," that is, of the ethnocentric diffusion of what is at root Latin and increasingly becomes "European-Anglo-*American* in its idiom" ("Faith and Knowledge" 79). That is what Nancy touches on in *Dis-Enclosure* where, looking at the contemporary confrontation between the West and Islamic fundamentalism, he argues that "th[e] Unifying, Unitary, and Universal model [of the former], also Unidimensional, and finally Unilateral [...] has made possible the symmetrical and no less nihilistic mobilization of a monotheistic and no less unilateralist model [that is, Islamic fundamentalism]" (41).

the deaths *of* god

Against this fear-driven *return to identity*, Nancy argues – quite cryptically, admittedly – that "Among the phenomena of repetition, resurgence, revival, or haunting, it is not the identical but the different that invariably counts the most" (*Dis-Enclosure* 1). More

specifically, he suggests that "the question should [...] be asked, ceaselessly and with new risks, what 'secularization' might denote, inevitably, other than a mere transferal of the identical" (1).[12] Whereas discourses on the return of religion tend to depict secularisation as a momentary crisis and the death of God as "some past [event] *that quite simply did not take place*" (Nancy, "The Forgetting of Philosophy" 22), he suspects that this event has played a determining role in the transformations that have recently challenged the traditional definition of religion. This seems to be confirmed by Charles Taylor who, in *A Secular Age*, remarks that the diffusion of atheism in the West turned the hitherto axiomatic belief in a form of transcendence into a mere *option*. "The shift to secularity," he explains "[...] consists, among other things, of a move from a society where belief in God is unchallenged and indeed, unproblematic, to one in which it is understood to be one option among others" (Taylor 3). Taylor describes this shift in terms of the installation of an "immanent frame" over Western minds, for the latter "come to understand [their] lives as taking place within a self-sufficient immanent order" (543).[13] Because it seems to have first liberated thought from the hitherto axiomatic notion of transcendence, the death of God appears as a privileged starting point for any attempt at appreciating and accounting for the plurality of religion(s) today, beyond the sole limits of transcendence. A quick look at the history of the concept of the death of God however goes against this observation: God's death does not seem to have *really* challenged the axiomatic value of transcendence. If anything, it has emphasised its dialectical resilience.

If the death of God is now generally associated with the emergence of atheism in a world previously dominated by theism, indeed, the concept was first theorised as part of the Christian doctrine. The death of Christ on the cross constitutes not only the birth-act of Christianity – what distinguishes it from Judaism – but also the heart of its dogma. It is only by exposing Himself to His negation that Christ may revive, and His sacrifice redeem humankind. God's death is, therefore, not a threat to Christianity; rather the opposite, it takes part in and reinforces its moral order.[14] It is this dialectical structure that one finds today in the *postsecular* return of religion. Drawing attention to the oecumenical efforts of reformist Christianity, Derrida observes in "Faith and Knowledge" that: "When one hears the official representatives of the religious hierarchy, beginning with [...] the Pope, speak of this sort of ecumenical reconciliation, one also hears [...] the announcement or reminder of a certain 'death of God'" (79). In *The Metamorphosis of Finitude*, Emmanuel Falque makes a similar point about Marion's treatment of God's death. For Marion, Falque argues,

> That God is dead is [...] not, or is no longer, a simple profession of atheism, but it is the highest truth of a Christianity properly understood – that is to say, in one centered on the mystery of the death and the resurrection of Christ. (31)

"Some people, however," Falque continues, "will see this recycling of the famous phrase as a kind of trick" (31). Is it not what dialectics as a whole is, a sleight of hand?

As Gilles Deleuze observes in *Nietzsche and Philosophy*, however, by staging for the first time the putting to death of God, Christianity did open thought to a world in which God is not. The Christian dogma thus "secretes its own atheism" (Deleuze, *Nietzsche and Philosophy* 154), a second death of God, thereby confirming Nietzsche's statement in *Thus Spoke Zarathustra* that "When gods die, they always die many kinds of deaths" (211). This second death of God, however, proved no less dialectical than the first. As Deleuze explains in "On the Death of Man and Superman," the disappearance of the Christian God threatened to exhaust the transcendent values that supported human existence. In the late eighteenth and nineteenth centuries, thinkers such as Auguste Comte, Immanuel Kant and Ludwig Feuerbach therefore modelled new values based on human finitude (Deleuze, "On the Death of Man and Superman" 126–27). Thus

was born the humanistic idea of Man in Western philosophy. Yet as Deleuze rhetorically asks, "by putting man in God's place, do we abolish the essential, that is to say, the place?" (*Nietzsche and Philosophy* 88–89). In *Difficult Atheism*, Christopher Watkin highlights that the atheistic death of God merely replaced theological values with humanistic or rationalist ones, the God-Man with the Man-God, thereby "explicitly rejecting but implicitly imitating theology's categories of thinking" (2). One may therefore criticise Taylor's use of the concept of "immanent frame." The "frame" of secularism is only immanent insofar as it does not depend on a belief in God but it does still appeal to atheistic figures of transcendence, as testified by the emergence of quasi-religious humanist or rationalist currents in most Western countries.[15] Most emblematic of all is Robespierre's Cult of the Supreme Being and the installation in November 1793 of the "goddess of reason" on the altar of Notre Dame.[16]

As Roberto Esposito stresses in "Flesh and Body in the Deconstruction of Christianity" ["Chair et corps dans la déconstruction du christianisme"], then, it appears that both the Christian and atheistic deaths of God are "*of* God, in both the objective and subjective sense of the genitive; these deaths, after all, if not above all, belong to him from the beginning in the figure of the God dying on the cross" (157).[17] This confirms Nietzsche's intuition that "God is dead; but given the way people are, there may still for millennia be caves in which they show his shadow" (*The Gay Science* 109). The definitional crisis evoked earlier leaves no doubt, however: the notion of transcendence, as it is traditionally understood, is not sufficient to account for the plurality of religious experiences in the contemporary world, much like, as Derrida rightly notes in *Paper Machine*, "Church attendance aren't the only way of measuring religion" (116). There must, therefore, be more to the death of God than what mainstream interpretations so far have suggested. By proposing that the "return of religion" deserves no more attention than any other "return," Nancy calls us to finally realise that the death of God must be interpreted in a way that does *not* leave His shadow intact, but rather fosters non-recuperable difference. He argues, in other words, that it is now time to do justice to the second, often forgotten, part of Zarathustra's exclamation: "God is dead! God remains dead!" (Nietzsche, *The Gay Science* 120).

the deconstruction *of* monotheism

To do so, Nancy turns to the successive episodes of death of God which facilitated the passage from polytheism to monotheism, as well as from monotheism to atheism, and remarks that, if these largely follow the schema of the return, they also "mar[k] out intaglio [...] the place of what will finally have to abandon the simplistic alternative of theism or atheism" (*Noli me tangere* 108).

He observes that the flight of the gods of polytheism functioned as a retreat of the gods from effective presence in the world, a retreat which rendered truth unnarratable. "When the gods have withdrawn," Nancy argues in "One Day, the Gods Withdraw ... ," "their history can no longer be simply true, nor their truth simply narrated. The presence that would attest to the existence of what is narrated as well as the veracity of the speech that narrates is lacking" (26). Truth and narration, logos and *muthos* thus emerge as distinct categories. Yet Nancy warns that the latter "separate in such a way that it's their separation that establishes them both" (26). What one is left with is "a scene of mourning and desire" (27–28); humanity mourns the loss of (divine) truth, the loss of foundation. It is faced with a perceived finitude which Hegel terms "*unhappy consciousness*" (126). Thus started the disenchantment of the West: before the gods' flight, the adequacy of *logos* and *muthos* allowed for the existence of magic, whose spells function as the unfolding of truth in language, and myth, which consists in the structuration in language of a cosmos seen as pure, proper, well-ordered – as per the etymology of *mundus* in Latin – , that is to say, as *Logos*. The withdrawal of divine presence,

however, came with a loss of foundation which exhausted both magic and mythical speech. Or did it? The end of polytheism also marked the advent of monotheism. Nancy warns that this should not be interpreted as a mere numeric reduction of the number of the gods, but rather as a profound transformation of divinity itself. Westerners eager to find consolation for their finitude recuperated divine "absencing" by means of a dialectical gesture of abstraction and hyperessentialisation. "From a present power or person," Nancy explains, "it changes divinity into a principle, a basis, and/or a law, always by definition absent or withdrawn in the depths of being" (*Dis-Enclosure* 22). This is exemplified by the "half-proper, half-common" name of the God of monotheism (Nancy, "Of Divine Places" 116). Whereas polytheist religions give *proper* names to their gods – whether it be Osiris, Zeus, Neptune, Quetzalcoatl or Amaterasu – , monotheist religions refer to God using the *common* name which designates all divine entities. As Nancy remarks, "It is as if we were to say that the name of a 'poplar' tree is simply *tree* [...] [God] is not the proper name of someone, but names the divine as such" (*God, Justice, Love, Beauty* 11). The God of monotheism emerges as the *alpha* and *omega* of the world. It is, therefore, insufficient to suggest that the gods' flight deprived the West of (divine) foundation.

Yet it is not sufficient to approach the advent of the monotheistic God as a mere transferal of the identical either, for in addition to referring to God using a common name, the three monotheisms deny the simple possibility of nomination (Nancy et al. 329). To be sure, in Judaism, God has a name, but this name cannot be spoken. In Islam, God even has a hundred names, but ninety-nine of these are mere superlatives while the hundredth designates God as the Unknowable. As for Christianity, the name "Jesus" only applies to a fraction of the Trinitarian divine. In "Of Divine Places," Nancy warns that this lack of divine names should not be mistaken for "a surface lack concealing *and* manifesting the depths of a sacred held in reserve" (120). Terminological instability rather testifies to the inability of the divine to inaugurate itself as God-*Logos*. The divine "strangles itself [...] with a literature that is *its own* impossible" (Nancy, "One Day, the Gods Withdraw ... " 29). It emerges as an open mouth choking on the word "God" as "the name of an impossible Name" (Nancy, "Dei Paralysis Progressiva" 52). The monotheistic sublation of divine "absencing" thus appears to fail to reach a point of closure. For Nancy, this is most visible in Christianity. Unlike in Judaism and Islam, the Christian God is literally put to death on the cross. The doctrine of God's incarnation has also been read as a retreat of God from Himself, while God's Trinitarian nature prevents Him from being viewed as a sufficient subject or an all-absorbing totality. Yet by withdrawing the ground under God's feet, Christianity paves the way for its own exhaustion. That is what Nancy calls "the deconstruction of Christianity," playing on both senses of the genitive: the deconstruction *of* Christianity (subjective genitive) leads to the deconstruction *of* Christianity (objective genitive). He therefore agrees with Marcel Gauchet: Christianity is "the religion of the egress from religion" (Nancy, *Dis-Enclosure* 146).

This self-deconstruction of the monotheistic divine should not come as a surprise. In "Atheism and Monotheism," Nancy stresses that, insofar as it is not given but posited, a foundation such as the God-*Logos* can only be established as an exception to its own rule – contrary to everything that follows it, it cannot be accounted for on its own terms – or else it sinks into an infinite regression, constantly trying to confirm its principle, the principle of its principle, and so on and so forth (*Dis-Enclosure* 22–23). The unicity of the God of monotheism was therefore condemned to be subsumed by the unity of the principle, to withdraw in the depths of being, thereby facilitating the passage from monotheism to atheism. The sublation of divine "absencing" that gave rise to monotheism carried within itself the seeds of its own exhaustion, and more generally, to quote *Noli me tangere* again, "of what will finally have to abandon

the simplistic alternative of theism or atheism" (108). Given that mainstream atheism has only replaced God with humanist and rationalist placeholders which similarly stand for the *alpha* and *omega* of the world, indeed, it similarly lacks a confirmation of their own principle. In turn, "the very principle of the premise [...] collapses by itself and, in this collapse, signals the possibility, even the requirement of and the call for, a wholly other, anarchic configuration" (24). On Nancy's account, then, if the history of religion in the West is driven by "the necessity of a resurrection that restores both man and God to a common immanence" ("Inoperative Community" 10), as testified by Westerners' repeated attempt at self-founding, this resurrection – or transferal of the identical – however *never quite takes place*.[18]

the *anastasis* of the dead god

It is here that *Noli me tangere* can be seen to be of key significance. In this 2003 essay, Nancy stresses that resurrection need not to be reduced to the return of the Same. He draws attention to an episode from the Gospel of John in which the arisen Jesus instructs Mary Magdalene not to touch him. This instruction is surprising considering that Jesus had never refused to be touched before. Nancy therefore suggests that death must have altered Christ's body, rendering it *untouchable*. He even wonders: "Is it not thus that the dead appear? [...] – [as] the appearing of that which or of he who can no longer properly appear[?]" (Nancy, *Noli me tangere* 28). Evoking Zarathustra's cry that "God remains dead!," Nancy argues that Christ's "*noli me tangere*" testifies to the fact that the dead God remains dead, which leads to a recasting of the Christian thinking of resurrection. The latter should not be seen as death vanquished, that is to say, as the return of the Same, but rather as the raising up – *anastasis*, in Greek – of the dead God. In "Dei Paralysis Progressiva," Nancy had already interpreted Nietzsche's paralysis as the *anastasis* of the one who has passed: "the scene in Turin, shows us someone who 'attended his own funeral twice'" (50). Both the paralysed and arisen body signal the appearing of the disappearing; not the rebirth of the one who has passed, but "the raising of a salute, of an 'adieu'" (Nancy, *Dis-Enclosure* 102).

To be sure, Nancy makes a rod for his own back by using the term *Wink* to speak of this salute. While this term designates a farewell gesture, as illustrated by the "*Winke, Winke*" of German children saying goodbye (Nancy, *Dis-Enclosure* 184), it is also imbued with redemptive potential. Heidegger argues, indeed, that the *Wink* signals the passing *of* the "last god" (*Contributions to Philosophy* 288). Despite his assertion that "Here no redemption takes place" (290), however, Nancy is quick to note that the passing *of* God unfolds as a mere transferal of a self-identical divine from presence to absence, from life to death, thereby dialectically guaranteeing its survival (*Dis-Enclosure* 115).[19] In Nancy's thinking, by contrast, what waves at us is not God Himself but the dead God. Death is the true subject of resurrection. Unlike Heidegger, then, Nancy speaks of the passing *of* God in both senses of the genitive: God passes *and is Himself passed*. Playing on the French word "pas," which refers both to a step and a gesture of negation, he writes that "God is the passerby and the step [*pas*] of the passerby [...] which, in passing, *winkt* and differentiates itself from itself" (Nancy, *Dis-Enclosure* 115). If God, in Nancy's thinking, may still be referred to as the last god, then, it is only "in the sense of extreme, and that extremity, being the extremity of the divine, delivers [*délivre*] the divine from itself in both senses of the expression: it frees it from the theological and disengages it from its own gesture" (114). Nancy thereby breaks with dialectical approaches to the death of God focusing rather on the movement by which God sur-*passes* Himself according to a transcendence "that does not go outside itself in transcending" (*The Muses* 34–35), a *transimmanence*.

Such a return of the Same to its own differen-tiation resonates with the rewriting of Nietzsche's doctrine of the eternal return as a radical contestation of identity popularised by thinkers of the so-called second and third "French moment of Nietzsche" (Le Rider).[20] In *Thus Spoke Zarathustra*, Nietzsche describes eternal recurrence as a working hypothesis encouraging human beings to live their lives in such a way that they would not want anything to be different should they have to relive it (178). As Jeremy Biles eluci-dates in *Ecce Monstrum*, Nietzsche thus lays the ground for "the rationally motivated pro-duction of an identity" (65). In the twentieth century, a number of French thinkers, starting with Pierre Klossowski and Georges Bataille, have however reworked the concept in terms of the return of a differentiating gesture.[21] I argue that Nancy follows in their footsteps by approaching the resurrection of Christ as a metaphor for the fact that nothing ever returns but what does not return, which is another way of saying that nothing remains self-identical in its own return or that, as he stressed as early as in "The Forgetting of Phil-osophy," "difference is what makes identity possible" (64). By locating the divine in the "pas" of the passerby, indeed, Nancy sheds light on the fact that the sense of unity that allows one to speak of the divine in the singular occurs *in* and *as* the passing, through the *anastasis* of the step (*Dis-Enclosure* 115); its conti-nuity unfolds as the Rimbaldian eternity found again through the return of each passing instant (120). A helpful illustration is found in *The Evidence of the Film*, in which Nancy high-lights that the continuity of a film arises from the discontinuation of images coming one after the other (60). I contend that the divine, in Nancy's thinking, similarly unfolds as the eternally recurring step not beyond [*pas au-delà*] God.

Nancy thereby shares Foucault's assessment in "Preface to Transgression" that God's death in the modern world "should [not] be under-stood as the end of his historical reign or as the finally delivered judgement of his nonexis-tence, but as the now constant space of our experience" (31–32), a constancy which should only ever be understood as the eternal return of the discontinuous, as infinite inconstancy. For Nancy, indeed, the Western history of religion unfolds as a process of secularisation through successive unsuccessful dialectical deaths of God. Far from offering some consolation for unhappy consciousness by identifying a foundation on to which humanity can hold, these episodes highlight that gestures of self-founding always carry within themselves "a gesture of an opening or reopening in the direction of what must have preceded all construction" (189). For François Raffoul, this gesture which Nancy calls "dis-enclosure" is extrapolated from Heidegger's *Destruktion*: far from proposing a dialectical ascent towards higher truths, dis-enclosure unfold as "a 'descent,' as Heidegger would write in his 'Letter on Humanism,' into the poverty of essence" (50). Crucially, by exposing the difference or finitude that always already prevents the return of identity, Nancy points at "a future for the world that would no longer be either Christian or anti-Christian, either monotheist or atheist or even polytheist, but that would advance precisely beyond all these categories" (*Dis-Enclosure* 34), beyond all *-theisms*. Hence his assertion that "It is not our concern to save religion, even less to return to it" (1).

postsecular temptations

Nancy's insistence that dis-enclosure is found exemplarily in the self-deconstruction of the *Christian* God however threatens to circumscribe his thinking within a postsecular horizon of determination. As Derrida observes in *On Touching*, following Nancy's deconstruction of Christianity, "Dechristianization will be a Christian victory" (54), thereby guaranteeing Christianity's relevance in the modern world. The fact that Nancy illustrates his rewriting of resurrection by turning to an episode from the Gospel of John also raises the question of whether his approach to the *anastasis* of the dead God should be considered as yet another Christian parabola. This accusation finds strength in the fact that, though Nancy asserts that he stands "completely outside any religion" (*God, Justice, Love, Beauty* 12), he received a Jesuit

education and has been involved in the Jeunesse Etudiante Chrétienne. To be sure, his relationship with Christianity hit a wall in 1956, when Jeunesse Etudiante Chrétienne was condemned by the Pope for its support of the decolonisation of Algeria. "It was an earthquake for all of the activists," Nancy recalls. "The question then became whether to stay or leave" (*The Possibility of a World* 10). Though he claims to have chosen neither option to focus, instead, on the study of "[h]ow and to what degree [...] *we hold* to Christianity" (Nancy, *Dis-Enclosure* 139), his suggestion that "*all* our thought is Christian through and through" (142) seems enough to justify accusations of residual Christianism.

I argue, however, that this interpretation does not withstand an examination of Nancy's recent works. In *Adoration*, in particular, Nancy nuances his position with regards to Christianity by clarifying sentences from *Dis-Enclosure* which he recognises as misleading, such as that which states that "the gesture of deconstruction [...] is only possible within Christianity" (148). He explains that he never meant to imply that deconstruction is essentially Christian but rather wanted to suggest that it is a deeper truth than Christianity found *within* the latter. Building on the Bible study training he received as a youth, which presented the Bible as an infinite reserve of sense, including of sense exceeding institutional teachings, he suggested in one of his first published essays, "Catechism of Perseverance" ["Cathéchisme de persévérance"], that "beyond belonging to the Church, there remain[s] something for which one should persevere" (Nancy, *The Possibility of a World* 12). Four decades later, Nancy continues to draw attention to "the movement that this name [of Christianity] has covered" (*Adoration* 22),[22] in both senses of the term, that is to say, what Christianity, through its ambiguous combination of gestures of self-deconstruction and dialectical attempts at self-founding, included *and* masked, indicated *and* obscured, namely, the fact that the divine fails to inaugurate itself as founding and essential, and that humanity is thereby abandoned to finitude without any possibility of consolation. Nancy's clarification has however largely failed to convince for, as Watkin observes in *Difficult Atheism*, "the very move of discerning in Christianity a truth deeper than itself once more repeats a Christian move, namely the opposition between the outward appearance and the heart (*kardia*) and a preference for the latter" (40). That is not to say that Nancy's "catechism of perseverance" should be seen as a *post-secular* "Rousseauism of Christianity" seeking to *return* to a "purer" version of Christianity (*Dis-Enclosure* 150), but rather that he extrapolates the dis-enclosing gesture from the internal logic of Christianity, as per his Christian education.

One should keep in mind, however, that Nancy identifies deconstruction in other religions than Christianity. As early as in "Of Divine Places," he remarks that Judaism and Islam deny the possibility of *naming* God in much the same way as Christianity. From the mid-1990s, he even describes dis-enclosure as a general structure of religiosity running through every religion, a term which he reserves for institutions of salvation. Commenting on a draft of this paper, he has confirmed that, when it comes to the religious, "I am increasingly telling myself that there is indeed something identical with itself (to speak against Derrida on this point) which returns everywhere and always" (unpublished).[23] This intuition was already visible in "Of Divine Places," where Nancy draws attention to Marion's postsecular dissemination of the divine so that it fits into the modern world and argues that this gesture dissolves into "polyatheism," one being left without "any statement about the divine that can henceforth be distinguished, strictly speaking, from another about 'the subject' (or its 'absence'), 'desire,' 'history,' 'others,' 'the Other,' 'being,' 'speech,' 'the sublime,' 'community,' and so on and so forth" (112). Marion preserves God under an infinite number of names, his definition of the religious thereby "show [ing] by its breadth its insufficiency operating the partition that we expect" (Nancy, "Religion Without Past nor Future" ["Religion sans passé ni avenir"] 2).[24] Yet by criticising

Marion's dissolution of the concept of religion, Nancy demonstrates a desire for a definition of the religious *in the singular*.

Crucially, whereas this definition is usually framed in terms of transcendent belief, that is to say, in terms of adherence to a signifying message, albeit without proof, Nancy focuses on faith understood as trust without postulation, as per the Latin etymology *fides*, which also gave "fidelity." In "The Judeo-Christian," he illustrates the distinction between "faith" and "belief" by drawing attention to two different readings of the story of Abraham, by Paul and James the Less. Paul, Nancy observes, focuses on the fact that Abraham *believed* that God could give him a son, "[h]is act thus depended on a knowledge postulate" (*Dis-Enclosure* 53). James, by contrast, emphasises the fact that Abraham decided to offer Isaac in sacrifice without postulating anything. "In a certain sense," Nancy notes, "James's Abraham believes nothing" (53). Unlike belief, faith is about being disposed to trust what remains unavailable, to let go of assurance. This recalls Christ's instruction to Mary Magdalene. Turning to the Greek of John, Nancy remarks in *Noli me tangere* that the phrase "*Me mou haptou*" implies a refusal of being *held back* from passing. Christ's instruction may therefore be translated thus: "don't try to touch or to hold back what essentially distances itself" (16). Christ calls Mary Magdalene to respect *the infinite passing of the identical*. In "Religion Without Past nor Future" ["Religion sans passé ni avenir"], Nancy argues that this "somehow non-religious truth of religion" (3), "is unknown to no form of religion in the West, including Islam, nor to Buddhism, Hinduism or Shintoism" (4). He even identifies faith in activities as diverse as the practice of music, the commitment to a social cause or the raising of a child. To be sure, these activities may be performed according to calculating determinations, much as religions tend to obscure their faithful heart with gestures of self-founding, such as the establishment of transcendent beliefs. Only when these activities come with a withdrawal of assurance, opening "a world without religion if we understand by this word the observance of behaviours and representations that respond to a claim for [...] assurance, destination, accomplishment" (Nancy, *Adoration* 39), may they be considered as *faith-ful*. From this, Derrida should have deduced that there can be no "victory" in Nancy's thinking. There is no religion to return to, only the opening to the withdrawal of ground.

The question remains, however, whether this faithful gesture is guilty of establishing itself as a new foundation. We have already noted that referring to the religious as a universal anthropological category is an ethnocentric move which flattens out the plurality of the religious through an artificial but comforting privileging of the principle of identity. The question therefore arises whether, by dodging one postsecular bullet, namely, the recuperation within the limits of a given religious revelation (here, Christianity), Nancy is hit by another one, namely, the identification, like Heidegger before him, of a general structure of revealability found at the heart of, and conditioning, every revelation. As Derrida explains, according to Heidegger, "[f]or some revelation to take place, *Dasein* must be able to open itself to revelation and this revealability [*Offenbarkeit*, in German] is, let's say, ontologically – not chronologically, not logically – prior to *Offenbarung*, to revelation" (Sherwood and Hart 43). Derrida denounces this move as a dialectical return to religion by means of "a theology with and without God" ("How to Avoid Speaking" 128), without the God of *Offenbarung*, but with the prime mover that is *Offenbarkeit*, whom Heidegger associates with the figure of the "last god" (*Contributions to Philosophy* 289). Derrida warned Nancy against this trap: "Are you not, in some way, replacing the fullness of the unique god of monotheism by the opening to which this god must himself yield?" (Derrida and Nancy 76). In line with Heidegger, Nancy does describe faith as *openness* to the unavailable and even writes in *Dis-Enclosure* that, through the self-deconstruction of God, "what is revealed is the revealable" (148).[25] Does his approach to faith in the singular fall guilty of erecting a new natural religion of the Open with a capital O, then?

a singular plurality

I argue that an answer to this question is found in "The Judeo-Christian." Insofar as he approaches faith as *trust without postulation*, Nancy decisively breaks with both *Offenbarkeit* and *Offenbarung* as structures of *unveiling*. Faith, in Nancy's thinking, is not even between or before the decision for the primacy of *Offenbarung* or *Offenbarkeit*, as Derrida's *khôra* arguably still is through the suspension of these two poles in undecidability.[26] Rather, it is otherwise than this decision; it is the act of decision itself, the authentically free act of decision that breaks with presupposition and all criteria of decision, which Nancy has called "the decision of existence" ("The Decision of Existence" 82). Nancy's thinking, much as James's epistle, does not postulate anything, including about the supposed essence of faith. It does even not carry within itself the possibility, albeit suspended, of an unveiling to come. Rather, it is "wholly given over [...] to the act of faith" (Nancy, *Dis-Enclosure* 48).

Nancy does however still speak of faith *in the singular*. This should not come as a surprise given that, as an attitude of fidelity to the infinite passing of the identical, Nancean faith necessarily shares the latter's *continuous discontinuity*. I contend that the sense of continuity that justifies Nancy's approach to faith in the singular arises from the recurring performation of singular acts of faith – in the plural. In *Being Singular Plural*, Nancy does remark that, in Latin, *singuli* only exists in the plural for singularity "designates the 'one' as belonging to 'one by one.' The singular is primarily *each* one and, therefore, also *with* and *among* all the others" (32). This resonates with his refusal to subsume singular artforms, from photography and poetry to music, portraiture and dance, into a unified theory of Art with a capital A. If one cannot deny that a sense of continuity emerges from the plurality of singular artforms, Nancy remarks in "Arts Make Themselves Against Each Other" ["Les arts se font les uns contre les autres"] that "this identity [...] is only formed by the ensemble of practices in all their differences, without this 'ensemble' absorbing even a little bit their heterogeneity" (164).[27] I argue that this may be extrapolated to Nancy's thinking of faith. He did recently admit that, for him, the religious in the singular is "something identical with itself [...] which *returns everywhere and always*" (unpublished).[28] Nancean faith does not, therefore, carry the possibility of redemption: it does not "save" God from passing by establishing the primacy of *Offenbarkeit*, the Open with a capital O, but rather accompanies God's infinite passage through the eternal recurrence of singular acts of faith, in the plural. It thereby proves faithful to – and echoes – the divine *adieu*, waving goodbye in turn, in the form of what Derrida has called a "*salut* [...] without salvation" (*On Touching* 310).

This explains Nancy's assertion in "Of Divine Places" that, in his thinking, "There is no return of the religious: there are the contortions and the turgescence of its exhaustion" (136). In *Difficult Atheism*, Watkin reads this sentence stands as an assertion that there will or should be a *complete* exhaustion of religion and argues that "Nancy [...] must finally acknowledge the impossibility of atheism's 'last step' to completion and consistency, and thereby come up short of a post-theological integration" (123). It should now be clear, however, that completion and consistency were never what Nancy looked for. He has recently clarified that, though he stands by his assertion that "an open world is [...] a world without religion" (Nancy, *Adoration* 39), he understands that one may feel the need to use the name "God." "Why even outside of religion is it not so easy to do without naming god in one way or another?" Nancy asks in *God, Justice, Love, Beauty* (16). "Because it [...] is necessary to be able to address oneself to or to relate to this dimension [i.e., the passing of the identical]" (16). Far from vouching for the disappearance of all transcendent religions, then, Nancy admits that there must still be institutions, structures and scaffoldings (Forestier).[29] Yet he calls us to cultivate the continuously discontinuous experience of the religious exhaustion of religion *from within these institutional*

constructions through the repeated performation of singular acts of faith. By shedding light on the fact that difference is what makes identity possible, Nancy draws our attention to the *struction* in "construction": "it is not 'construction' if the 'con-' designates architectonic reason [...] It is a jumble or an 'agglomeration' [...] in which all goes in every direction" (Forestier). Constructions including institutional religions are only ever the sum of a *plurality* of *singular* acts of faith that always already – and must unceasingly again – challenge what is too often perceived as the unity of their edifice. For Nancy, then, one should never take values, dogmas or institutions for granted for:

> the truth of "god" awaits us elsewhere than in fetishism [...], truly elsewhere, to the infinite [...] The "infinite" is nothing huge or unreachable. It is simply this: to settle for nothing determined, fixed, identified, named with a supposedly proper name. ("God, Charlie, Nobody" ["Dieu, Charlie, Personne"])[30,31]

I argue that Nancy thus offers a way out of the definitional impasse evoked in the introduction: one can still speak of religion in the singular(-plural), without compromising its diversity. Both immanent and transcendent forms of religiosity do have a place in Nancy's thinking, yet only to the extent that one keeps *acting* in such a way that they are not left to close in on themselves, whether on a dogmatic structure or a supposed "essence" of religion. Nancy thereby lays the ground for an inclusive religious coexistence, at least more so than that currently secured by secularism – he provides us with "an elementary guide for the use of all in a secular regime of denominational plurality," as he puts it in "God, Charlie, Nobody" ["Dieu, Charlie, Personne"] – while countering the dogmatism and universalism that feeds post(-)secular currents today.

What one should learn from Nancy's thinking up to its most recent developments, then, is *not* that the so-called "return of religion" in the contemporary world does not deserve much attention. It would be a mistake to assume that

Nancy's understanding of the "return" is limited to the return to identity, just as it is a mistake to assume that the phenomenon referred to as the "return of religion" merely consists of the dialectical resurgence of the Same, a step backwards in history. Nancy makes really clear that the "return of religion" *should* be carefully studied and appreciated for the way in which it breaks with the logic of the return of the Same and testifies to an eternal return of difference which, paraphrasing Nancy, open religion to the limitlessness that constitutes its truth (*Dis-Enclosure* 1). I argue that recognising this is necessary in order to understand that contemporary spiritual developments – and the secularisation of which they are a manifestation – participate in a radical transformation of the Western understanding of the term "religion." I therefore make the case that Nancy should be considered as a most rigorous thinker of the (eternal) return of religion, in the singular-plural.

echo by jean-luc nancy

I am infinitely grateful to Marie Chabbert for having grasped so well the finest and sharpest extremity of the effort which consists in continuing to pursue – to persevere, I would say, using a term formerly used by the "catechism of perseverance" (the catechism of those who wished to pursue further instruction after completing the formation required in preparation for communion and subsequently confirmation, i.e., complete integration into the church – the Catholic as well as the Protestant one, with a few variations). To persevere, not in staging a return, but in the tension and desire for an "eternal return" of nothing less than – if I may say so – eternity itself. The one that Rimbaud says was found again in "the sea mingled with the sun." In other words, perhaps a night and an engulfment – but isn't it precisely to a night, a non-knowledge, a sensibility of the insensible that one must be waking up?

If what disappeared with "God" is the representation of a power (*puissance*) and origin – so, stripped of this representation and with it of all representation, we reach an abandonment that cannot but have to do with the mystical demands of triple monotheism (and, *mutatis mutandis*, of Buddhism, which could very well be its oriental version). I indeed mean demands, not necessarily outpourings. When Meister Eckhart prays to keep us "free of God," he is less adopting an approach centred around outpouring than one of rigour. To be delivered from God means to experience that "something other than thought itself can be manifested in thought" (according to a formula by Valéry, a non-religious spirit if ever there was one). In a sense, this sentence takes up or replays Anselm's argument, from which the absurd "proof for the existence of God" was drawn and so well dismantled by Kant.

We are no longer in the order of predicating anything of the subject by way of attributes, we are beyond language and conceptuality but at the heart of what animates and drives them: an experience, not of transcendence, but of being pushed, projected beyond what can be grasped and beyond being, we are instead ourselves grasped and carried away.

Now, the situation today – for Western man, but what is not Western nowadays? – is the impossibility of this experience; or rather, and this is more serious, its transformation into the experience of man being surpassed in a "transhuman," designating nothing other than the techno-economic expansion of a self-productive and self-consuming – in other words, self-destructive – machine.

Of course, this could mean that human experience has had its time, and with it
all that has suffered its misery.
But even that, even a last breath
could still let itself be carried
away divinely ... nowhere.

disclosure statement

No potential conflict of interest was reported by the author.

notes

1 All emphases in quotes are in the original sources, except where indicated otherwise.

2 See Billington 1–8.

3 On the question of whether the appellation "New Age" should be reserved for the spiritual movement which developed in the 1970s and disappeared twenty years later or should be extended to these recent forms of spiritual commitments, see MacKian 7 and Kemp 179.

4 I translate all the quotes from Bidar's work.

5 See, for instance, Lopez, Taylor, Latour, Benkirane, and Feneuil and Schmitt.

6 A similar play on hyphenation has been used to distinguish the "post-colonial" from the "postcolonial" (see Hiddleston 3–4 and Shohat 101), and in relation to other "posts," including post(-)modernism and post(-)structuralism (see Bennington and Derrida, "Some Statements and Truisms about Neologisms").

7 On the parallel between the Freudian "return of the repressed" and the return of religion, see Derrida, "Faith and Knowledge" 62 and Mercier.

8 See McCaffrey.

9 My translation.

10 My translation.

11 As many have noted – and criticised – Marion identifies the phenomenological regime of revelation with Christian theophany by designating the latter as universally accessible (see, for instance, Janicaud and Caputo); a dangerous move which threatens to redirect Marion's trajectory from postsecularism to post-secularism.

12 Translation altered.

13 In secular societies, this frame is kept ajar: one is free to believe in a transcendent divine, provided that this remains a private matter. Not everyone agrees on what the private sphere includes in this specific case, though, as demonstrated by the debates surrounding the right for women to wear a veil when accompanying school trips in France.

14 See Hegel 475–76.

15 See Kapferer 341–44 and Engelke 292–301.

16 See Watkin 2.

17 My translation.

18 See *The Speculative Remark* 17.

19 Heidegger's residual attachment to the possibility of redemption is visible in his assertion in 1966 that "Only a god can save us" ("Only a God Can Save Us" 57; see Greisch 261). It might also account for the banality of Heidegger's drift towards Nazism's project to facilitate the restoration of the supposedly lost pure Aryan community, as Nancy puts it using Arendt's terms (*The Banality of Heidegger*).

20 My translation.

21 For more details, see Le Rider 194–99.

22 Translation altered. I contend that John McKeane's translation of the original "recouvert" in French by "named" fails to account for the twofold meaning of the term in French, which is however intended to reflect the ambiguity of Christianity's position "at the heart of the disenclosure just as it is at the center of the enclosure" (Nancy, *Dis-Enclosure* 10).

23 My translation. See Derrida, "Faith and Knowledge" 72–73.

24 All the quotes from Nancy's "Religion Without Past nor Future" ["Religion sans passé ni avenir"] article are mine.

25 Also see Derrida and Nancy 81.

26 For more details on Nancy's critique of Derrida's undecidability, see "Of Divine Places" 120 and Derrida, Lacoue-Labarthe, and Nancy 93–94.

27 My translation.

28 My emphasis.

29 I translate all the quotes from Forestier's interview.

30 I translate all the quotes from Nancy's article.

31 That is no easy task, however. Nancy himself has been accused of cultivating Christian exemplarism (see, for instance, Watkin 120). To be sure, that Nancy mainly focuses on Christianity is understandable given his intellectual background. Yet that it took him no less than twenty-three years – from 1995, when the first article later collected in *Dis-Enclosure*, namely, "The Deconstruction of Christianity" was published, to the publication of "Religion Without Past nor Future" ["Religion sans passé ni avenir"] in 2018 – to extend his conclusions regarding the deconstruction of Christianity and the gesture of dis-

enclosure to non-Abrahamic traditions testifies to his unavowed – and perhaps even unconscious – willingness to keep a certain place for the mono-theistic – a fortiori Christian – divine.

bibliography

Asad, Talal. *Genealogies of Religion: Discipline and Reasons of Power in Christianity and Islam.* Baltimore: Johns Hopkins UP, 1993. Print.

Benkirane, Reda. *Islam, à la reconquête du sens.* Paris: Le Pommier, 2017. Print.

Bennington, Geoffrey. "Post." *Cross-References.* Ed. David Kelley and Isabelle Llasera. London: Society for French Studies, 1986. 65–73. Print.

Bidar, Abdennour. *L'Islam face à la mort de Dieu: Actualité de Mohammed Iqbal.* Paris: François Bourin, 2010. Print.

Biles, Jeremy. *Ecce Monstrum: Georges Bataille and the Sacrifice of Form.* New York: Fordham UP, 2007. Print.

Billington, Ray. *Understanding Eastern Philosophy.* London: Routledge, 1997. Print.

Caputo, John D. "The Hyperbolization of Phenomenology: Two Possibilities for Religion in Recent Continental Philosophy." *Counter-Experiences: Reading Jean-Luc Marion.* Ed. Kevin Hart. Notre Dame: U of Notre Dame P, 2007. 67–93. Print.

Deleuze, Gilles. *Nietzsche and Philosophy.* Trans. Hugh Tomlinson. London: Continuum, 2002. Print.

Deleuze, Gilles. "On the Death of Man and Superman." *Foucault.* Trans. Seán Hand. London: U of Minnesota P, 1988. 124–32. Print.

Derrida, Jacques. "Faith and Knowledge: The Two Sources of 'Religion' at the Limits of Reason Alone." Trans. Samuel Weber. *Acts of Faith.* Ed. Gil Anidjar. New York: Routledge, 2002. 42–101. Print.

Derrida, Jacques. "How to Avoid Speaking: Denials." Trans. Ken Frieden. *Derrida and Negative Theology.* Ed. Harold Coward and Toby Foshay. Albany: SUNY P, 1992. 73–142. Print.

Derrida, Jacques. *On Touching – Jean-Luc Nancy.* Trans. Christine Irizarry. Stanford: Stanford UP, 2005. Print.

Derrida, Jacques. *Paper Machine.* Trans. Rachel Bowlby. Stanford: Stanford UP, 2005. Print.

Derrida, Jacques. "Some Statements and Truisms about Neologisms, Newisms, Postisms, Parasitisms, and Other Small Seisms." *The States of "Theory."* Ed. David Carroll. New York: Columbia UP, 1990. 63–94. Print.

Derrida, Jacques, Philippe Lacoue-Labarthe, and Jean-Luc Nancy. "Dialogue entre Jacques Derrida, Philippe Lacoue-Labarthe et Jean-Luc Nancy." *Rue Descartes* 52.2 (2006): 86–99. Print.

Derrida, Jacques, and Jean-Luc Nancy. "Responsibility – Of the Sense to Come." *For Strasbourg: Conversations of Friendship and Philosophy.* Trans. and ed. Pascale-Anne Brault and Michael Naas. New York: Fordham UP, 2014. 56–86. Print.

de Vries, Hent. *Philosophy and the Turn to Religion.* Baltimore: Johns Hopkins UP, 1999. Print.

Engelke, Matthew. "Christianity and the Anthropology of Secular Humanism." *Current Anthropology* 55.10 (2014): 292–301. Print.

Esposito, Roberto. "Chair et corps dans la déconstruction du christianisme." *Sens en tous sens: Autour des travaux de Jean-Luc Nancy.* Ed. Francis Guibal and Jean-Clet Martin. Paris: Galilée, 2004. 153–64. Print.

Falque, Emmanuel. *The Metamorphosis of Finitude: An Essay on Birth and Resurrection.* Trans. George Hughes. New York: Fordham UP, 2012. Print.

Feneuil, Anthony, and Yann Schmitt, eds. "L'incroyance religieuse." *ThéoRèmes* 5 (2013). Print.

Forestier, Florian. "Entretien avec Jean-Luc Nancy (1): autour de *Dans quels mondes vivons-nous?*" *Actu Philosophia* 22.04 (2012): n. pag. Web. 6 May 2018. <http://www.actu-philosophia.com/entretien-avec-jean-luc-nancy-1-autour-de-dans/>.

Foucault, Michel. "Preface to Transgression." Trans. Donald F. Bouchard and Sherry Simon. *Language, Counter-Memory, Practice: Selected Essays and Interviews.* Ed. Donald F. Bouchard. Ithaca: Cornell UP, 1977. 29–52. Print.

Gauchet, Marcel. *The Disenchantment of the World: A Political History of Religion.* Trans. Oscar Burge. Princeton: Princeton UP, 1997. Print.

Greisch, Jean. "The Poverty of Heidegger's 'Last God.'" *French Interpretations of Heidegger: An Exceptional Reception*. Ed. David Pettigrew and François Raffoul. Albany: SUNY P, 2008. 245–64. Print.

Halbertal, Moshe, and Avishai Margalit. *Idolatry*. Cambridge, MA: Harvard UP, 1992. Print.

Hegel, Georg W.F. *Phenomenology of Spirit*. Trans. A.V. Miller. Oxford: Oxford UP, 2004. Print.

Heidegger, Martin. *Contributions to Philosophy (From Enowning)*. Trans. and ed. Parvis Emad and Kenneth Maly. Bloomington: Indiana UP, 1999. Print.

Heidegger, Martin. *Identity and Difference*. Trans. Joan Stambaugh. New York: Harper, 1969. Print.

Heidegger, Martin. "Only a God Can Save Us." Trans. William Richardson. *Heidegger: The Man and the Thinker*. Ed. Thomas Sheehan. Chicago: Precedent, 1981. 4–67. Print.

Hiddleston, Jane. *Understanding Postcolonialism*. London: Routledge, 2009. Print.

Janicaud, Dominique. *Le Tournant théologique de la phénoménologie française*. Combas: Editions de l'Éclat, 1991. Print.

Kapferer, Bruce. "Anthropology. The Paradox of the Secular." *Social Anthropology* 9.3 (2001): 341–44. Print.

Kemp, Daren. *New Age: A Guide*. Edinburgh: Edinburgh UP, 2004. Print.

Latour, Bruno. "'Thou Shall Not Freeze-Frame,' or, How Not to Misunderstand the Science and Religion Debate." *Science, Religion, and the Human Experience*. Ed. James D. Proctor. Oxford: Oxford UP, 2005. 27–48. Print.

Le Rider, Jacques. *Nietzsche en France. De la fin du XIXème siècle au temps présent*. Paris: Presses Universitaires de France, 1999. Print.

Lopez, Donald S. "Belief." *Critical Terms for Religious Studies*. Ed. Mark C. Taylor. Chicago: U of Chicago P, 1998. 21–35. Print.

Lyotard, Jean-François. *La Phénoménologie*. "Que sais-je?" Paris: Presses Universitaires de France, 1999. Print.

MacKian, Sara. *Everyday Spirituality: Social and Spatial Worlds of Enchantment*. New York: Palgrave Macmillan, 2012. Print.

Marion, Jean-Luc. *Being Given: Towards a Phenomenology of Givenness*. Trans. Jeffrey L. Kosky. Stanford: Stanford UP, 2002. Print.

Marion, Jean-Luc. "L'événement, le phénomène et le révélé." *Transversalités* 70 (1999): 4–26. Print.

McCaffrey, Enda. *The Return of Religion in France. From Democratisation to Postmetaphysics*. New York: Palgrave Macmillan, 2009. Print.

Mercier, Thomas Clément. "Pensées magiques: Retour sur le 'retour du religieux.'" *L'à venir de la religion. Revue ITER* 1 (2018): n. pag. Web. 3 Feb. 2019. <http://lire-travailler-derrida.org/revue/thomas-clement-mercier-pensees-magiques-retour-sur-le-retour-du-religieux/>.

Milbank, John. *Theology and Social Theory: Beyond Secular Reason*. Oxford: Basil Blackwell, 1990. Print.

Nancy, Jean-Luc. *Adoration. The Deconstruction of Christianity, I*. Trans. John McKeane. New York: Fordham UP, 2013. Print.

Nancy, Jean-Luc. *The Banality of Heidegger*. Trans. Jeff Fort. New York: Fordham UP, 2017. Print.

Nancy, Jean-Luc. *Being Singular Plural*. Trans. Robert D. Richardson and Anne E. O'Byrne. Stanford: Stanford UP, 2000. Print.

Nancy, Jean-Luc. "Catéchisme de persévérance." *Esprit* 364.10 (1967): 368–81. Print.

Nancy, Jean-Luc. "The Decision of Existence." Trans. Thomas Harrison. *The Birth to Presence*. Ed. Werner Hamacher and David E. Wellbery. Stanford: Stanford UP, 1993. 82–109. Print.

Nancy, Jean-Luc. "Dei Paralysis Progressiva." Trans. Thomas Harrison. *The Birth to Presence*. Ed. Werner Hamacher and David E. Wellbery. Stanford: Stanford UP, 1993. 48–57. Print.

Nancy, Jean-Luc. "Dieu, Charlie, Personne." *Mediapart* 27.01 (2015): n. pag. Web. 6 May 2018. <https://blogs.mediapart.fr/edition/les-invites-de-mediapart/article/270115/dieu-charlie-personne>.

Nancy, Jean-Luc. *Dis-Enclosure. The Deconstruction of Christianity, I*. Trans. Bettina Bergo, Gabriel Malenfant, and Michael B. Smith. New York: Fordham UP, 2008. Print.

Nancy, Jean-Luc. *The Evidence of the Film – Abbas Kiarostami*. Trans. Christine Irizarry and Verena

Andermatt Conley. Bruxelles: Yves Gevaert, 2001. Print.

Nancy, Jean-Luc. "The Forgetting of Philosophy." Trans. François Raffoul and Gregory Recco. *The Gravity of Thought*. Atlantic Highlands: Humanities, 1997. 7–74. Print.

Nancy, Jean-Luc. *God, Justice, Love, Beauty*. Trans. Sarah Clift. New York: Fordham UP, 2011. Print.

Nancy, Jean-Luc. "The Inoperative Community." Trans. Peter Connor, Lisa Garbus, Michael Holland, and Simona Sawhney. *The Inoperative Community*. Ed. Peter Connor. Minneapolis: U of Minnesota P, 1991. 1–42. Print.

Nancy, Jean-Luc. "Les arts se font les uns contre les autres." *Les Muses*. Paris: Galilée, 1994. 161–74. Print.

Nancy, Jean-Luc. *The Muses*. Trans. Peggy Kamuf. Stanford: Stanford UP, 1996. Print.

Nancy, Jean-Luc. *Noli me tangere: On the Raising of the Body*. Trans. Sarah Clift, Pascale-Anne Brault, and Michael Naas. New York: Fordham UP, 2008. Print.

Nancy, Jean-Luc. "Of Divine Places." Trans. Peter Connor, Lisa Garbus, Michael Holland, and Simona Sawhney. *The Inoperative Community*. Ed. Peter Connor. Minneapolis: U of Minnesota P, 1991. 110–50. Print.

Nancy, Jean-Luc. "One Day, the Gods Withdraw …" Trans. Robert Bononno. *Expectation: Philosophy, Literature*. New York: Fordham UP, 2018. 25–31. Print.

Nancy, Jean-Luc. *The Possibility of a World: Conversations with Pierre-Philippe Jandin*. Trans. Travis Holloway and Flor Méchain. New York: Fordham UP, 2017. Print.

Nancy, Jean-Luc. "Religion sans passé ni avenir." *L'à venir de la religion, Revue ITER* 1 (2018): n. pag. Web. 6 Feb. 2019. <http://lire-travailler-derrida.org/revue/religion-sans-passe-ni-avenir/>.

Nancy, Jean-Luc. *The Speculative Remark: One of Hegel's Bon Mots*. Trans. Céline Surprenant. Stanford: Stanford UP, 2001. Print.

Nancy, Jean-Luc, Alena Alexandrova, Ignaas Devisch, Laurens ten Kate, and Aukje van Rooden. "On Dis-enclosure and Its Gesture, Adoration: A Concluding Dialogue with Jean-Luc Nancy." *Re-treating Religion: Deconstructing Christianity with Jean-Luc Nancy*. Ed. Alena Alexandrova, Ignaas Devisch, Laurens ten Kate, and Aukje van Rooden. New York: Fordham UP, 2012. 304–44. Print.

Nietzsche, Friedrich. *The Gay Science*. Trans. Josephine Nauckhoff. Ed. Bernard Williams. Cambridge: Cambridge UP, 2007. Print.

Nietzsche, Friedrich. *Thus Spoke Zarathustra*. Trans. Adrian Del Caro. Ed. Adrian Del Caro and Robert B. Pippin. Cambridge: Cambridge UP, 2006. Print.

Raffoul, François. "The Self-Deconstruction of Christianity." *Re-treating Religion: Deconstructing Christianity with Jean-Luc Nancy*. Ed. Alena Alexandrova, Ignaas Devisch, Laurens ten Kate, and Aukje van Rooden. New York: Fordham UP, 2012. 46–62. Print.

Scott, Michael. "What I'm Reading: The Anthropology of Ontology." *Journal of the Royal Anthropological Institute* 19 (2013): 859–72. Print.

Sherwood, Yvonne, and Kevin Hart, eds. *Derrida and Religion: Other Testaments*. New York: Routledge, 2005. Print.

Shohat, Ella. "Notes on the 'Post-Colonial.'" *Social Text* 31–32 (1992): 99–113. Print.

Taylor, Charles. *A Secular Age*. Cambridge, MA: Harvard UP, 2007. Print.

Watkin, Christopher. *Difficult Atheism. Post-Theological Thinking in Alain Badiou, Jean-Luc Nancy and Quentin Meillassoux*. Edinburgh: Edinburgh UP, 2011. Print.

nancy against the emancipation narrative

It is not an uncommon view, and it is one fuelled in part by Nancy himself, that his thought is inimical to an agenda of radical emancipation. Two of his most explicit engagements with emancipation can be found in a 2009 interview entitled "Le sens de l'histoire a été suspendu" ["The Meaning/Direction of History has been Suspended"] ("Le sens de l'histoire")[1] and a passage in *The Possibility of a World* (*La Possibilité d'un monde*; *The Possibility of a World*) both of which distance him from even a lukewarm embrace of emancipation. In the course of the former interview he affirms that the modern narrative of "history represented as the emancipation of humanity" – the narrative that began with the Enlightenment, endured through the workers' struggles of the nineteenth century and survived two World Wars – has now come to an end.

What Nancy has in mind here is the "emancipation narrative" discussed by Jean-François Lyotard in *The Postmodern Condition* and elsewhere ("Memorandum"; *The Hyphen*; "Randbemerkungen"; *The Postmodern Explained*). This narrative is in fact told in two different ways that, for ease of identification, we can label "long" and "short." The long emancipation narrative stretches back to the ancient world, tracing the roots of our emancipatory paradigm to Paul, Augustine and beyond to the Hebrew exodus and Christian models of salvation (Lyotard and Gruber, *The Hyphen* 6). The shorter version, equally insistent on the central importance of liberation both for individual and corporate identity, dates from the Enlightenment and the revolutions of the late

christopher watkin

NANCY IS A THINKER OF RADICAL EMANCIPATION

eighteenth century. Lyotard treats the long and short emancipation narratives alongside each other in a "Missive on Universal History" written to Mathias Khan in November 1984:

The thought and action of the nineteenth and twentieth centuries are governed by an Idea (in the Kantian sense): the Idea of emancipation. It is, of course, framed in quite different ways, depending on what we call the philosophies of history, the grand narratives that attempt to organize this mass of events: the Christian narrative of the redemption of original sin through love; the Aufklärer narrative of emancipation from ignorance and servitude through knowledge and egalitarianism; the speculative narrative of the realization of the universal idea through the dialectic of the concrete; the Marxist narrative of emancipation from exploitation and alienation through the socialization of work; and the capitalist narrative of emancipation from poverty through technological development. Between these narratives there are grounds for litigation and even for difference. But in all of them, the givens arising from events are situated in the course of a history whose end, even if it remains beyond reach, is called universal freedom, the fulfillment of all humanity. (*The Postmodern Explained* 25)

As Lyotard argues here, the emancipation narrative spans the political spectrum and remains decisive throughout the post-Enlightenment era. It is, as Charles Taylor later argued, the way in which the West as a whole, and Western individuals, understand themselves (28–29): as those who have been liberated from a series of historical oppressions and constraints, from slavery and superstition, patriarchy and poverty.

This emancipation narrative runs as a fault line through recent French philosophy, with thinkers such as Alain Badiou and Jacques Rancière foregrounding the theme of emancipation in their accounts of everything from ontology and politics to art and science. On the other side of the fault line we find an unlikely coalition including Michel Foucault, Gilles Deleuze, Jacques Derrida, Bruno Latour and strands of speculative realism that resist or problematise the emancipation narrative in a variety of ways. Let us begin this investigation into Nancy's attitude to emancipation by preliminarily situating him in the latter group, though as we shall shortly see this designation is of only heuristic value, and his rejection of the emancipation narrative is far from straightforward.

Nancy details three decisive hammer blows that have driven the nails into the coffin of the emancipation narrative. The first is the demise of the assumption that historical progress is inevitable. This fantasy was nourished by a theory of historical ruptures, sometimes understood as linear and sometimes dialectical, each one interrupting the smooth flow of history and creating a decisive "before" and "after" in terms of which progress can be measured. In *Dis-Enclosure*, Nancy calls these moments "Christmas projections" (*La Déclosion* 121; *Dis-Enclosure* 145), modelled as they are on the incarnation of the second person of the Christian Trinity into a first-century artisanal family: a decisive intervention in history that changes everything and propels history itself forwards. We can call this the "progress as rupture" thesis. It tells "the illusion of an edifying tale of the liberation of modern reason, rising forth fully armed out of Bacon or Galileo's head and reconquering by its strength alone the whole terrain that was in thrall to metaphysical belief," a story which "is doubtless the most tenacious and insidious illusion ever to be concealed in the nooks of our many discourses" (*La Déclosion* 17; *Dis-Enclosure* 7).

This assumption of inevitable progress characterised the post-war left throughout the *Trente Glorieuses*, but for Nancy it has now run its course. To the question "What has ended?," he replies

> History represented as the emancipation of humanity. The direction and meaning [*sens*] of history has been suspended, and this suspension is not provisional. I am not saying that history won't start again, otherwise. But to be on the left was to feel that you were participating in a history and a story [*histoire*] that was progressing, year in year out, towards the possibility of greater social justice, and a more just, happy and peaceful society. We were in a democratic and humanist bubble that was paradoxically inherited from the cold war, and that has not outlasted it. (Nancy, "Le sens de l'histoire")

It is with the events of 1968, Nancy continues, that the change began to become apparent; this was the moment when, instead of aspiring to a better future, the protesters focused on questioning the present, leading eventually to the

Punk slogan "no future" and to a dark and tragic version of history ("Le sens de l'histoire"). We have lost the idea of progress, the "dorsal fin of humanism" that led the militant to sacrifice "all his present life – affectionate, sexual, artistic, sensitive – to the service of a future project" ("Le sens de l'histoire").

The second hammer blow to the emancipation narrative exposes it as perversely oppressive. It fetishises emancipation itself, according it an ultimate, ossified and unchanging meaning, elevating it to the status of a brute, self-justifying dogma that can be neither questioned nor modified (see Nancy, "Le sens de l'histoire"), and that therefore participates in the very logic of closure to which it superficially tries to oppose itself. From this perspective, the ideology of the free individual is just as immanent and closed as the totalitarian communities from which the emancipation narrative assumed it had won freedom. In *The Inoperative Community*, Nancy explains that both totalitarianism and the ideology of the free individual are products of the auto-production of identity, individual auto-production in the case of emancipated autonomy, and communal auto-production in the case of totalitarian or exclusionary collectivities (*La Communauté désœuvrée* 14; *The Inoperative Community* 2–3). The autonomous individual and the community of those who have something in common are both instances of the auto-production of identity, and both deny singular-plural being.

Allied to this logic of closure, the third and final death blow to the modern emancipation narrative is that it assumes the essence of the individual to be liberated. In the 2009 interview Nancy gives a concrete example of this assumption, along with the difficulties it encounters:

> We assumed that emancipation would make people more fraternal, friendly, and dispose them to the free creation of forms of life and art. In *The German Ideology* Marx imagines a world where the labourer can work in a forge in the morning and play the violin in the afternoon. That implicitly meant that there was an essence of man waiting to be

discovered. This dream was in very small part realised with paid holidays. And yet, are we so sure about this human essence? Or take the medical technology that has freed us from illness, suffering, and the brevity of life. When a new heart was grafted into my body, my life was extended by eighteen years; very good. But, in the final analysis, from where do we get the idea that duration is an end in itself? Some will say "yes, but it's more life," but lives become weighed down when there is too much treatment, too many chemicals. We could say: we shouldn't live so that we can be in good health, but we should be in good health so that we can live. ("Le sens de l'histoire"; see also *L'Adoration* 13; *Adoration* 4–5; *La Possibilité d'un monde* 65–66; *The Possibility of a World* 64)

The modern emancipation narrative assumes, indeed it must assume, that it knows who is to be liberated, and therefore what sort of liberation is required, but for Nancy this is both presumptive and far from obvious.

Not only is this human essence assumed, however, it is also created by the modern drive for emancipation (Nancy, *L'Adoration* 13; *Adoration* 5). Requiring a human essence that it could emancipate from its presumed shackles, modernity obliged by reverse engineering a figure of the human entirely exposed to itself, whose truth is apparent to itself. Only this figure was capable of the emancipation that modernity mandated for it, because its self-transparency made both the means and goal of its emancipation conveniently unambiguous. Modernity required the essence of liberated humanity to be generally agreed upon, but in reality, this essence proved stubbornly elusive to articulate: "[i]n the ancient world, when a slave was emancipated we knew *who* was coming into the picture as a 'free man' [...] When modern man emancipates himself, he does not know *who* he is bringing into the picture" (*L'Adoration* 13; *Adoration* 5; trans. mod.).

So for Nancy the modern emancipation narrative stands under the threefold condemnation of promoting progress through rupture, entertaining a logic of closure, and assuming the essence of humanity, complicating its simple emancipatory story with a counter-narrative of oppression and enclosure. The hammer blows to the emancipation narrative, it turns out, were struck by its own hand.

These arguments, combined with the relative scarcity of the explicit lexicon of emancipation in Nancy's œuvre, has led some to consider his thought inimical to the idea. Alain Badiou, for example, holds Nancy's finitude – his refusal to embrace a fixed essence of the human to be liberated and the refusal of a closed meaning of emancipation – to foreclose any emancipatory aspirations:

> Let it be said and proclaimed: that with which we must urgently break, that with which we must have done, is finitude [...] In the motif of finitude are concentrated the renunciation of emancipation, the deadening reign of the present, the absence of peoples to themselves and the eradication of truths. ("L'Offrande réservée" 15)

For Badiou himself, emancipation must come by way of historical rupture and decisive intervention, and must be sustained by its faithfulness to an unchanging idea that he calls communism, where "'communist' designates the transtemporal subjectivity of emancipation, the egalitarian passion" (*D'un désastre obscur* 13; my trans.).

For Andrew Norris, Nancy's distinction between politics and the political means that he "all but abandons politics" because he takes away from politics the transcendence which it needs to effect decisive historical change: "Nancy's distinction between these political freedoms and the political thus has the force of robbing practical, enforceable freedoms of philosophical significance" (155) in favour of a notion of "the political" which is dislocated from all practical politics. Norris complains that, on Nancy's account, every position is caught up in a metaphysics, with the result that it is almost impossible to know who needs liberating, or which metaphysical entanglements are the most grievous, with the result that "his account of the practical is one

in which all cows are pretty much black" (155). Similarly, David Ingram argues that, "without some global idea of the good to be attained, of the subject to be emancipated, or of justice pure and simple, there would probably be no reason for judging at all, let alone engaging in politics" (116). Gary Gutting, commenting on "poststructuralist thinkers" in general, bemoans that they "contributed little to our philosophical understanding of freedom" because they "remain content with a naïve, prereflexive commitment to the unquestionable status of transgression, novelty, plurality, and difference as absolute ethical ideals" and "endorse the most radical liberation without stopping to ask just what it would consist in and why it is so important" (389).

nancean emancipation

In the remainder of this article I would like to offer a reading of Nancy's position on emancipation that pushes back against some of the criticisms he has faced, while also highlighting new problems and complexities in his account. When Nancy espouses the lexicon of emancipation and liberation, he does so in what may at first seem a surprising way: in order precisely to reject the closed idea of emancipation. One refrain running through his work from *The Experience of Freedom* (pub. in French in 1988) to *Dis-Enclosure* (pub. in French in 2005) is that what we need to be emancipated from is nothing other than emancipation itself, or rather the particular understanding of emancipation that shares the three features identified above: progress as rupture, closure of the idea of emancipation itself, and an assumed essence of the individual to be emancipated:

> [freedom] renders [*se livre*] itself to itself, it de-livers itself [*se délivre*] for itself or delivers itself from itself. The fact of freedom is this de-liverance of existence from every law and from itself as law: freedom there delivers itself as will, which is itself only the existent's being-delivered-an-decided. (Nancy, *L'Expérience de la liberté* 37–38; *The Experience of Freedom* 30)

What we must emancipate ourselves from is "a certain conception of emancipation that saw in it the cure for a shameful illness" (Nancy, *La Déclosion* 19; *Dis-Enclosure* 9; trans. mod.) of primitivism and clericalism. Having liberated us from the prisonhouse of these regressive superstitions, the emancipation narrative marched us directly into the modern penitentiary of progress, an inflexible concept of liberation and a determinate human essence.

The call for an emancipation from emancipation is not a cute apolitical self-reflexivity on Nancy's part, but a recognition of the self-defeating totalitarianism of emancipatory ideology. In *The Experience of Freedom* he insists that we have the task "of delivering ourselves from the thought of 'freedom' as the property of an individual 'subject'" (Nancy, *L'Expérience de la liberté* 47; *The Experience of Freedom* 7). One problem with the unquestioned concept of freedom is that it hangs over us like a "discretionary authority," dictating what we must desire and that for which we must strive in a way that uncannily mimes its purported antagonists: "despotism and freedom form a couple: the former figures, in particular subjectivity, the ontology of the latter, whose benefits it simultaneously withdraws from other particular subjectivities" (*L'Expérience de la liberté* 47; *The Experience of Freedom* 6). Nancy is not arguing that we abandon freedom, but that we abandon always knowing, from the outset, what freedom will mean or for whom it will be won.

He returns to this argument in *Dis-Enclosure*, insisting that "[p]erhaps we should also emancipate ourselves from a certain thinking of emancipation" (Nancy, *La Déclosion* 19; *Dis-Enclosure* 9) that can see nothing but illness and shame in Christianity and nothing but sweetness and light in the rationality, freedom and autonomy that triumphed over the old religion in the "saga of the emancipation of the human race" (*La Déclosion* 19; *Dis-Enclosure* 9). In a 2016 interview Nancy once again affirms the necessity of being liberated from, not merely by, the emancipation narrative:

We are not free if that means "to be able to do what one wants" and "be independent of everything" because we depend on a lot of things, and most times our "will" consists only of propensities, hopes and yearnings that come from somewhere else. Understanding this and what it means is the beginning of liberation. And that is why liberty surprises us, because we discover that there is something other than what we thought was obvious. ("The West is No More")

Nancy's account of liberation is one that retains the capacity to surprise us, to free us not only from our oppression but also from our preconceptions of what it is that oppresses us. Nancy repeatedly affirms the value of liberation but warns that it is not to be found through the dogmatic and closed means by which it is customarily pursued. In the place of these inadequate means he advances an alternative, more radical model of emancipation articulated not in terms of rupture, closure and essence, but of *ressourcement*, dis-enclosure and self-surpassing.

from progress as rupture to ressourcement

Whereas the ruptures of the historical progress model of emancipation create an incremental schema of "before" and "after" and a relationship between an unchanging idea of freedom and its progressive realisation in a specific historical context, the temporality of Nancy's account of emancipation is more complex. Emancipation for Nancy is not simply emancipation-from, but emancipation-by-and-from, in what we might think of as a "hair of the dog that bit you" approach, or an inflection of the Eckhartian maxim "I pray God to rid me of God" (*Wandering Joy* 112).

He explores this temporality at length in his account of the deconstruction of Christianity, which frames post-Enlightenment modernity *both* as an overcoming *and* as a culmination of Christianity. In his articulation of an argument adopted and adapted from Karl Löwith, Claude Lefort and Marcel Gauchet among others, Nancy insists that the modern world is – in a carefully chosen phrase – "itself the unfolding of Christianity" (*La Déclosion* 209; *Dis-Enclosure* 143–44). This is of course neither a straightforward continuity nor a simple rupture between modernity and Christianity, but a complex dynamic of non-linear continuation. Modernity is liberation from Christianity, but it is also the culmination of Christianity, with "Christianity" carrying two different meanings in these two propositions. It is on the nature of the difference (and indeed the possibility of the difference) between these two meanings that Nancy's alternative to incremental progress hangs.

Let us approach this crucial question of the difference between the Christianity that is overcome and the Christianity that finds its culmination in that very overcoming through Nancy's account of what it is in Christianity that persists in modernity:

> the question is to find out whether we can, by revisiting our Christian provenance, designate in the heart of Christianity a provenance that might bring about another resource – with an ambiguity that I for now take entirely upon myself – between a gesture of Hegelian dialectical *Aufhebung* and a different one that is not dialectical sublation. (*La Déclosion* 208; *Dis-Enclosure* 144)

In a 2007 article Nancy expands on the nature of this "resource" in Christianity:

> Deconstructing Christianity does not mean being content with the critique of religious illusion as with Marx or Freud, but asking what we can perhaps now uncover in the depths of Christianity, that is to say: finding something hidden in the theological, dogmatic, ecclesiastical heart of Christianity itself, and asking ourselves if, among all this, there isn't a resource that is not religious, but deeper still than that, neither philosophical nor religious, but that perhaps would be the great opening of Western thought. ("Il faut remettre" 784; see also *La Déclosion* 208–09; *Dis-Enclosure* 144)

The key term for our purposes here, the term Nancy uses to describe this "something in

Christianity deeper than Christianity itself" is a "resource," a return to the source that is freed from the historically contingent Christian forms it has taken. This *ressourcement* is not an object of thought but a gesture of thought, a gesture of "turning back on our Christian origins" in order to find something deeper than their manifest tradition, something that "comes to the West and Christianity from beyond themselves, what comes toward us from the depths of our tradition as more archaic than Christianity" (Nancy, *La Déclosion* 208; *Dis-Enclosure* 143). It is this more archaic "something" that needs liberating from its contingent theological expression. In Nancy's deconstruction of Christianity there is a clear hierarchy of gesture over content, deep ahistorical form over contingent historical expression: "it is necessary, if possible, to extract from a ground deeper than the ground of the religious thing that of which it will have been a form and a misrecognition" (*L'Adoration* 40; *Adoration* 26), and "'God' is only the name adopted by a pure excess – indeed vain, indeed exorbitant" (*L'Adoration* 31–32; *Adoration* 20). Thus it is that Christianity is understood as the contingent historical husk, the "front-man," for a gesture that is deeper than Christianity, a gesture that provides the essence and truth of Christianity, and which Christianity itself misunderstands. It is, once more, this deep pre-theological and pre-religious gesture that needs to be liberated from its theological and ecclesiastical husk.

Nevertheless, though this gesture is transtemporal it is not atemporal; the gesture to be unearthed in Christianity is not the key to the meaning of life or a universal, eternal truth, but a gesture that opens Western thought onto something other than itself. *Ressourcement*, in other words, is a local intervention into a specific tradition, not a passepartout method to unearth a universal cultural truth. This depth and locality together make for a double emancipation: from the oppression of the present, and from the oppression of an absolute yardstick of freedom. The "something in Christianity deeper than Christianity itself" is not an atemporal idea, but a historical gesture that exists across, but not independently of, its historical instantiations. As such, the gesture itself is not a closed, atemporal absolute.

This gesture is also a continuation and even a culmination of Christianity to the extent that Christianity itself performs it repeatedly. For example, for the New Testament there is, so to speak, "something in Moses deeper than Moses himself, which Moses misunderstands," namely, that Moses is a type of Christ. Nancy similarly argues that the crucifixion shows that there is something in pagan sacrifice deeper than that sacrifice itself and that paganism misunderstands, such that for Christ (and for Socrates as well)

> the ancient sacrifice is reproduced – up to a certain point, *in its form or in its schema*, but it is reproduced in such a way as to reveal in it an entirely new content, a truth until then buried or misunderstood, if not perverted (*Une Pensée finie* 71; *A Finite Thinking* 55; emphasis added, trans. mod.)

and the former modes of sacrifice are retroactively revealed to have been "a previous imitation, a crude image of what *transfigured* sacrifice will henceforth bring about," and the new form of sacrifice is "a higher, truer mode of sacrificial logic" (*Une Pensée finie* 78; *A Finite Thinking* 59).

What Christianity does to sacrifice here, making previous modes of sacrifice an imperfect foreshadow of Christ's death, is precisely, for Nancy, the operation performed on Christianity itself by secular modernity. So we are now in a position to draw an important distinction: when Nancy says that there is "something in Christianity deeper than Christianity," he means that there is a gesture of purifying "transfiguration" or of *ressourcement* in Christianity deeper than the contingent historical details of Christian doctrine and religious expression; there is an excess of the truth of sacrifice deeper than the historical forms of sacrifice, an excess of the truth of the Mosaic exodus over the determinate exodus narrative in the Pentateuch.

Ressourcement therefore enacts a complex temporality. Yes, there is a repeated return to

the sources of the faith, but this does not mean that *ressourcement* is flatly retrospective, much less conservative. Its return to the past is in the service of reinventing the faith each time anew, as if for the first time. The reaching back in time to the source is not for Nancy a gesture that grounds the faith on an unchanging foundation, but a way of reimagining the faith and even, to use Gauchet's expression, of exiting it. When Christianity reaches back into Judaism its gesture is not to reinforce Judaism's own foundations, but simultaneously to subvert and fulfil them in something radically new. This complex movement of *ressourcement* provides a liberation not only from the determinate forms of the present but also from the ideology of the present, because the creation of the future is always in conversation with a past that does not simply hold up a mirror to contemporary concerns but criticises, reframes and reinterprets them. This is what Nancy calls Christianity's "essential historicity" (*La Déclosion* 213; *Dis-Enclosure* 146), a historicity not merely of the act of faith but of the content of faith, a feature which for Nancy "ends up rigorously and implacably separating Christianity from the element of religion in general" (*La Déclosion* 213; *Dis-Enclosure* 146; trans. mod.). The temporality of Christianity – and of Nancy's account of emancipation – therefore is one "constitutively held between passage and presence" (*La Déclosion* 213; *Dis-Enclosure* 147), between the gesture of reinvention and the particular form the faith takes at any given moment. The model of temporality at work here, with its reaching back into the past to reinvent and transform the meaning of the past as well as the future clearly draws heavily on the movement of *ressourcement* that influenced the discussions of Vatican II (Flynn and Murray). The defining dogma of Christianity is overcome through a characteristic gesture of Christianity; nothing could be more deeply and quintessentially affirmative of this Christianity than the secularism that exits Christianity. Once more the nails of the coffin are, *per impossibile*, hammered in by the corpse it supposedly encases.

from closure to dis-enclosure

Secondly, Nancy's radical emancipation is not one of closure, but of dis-enclosure. In *The Experience of Freedom* he sets himself against "a 'liberation' whose principle and end would themselves be established," which would amount to "the material destruction of all freedom" (Nancy, *L'Expérience de la liberté* 106; *The Experience of Freedom* 79). The mistake he is highlighting here is to think that there is one and only one way of thinking freedom, to posit an emancipatory *pensée unique*. Thinking itself must be freed from this thinking of freedom (*L'Expérience de la liberté* 193; *The Experience of Freedom* 206). Freedom becomes that from which we need liberation when it shows itself as an "infinite foundation or finality" with an "infinite projection to infinity": unchanging, unimpeachable and closed (*L'Expérience de la liberté* 18; *The Experience of Freedom* 13–14). It follows that the task of politics is a liberation of liberty, "the liberation from every establishment, or its overflowing, by freedom in its *each time* irreducible (re)beginning" (*L'Expérience de la liberté* 106; *The Experience of Freedom* 79). This is one reason why Nancy is drawn to the dis-enclosure of Christianity: it is constantly un-closing its own closure and opening itself to other, unheard-of trajectories.

It follows that, as Nancy insists in *La Possibilité d'un monde*, emancipation is always local, and always partial: one is emancipated from a particular authority, guardianship, despotism or tyranny, but "all experience of the modern world leads to the conclusion that there's no absolutely emancipated subject" (*La Possibilité d'un monde* 65; *The Possibility of a World* 65; trans. mod.). Similarly reason, that great weapon of emancipation for the radical enlightenment, needs liberating from itself insofar as it takes itself to be infinite and self-enclosed. In a memorable phrase, Nancy insists that we must allow "the obscure to emit its own clarity" (*La Déclosion* 6; *Dis-Enclosure* 6). For Nancy, to liberate reason is not to assert its infinite capacity for procuring emancipation, but to insist precisely on its

ontological incompleteness (see Karolis). Why should we think that reason, any more than the God of Abraham, will be the universal, trans-temporal means of liberation for all people at all times and in all places, particularly when we, even in our own social-cultural moment, have seen rational principles deployed in the service of oppressive or murderous ends? A particular enlightenment conception of reason provided the means of liberation in one specific context, as indeed did the God from which reason itself sought emancipation. This should not *eo ipso* elevate either to the status of providing the only means of emancipation for all people in all places at all times.

In the movement from closure to dis-enclosure we can also once more discern the privilege of gesture over content that we encountered in Nancy's treatment of *ressourcement*. The closure of freedom and reason determine and ossify those concepts, but dis-enclosure is a gesture that overflows and liberates thinking from becoming imprisoned in any particular content.

But what of the political stakes of this dis-enclosure? In the 2009 *Libération* interview, Nancy is asked whether this non-essential account of emancipation is removed from daily preoccupations. His response is both emphatic and illuminating:

> No, because the present crises have something to do with five centuries of failure or error, of confusion or blindness, even duplicity, in "the emancipation of humanity" (despite all the successes and creations of these same centuries). It is just as pressing to think seriously about the stakes of our "humanist" civilization as it is finally and seriously to prevent the richest from multiplying their wealth by the number of poor they create. (Nancy, "Le sens de l'histoire")

This nuanced response illustrates that Nancy is by no means opposed to the concrete, street-level successes that have been won in the name of the closed model of emancipation, but he insists that they have been wrought by the means of a humanism that is itself not without consequences, and that these consequences should not be kept off balance sheet. To question this humanism is not to reject out of hand the successes it has brought; it is to seek to enlarge the sphere of the emancipation it can win.

from essence to self-surpassing

Thirdly, Nancy's radical emancipation rejects any determination of the essence of the human in favour of understanding the human as a gesture self-surpassing, in so doing emancipating the human from any constraining, essential concept of subjectivity. This key gesture of self-surpassing structures both Nancy's account of Christianity and of the human. In terms of Christianity, "Christianity, as such, is surpassed, because it is itself, and by itself, in a state of being surpassed [*en état de dépassement*]" (*La Déclosion* 141; *Dis-Enclosure* 206). Christianity, in other words, is never more itself than when it goes beyond itself. In fact, "[t]hat state of self-surpassing may be very profoundly proper to it; it is perhaps its deepest tradition – which is obviously not without its ambiguities" (*La Déclosion* 206; *Dis-Enclosure* 141), not least the ambiguity of the distinction between gesture and content itself. In self-surpassing, the gesture of Christianity surpasses its content. So when we say that Christianity is in a state of self-deconstruction, we mean that its gesture deconstructs its content at any given moment.

Self-surpassing is not the preserve of explicit theology, however. In terms of the human, Nancy regularly returns to Pascal's phrase "l'homme passe infiniment l'homme" [man infinitely surpasses man], identifying it with the inauguration of the modern West (*Vérité de la démocratie* 25; *The Truth of Democracy* 11). The phrase indicates that man is "in an infinite relation with himself" ("Il faut remettre l'homme" 790), and it frames the human neither as a self-enclosed immanence nor as a transcendence that makes the human a creature of God. What it does, in contrast, is "put man back in an infinite relationship with himself" (790) and frame the human as "the being fundamentally unfinished" (789). Which is to say that

it puts the concept of the human at any given moment in relation to the characteristic gesture of the human as self-surpassing, denying to the human any abiding essence other than this gesture itself. This is an emancipation of "man" from any fixed determination (Nancy, "Le sens de l'histoire").

The self-surpassing of Christianity and the self-surpassing of the Western notion of humanity are intimately linked for Nancy, and together they signal the persistence of the Christian gesture in the West:

> Independently of any profession of faith, of any ecclesiastical affiliation, of any church whatsoever, we are Christian [...] but what makes us Christians? It is the phrase of Pascal: "Man infinitely surpasses man." There you go, that's it. (Stiegler and Nancy)

So, when Christianity or the figure of the human are described in terms of a self-surpassing, it is only a surpassing of determinate content, not of the repeated gesture that characterises them both. Indeed, it is an affirmation of the gesture itself as the essence, the truth, both of Christianity and of the human.

problems with Nancy's account of emancipation

The important distinction between gesture and content gives rise to four problems that Nancy's account of emancipation needs to face. The first is this: is a constant and unchanging gesture just as closed and essential as a constant and unchanging content? Why is the gesture of self-surpassing, *qua* gesture, not as closed as humanism's essence of the human? It could in fact be argued that a gesture is more pervasive and constraining than any determinate content, precisely because it can operate on any given content.[2] It is relatively easy to see how we might overturn or surpass an oppressive definition of the human; it is much harder to see how we might surpass the gesture of surpassing. Nancy has relocated the thorny problem of the relation between oppression and emancipation from content to gesture, but he has by no means got rid of the problem. To deconstruct

THE PULSE OF SENSE

is not to overcome; in fact, as Derrida warns, it might well be to hyperbolise (*Le Toucher* 249; *On Touching* 220). This first problem cannot be conclusively resolved: the gestures of *ressourcement*, dis-enclosure and self-surpassing can always tip over into a hyperessentialism that repeats, at a more radical level, the errors they seek to mitigate. But, then again, so can the closed, progressive, essential account of emancipation they deconstruct.

A second problem Nancy's account of emancipation needs to face is whether this relocation of the problem from content to gesture also risks falling into an awkward Platonism that he is elsewhere at pains to resist. If the gesture is, as Nancy says, "deeper" than any determinate content, and the "truth" of any given historical instantiation of it, then there is a risk – as Badiou and others intuit – of devaluing the historical, the particular and the material. Nancy's gesture of self-surpassing draws heavily, via Gauchet, on a kenotic understanding of incarnation, but there is a sense in which it might not take the fleshiness of the Christian figure of incarnation seriously enough. An orthodox understanding of incarnation would assert that Christ is not merely an instantiation of a movement, truth or reality that exceeds him; he is God himself, presenting theology with the threefold scandal of the particular (for the universal Christ bore all the particularities of human life such as a language, a geographical location and a gender), of the historical (for the incarnation of the one true God took place at a particular moment in history and not eternally) and of the material (for the embodied Christ himself, in his flesh, was God, and not merely a vessel for a fleshless God). This Chalcedonian account of the incarnation, in which the fullest depth of reality is completely identified with a specific historical, material, personal individual, not as an admixture but in a way in which Christ is both "fully God and fully man," is present at other points in Nancy's work, where he draws his distinction between gesture and content away from the charge of paying insufficient attention to particular, historical political situations and causes, and of focusing only on abstract,

metaphysical realities. By contrast, in the assertion that Christianity "misunderstands" self-surpassing or that it is merely a "front-man" for a non-specific gesture that exceeds it, Nancy risks delegitimising the determinate and minimising the material, thereby driving a wedge between any specific, determinate historical political context and the reality it instantiates, which is always construed as a trans-temporal and therefore non-immediate gesture. The focus on the "something in Christianity deeper than Christianity" risks a hierarchy of (enduring) gesture over (ephemeral) material and historical support.

This brings us to the third problem with Nancy's position. If we allow him the distinction between content and gesture, between "Christianity" and "something in Christianity deeper than Christianity," then his thought does not operate after the end of the modern emancipation narrative at all; it merely transposes this narrative into another key, in just the same way that it has been repeatedly transposed throughout its history. The gesture Nancy performs repeats that of the modern emancipation narrative he ostensibly rejects: the gesture of turning the means of emancipation into that from which emancipation is sought. Secular modernity took the deity that had been the means of emancipation in the Hebrew Exodus and the New Testament figures of salvation, and made it into that from which emancipation was to be sought, by means of reason. Nancy similarly takes reason, the means of emancipation in modernity, and makes self-enclosed and self-sufficient reason that from which emancipation must be sought. Same gesture: different content. Understood in this way, Nancy's thought is not the end of the emancipation narrative at all, but the next iteration of its repeated gesture.

The fourth and final problem with Nancy's account of emancipation is perhaps the hardest of all to clarify. If the gesture of self-surpassing is deeper than Christianity, to what extent is that gesture itself a "Christian" gesture; to what extent does Christianity, so to speak, "own the copyright" on *ressourcement*, dis-enclosure and self-surpassing? This is a complex question that cannot receive a full treatment in the present article, but let me indicate the terms in which I think any future response should be framed.

As we have already seen, Nancy claims at points that these gestures are deeper than Christianity, but he does not make clear where they are to be found in pre- or non-Christian sources. Moreover, across different texts as well as within *Dis-Enclosure* itself, he seems at times to assert the contrary, namely, that *ressourcement*, dis-enclosure and self-surpassing are in fact at bottom Christian. He affirms, for example, that "all our thought is Christian through and through. Through and through and entirely, which is to say, all of us, all of us to the end [jusqu'au bout]" (Nancy, *La Déclosion* 142; *Dis-Enclosure* 207–08; trans. mod.). The claim here is notably not that all of our thought is one of *ressourcement* through and through, which would be consistent with the affirmation that the gesture of *ressourcement* is deeper than Christianity. In *Dis-Enclosure*, Nancy similarly asserts that "Christianity is inseparable from the West" (*La Déclosion* 142; *Dis-Enclosure* 207). What, then, of something in Christianity deeper than Christianity? These affirmations are quite explicit that the "self-absorption" and "self-surpassing" of Christianity that constitute its characteristic gesture are to be unequivocally identified with Christianity itself, not with something deeper.

How, then, should we square these seemingly contradictory statements? It would be too hasty to jump to the conclusion that Nancy is being inconsistent, a haste that would overlook the complex structure of the gestures themselves. A more nuanced reading would recast this supposed contradiction as the "paradoxical fulfilment of Christianity in its own exhaustion" (Nancy, *La Déclosion* 102; *Dis-Enclosure* 71) that it is strictly impossible to collapse either into a simple story of fulfilment, or one of exhaustion. Yes, there is a gesture of emancipation in Christianity deeper than Christianity, which can be rescued from the husk of Christianity; and yes, Christianity itself is coextensive with the West, and our thinking is

thoroughly Christian such that any possible emancipation from Christianity is a Christian emancipation. Modernity makes Christianity secular by following the pattern laid down by Christianity itself when it made Judaism Christian. It is in this way that two affirmations are equally true: "The only Christianity that can be actual is one that contemplates the present possibility of its negation," and "The only thing that can be actual is an atheism that contemplates the reality of its Christian origins" (*La Déclosion* 140; *Dis-Enclosure* 204–05). We are those who pray to God to emancipate us from God, not as a contradiction, not as a compromise, but as a necessity.

Further investigation into this question will need to distinguish more precisely the various degrees of identification between Christianity and the gesture of self-surpassing. Four such degrees at least are possible. The first is coincidence: self-surpassing happens to have been identified with Christianity, but this is a historical contingency that could well have been otherwise. The second is derivation: self-surpassing draws directly on explicitly Christian themes such as the critique of idolatry, though it is conceivable that it might have emerged independently of these themes. The third is internal necessity: self-surpassing is logically unthinkable outside a Christian or post-Christian frame. This is a necessary reliance of the gesture on its context. The final degree is external necessity: the West is unthinkable without the gesture of self-surpassing. This is a necessary reliance of the context on the gesture. To claim, for example, that Christianity is "coextensive" with the West, as Nancy does (*La Déclosion* 142; *Dis-Enclosure* 207–08), could fall into any of these four very different categories. The all-too common assertion – not from Nancy but from others – that some concept or other has "Christian roots" could similarly encode any one of these four claims.

conclusion

In the introduction to this article I suggested that the emancipation narrative runs like a fault line through recent French thought. As I close now I would like to return to that characterisation both to affirm and to contest it. I affirm it in the following way: the emancipation narrative does indeed divide most modern and contemporary thinkers into two broad camps. But what needs to be contested is that what divides these two camps is whether they embrace or reject emancipation.

As we have seen in Nancy's case, and as we could also show in relation to other thinkers would space allow, what is rejected is not emancipation per se but a particular, dogmatic account of emancipation that insists upon progress as rupture, a fetishised closure of the concept of emancipation itself, and a fixed essence of humanity. It is an account of emancipation that considers any position that fails to sign up to this threefold creed to be de facto anti-emancipatory. What Nancy embraces as he rejects this narrow vision is, in his eyes at least, a deeper, more rigorous and, yes, a more emancipatory account of emancipation, one that does not construct itself as the mirror image of the totalitarianism it resists and that is therefore in a position to perform a more radically emancipatory gesture. What we need to be emancipated from is the narrow conception of emancipation itself.

We might venture to label these two accounts of emancipation as a "parasitic" and "ascetic," respectively.[3] The emancipation propounded by Badiou, Rancière and others is, on Nancy's account, parasitic on the structures of progress, essence and totality that constitute the very oppression from which emancipation needs to be sought, and the liberation it brings can only ever come at the expense of reinforcing these structures. Nancy's own account of emancipation, by contrast, problematises these same structures and seeks a liberation from, not merely a redeployment of, progress, essence and closure, and in so doing ascetically denies itself, in the eyes of Badiou et al., the possibility of incisive social transformation available to the proponents of the closed version of emancipation. The choice, then, is not between embracing or rejecting radical emancipation, but between an emancipation that is radical in its disruption of limiting structures, and an emancipation that is radical in its potential for incisive social transformation. Nancy is a thinker of radical emancipation, but we must be careful to discern where the radicality of his account lies.

echo by jean-luc nancy

Where the desire for emancipation comes from is certainly an excellent question, because it is undoubtedly the appearance of such a desire that signals the birth of the West. It seems that throughout Egyptian history such a desire did not manifest itself, nor in Assyria or the other pre-political groups around the Mediterranean, nor anywhere else in the world. Power was overthrown, dynasties changed, new foundations, but it does not seem that one can speak of desire for emancipation. By contrast, it characterises both what is called "Hellenism" as well as what is called "Judaism." These two phenomena emerged after a great rupture at the beginning of the twelfth century. The great imperial or palatial structures collapsed, and it seems that entire populations were left to their own devices. It is as if the protecting, titular order broke down, alongside religious transformation of which the most important one was the effacement of human sacrifice. One can therefore wonder whether there was not first a loss, then the need to organise oneself in a new way and hence the desire to do so autonomously – above all because there were no other resources left. In particular, no more mythical resources, since it is also in this period that myths were written down, hence the end of their active role. To be sure, from either side, a new edifice of grounding or inaugural discourse (*parole*) is erected, but each time with new characteristics: from the Greek side, it is the *logos*; and from the Jewish side, the creative Word (*parole*) of God. Both are disposed to invention or responsibility, which remains foreign to myth.

All of this is accompanied by – or supported by – important technological transformations. To those, there is no end in sight ... : the important thing is that "emancipation" begins with the disappearance of forms of domination. In a way, there was a first emancipation, one that threw these peoples into an absence of reference points such that it is from that absence that one had to emancipate oneself so as not to sink into chaos (unless one took back the old orders, but they had gone out of use).

There is much to explore in this direction ...

disclosure statement

No potential conflict of interest was reported by the author.

notes

1 All translations from the interview are my own.

2 This point follows the shape of the argument in Watkin, "Rewriting the Death of the Author," in which I suggest that formal gestures that seek to escape the control of ownership and attribution are inevitably recuperated into that very same logic, not as voice but as style.

3 These appellations borrow from terms I first deployed in relation to atheism. See Watkin, *Difficult Atheism*.

bibliography

Badiou, Alain. *D'un désastre obscur: Droit, État, Politique.* Paris: Nouvelles éditions de l'Aube, 2013. Print.

Badiou, Alain. "L'Offrande réservée." *Sens en tous sens: autour des travaux de Jean-Luc Nancy.* Ed. François Guibal and Jean-Clet Martin. Paris: Galilée, 2004. 13–24. Print.

Derrida, Jacques. *Le Toucher, Jean-Luc Nancy.* Paris: Galilée, 2000. Print.

Derrida, Jacques. *On Touching – Jean-Luc Nancy.* Trans. Christine Irizarry. Stanford: Stanford UP, 2005. Print.

Eckhart, Meister. *Wandering Joy: Meister Eckhart's Mystical Philosophy.* Ed. David Applebaum. Trans. and commentary by Reiner Schürmann. Great Barrington, MA: Lindisfarne, 2001. Print.

Flynn, Gabriel, and Paul D. Murray. *Ressourcement: A Movement for Renewal in Twentieth-Century Catholic Theology.* Oxford: Oxford UP, 2011. Print.

Gutting, Gary. *French Philosophy in the Twentieth Century.* Cambridge: Cambridge UP, 2001. Print.

Ingram, David. "The Retreat of the Political in the Modern Age: Jean-Luc Nancy on Totalitarianism and Community." *Research in Phenomenology* 18 (1988): 93–124. Print.

Karolis, Alexander C. "Sense in Competing Narratives of Secularization: Charles Taylor and Jean-Luc Nancy." *Sophia* 52.4 (2013): 673–94. Print.

Lyotard, Jean-François. "Memorandum über die Legitimität." *Postmodernism: A Reader.* Ed. Thomas Docherty. New York: Harvester Wheatsheaf, 1993. 244–56. Print.

Lyotard, Jean-François. *The Postmodern Condition.* Trans. Geoff Bennington and Brian Massumi. Minneapolis: U of Minnesota P, 1984. Print.

Lyotard, Jean-François. *The Postmodern Explained: Correspondence, 1982–1985.* Trans. Don Barry, Bernadette Maher, Julian Perfanis, Virginia Spate, and Morgan Thomas. Minneapolis: U of Minnesota P, 1993. 25–38. Print.

Lyotard, Jean-François. "Randbemerkungen zu den Erzählungen." *Postmoderne und Dekonstruktion. Texte franzosischer Philosophen der Gegenwart.* Ed. Peter Engelmann. Stuttgart: Reclam, 1990. 49–53. Print.

Lyotard, Jean-François, and Eberhard Gruber. *The Hyphen: Between Christianity and Judaism.* Trans. Pascale-Anne Brault and Michael Nass. Amherst, NY: Humanity, 1999. Print.

Nancy, Jean-Luc. *Adoration: The Deconstruction of Christianity II.* New York: Fordham UP, 2012. Print.

Nancy, Jean-Luc. *Dis-Enclosure: The Deconstruction of Christianity.* Trans. Bettina Bergo, Gabriel Melenfant, and Michael B. Smith. New York: Fordham UP, 2008. Print.

Nancy, Jean-Luc. *The Experience of Freedom.* Trans. Bridget McDonald. Stanford: Stanford UP, 1993. Print.

Nancy, Jean-Luc. *A Finite Thinking.* Ed. Simon Sparks. Stanford: Stanford UP, 2003. Print.

Nancy, Jean-Luc [Interview with Silvia Romani]. "Il faut remettre l'homme dans un rapport infini avec lui même." *Rivista di Filosofia Neo-Scolastica* 99.4 (Oct.–Dec. 2007): 771–94. Print.

Nancy, Jean-Luc. *The Inoperative Community.* Ed. Peter Connor. Trans. Peter Connor, Lisa Garbus, Michael Holland, and Simona Sawhney. Minneapolis: U of Minnesota P, 1991. Print.

Nancy, Jean-Luc. *La Communauté désœuvrée.* Paris: Christian Bourgeois, 1986. Print.

Nancy, Jean-Luc. *La Déclosion: déconstruction du christianisme I.* Paris: Galilée, 2005. Print.

Nancy, Jean-Luc. *L'Adoration: Déconstruction du christianisme, 2.* Paris: Galilée, 2010. Print.

Nancy, Jean-Luc. *La Possibilité d'un monde: Dialogue avec Pierre-Philippe Jandin.* Paris: Les Petits Platons, 2013. Print.

Nancy, Jean-Luc [Interview by Eric Aeschimann]. "Le sens de l'histoire a été suspendu." *Libération* 4 Jun. 2009. Web. 30 Mar. 2020. <https://web.archive.org/web/20200225123220/https://next.liberation.fr/livres/2009/06/04/le-sens-de-l-histoire-a-ete-suspendu_561906>.

Nancy, Jean-Luc. *L'Expérience de la liberté.* Paris: Galilée, 1988. Print.

Nancy, Jean-Luc. *The Possibility of a World: Conversations with Pierre-Philippe Jandin.* Trans. Travis Holloway and Flor Méchain. New York: Fordham UP, 2017. Print.

Nancy, Jean-Luc. *The Truth of Democracy.* Trans. Pascale-Anne Brault and Michael Naas. New York: Fordham UP, 2010. Print.

Nancy, Jean-Luc. *Une Pensée finie.* Paris: Galilée, 1990. Print.

Nancy, Jean-Luc. *Vérité de la démocratie.* Paris: Galilée, 2008. Print.

Nancy, Jean-Luc [Interview by Elena Cué]. "The West is No More." 13 July 2016. Web. 30 Mar. 2020. <https://web.archive.org/web/20190306170811/https://www.alejandradeargos.com/index.php/en/all-articles/21-guests-with-art/1418-interview-with-jean-luc-nancy-the-west-is-no-more>.

Norris, Andrew. "Jean-Luc Nancy on the Political After Heidegger and Schmitt." *Jean-Luc Nancy and Plural Thinking: Expositions of World, Ontology, Politics, and Sense.* Ed. Peter Gratton and Marie-Eve Morin. Albany: SUNY P, 2012. 143–58. Print.

Stiegler, Bernard, and Jean-Luc Nancy. "Entretien sur le christianisme, 23 avril 2008, Paris." *Pourquoi nous ne sommes pas chrétiens: 40 écrivains et philosophes, 40 réponses.* Kindle book. Paris: Max Milo, 2009. Print.

Taylor, Charles. *A Secular Age.* Cambridge, MA: Harvard UP, 2006. Print.

Watkin, Christopher. *Difficult Atheism: Post-Theological Thinking in Alain Badiou, Jean-Luc Nancy and Quentin Meillassoux.* Edinburgh: Edinburgh UP, 2011. Print.

Watkin, Christopher. "Rewriting the Death of the Author: Rancièrian Reflections." *Philosophy and Literature* 39.1 (2015): 32–46. Print.

Coda

Coda

Tireless, Marie and Nikolaas, the architects of this special issue and the accompanying conference, asked me to retrace my "international trajectory." I find this somewhat awkward for two reasons: first of all, I'm not very good at telling stories; secondly, my "trajectory" is rather unexceptional. Nevertheless, they insisted, my readers might find it useful.

Yet, how are we to speak of things "international" today, in a time when this term – which once belonged to the epic of communism and socialism – resonates only as a narrow category, confronted as it is with a global reality of interdependence and interconnection within which national realities certainly persist, but hardly refer to an "international" dimension? "Cosmopolitan" would be my preference, but this is ambitious since nothing is less certain today than cosmopolitanism. In fact, as I reflect on this "trajectory" – which I have never thought or been asked about – , I realise first of all that for me it has for a long time simply been part of philosophical labour, and then that it is a question of a complex interplay of near and far: in terms of space, certainly, but also in terms of thinking, in terms of the extent and limits of all "communication," or conversation, lectures, conferences, meetings, palaver, discussion; all figures of the same playing of the accordion where the moving walls of a bellows must in turn be pulled apart and pushed together.

Let's therefore attempt to play a little tune on the accordion.

Undoubtedly, we should start with the experience of my childhood. In 1945, my

jean-luc nancy

translated by marie chabbert and nikolaas deketelaere

AN ACCORDION TUNE

father, a military engineer, was sent to Germany as part of the occupation. I spent five years in Baden-Baden – so from my fifth to my tenth year. I did not have even the slightest awareness as to the reasons for why we were there. Due to random encounters, I took quickly to speaking German and by the time I returned to France I was almost bilingual. That did not last, but I nevertheless kept the taste for this other language and for the pleasure of switching from one to the other. Later, this allowed me to teach in German in Berlin – which I will say more about later. What was

---

This is an Open Access article distributed under the terms of the Creative Commons Attribution-NonCommercial-NoDerivatives License (http://creativecommons.org/licenses/by-nc-nd/4.0/), which permits non-commercial re-use, distribution, and reproduction in any medium, provided the original work is properly cited, and is not altered, transformed, or built upon in any way.

far away undoubtedly joined paths with me very early on.

I did not leave France during my studies. There was no Erasmus at that time, nor the desire to go gallivanting across the globe. There was nevertheless an attraction to "under-developed" countries, and some of my friends went to stay there or did their military service there (with the system of postponements for studies, we did not do it at the time of the Algerian war). One of my friends was in Oran in this capacity when I was finishing my studies and I stayed with him for a few days. I was very curious about this new country, but did not have the time to really get to know it. I returned there about forty years later, with great interest; but on this occasion again for too short a stay, divided up for a series of lectures.

Speaking of lectures immediately prompts me to introduce this remark, which applies to everything that follows: giving lectures or attending conferences is the worst way to travel abroad. For two reasons: the first is that time is always too short; the second is that, between philosophers of different countries, a stage is set up that essentially effaces countries, peoples and even languages (we translate). I did it often, for quite a long time, and ended up feeling regretful: the idea of being far away in order to turn to the same circle of interests and references, without any real connection to a country, has something off-putting. This has nothing to do with the welcome provided by the hosts, nor with the generally warm climate. But it's the overwhelming feeling of having stepped out of a plane to go speak in a room, followed by dinner with colleagues before returning to one's hotel whilst asking oneself "What am I doing here?" (here being Austria or Massachusetts). Of course, sometimes something happens and a discussion can be full of life, fire even. But we don't stay, that's the major error. When you have at least three days, when you can wonder about a bit and recognise people – that point is crucial to me: you have to be able to recognise and return to (retrouver) someone – at least once or twice – in order for things to start happening.

If not, the accordion is stuck, there is no bellowing.

Having said that, my earliest memory of travelling abroad is a mission to Romania in Ceausescu's time (I forget the year, but around 1975). It was a mission of the Ministry of Foreign Affairs intended to facilitate academic contacts in spite of the circumstances. The project was so poorly put together that the Romanians didn't know what to do with me. There was no question of me attending faculties of philosophy. Instead, I was taken for a visit to an anthropology laboratory where everyone was very embarrassed. We mostly drank tea. Through I don't know what channel, I was offered to go and see a retired philosopher who was suspected by the authorities. This visit – curtains drawn, with a man who spoke elegant French but did not wish to say much as he let me know through gestures – made a huge impression on me. For the remainder, I made some very pleasant little trips in the company of young sociologists eager to show me their country: in Cluj, I listened to *La Traviata* in Hungarian; in Iași, I slept in a nuns' convent who awaited the exceptional visit of a Moldovan patriarch who had been authorised to come see them; in Budapest, I had a guide, a very kind student, very careful but giving clear indications as to his feelings. I walked around a lot, I believe to have seen something of this country. Of course, this exception remained unique. At the same time, two other offers came in: a trip to the United States and a teaching post in Berlin.

The trip to the United States was part of the profusion of trips trigged by the aftermath of the famous 1966 conference in Baltimore. The Americans wanted to discover the "structuralists" (this was the overall category) and the French (like the Germans) were still to discover America. I will return to this.

In Berlin, after his sudden death (in 1971), Peter Szondi's students and assistants wanted to organise a seminar. I've forgotten how – probably through Derrida – , but I was invited to do so since I spoke German. I went there for two days every two weeks. This continued for several years, with stays of two to three months that I spent at Jakob Taubes' Institute for Hermeneutics. The experience of Berlin – insofar as teaching is concerned – was the richest one I've had abroad. It was still the Berlin of the wall, of the occupation of buildings and – on the horizon – of the Rote Armee Fraktion. The students were impressively present and active, and everything took place in an atmosphere of permanent inventiveness. But at the beginning of the 1980s, the Berlin Senate began to put things in order ... For the first time, I was not visiting, I was working whilst living there; I was in – not the country, for sure, because it was an island apart – but in what we now call an ecosystem. That is to say, that which specifies, organises and sometimes also displaces, the very notions of near and far.

It was an entirely different ecology in the United States where, after several trips for lectures, I had regular stays at the University of Irvine. This system had been inaugurated (at least insofar as "French theory" was concerned) by Derrida, Lyotard, Marin, Goux, Damisch, Lacoue-Labarthe and many others. Lacan, Deleuze and Foucault appeared there frequently, but in other forms than extended stays. It was the rise of "French theory" and I find it painful to say to what extent this long episode, overloaded with rivalries but also worked by deep tectonic movements, became insufferable to me – even though I was myself part of it: it accumulated so many misinterpretations and so much nonsense. In this case, there is no question of an accordion, there is instead a cacophony against a background of deafness.

It is, in fact, a matter of one of the great shockwaves taking place in the world – let us say, for the sake of simplicity, since 1945. One of the consequences of what had happened to Germany, and which somehow transported the thought of Husserl and Heidegger to France. This had certainly begun before the war, but afterwards Germany was bled dry. Through Corbin, Levinas, Sartre, Merleau-Ponty, Beaufret, a transfer took place that – complex and polymorphous for sure, but nevertheless a transfer of an intellectual inspiration – had been trigged by Husserl: namely, a sense of the need to re-establish

philosophy, nothing less, which was in fact a response to the shaking felt by European society since at least Nietzsche. "French" thus had both empirical and "historical" motives, and France was there a guide who in turn proved to be an instigator. As for "theory," it is a term whose indeterminacy betrays perplexity. Since we do not know whether its philosophy, literary criticism, anthropology, etc., we call this vagueness "theory." And this is accompanied by enormous misunderstandings, which I cannot dwell on here.

I would like to add that it was a subdivision of that other vague term that constituted the "linguistic turn." A very clumsy (but understandably so, given the role played by various disciplines of language) way of grasping a phenomenon that was basically that of a general suspension of acquired meanings (such as history, man, sense, etc.). Today, it can be reversed in favour of a demand for the "real," as if the preoccupation with language did not concern precisely the very "reality" of the supposedly "real."

I will not dwell on it any further: this is just to indicate that, for me, the role played by the United States at this time was but a banal effect of this overall movement.

Later on, for entirely different and pragmatic reasons, I spent two years in San Diego and then Berkeley. So I could have pursued an American career, but I had no interest in that whatsoever. The favourable conditions, the undeniable friendships, could not prevent a malaise due to the deep separation between the university and the country (especially in California). I much preferred to be in Europe, where the university was for me – at least then – as much part of the country as my childhood school was part of its little town. The accordion did not work well for me in the United States.

Other reasons – health reasons – prevented me from returning to the other side of the Atlantic anyway. Unfortunately, the same was true for South America, where I was never able to go despite all my interest in this so very carnal culture.

In Europe, throughout this period, many relationships were forged: especially with Italy, Germany – no longer that of the Berlin wall –

and Spain; to say nothing of almost all the other countries (including, in the 1990s, those of Central Europe and former Yugoslavia, around which militant fervour of course reigned). The regime of the visits prevailed everywhere, but I stayed in Italy and Germany on multiple occasions as a visiting professor. I cannot go into detail, nor make a typology of the intellectual climates (fascinating in itself), but detailing the variations of what had become more European rather than just "French," and partly more Latin than Nordic, is necessary. Certainly, there were contacts and echoes everywhere; but in the North and East of Europe, little by little, a pragmatic, sociologising or psychologising rather than philosophical thinking had taken root. The accordion sometimes produces too discordant sounds.

England, it turned out, was a little bit out of the way – only a little bit, because I made several visits there, but must say that the 2019 conference in Oxford was a great surprise. I had at times been invited – each time prevented by my health – but from there to such a conference was a big step. Moreover, the organisers were French and Flemish – which is at the same time indicative of the increased mobility of students. I might add this sign of the times: it was the very same year that my grandson was staying in Oxford, where he practices so-called "analytic" philosophy, which already formed the core of his studies in France.

Once again, it is a question here of profound movements accompanying the major techno-economic and geopolitical evolutions or involutions of the last twenty years.

Outside Europe, Japan unsurprisingly not only comes first but is also a place where I breathed the same philosophical air as in France, surrounded by entirely different fragrances and hues. As well as the same air of friendship. For health reasons, I have not been elsewhere in Asia. I have some correspondents in China and Korea. I have forged promising connections in India around the journal *PWD* (*Philosophy World Democracy*).

Then there is Africa, the North of which I have visited quite often – going as far as Egypt – and with which I have relationships that history has committed our countries to. But I have only enjoyed a friendly stay south of the Sahara, in Burkina Faso – around 1985 – , after which my health forever closed off for me a continent that fascinates me all the more. Nevertheless, students from Burkina Faso came to Strasbourg for several years.

Today, from whatever region, Skype, Zoom, WhatsApp, e-mail operators and many other agents of connection, make another accordion resound – whose music is still to be deciphered.

This exposition is dry, I am aware of that. To tell a real story – of which I am incapable – would take a hundred times the space. It would allow me to name all those, so many, who have opened their doors and their work to me, many of whom are still friends. In responding to Marie's and Nikolaas' request, I am conscious both of the insignificance of a trajectory blended with a thousand others and carried by an even greater number of events, as well as the wealth of encounters that are in turn much richer and stronger than a schematic outline could even suggest. And they go, when luck intervenes, far beyond philosophical exchanges. The accordion accompanies the dance very well.

Jean-Luc Nancy, November 2020

disclosure statement

No potential conflict of interest was reported by the author.

Index

Note: Page numbers followed by "n" denote endnotes.

"Abandoned Being" 24
abandonment 20, 24, 32, 37, 39, 64, 146, 227; of beings 146
Abraham 72, 75–82, 224, 239; life 75–77, 83; ordeal 71–85
Abrahamic religions 215, 217
access 2, 39, 60–61, 66–67, 77, 83, 108, 143, 191
accordion 249–52
act of faith 183, 225, 238
adoration 83, 92, 95, 169, 178–79, 182, 190, 223, 225–26, 234, 237
aesthetics 17, 104–6, 110, 112
affectivity 159, 162–65
anastasis 221–23
anthropocentrism 144–45, 154
anthropomorphism 145, 151, 154
æsthetic religion 103, 105–6, 108, 110–11
atheism 19, 45, 132–33, 146, 172, 176, 192, 204, 215, 217–21, 226

being-in-common 18–20, 146–47
being-in-the-world 2, 25, 74–76, 81–84, 106
being-of-the-world 83–85
being-to-itself 13, 152
belief 63, 180–81, 183, 203–5, 208, 215, 218–19, 224
Berlin 249–51
biological body 160–61, 164
biological life 7, 159, 163–65
biological organism 159, 162–64
biological philosophy 162
biological thought 162, 164
Blanchot, Maurice 6, 43, 123, 209

Canguilhem, Georges 162–65
capitalism 178–79
Caputo, John 72, 75–76, 78–79, 81, 85, 187–88, 192–93, 197
Chabbert, Marie 7, 11, 130, 214, 227
Christian culture 133, 169, 176, 178–79, 182

Christianity 50–51, 71, 83, 131–33, 138–40, 169–72, 174–79, 182–83, 186–88, 190–93, 195–96, 202–4, 218–21, 223–25, 236–42
Christian religion 105, 172, 176, 203–4
Christians 131–33, 139, 146, 172, 177–79, 182, 190, 219, 223–24, 240, 242
Churchland, Paul 162
classical empiricism 60, 67–69
clericalism 236
communication 6, 53, 93, 98–100, 177, 179, 181, 249
conduct of sense 3–4
consciousness 6, 24, 61, 73, 79, 143, 149, 160, 162, 164–65, 215
continental philosophy 143, 154
corporeality 6, 131, 133–34, 139–40
corpus meum 131–33, 137–40
correlationism 143–44
crime 33–34, 36, 38
culture 13, 131, 133, 136–37, 139, 169, 172–74, 176–78, 182, 193, 195

decision of existence 153, 225
deconstruction 50–51, 132, 143, 146, 151, 177, 179, 181–82, 185–86, 188–89, 191, 196–98, 203–4, 206, 223–24; of Christianity 7, 50, 132–33, 138, 169–70, 174–75, 177–79, 182, 203–4, 211, 219, 221
Derrida, Jacques 7, 17, 40–42, 71, 79–80, 97, 119–20, 147, 173–74, 176–82, 185–86, 189, 191–92, 214–16, 218–19, 223–26, 233, 250–51
desacralisation 185–86, 189, 191, 193–96, 198
desecularisation 7, 185–93, 195–98
detheologization 177–78
dialectical reciprocity 41, 43
dialectics 42, 45, 47, 66, 104, 111, 192, 216, 219, 233
dis-enclosure 81–85, 132, 169, 171–72, 174–77, 179–80, 185–86, 189–91, 196, 216–18, 220–25, 227, 233, 235–42

254 INDEX

divine 75–76, 81, 97–101, 105, 108, 120–21, 171, 173, 190, 194, 217, 220–24; force 94–95; spirit 99–101; voice 93–100

emancipation 7, 189, 193, 204, 232–36, 238–44; account of 239, 243
emotions 7, 112, 159–65
empirical experience 60, 66, 68, 73–74
empiricism 6, 59–63, 68–70
empirico-transcendentalism 60
Erlebnis 73, 75
essence 2, 4, 61, 65–67, 69, 118, 138–39, 145–48, 174–75, 177, 181–82, 223, 234–37, 240, 243
ethics 31, 72, 76–79, 81, 130–31, 133–38, 160
Europe 161, 196, 207, 251–52
ex nihilo 38, 111, 146, 174, 177, 179, 181–83
experience of being 74, 78, 160
experience of faith 71, 76, 81–82
Experience of Freedom 6, 17, 39, 59, 62–63, 65–66, 70, 74–75, 235–36, 239
exteriority 141, 147–48, 150–52, 163

factuality 60–61, 65–69, 181; of being 61
faith 6, 71–72, 75–85, 131–32, 138, 179–83, 192, 197, 208–9, 214, 224–26, 238, 240
fate 111, 179, 182
father of faith 72
fictions 34–37, 39, 44, 92, 124, 207
finitude 2–4, 34, 36, 106, 143, 148, 176, 219–20, 223, 235; of being 2, 4
flat ontology 144–45, 148, 151, 154
foreign body 13, 130, 133–34
forgetfulness of being 119
form-of-life 76, 79, 83, 85
foundation of freedom 62
fragility 5–6, 45–47, 49, 52–54; of thinking 6, 51
France 16, 132, 162, 187, 194, 249–52
freedom 17, 19–20, 22, 24, 38–39, 59–70, 74–75, 146–50, 153, 215, 217, 234–37, 239; of existence 67
functional relationships 163
fundamental spiritual dissatisfaction 215

Gadamer, H.-G. 73, 84, 94
game of truth 208–9
generosity 63–65; of being 63–64, 68
genres 46, 122, 124
Germany 249, 251–52
gesture 7, 14, 37, 44, 69, 85, 112, 217, 222–25, 237–42, 250
givenness 3, 60, 63–65, 67–69, 143, 170, 174, 182
globalisation 11, 214

Habermas, Jürgen 203
Hegel, Georg W.F. 6, 24, 50, 52, 60, 76–77, 103–5, 107–12, 183, 210, 216
Heidegger, Martin 2, 4–5, 59–60, 63, 94, 132–33, 171–74, 176, 186, 189–91, 193, 204, 216–17, 222–23, 225

hermeneutics 93–97, 100, 133–34, 143, 186, 193, 251
historicity 191, 238
history 61–62, 107–8, 170, 178, 180, 187–92, 196–98, 202–3, 215–16, 218, 220–21, 224, 232–34, 241, 251–52; of Christianity 187–88, 191, 193
hospitality 131, 181
human beings 4–5, 7, 40, 144–45, 152–53, 165, 171, 222
humanities 11, 159, 161, 164, 172, 178, 182–83, 194, 223, 232–33, 235, 240, 243
human life 165, 204, 206, 210, 241
human speech 92–93
humiliation 187, 195, 204
Husserl, Edmund 217
hyper-reality 79–80

ideality 66, 181–82
identity 47, 108, 134, 140, 149–51, 196, 216, 218, 222–23, 225–27, 234
immanent transcendence 204
impossibility 40, 42, 47, 53, 77, 79–80, 134–35, 160, 192, 198, 226–27
inadequation 82–84
incapacity 22, 96–98, 144
incarnation 112, 165, 175–77, 190, 193, 195, 204, 221, 233, 241
insistence 16–22, 112
interpretations 5, 46, 48, 93–94, 100, 133–34, 136, 138, 192, 196, 203, 209–10, 217
interpreters 6, 92–94, 97, 99–101, 109

Jena Romanticism 122–23
Jeremiah 92, 96–98
Jesus Christ 46, 112, 139, 171, 194, 203–10, 218–22, 224, 238, 241
Jeunesse Etudiante Chrétienne 223
Johannes 72, 76–80, 83
judgment 32, 34–35, 37–38
jurisdiction 33–39, 69
jurisprudence 36, 39–40
jurisprudentialism 33
justice 31–32, 39–40, 151, 161, 220, 223, 226, 235

Kafkaesque proceduralism 39
Kant, Immanuel 32–34, 36–37, 40, 42–43, 59–60, 63, 69–70, 78, 81, 104, 170–71
kenosis 82, 193, 195
kenotic movement 192
Kierkegaard, Søren 71–72, 75–84, 99, 101, 122

Lacoue-Labarthe, Philippe 25, 45, 47, 49, 73, 103–4, 106–11, 122–23, 204, 251
language 32, 39–40, 65, 67–68, 92–94, 100–1, 119–22, 124, 130–31, 136, 138, 180, 182, 220, 249–51
law of love 119
Lazarus 51, 209–10

INDEX

liberation 66, 204, 232–39, 243
life force 21
lived experience 73, 131, 136–37, 215
love 6, 20–22, 24–25, 83, 85, 117–24, 125n9, 190, 194–96, 220, 223, 226, 232; relation 118, 120; of thinking 17, 118, 123
Lubac, Henri de 132
Lyotard, J.-F. 232–33

Magdalene, Mary 46, 204–5, 221, 224
Marion, Jean-Luc 217
material transcendentality 68
melancholics 25–26
metamorphosis 169, 174, 178–79, 182
metaphysical principles 151, 192
metaphysics 7, 63, 146–48, 151, 154, 161, 169–74, 176–77, 179–80, 182, 185–86, 188–92, 195–98
Michaud, Ginette 41
modern art 103–4, 106–8
modern emancipation 234, 241
modernity 105, 108, 170–71, 178, 187–89, 191, 195, 197, 202–4, 234, 237, 241–42
modern metaphysics 191
mondialisation 11, 153
monotheism 45, 169, 190, 202, 204, 220–21, 225
monotheistic divine 221
Morton, Tim 155n2
mutation 123, 169, 173–74, 178–79, 182, 185–86
myth 42, 44–45, 48–50, 52, 194, 198, 220, 243

Nancy, Jean-Luc 2–7, 16–25, 31–53, 59–69, 71, 74–75, 81–85, 92–95, 97–99, 103–6, 110–12, 117–24, 130–40, 145–54, 164, 169–82, 189–91, 202–10, 216–27, 232–43; account of emancipation 235, 236, 238, 240–41; claims 32–33, 242; deconstruction of Christianity 172, 178, 223, 237; ontology 38, 145, 147–52; philosophy of love 6, 118; project 7, 64, 203–4; resistance 18–19; thinking 4–8, 17, 20, 24, 42, 48, 118, 174, 179, 222, 225–26; work 17, 35, 60, 68–69, 93–94, 117, 120, 124, 179–80, 208, 241
narration 43–44, 220
naturalism 160–61, 203
negative force 18, 25
Nietzsche, Friedrich 77, 83, 104–5, 154, 161, 171–73, 186, 189, 191–92, 194, 196, 220, 222
nihilism 39, 104, 146, 151, 154, 172–74, 178–79, 186, 192–93, 195

obligation 32, 78–79
ontological force 18, 20
ontotheology 94, 170–73, 182, 216
optimism 21–25, 189
ordeal of faith 76, 80, 85
original violence 193–95
otherness 22, 101, 147, 150, 174, 180

parabolic truth 203, 208–9
partage 39, 94–95, 98–99

passionate love 119–20
philosophical discourse 6, 16, 42, 47, 60, 63, 154, 182
philosophical thinking 6, 118, 122, 252
poetics 6, 76, 79, 85; of faith 71, 85
poïēsis 71, 82, 84
posthumous existence 24–25
praxis 32, 62, 65–67, 82
primitivism 236
prophet 92–93, 96–101, 111; existence 97–98, 101
pulse of sense 5–6

qualitative experience 161–62, 164

Rabate, Jean-Michel 123
radical politics 7
radical secularisation 186, 189, 192, 198
realism 140, 180
relational events 149
religion 103–6, 108, 176, 178–79, 182–83, 186–89, 194–97, 202–4, 214–19, 221, 223–27, 236, 238
ressourcement 236–39, 241–42
resurrection 7, 49–51, 53, 202–11, 219, 221–23
return of religion 7, 203, 215–16, 218–19, 226–27
revelation 4, 53, 104, 109–10, 154, 206, 215, 217, 225
Romanticism 45, 104, 106–8, 111, 117, 120, 123–24

sacrifice 18–19, 72, 80–81, 194, 207, 224, 234, 238
Saint Paul 6, 93–94, 99–100
Schrijvers, Joeri 7, 183
Schürmann, Reiner 170
science 32–33, 159–62, 178, 188, 196, 233
Scott, Michael 215
secularisation 7, 177–79, 185–98, 202–3, 218, 223, 227; thesis 186–89, 191, 197–98
secularism 186, 190, 198, 202–3, 214–15, 217, 219, 226, 238
self 16, 24, 64, 73–74, 81–82, 93, 120, 123, 138, 147, 150–51
self-surpassing 7, 236, 240–42
sense of being 2, 137
sense of continuity 225
Sexistence 17, 20, 117, 120–23
"Shattered Love" 21, 24, 117–21, 125n8
singular acts of faith 225–26
singular existence 77–78, 81, 150, 181
singularities 37–39, 61–62, 78–79, 140, 147–54, 164, 182, 225
singular plurality 121, 225

techno-economic development 11
technology 172, 178, 188
threshold of speech 92–93, 100
transcendental experience 67–68, 75
transcendent beliefs 214–15, 217, 224
transition 171–72, 190, 195

256 INDEX

transmission 95–96, 101, 178
transubstantiation 138–39
truth 4–5, 7, 32–33, 41–44, 53, 84–85, 105–8, 110,
    118–21, 207–10, 220, 223–24, 226–27, 234–35,
    238, 240–41

unavowable community 48, 51,
    53–54
unfaith 76–77, 79
United States 161, 196, 250–51

violence 13, 17, 20, 35, 37–38, 40, 43, 64, 85,
    193–95, 216–17

Watkin, Christopher 7, 232
Williams, Raymond 17
wisdom 42, 49, 118
witness 37–38, 43, 49, 53–54, 92–98,
    100–1, 112, 170
world-disclosure 74–75
worldly sovereignty 18–19